Windows® 2000 Deployment & Desktop Management

Other Books by New Riders Publishing

Windows NT Power Toolkit
Stu Sjouwerman and Ed Tittel, 0-7357-0922-X

Planning for Windows 2000
Eric Cone, Jon Boggs, and Sergio Perez, 0-7357-0048-6

Windows NT DNS
Michael Masterson, Herman Kneif, Scott Vinick, and Eric Roul, 1-56205-943-2

Windows NT Network Management: Reducing Total Cost of Ownership
Anil Desai, 1-56205-946-7

Windows NT Performance Monitoring, Benchmarking and Tuning
Mark Edmead and Paul Hinsburg, 1-56205-942-4

Windows NT Registry: A Settings Reference
Sandra Osborne, 1-56205-941-6

Windows NT TCP/IP
Karanjit Siyan, 1-56205-887-8

Windows NT Terminal Server & Citrix MetaFrame
Ted Harwood, 1-56205-944-0

Cisco Router Configuration & Troubleshooting
Mark Tripod, 0-7357-0024-9

Exchange System Administration
Janice Rice Howd, 0-7357-0081-8

Implementing Exchange Server
Doug Hauger, Marywynne Leon, and William C. Wade III, 1-56205-931-9

Network Intrusion Detection: An Analyst's Handbook
Stephen Northcutt, 0-7357-0868-1

Understanding Data Communications, Sixth Ed.
Gilbert Held, 0-7357-0036-2

SQL Server System Administration
Sean Baird, Chris Miller, et al., 1-56205-955-6

Domino System Administration
Rob Kirkland, 1-56205-948-3

Understanding Directory Services
Beth & Doug Sheresh, 0-7357-0910-6

Understanding the Network: A Practical Guide to Internetworking
Michael Martin, 0-7357-0977-7

Internet Information Services Administration
Kelli Adam, 0-7357-0022-2

Inside Windows 2000 Server
William Boswell, 1-56205-929-7

Windows 2000 Active Directory
Edgar Brovick, Doug Hauger, William C. Wade III, 0-7357-0870-3

SMS 2 Administration
Michael Lubanski and Darshan Doshi, 0-7357-0082-6

Windows® 2000 Deployment & Desktop Management

New Riders
201 West 103rd Street,
Indianapolis, Indiana 46290

Jeffrey A. Ferris

Windows® 2000 Deployment & Desktop Management

Jeffrey A. Ferris

FIRST EDITION: *April, 2000*

International Standard Book Number: 0-7357-0975-0

Library of Congress Catalog Card Number: 00-100404

04 03 02 01 00 7 6 5 4 3 2 1

Interpretation of the printing code: The rightmost double-digit number is the year of the book's printing; the rightmost single-digit number is the number of the book's printing. For example, the printing code 00-1 shows that the first printing of the book occurred in 2000.

Composed in Bembo and MCPdigital by New Riders Publishing

Printed in the United States of America

Trademarks

All terms mentioned in this book that are known to be trademarks or service marks have been appropriately capitalized. New Riders Publishing cannot attest to the accuracy of this information. Use of a term in this book should not be regarded as affecting the validity of any trademark or service mark. Windows and Microsoft are registered trademarks of Microsoft Corporation.

Warning and Disclaimer

This book is designed to provide information about Windows 2000. Every effort has been made to make this book as complete and as accurate as possible, but no warranty or fitness is implied.

The information is provided on an as-is basis. The authors and New Riders Publishing shall have neither liability nor responsibility to any person or entity with respect to any loss or damages arising from the information contained in this book or from the use of the discs or programs that may accompany it.

Publisher
David Dwyer

Associate Publisher
Brad Koch

Executive Editor
Al Valvano

Managing Editor
Gina Brown

Product Marketing Manager
Stephanie Layton

Acquisitions Editor
Theresa Gheen

Editor
Robin Drake

Indexer
Miriam Rodríguez Lowe

Manufacturing Coordinator
Chris Moos

Book Designer
Louisa Klucznik

Cover Designer
Aren Howell

Composition
Scan Communications Group, Inc.

Contents at a Glance

Contents

About the Author

Jeffrey A. Ferris, MCSE, currently works as Systems Engineer for a large technology firm in Austin, Texas, where his responsibilities include technical development for emerging technologies, focusing on implementation recommendations and deployment of the Microsoft Windows 2000 operating system. Jeffrey has been working with computers since just after learning to walk, focusing on operating systems deployments and Windows NT enterprise technologies for the past six years. Prior to moving to Texas, Jeffrey was an associate consultant with Celeritas Technologies, LLC, a prominent consulting firm in the Kansas City area. While in Kansas, Jeffrey fulfilled a critical role in the development and implementation of the first nationwide rollout of a Windows NT 4.0 domain architecture for the Call Center Services division of Sprint Communications Company, L.P. This is Jeffrey's fifth published work; he has co-authored four other titles covering Windows NT Server 4.0, Windows NT 4.0 Enterprise, A+, and Network+ certification exams. Jeffrey can be reached online at `jeff@ferristech.net`; a companion Web site for this book can be found at `http://www.ferristech.net/win2k`.

About the Technical Reviewers

These reviewers contributed their considerable hands-on expertise to the entire development process for *Windows 2000 Deployment & Desktop Management*. As the book was being written, these dedicated professionals reviewed all the material for technical content, organization, and flow. Their feedback was critical to ensuring that *Windows 2000 Deployment & Desktop Management* fits our readers' need for the highest quality technical information.

Andrej Budja, MCSE+I, MCT, MVP, is currently studying computer science at the University of Maribor, Slovenia. He is the author of more than 100 articles about computer hardware, Windows NT, and Windows 2000. Lately, he is devoting all his time to Windows 2000. He speaks about Windows 2000 at various local events in Slovenia and helps users solve problems in Microsoft newsgroups. Andrej is a Microsoft Certified System Engineer + Internet (MCSE+I), Microsoft Certified Trainer (MCT), and Microsoft Most Valued Professional (MVP).

Thomas Lee, MCSE, MCT, MVP, is an independent computer consultant who has been working with Windows NT since 1993. After graduating with a B.S. in Computer Problem Solving from Carnegie Mellon University, he worked on two successful operating system projects (Comshare's Commander II and ICL's VME) before joining Andersen Consulting in 1981, where he was a manager in the London office. He has been an independent consultant since 1987. Most recently, he has worked in Redmond, Washington, developing Windows 2000 Microsoft Official Curriculum (MOC) training material and is presently engaged in several consulting projects related to Windows 2000. Thomas is a Fellow of the British Computer Society, a Member of the Institute of IT Trainers, as well as a Microsoft Certified Systems Engineer (MCSE), Microsoft Certified Trainer (MCT), and Microsoft Valued Professional (MVP). He lives in a cottage in the English countryside with his wife, Susan, and daughter, Rebecca.

"He is the half part of a blessed man,
Left to be finished by such as she;
And she a fair divided excellence,
Whose fullness of perfection lies in him."

- Shakespeare

To my love Amy, thank you for putting up with the eight months of late nights, sunny days, and long weekends, the majority of which I spent behind the keyboard instead of by your side.

I'd like to make it up to you. . . I'd like to be by your side for the rest of our lives. . . I love you so much. . .

Amy Gayle O'Brien, will you marry me?

Acknowledgments

Although this is my fifth published work, this book is the first I've composed cover-to-cover, proposal to publication. There are a surprising number of people behind the scenes, without whom this book would never have made it to the shelves. I'd especially like to thank Al Valvano for listening to my pitch at TechEd; Theresa Gheen for the project management assistance during the end game; Robin Drake for making everything coherent; and Thomas Lee and Andrej Budja, the technical reviewers, for calling my bluffs and keeping me accurate.

Thanks to my parents for not killing me as a child when I'd take apart the appliances (at least we were the first family in the nation to have a microwave/VCR combo unit). Dad, I knew you'd get better. Hang in there, you always have. Mom, I'm sorry I moved to Texas. To my little brother Tim, I'm sorry for all those times I broke your nose when we were growing up. And Grandma and Grandpa, if you keep collecting my books, people are going to expect you to get your MCSEs.

Thanks to all my friends for supporting me and cheering me on, even though you knew it meant I'd have to move away. To Matt, thanks for always setting up my jokes, no matter how many times it meant you'd have to hear my same stories. To Shawn, thanks for showing me how to keep things in perspective. And to Barb Coleman and Dangerous Dave, thanks for helping me find my way through those first few levels. I shudder to think that, without your guidance, I might have become an accountant. . .

Tell Us What You Think

As the reader of this book, you are the most important critic and commentator. We value your opinion and want to know what we're doing right, what we could do better, what areas you'd like to see us publish in, and any other words of wisdom you're willing to pass our way.

As the Executive Editor for the Networking team at New Riders Publishing, I welcome your comments. You can fax, email, or write me directly to let me know what you did or didn't like about this book—as well as what we can do to make our books stronger.

Please note that I cannot help you with technical problems related to the topic of this book, and that due to the high volume of mail I receive, I might not be able to reply to every message.

When you write, please be sure to include this book's title and author as well as your name and phone or fax number. I will carefully review your comments and share them with the author and editors who worked on the book.

Fax: 317-581-4663
Email: `nrfeedback@newriders.com`
Mail: Al Valvano
Executive Editor
New Riders Publishing
201 West 103rd Street
Indianapolis, IN 46290 USA

Introduction

This book is geared toward experienced system administrators, system integrators, system engineers, and other IT professionals responsible for rolling out and supporting Windows 2000 Professional clients in an enterprise environment.

The contents of this book touch on business benefits, but focus on in-depth technical aspects involved in deploying Windows 2000 Professional to corporate workstations. My goal in authoring this work was to provide a reference that you can use as a strategy guide during the planning and implementation phases of your corporate Windows 2000 rollout, and as a technical reference as you continue into the post-installation support of your Windows 2000 Professional environment from a desktop-management perspective.

This work is *not* a simple rewording of white papers. The technical procedures are described in great detail, with commentary on best practices, lessons learned from the field, and sample implementation scenarios based on real-world cases. Where applicable, the text discusses undocumented switches, side effects—either beneficial or dangerous—of various technologies, third-party solutions/utilities, and suggestions on enhancing the processes.

One of the biggest complaints I heard during the initial months following the release of Windows NT 4.0 was the lack of resources explaining deployment and management strategies for a complex environment. Microsoft heard those same complaints. As time went on, people developed their own solutions for deployment and management. With this new revision of Windows NT—Windows 2000—Microsoft has responded to this shortcoming of Windows NT 4.0 by incorporating the most popular technologies as core features of the new operating system. By spending a little extra development time, you'll be able to exploit these technologies to fully customize the Windows 2000 Professional installation process in your environment.

Contents

This book has three major sections. The first part of the book deals with getting Windows 2000 to the desktop, providing a top-level summary of some of the business benefits behind automated desktop deployment, comparing the various deployment methods available under Windows 2000, and exploring in detail the technical process involved when implementing the various deployment methods.

The second part of the book explores management and maintenance of the desktop once Windows 2000 is installed in the enterprise. This involves the use of technologies such as group policy objects (GPOs), IntelliMirror (Software Installation and Maintenance, User Settings Management, and User Data Management), and securing the workstation.

The third part of the book contains the appendixes and the glossary. The appendixes contain frequently needed references for use when developing your installation and management processes.

Users familiar with the Windows 2000 operating system but not the automated deployment process might skip all but the last section of Chapter 1. Users familiar with both Windows 2000 and the concepts behind automated deployment could jump straight to Chapter 3, which begins the discussion of automated deployment methods available in Windows 2000. If you've already deployed Windows 2000 in your environment and your interests lie more with post-deployment workstation management, direct your focus to Part II of the book, which focuses on managing and maintaining the desktop.

Part I: Deploying Windows 2000 Professional in the Enterprise

Chapter 1, "Why Upgrade?," discusses some of the basic reasons, both business and technical, for moving your environment to Windows 2000. This chapter also contains some brief introductory material on the various flavors and features of Windows 2000, including a high-level comparison of some of the major differences between the various Microsoft operating systems.

Chapter 2, "Setting the Standards," looks at one of the most-often-overlooked first steps of deployment and management strategies: evaluating your existing environment and planning your standards for going forward. This chapter discusses setting up your deployment team, reviewing your current standards, upgrading clients versus clean installs, and the development of a standardized desktop.

Chapter 3, "Deployment Options," introduces the various solutions available for the deployment of Windows 2000 Professional. Technologies discussed include distribution share points, Remote Installation Services, system cloning with SYSPREP, using the Windows 2000 Professional CD-ROM, and integrating installation with Microsoft's SMS 2.0 (Systems Management Server).

Chapter 4, "Answer Files and the Setup Manager Wizard," provides an in-depth look at building and using unattended answer files for installing and upgrading Windows 2000. The chapter also looks at some Resource Kit utilities that can assist you in the creation and maintenance of unattended answer files.

Chapter 5, "Remote Installation Services (RIS)," explores in detail the use of Remote Installation Services, included with Windows 2000 Server, in deploying your Windows 2000 Professional environment. Architectural requirements, the workstation image-development process, and the install procedures are among the main topics covered in this chapter.

Part II: Managing and Maintaining the Desktop

Chapter 6, "Group Policy Objects," describes the development and implementation of group policy objects as a tool for managing your corporate environment. This chapter also looks at script events for logon, logoff, startup, and shutdown.

Chapter 7, "IntelliMirror," presents an overview of the IntelliMirror technology suite, from introduction to implementation and integration of the various technologies that comprise IntelliMirror. IntelliMirror technologies include the Windows 2000 Software Installation and Maintenance component, User Data Management, and User Settings Management.

Chapter 8, "Application Management and Software Installation," takes a more in-depth look at the Software Installation and Maintenance component of the IntelliMirror technology suite. Major sections in this chapter include setting up the server for the Software Installation and Maintenance component, preparing applications, installing and managing applications, automatic application-repair features, and integrated protection from the administrative nightmare commonly referred to as "DLL hell."

Chapter 9, "Desktop Security," examines the integration of technologies described in this book that will ultimately enable you to secure your systems and lock down your users' desktops. The chapter explores the Windows 2000 security toolset, including the Security Configuration and Analysis snap-in, security templates, and the SECEDIT command-line tool. In addition, I provide some reasons why you might want to lock down desktops, as well as what issues to consider when profiling users.

Part III: Reference

The appendixes contain frequently needed references for use when developing deployment and management processes. The glossary includes definitions of terms and technologies referenced in this book as they apply to Windows 2000 deployment, customization, and management.

Appendix A, "Common File Extensions," provides an alphabetic listing of a large number of file extensions and their descriptions. This information is intended for use in determining which files to back up during a data-migration process. Information in this appendix is reprinted with permission of whatis.com Inc. (`http://whatis.com`) from their online feature, "Every file format in the world." Updates can be found at `http://whatis.com`.

Appendix B, "Complete Answer File Syntax," contains a complete listing of available sections, keys, and data values for use with unattended install answer files. This information applies to SYSPREP, Remote Installation Services, distribution share points, and CD-based installation automation processes.

Appendix C, "Sample Answer Files," contains four different types of sample answer files (with comments).

On the Web

News and important information about this title and other titles on Windows 2000 can be found on the New Riders home page at `http://www.newriders.com`. A companion Web site for this book is available at `http://www.ferristech.net/win2k`.

Conventions Used in this Book

The following conventions are used in this book:

Convention	Usage
italic	New terms being defined.
boldface	Text that you type, such as a domain name.
`monospace text`	Commands, syntax lines, and so on, as well as Internet addresses such as `www.microsoft.com`.
➥	Code-continuation characters are inserted into code when a line shouldn't be broken, but we simply ran out of room on the page.

I

Deploying Windows 2000 Professional in the Enterprise

1

Why Upgrade?

This chapter covers:

- Introduction to Windows 2000, and a brief history
- Comparison of the features of Windows 2000 versus other Microsoft operating systems
- Hardware requirements in the real world
- Benefits of deployment automation

After reading this chapter, you should be able to do the following:

- Understand where Windows 2000 fits in relation to other Microsoft operating systems
- Identify some of the major technological improvements in Windows 2000
- Differentiate between the four flavors of Windows 2000: Professional, Server, Advanced Server, and Datacenter Server
- Recognize the business and technical benefits of using deployment automation

Whenever Microsoft—or any other vendor, for that matter—releases a new software revision, the first question we all ask ourselves is, "Why should I upgrade?" This question is particularly important when dealing with a core component of your enterprise infrastructure such as the operating system—a change with the potential to affect every system in your organization.

Obviously, changing the operating system on every machine in an organization is no small task. It makes no sense to go through all that trouble if upgrading offers no benefits. This chapter starts off by providing a brief introduction to Windows 2000, discussing some of the benefits—and, in some cases, the drawbacks—of Windows 2000 versus Microsoft's other operating systems. The last part of the chapter looks at the real-world hardware requirements for rolling out Windows 2000 and explores the benefits of automating your deployment.

Readers who are familiar with the concepts and technologies behind Windows 2000 but not with the advantages of automated Windows 2000 deployment may prefer to skip the introductory material and go directly to the final section of this chapter, "Benefits of Deployment Automation."

Related Publications

This book focuses on deployment and management of Windows 2000. For a more detailed introduction to Windows 2000 basics (such as detailed changes from NT 4.0 to Windows 2000), consider these titles from New Riders Publishing:

- *Planning for Windows 2000* by Eric K. Cone, Jon Boggs, and Sergio Perez, ISBN 0-7357-0048-6.
- *Inside Windows 2000 Server* by William Boswell, ISBN 1-5620-5929-7.
- *Inside Windows 2000 Professional* by Jerry Honeycutt, ISBN 0-7357-0950-5.

In addition, the Microsoft Windows 2000 Web site at `http://www.Microsoft.com/windows2000` provides links to a number of introductory, technical, and training documents.

A Brief History of Windows 2000

As you may already be aware, Windows 2000 is the latest version of Microsoft's popular Windows NT operating system product line. Originally named Windows NT 5.0, this enterprise-class operating system was designed to build on the strengths of Windows NT 4.0, incorporate the best features of Windows 98, and take advantage of the latest advances in hardware. The official announcement of the name change from Windows NT 5.0 to Windows 2000 came during the fourth quarter of 1998.

From the beginning, an important goal of Windows 2000 was to provide a better out-of-the-box experience for both end users and system administrators. There are four basic releases of Windows 2000, one for workstations and three for servers, all four based on the same core programming code. While all of these versions share a common kernel, common user interface, and common base of features, each version has a few special features, and all the versions are tuned for different uses in the enterprise environment.

- **Windows 2000 Professional.** This is the workstation-class version of Windows 2000, with a target audience similar to that of Windows NT Workstation 4.0. For most users in a corporate environment, Windows 2000 Professional is the operating system (OS) installed on the desktop, workstation, and notebook-class systems. Windows 2000 Professional supports single-processor and two-way *symmetric multiprocessing* (*SMP*) systems with up to 4GB of RAM. In addition, the inclusion of features modeled after Windows 98 makes Windows 2000 Professional the first NT-class operating system feasible for widespread use by the typical home office user. Windows 2000 Professional is *not* positioned for use by casual home users, Internet-focused users, or heavy gamers. Windows 98 remains the consumer-focused desktop OS.

- **Windows 2000 Server.** As its name implies, Windows 2000 Server is the server-class version of Windows 2000, with a target audience similar to that of Windows NT Server 4.0. Windows 2000 Server, sometimes referred to as Windows 2000 Server Standard Edition, will be the most popular version of the server family for small and medium-sized businesses. This version supports single-processor systems as well as two- and four-way SMP systems, with a maximum of 4GB of RAM.
- **Windows 2000 Advanced Server.** This enterprise-level server-class version of Windows 2000 targets a similar audience to that of Windows NT Server 4.0, Enterprise Edition. Windows 2000 Advanced Server supports systems with up to eight processors (eight-way SMP), with a maximum of 8GB of RAM. In addition, Advanced Server includes the Clustering service for high-availability clustering and application failover, and the Network Load Balancing service to distribute network application tasks among groups of servers. Advanced Server is well suited for highly available, mission-critical servers used in medium and large businesses. The Advanced Server Clustering service supports two-node clustering.
- **Windows 2000 Datacenter Server.** This version is a high-end enterprise-level server-class version of Windows 2000. As with Advanced Server, Datacenter Server supports a maximum of 8GB of RAM and includes services for high-availability clustering and load balancing; but instead of just eight processors, Datacenter Server supports up to 32-way SMP (16-way native, 32-way through some OEMs). Datacenter Server is optimized for use with large-scale enterprise solutions, including data warehousing, engineering simulations, and high-demand e-commerce applications. Datacenter Server supports four-node clustering.

New Features in Windows 2000

Other than the name change and the nifty new startup sound, what are the real advantages of Windows 2000? This section outlines some of the general features and improvements, and provides a comparison of Windows 2000 to other recent Microsoft operating systems.

The "Big Three" Enhancements

Windows 2000 includes a number of features for both end users and administrators, geared toward improving the overall customer experience and reducing *Total Cost of Ownership* (*TCO*). Probably the three most noticeable improvements are the inclusion of directory services, the new disaster-recovery and workstation-management features, and the wide range of enhanced security features.

The directory service in Windows 2000 is called *Active Directory* (*AD*). Active Directory, based loosely on the X.500 directory protocol, provides a centralized information repository for network objects (see `http://www.whatis.com/x500.htm` for background information on X.500 directories). Users, network administrators, and even applications can benefit from a well-designed directory structure:

- Active Directory benefits administrators by allowing for a single point of administration for all objects in a network.
- All users can benefit from enhanced search capabilities; for example, through a simple search interface, a user could search for all color printers on the third floor of a certain building, or for all users with the last name Smith.
- Applications benefit from the ability to pull data from the Active Directory without requiring separate databases on the back end. For example, the corporate directory could display phone numbers and physical addresses for all users in the corporation by pulling the data from the Active Directory. Microsoft Exchange is another example. In a Windows NT 4.0 domain with Exchange 5.x environment, there are two directory repositories; one directory for NT, and a separate directory for Exchange. Exchange 2000, however, leverages the Active Directory for its directory repository, reducing the administrative overhead required to maintain multiple directories.

Workstation-management and disaster-recovery features are provided through the *IntelliMirror* technologies. IntelliMirror is a suite of technologies including User Data Management, User Settings Management, and Software Installation and Maintenance components. In addition to disaster recovery, IntelliMirror allows the user's environment to "follow" the user, meaning that the user will be presented with the same desktop environment regardless of where he or she logs on. *Remote Installation Services* (*RIS*) is often included in discussions of IntelliMirror, although Microsoft doesn't actually consider RIS to be part of the IntelliMirror suite. IntelliMirror is discussed in detail in Chapter 7, "IntelliMirror."

Windows 2000 includes a number of enhancements and additions to security. In addition to the familiar username/password–based logon, Windows 2000 supports hardware-based logons such as smart cards and biometric devices. In fact, the old NTLM authentication protocol is no longer the default; Windows 2000 authentication utilizes Microsoft's implementation of the Kerberos 5 user authentication protocol. Microsoft's Windows 2000 Kerberos 5 implementation can interoperate with the MIT-based Kerberos 5 authentication protocol.

Basic file and folder security is still available through the use of NTFS permissions, but the new version of NTFS adds support for the *Encrypted File System* (*EFS*) to encrypt files and prevent unauthorized users from viewing the contents. Security for remote users is enhanced through the use of *Layer 2 Tunneling Protocol* (*L2TP*), *Extensible Authentication Protocol* (*EAP*), and *Internet Protocol Security* (*IPSec*). In addition to enhancing security for remote users, IPSec can provide an encrypted network communication path between Windows 2000 workstations and servers on the local network.

Windows 2000 Versus Windows 9x and Windows NT 4.0

Windows 2000 differs in quite a few ways from older versions of Microsoft operating systems. Although it's not the purpose of this book to outline all the changes, a handful of differences deserve mentioning, and are briefly outlined in this section. (For more in-depth information on the differences between the various Windows product lines, check the Microsoft Web site at `http://www.microsoft.com/windows`.)

Security

While the Windows 9x product line focuses primarily on the home user, the Windows NT family—which includes Windows NT 4.0 and Windows 2000—is geared more toward corporate environments. As such, an important difference between a Windows 9x client and a Windows NT or Windows 2000 client is security; Windows 9x clients are not nearly as secure as their corporate counterparts, from either a network or file system perspective.

On the network side, Windows 9x clients can have password-protected shares, a low-security access method in which multiple users utilize a single password to access a network resource. There is no resource-level security—such as NTFS permissions in the NT world—for Windows 9x clients when a user is logged on locally. Neither Windows NT nor Windows 2000 supports password-protected shares.

Windows 9x, Windows NT, and Windows 2000 all support user-level security, in which access to a resource is granted on a user-by-user basis, requiring a unique username and password for logon. Windows NT 4.0 and Windows 2000 also contain built-in support for group-level security. Although group-level security can be applied to Windows 9x network shares, a stand-alone Windows 9x client has no built-in support for local groups; the client machine must use NT domain-based user and group security.

In terms of the file system options, FAT and FAT32 drives are not secure or robust in case of failure. Any user can boot with a boot floppy to access files stored on a FAT or FAT32 partition. User-level security can't be set on a local machine for FAT or

Kerberos, Active Directory, and Authentication

Kerberos 5 only works in an Active Directory domain for Windows 2000 to Windows 2000 authentication. When network authentication involves one or more pre-Windows 2000 clients, the authentication method reverts to NTLM. Also, Windows 2000 systems operating in workgroups or in stand-alone environments will revert to NTLM authentication.

FAT32 files or folders. NTFS, on the other hand, is an enhanced, more secure file system, which allows an administrator to set file-level permissions on a user-by-user or group-by-group basis. In addition, NTFS drives allow auditing for successful or unsuccessful attempts to access a resource. Windows 9x clients support only FAT- and FAT32-formatted drives (although FAT32 was not supported in the initial release of Windows 95), Windows NT 4.0 supports only FAT or NTFS, and Windows 2000 clients support FAT, FAT32, or NTFS. While local NTFS files could still be accessed by reinstalling Windows NT or by physically removing the drive and inserting it into a machine on which you have local administrator rights, Windows 2000 includes EFS (Encrypted File System) for NTFS, which can encrypt local files, making them inaccessible through either of these methods.

Windows 2000 also adds support for user-level disk quotas. Unfortunately, you can't apply disk quotas across groups; you can only apply quotas to individual user accounts. Quotas are defined per user at the level of the physical drive volume, meaning that a single user can't have separate quotas for different shares or folders located on the same physical volume.

In addition to network and file-system security, the default authentication protocol and system-to-system network communication in a Windows 2000 Active Directory environment is much more secure. Windows 2000 clients and servers authenticate with each other using Kerberos 5. Kerberos 5 authentication is not supported with pre–Windows 2000 machines. Windows 2000 machines can communicate with each other using IPSec, an encrypted IP protocol requiring a machine account in the Active Directory. Since Windows 9x clients can't have machine accounts, they're unable to utilize IPSec.

User Interface

The user interface for Windows 2000 follows the same evolutionary path as the GUI introduced with Windows 95 and extended to Windows NT 4.0 and Windows 98. Windows 2000 introduces the Device Manager to the NT product line; Device Manager was present in Windows 95 and Windows 98 but not available in Windows NT 4.0.

Device Support

Unlike Windows NT 4.0, Windows 2000 adds support for plug and play, Universal Serial Bus (USB) devices, Advanced Configuration and Power Interface (ACPI) power management, and full DirectX 7.x compatibility. All of these enhancements make Windows 2000 run better on portable computers than prior versions of Windows NT.

Interoperability in a Mixed Environment

Windows 2000 Professional can interoperate to some degree with existing Windows NT Server 4.0–based domains. Windows NT Server 4.0–based printer drivers will work on Windows 2000; if you currently use printer shares on NT 4.0 servers, you won't have to load server-side drivers to support Windows 2000 or load Windows 2000-specific drivers on the client end. The Event Viewer, Performance Monitor, and Server Manager tools for NT 4.0 are not included with Windows 2000, but the executables can be copied to a Windows 2000 machine to enable remote management of NT 4.0 environments. Windows 2000 Professional can use—to a degree—system policies built with the Windows NT 4.0 Policy Editor, such as the NTCONFIG.POL file. Such down-level policy inheritance is not enabled by default; group policy objects provide much greater flexibility and granularity for Windows 2000 management and configuration tasks, and NT 4.0 policies don't contain policy settings for the enhanced features available on a Windows 2000 client.

With the Active Directory, domains can be one of two types: *mixed mode* or *native mode*. In mixed mode, Windows 2000 domain controllers emulate NT 4.0 domain controllers and support the same range of facilities. Thus, Windows 2000 domain controllers can also interoperate with existing Windows NT Server 4.0–based domains. Windows 2000 domains can also be native mode, which means that all Windows NT 4.0 domain controllers have been removed or upgraded. You can't have an NT 4.0 domain controller in a native-mode environment. Native-mode domains offer more functionality, such as universal groups, which aren't supported in a mixed-mode domain.

Inclusion of Windows 2000 member servers in a Windows NT 4.0 domain works no differently than using Windows NT Server 4.0 member servers. Windows 2000 member servers can be added to a Windows NT 4.0 domain, and Windows NT 4.0 member servers can be added to a Windows 2000 domain.

Using a Windows 2000 server as a domain controller in a Windows NT 4.0 domain means that you'll be running in a mixed-mode environment. Adding a Windows 2000 domain controller to a Windows NT 4.0 domain requires installing the Windows 2000 domain controller as the primary domain controller (PDC). More accurately, the first Windows 2000 domain controller in your environment becomes the PDC emulator; there are no Windows 2000 PDCs or backup domain controllers (BDCs), just domain controllers. All NT 4.0 domain controllers become BDCs. Subsequent Windows 2000 domain controllers act as additional BDCs as far as the Windows NT 4.0 BDCs are concerned.

If you want to introduce a Windows 2000 domain controller in a Windows NT 4.0 domain environment, you must first upgrade the existing primary domain controller to Windows 2000. Down-level clients—such as Windows NT 4.0 Workstation systems—

NT 4.0 Policy in a Windows 2000 World

Windows 2000 Professional can use the same system policy files (*.pol files) as Windows NT 4.0, but I wouldn't recommend it for two reasons. First, NT 4.0 policies address a more limited set of features than Windows 2000 group policy objects. Second, once an NT 4.0 policy has been applied to a Windows 2000 machine, the machine's local registry will be tattooed with the policy information. Deleting the NT 4.0 policy leaves the Windows 2000 machine in a modified state. When you move to Windows 2000 group policy objects at a later point, the resulting set of policies will be unpredictable.

can still access the mixed-mode domain by using the NetBIOS name of the old NT 4.0–based domain, while Active Directory clients can access the domain through the new directory services model. The upgrade of the domain controllers will be transparent to the down-level clients. They won't lose existing functions, but they also won't be able to take advantage of new features in Windows 2000—such as Software Installation and Maintenance, group policy objects, or User Data Management—until the clients are upgraded to Windows 2000. This feature keeps you from having to upgrade the entire network infrastructure to Windows 2000 at the same time, and allows older clients to operate in a mixed-mode environment with no change in network configuration, while still permitting newer Windows 2000 clients to benefit from features of the Active Directory.

Hardware Requirements in the Real World

It's quite fortunate that PC prices have plummeted over the past years, because one of the big disadvantages of Windows 2000 is the hefty hardware requirement. Long gone are the days of stretching the life of 486s and low-end Pentiums by adding more RAM and bigger hard drives. Microsoft states the minimum hardware configuration for Windows 2000 Professional as follows:

- Pentium-class 133 MHz processor
- 64MB RAM
- 2GB hard drive

These are the Microsoft-determined requirements for Windows 2000 Server, both Standard and Advanced:

- Pentium-class 133 MHz processor
- 128MB RAM
- 2GB hard drive
- PCI network interface card (recommended)

The hardware levels indicated here are Microsoft's *minimum* supported configuration. Obviously, installing Windows 2000 on either of those configurations would be guaranteed to cause headaches. Running any sort of application load on such a setup may cause the system to run unacceptably slowly. (This is, of course, a subjective issue.)

> **What About the Datacenter Server Requirements?**
>
> Windows 2000 Datacenter Server isn't available as a stand-alone product. Due to the nature of this high-end OS, Windows 2000 Datacenter Server is available only from an OEM with certified hardware. If you need Datacenter Server, you aren't likely to be ordering hardware that falls below the minimum requirements.

The following recommendations are based on minimum *usable* hardware configurations, gleaned from testing against a variety of systems for a large-scale corporate deployment:

Windows 2000 Professional:

- Pentium Pro class 200 MHz processor, Pentium II class 266 MHz or better recommended if you're running any applications
- 64MB RAM, 128MB recommended if you're running multiple applications
- 4GB hard drive
- CD-ROM

Windows 2000 Server (low end):

- Pentium Pro class 200 MHz processor, Pentium II class 266 MHz or better recommended
- 128MB RAM, 256MB on a domain controller
- 4GB hard drive
- CD-ROM
- PCI network interface card

Notice that this server configuration is designated as "low end." In reality, server requirements are very specific to your organization. These specifications serve only as a very basic guide to the absolute minimum hardware requirements to install and operate Windows 2000 Server. In my experience, when choosing between a faster processor or more RAM, an increase in RAM gives greater performance gains than stepping up the processor.

From a customer experience standpoint, there's no such thing as "too much server." Unfortunately, the price tag on a fully decked server may cause management to have a slightly different opinion. Unless you happen to have an unlimited budget, consider the purpose of the server in your hardware selection. For example:

- Application servers need more RAM.
- File and print servers need more storage space, although a large organization might consider a Storage Area Network (SAN).

Windows 2000 in the Real World—Microsoft's Setup

According to presentations from TechEd '99, Microsoft's Redmond domain contains over 27,300 user accounts and over 5,000 groups. The domain was initially mixed mode, with 10 Windows 2000 domain controllers. One Windows NT 4.0 BDC was initially left in place in case a back-out plan was needed, but the BDC has since been shut off, and the domain switched to native mode.

The Windows 2000 domain controllers are each Quad processor 450 MHz Xeons with 1GB RAM and 36GB storage space. The Active Directory database takes up 310MB; the Global Catalog adds 333MB. Servicing over 19,000 logons per day, CPU utilization is only around 10%.

- Domain controllers' need for RAM and storage space is proportional to the size of the Active Directory.
- Any mission-critical server should have on-the-fly data redundancy. I prefer hardware RAID 5, but if cost is really an issue mirrored disk sets are usually sufficient.

Benefits of Deployment Automation

With vendors turning out new versions of programs written for Windows 2000, your users may clamor for an operating system upgrade. Then again, once you discover some of the administrative benefits of Windows 2000, you may be looking forward to the upgrade even more than the users are. Either way, before you start installing Windows 2000 clients, you have to decide on the upgrade process.

A small organization running a relatively recent release of Windows may have little or no trouble doing in-place upgrades from the current operating system to Windows 2000 clients, using nothing more complex than the Windows 2000 Installation CD. After all, Windows 2000 can upgrade NT 4.0, Windows 98, and Windows 95 clients straight out of the box. On the other hand, if you plan to install Windows 2000 in a mid- to large-sized business, sneaker-netting from client to client and attending every installation from start to finish would be a costly, time-consuming process. Here's where deployment automation comes in.

Windows 2000 includes a number of technologies to simplify deployment automation and post-deployment management. For deployment, a number of enhancements are available for the unattended install technologies, including more detailed answer files, SYSPREP, and Remote Installation Services. For post-deployment management, Windows 2000 provides group policy objects, Software Installation and Maintenance, User Data Management, and User Settings Management. These technologies are the focus of this book.

Business Benefits

Automating the deployment process reaps a number of potential benefits over a manual install procedure. First of all, it's easier to standardize the load image because you remove the potential for human error by using an automated process. With no human interaction, there's no chance for typographical errors or forgotten steps, and every machine should look the same when the installation is complete. For example, if you roll out 1,000 machines with Windows 2000 Professional, Office 2000 Standard Edition, and your custom business application, you'll know how every user's machine is configured, and support should be cheaper because your staff won't have to guess at possible installation-induced configuration variants.

Second, an automated install can be initiated by less-skilled workers—in some cases, perhaps even by the end user—which lowers the cost associated with staffing or contracting for a rollout. If you develop a load that requires zero technician interaction on the majority of the user machines, you've just saved a bundle of budget money.

Third, post-installation support is easier. If your support staff knows how a system was initially installed, they'll have a better idea of where to start diagnosing unexpected anomalies. Together, these benefits can drastically reduce the cost of creating, completing, and supporting a Windows 2000 Professional rollout.

Technical Benefits

With an automated deployment process, you spend less time per system babysitting the install and waiting for Next buttons to become active. The install process runs much faster than a technician-attended process, and the chance of keying incorrect data drops dramatically. Plus, a person can watch that little "copying" bar creep across the text setup screen only so many times before going insane.

If a user accidentally destroys his or her system ("What did you do?" "Nothing! It just did this all by itself!"), getting the system up and running again is much easier with an automated deployment process in place. Not only is the rebuild faster, but the resulting system image will be very similar—if not identical—to the system image being replaced. If you use the IntelliMirror technologies in that environment, all user settings and user data will be restored automatically to the machine. For a technician, this means not having to fix the broken system to recover lost user data.

Because an automated deployment uses a standardized image, subsequent releases of the operating system are easier to manage. If every user in the environment has an identical system, any workstation upgrade procedures to the next major release of NT—let's say Windows 2003—should run the same on all systems. If a specific application requires a workaround before it works on the upgraded OS, that workaround will be required on every system, and you can build that workaround into the automated deployment process.

Example of Automated Deployment Savings

Suppose the environment includes 10,000 users, and the average technician hour is budgeted as a cost to the business of $40. If a standard install takes 1.5 technician-attended hours, you're looking at $600,000 (10,000 workstations × $40 × 1.5 hours = $600,000) just for the workstation rollout—and that's not even taking development time into account.

But if you could automate the install process to the point where 70% of the users could install their own systems, and the technician-assisted install time for the remaining 30% is cut down to 20 minutes, the workstation rollout cost drops to $40,000 (30% × 10,000 workstations = 3,000 workstations; 1/3 hour × $40 = $13.33; $13.33 × 3,000 workstations = $40,000). That's a savings of $560,000. Keep in mind that developing the unattended install process will cost a little more up front for research and development, but the minimal research and development expense should more than justify savings of half a million dollars. Using similar assumptions in an environment of only 1,000 users, you could potentially see cost savings of nearly $50,000.

An important part of the automated deployment is designing a system that the user can't corrupt easily. With proper security policies in place, users must go through proper channels before installing unsupported software on their systems. In theory, this means that you'll know the software configuration for every machine in the environment, and that makes providing user support quite a bit less painful.

The next chapter explores the project-planning portion of a Windows 2000 deployment strategy. Starting in Chapter 3, the focus shifts to the implementation of technological solutions in a Windows 2000 environment that facilitate the benefits of deployment automation.

2

Setting the Standards

This chapter covers:

- Who should be on the team that determines the standards and guidelines for Windows 2000
- Reviewing existing infrastructure architecture and desktop standards
- Upgrading clients versus clean installs
- Developing the standard desktop

After reading this chapter, you should be able to do the following:

- Identify individuals critical to the successful development of a Windows 2000 deployment strategy
- Define the standards that exist in your current environment and identify opportunities for standards going forward
- Understand and mitigate the risks pertaining to local user data storage
- Decide whether you should do in-place upgrades or clean installs for Windows 2000 Professional clients
- Design a standard desktop configuration for your Windows 2000 Professional clients

One of the most important aspects of a deployment strategy is the planning phase. Unfortunately, with the speed at which technologies change and the pressures to adapt corporate environments quickly to take advantage of these technological advances, the planning phase is often cut short—if not skipped altogether. By involving the right people, documenting the plan clearly, and taking just a bit of extra time at the beginning of such a complex undertaking as the deployment of a new operating system (OS), you stand to save an incomparable amount of time on the back end—time that might otherwise be spent reworking unexpected issues, reinstalling improperly configured workstations, and apologizing profusely for what you might have perceived as relatively minor oversights.

The first part of this chapter is written toward project managers. It addresses the importance of selecting the proper team members for your Windows 2000 deployment effort. The second section takes you into a review of your existing environment. By the way, if you choose to skim this section, I'd recommend paying particular attention to the section "Local User Data Storage." The chapter continues with a comparison between upgrading clients and performing clean installs, and concludes with a discussion on the development of a standard Windows 2000 Professional desktop.

Who's on the Team?

One of the most common technician errors in the evaluation and implementation of new technology is spending more time focusing on the technology than figuring out the actual customer requirements. Implementing a feature simply for the sake of technology can endanger your environment—and, depending on the outcome, your employment. This is why, when implementing major changes to a network environment, it's absolutely crucial to get buy-in from the representatives of various departments in your organization. The best way to get this buy-in is to involve the proper representatives from the beginning.

So who should be included in your deployment planning efforts? The following list provides some starting ideas. (Keep in mind that this list will vary depending on your corporate environment, and it's not uncommon for a single representative to be responsible for multiple aspects of the deployment.)

- **Account administrators.** Anyone responsible for user accounts, security policies, profiles, and logon scripts should be involved. These individuals will need to be in the loop for group policy objects.
- **Application developers.** These programmers are responsible for internal applications. If you're installing a new operating system, you need to make sure that important internal applications run on the new platform.
- **Core business representatives.** Core business representatives are usually managers or team leaders who can speak for the critical departments in your organization. These individuals vary depending on the business. For example, if the primary revenue in your company comes from consumer product sales, you

might want representatives from sales and marketing departments involved in your planning efforts so you don't accidentally schedule their system upgrades during a critical time in the business cycle. It might also be a bad idea to upgrade your accounting department during tax season or at the end of a fiscal period. If you can work in these kinds of exceptions at the beginning of a project, the process runs much smoother than when reactively trying to accommodate issues in the middle of a deployment.

- **Desktop engineers.** These engineers are responsible for workstation configuration and software installations. Additional responsibilities might include application-compatibility testing to make sure that critical third-party applications work with the new operating system. Desktop engineers are likely to be the people responsible for developing the installation process, including the user data backup-and-restore procedure, desktop-hardware inventory evaluation to determine systems needing upgrades, and the deployment mechanism used to load the OS.
- **Domain architects.** The engineers who design and maintain your existing domain structure (assuming that you have one), including account domains, resource domains, trusts, and directory design, will be integral to the development of the Active Directory.
- **LAN/WAN engineers.** These engineers are responsible for the network infrastructure, such as bandwidth planning, routing, IP security, name resolution, directory services, replication considerations, and DHCP/client configurations. They may also provide remote access solutions, such as VPNs, ISDN connectivity, RADIUS authentication, and other related network services.
- **Logistics.** Logistics personnel are responsible for setting the timeframe for the deployment. In a perfect world, they should also be able to provide information on the current user environment, from historical hardware deployment standards to supported software information.
- **Security.** These folks make sure that your network is safe from both internal and external threats, such as viruses, hackers, and evil gnomes. They may also set the standards and policies that minimize the opportunities for your users to hurt themselves, such as defining file permissions and group policy objects to restrict user access to sensitive OS areas, setting password policies to prevent users from selecting an easily guessed password, and specifying guidelines for security delegation practices.
- **Training.** The training department staff will be responsible for making sure that users know how to work in the new environment, whether by providing classes, handing out documentation, or providing assistance via telephone on an as-needed basis. They need to determine whether your deployment plans are too aggressive to meet user-training schedules; you don't want to deploy new software before the end users know what to do with it.

- **User support.** Field technicians and related user-support groups who interact face-to-face with users to diagnose issues will likely see an increase in their workload as users adjust to the new operating system. These support groups will need to make sure that their own skills are up to par before they can provide support to others on the new system. User support staff may also be responsible for developing handouts, technology primers, or Web content for your rollout project. This group also includes help desk staff, the technicians who will provide user support, technical support, application support, hardware maintenance, and similar services for the new platform via phone or email. Some organizations outsource help desk functions.

Obviously, the preceding list doesn't apply perfectly to every organization, but it should give you an idea of where to start when planning your deployment. Some of the listed tasks may be shared between multiple groups of people. In other cases, one person may be responsible for a number of the above categories. At the very least, I hope it helps some readers to come up with an "Oh, yeah, I wouldn't have thought about them," before the project plan is set in stone.

Evaluating the Current Standards

Standards are important in any organization, regardless of size. With standards in place, administration, maintenance, support, and implementation tasks are more efficient, and problem resolution becomes dramatically easier. As a result, organizations are able to increase output while decreasing administrative overhead.

Before you can decide how your new Windows 2000 Professional environment is going to be set up, you need to evaluate your existing environment. Among the questions you should consider are the following (and again, this is not a conclusive list):

- Can your existing infrastructure support the new requirements?
- Are your technicians ready to support a new operating system?
- Do your critical applications—the applications necessary to keep your users productive—run on Windows 2000?
- Are your users prepared for the upgrade?
- Will any third-party applications you use need to be upgraded?
- Is your desktop hardware adequate to support Windows 2000? If not, have you budgeted for a hardware upgrade?
- What's your deployment timeframe?
- Will the deployment schedule overlap or conflict with any other major projects or business milestones?
- What processes and procedures will need to be refined to be efficient in your new environment?

The following subsections break out some of the important considerations into two categories—architectural standards and desktop standards—and provide sample questions for each. Keep in mind that these are just examples to get you started; you'll need to fine-tune these questions for your environment.

Reviewing the Base Infrastructure

Before you can roll out Windows 2000 Professional, you need to evaluate existing standards in your base infrastructure. Use this section as a starting point to evaluate the complexity of your existing infrastructure. For each of the following subsections, determine whether you have standards in place. If so, describe the standard, and specify whether the component is maintained by a technological solution (such as password aging policies or policy files) or a political solution (such as a documented corporate policy). If no standards exist in a given area, consider using the rollout of Windows 2000 as a catalyst to drive the creation of a standard.

Operating Systems

Questions:

- Do you have a single operating system throughout your company, or is it a mixed environment? (This includes server and desktop operating systems.)
- Will all existing desktop or server operating systems be replaced with Windows 2000?

Possible issues:

With a single desktop OS, integration and testing tasks are simplified. With multiple server operating systems—such as Windows 2000, NetWare, and UNIX servers—you may need to select appropriate interoperability solutions, usually either through network client software installed on every workstation in the environment or through gateways installed on a selection of servers. Because you'll most likely stage the rollout of Windows 2000 Professional over weeks or months—rather than upgrading the entire desktop environment overnight—you must be prepared for the transitional period during which you'll be running mixed desktop clients. The costs of the upgrade would need to be balanced against the benefits.

Network Configuration

Questions:

- What network protocols are used?
- How are the clients configured?
- What's the physical composition of the network?

Possible issues:

Technology changes frequently, but ripping out and reinstalling your network infrastructure every time a new network standard comes along would be too expensive to consider. Nevertheless, any opportunity to reduce the number of older supported technology standards makes the network easier to use and support. Network standards include all of the following:

- Supported frame type
- IP addressing scheme
- Network infrastructure equipment such as routers, hubs, and switches
- Media, media access control, and network interface cards
- Client configuration, such as DHCP versus static IP assignment
- Domains, sites, and other logical network structures
- Network services such as email servers, application servers, name resolution, and print servers
- Data transmission and communication protocols

Windows 2000 clients must be configured properly to interoperate with your existing network configuration. If the network utilizes a standard or proprietary architectural component that conflicts with the supported features of Windows 2000, a workaround will be required before deployment can begin.

Naming Conventions

Question:

- Does your organization use any naming standards?

Possible issues:

Naming standards facilitate administrative tasks and organizational efficiency in a number of ways. Naming standards can be applied to almost any object in an information infrastructure. The most common naming structures include the following items:

- User accounts
- Server names
- IP address assignment and subnetting scheme
- Workstation names
- Directory shares
- Printer names

If naming standards exist, they may be integrated into network applications or protocols, such that changing the standards could cause service interruptions on your network. If your environment has no naming standards, the Windows 2000 deployment is a good opportunity for implementation.

Ideally, a naming convention for non-user objects will provide administrators with a way to identify, at a minimum, the location and purpose of a given object in the network. The standard should be flexible enough that future upgrades to your network won't require renaming critical components that are frequently accessed by users, such as file and print shares.

Consider computer accounts as an example. Computers in your environment may take a number of roles: workstations, domain controllers, file and print servers, application servers, and more. Your company may have offices located in a number of cities, or at multiple sites within those cities. Your naming convention could identify the type of system and the system's general physical location at a glance. For example, your computer names could be formatted as follows:

XXXYYYZZZ####

XXX	Three-letter city code, such as STL for St. Louis, Missouri; KCM for Kansas City, Missouri; or DAL for Dallas, Texas. You might consider using airport codes.
YYY	Three-letter building code, perhaps based on a street name and number such as MN1 and MN2 for two buildings on Main Street, or SX1 for a building on Sixth Street. If you already use mail stop codes for your buildings, consider using the same codes.
ZZZ	Three-letter function code identifying the role of the computer, such as WKS for workstation, ADC for Active Directory controller, FPS for file and print server, or APP for application server.
####	Numeric identifier used to create a unique ID for multiple computers in the same building with the same functions.

Network Security

Questions:

- What security mechanisms are in place for access control, data protection, and physical access?
- Will Windows 2000 require modification to any of those policies?
- Do you allow Internet access to or from your corporate network?

Possible issues:

The default security level in Windows 2000 is more secure than in Windows NT 4.0. Windows 2000 Professional contains a number of enhancements over older operating systems in terms of access control and data encryption, but security standards apply to a much broader range of technologies. When evaluating security standards, consider the following components:

- Access control (user logon)
- Virus protection
- Data encryption
- Digital signatures
- Backup procedures and disaster recovery
- Physical access control

Third-party security devices such as smart card solutions, secure ID tokens, or biometric devices in an environment may not be compatible with Windows 2000 out of the box. Legacy virus protection and backup applications are almost guaranteed to be incompatible with the new OS. These items must be addressed; a weakness in a single client could put the security of the entire network at risk.

Reviewing the Current Desktop Standards

Current desktop standards have quite a bit to do with how easily you'll be able to roll out Windows 2000 Professional in your environment. If your desktop standard is already locked down, you have much less to worry about from the logistics, recovery, and testing perspectives. If you don't have a standard, locked-down desktop, automating the deployment process may be a bit more difficult. You must then take into consideration user data migration, user-installed applications, and nonstandard software and hardware configurations.

Use this section as a starting point to determine which of the following workstation configuration components you'll need to document and evaluate in your environment. For each of the following subsections, determine whether you have standards in place. If so, describe the standard, and specify whether the component is maintained by a technological solution (such as NT security policies), or a political solution (such as a documented corporate policy).

Hardware

Questions:

- Does your environment have a standard desktop hardware configuration?
- If not, what's the range of desktop equipment you can expect to work with?
- What peripherals are in use?

> **Taking Advantage of Missed Opportunities**
>
> If you don't currently hold your users to any specific corporate policies, the rollout of Windows 2000 might be a good opportunity for you, as a system administrator, to implement such standards, through either technical or non-technical means. Doing so will make future software deployments or system upgrades much less painful.

Possible issues:

With a standard hardware configuration, you should know how many desktop machines would need to be upgraded before they could handle the minimum requirements of Windows 2000. With standard hardware, you're also more likely to have success using a disk-image–based deployment mechanism such as Norton Ghost or PowerQuest Drive Image. If no standard is in place, you're more likely to run into issues of hardware compatibility, and should choose a deployment method that lessens the risks associated with incompatible hardware platforms.

What peripherals do your users need? If the environment includes special devices such as scanners, CD burners, graphics tablets, or accessibility devices, you'll need to make sure that Windows 2000 will work with those devices. As you've probably guessed, there's both good news and bad news on this front. First, the good news: Windows 2000 can use drivers written to the Windows Driver Model (WDM). Windows 98 is able to use WDM drivers, so in theory any device written to the Windows 98 WDM can be installed under Windows 2000, right? Well, almost. Here's the bad news: Not all Windows 98 drivers are written to the WDM, and for many of the peripherals that are, the device still needs a controlling software application. For some devices, the base drivers are only available through a complete software installation.

For example, I have a parallel port scanner, included as a bundled companion accessory with my laser printer. It includes Windows 98 WDM drivers, which should work with Windows 2000, but the drivers are compressed with a proprietary algorithm, packed deep inside the setup files, and can only be installed through the execution of the included setup routine. If I attempt to run the setup under Windows NT, the setup routine checks the OS version, finds NT, and errors out, stating reasons of incompatibility. Although the scanner is incompatible with Windows NT Workstation 4.0, it's likely to be compatible with Windows 2000 Professional because of the WDM drivers. Unfortunately, the programmer who implemented version checking in the setup routine didn't anticipate a future version of Windows NT being compatible with the Windows 98 driver, so I can't use this device until the vendor provides an update to the setup program.

So what does this mean? Essentially, you can't expect all devices to work under Windows 2000 just because they're written to the Windows 98 WDM. To ensure compatibility, you'll still need to look for the "Certified for Windows 2000" logo.

Properly Utilizing Your Peripherals

Deployment of Windows 2000 gives you an opportunity to rearrange hardware—perhaps taking advantage of little-used peripherals, relieving some of the load on overused peripherals, or just restructuring the locations to be more economically or ergonomically beneficial. This sort of change does come with a hazard, though—users need to see this as an improvement in their environment. Balance economy with other aspects. For example, don't annoy users by making them walk halfway to another building to pick up a print job just because it lets you get rid of one underutilized high-end laser printer; instead, consider trading the printer for a lower-end model, and relocating the high-end printer to a more beneficial location.

Any device displaying this logo has been tested and certified to work with Microsoft Windows 2000. More information on the Certified for Windows logo is available at `http://msdn.microsoft.com/certification/description.asp`. The Windows 2000 Hardware Compatibility List—and more information on the Windows logo—is available at `http://www.microsoft.com/hcl`.

Desktop Security

Questions:

- Does the current desktop permit various levels of local user privileges?
- If so, is the local user a standard user, a power user, or an administrator on his or her machine?

Possible issues:

If you currently have NT 4.0 workstations and the user is an administrator on his or her local machine, it may not matter what other technological policies you've implemented in your environment; a savvy administrative-level user can override configuration settings, install applications, edit the registry, modify hardware settings, and otherwise completely circumvent most of your technology-enforced system policies.

On the other hand, for some of your more technical users, giving local administrative rights could potentially reduce the cost to support those users, for many of the same reasons. The user no longer needs to call a technician when he or she needs to install an application, modify hardware, apply a patch, or upgrade a driver.

Local User Data Storage

Question:

- Are users required to save data in a consolidated location, or can they save it in any folder on the local drive(s)?

Possible issues:

This touches a key component of your existing environment: user data. Chances are that almost everything in your software environment can be replaced with relative ease, compared to the user data. User data, such as word processing and desktop publishing documents, spreadsheets, presentations, image files, project-management files, custom programs, local email archives, and so on, is unique to each user in the environment. Applications can be reinstalled, and program settings can gradually be restored, but depending on the nature of the data, most locally stored items are unrecoverable once lost.

User data represents one of the highest risks to your project. Imagine if an organization's entire sales force were to lose their customer databases, or if invoices stored in locally saved email inboxes were accidentally destroyed. What if one of your application developers had the only recent copy of the source code for an important application saved to his local drive? You can see the potential for loss if you don't take proper precautions.

If you already have a standard in place, this risk can be mitigated quite easily. In the best-case current environment scenario, users save no data to local drives; you require all users to store data files on the network, and the network shares are backed up daily. If this is the case, you could, in theory, do anything to the local desktop without concern for local user data. But I'm willing to bet that the companies taking that level of precaution are in the minority.

Only slightly more likely, perhaps you have a corporate policy in place, requiring all user data to be stored in a common folder hierarchy, such as under the C:\DATA folder, or on a separate local partition. If this is the case, you could mitigate the risk of data loss with minimal effort, simply backing up the C:\DATA folder to a location on the network before the OS upgrade, and restoring it when the machine installation has been completed.

Unfortunately, most companies don't have such data storage policies in place. It's more likely that users have data randomly saved to favorite locations on their local drives, in a filing system no one else might understand. As you can guess, this makes data protection during the OS migration a much more daunting task; mitigating the risk of data loss in this type of environment takes a bit more work. Here are some suggestions:

1. Make the user partially responsible for his or her data. For example, have users move their data files to a standard location on the hard drive that will then be copied up to the network before beginning the installation process.
2. Either write a script or have an application developer create a small utility that searches for common data files and copies them to a safe location. Even technically adept users occasionally miss a folder.
3. Get users to sign off on whatever process you've used before upgrading their systems. Provide a small, easy-to-understand outline of the documents that will be backed up, a network location to save documents not explicitly mentioned on the list, the user's portion of the responsibility, a contact number indicating where to call for questions, and other pertinent information explaining the risk to the user's data.
4. Implement a user data storage policy going forward, so issues such as this won't come up with future upgrades.

Appendix A, "Common File Extensions," contains a listing of common file extensions. Refer to this list when determining which files to back up for user data migration purposes.

Applications

Questions:

- What applications are used in your environment?
- How widely do applications vary across your user groups?
- Which applications perform critical business functions?
- Are the applications from third-party providers, or were they developed in-house?

Possible issues:

Application compatibility is a significant risk with any major desktop software upgrade. To minimize this risk, you must know the application standards in place in your environment and whether those applications will run successfully on Windows 2000. You're likely to have a suite of standard applications installed on every system in your environment. These applications often include an office productivity suite, an email package, a virus scanner, and a file compression-and-expansion utility.

Beyond the enterprise-wide standard application suite, most businesses have standard applications specific to that business. For example, the HR department might have a résumé management system, the users in Accounting use Quicken, and the IT developers have Visual Studios installed.

In addition to these departmentalized applications, some individual users or groups might have their own applications installed. For example, staff responsible for transmitting sensitive financial documents to a government organization may have special encryption and communication software, or the CEO might be running a DigiPet for stress relief.

All of the preceding situations describe standard applications available from software vendors. The vendor should perform the Windows 2000 compatibility testing for such applications. But many businesses also use custom applications. Any application specialized for your organization, whether developed in-house or by a contract developer, will need to be tested on the new OS. It's unlikely that your in-house applications will show up on any industry-wide compatibility advisories. Make sure that everyone in your environment using a custom-built application is running the most recent version of that application, and then have both the users and the developers run tests against those applications to make sure that the apps are fully compliant.

Don't forget, just because an application is listed as compatible with Windows 2000 doesn't always mean it's compatible with Windows 2000 *in your environment.* There's always the potential for application conflicts when loading multiple application programs on a single machine. Or you could have a special combination of hardware with a conflict no one else has discovered. Always test applications in-house before rolling them out to your users to make sure that they work in your specific environment.

Ultimately, your goal is to reduce the number of applications in your environment to the minimum number required to support the business functions of the users. The fewer supported applications, the easier it is to manage and maintain an environment from user support, desktop design, and license tracking standpoints.

Are Your Applications Windows 2000-Compatible?

You can find a searchable directory of Windows 2000 Certified, Ready, and Planned applications at the following URL:

`http://www.microsoft.com/windows2000/upgrade/compat`

If one or more of your key applications isn't on the list, you should contact the application vendor for compatibility or upgrade information.

Application Installation

Questions:

- Who is responsible for installing application software?
- Can users install applications on their own machines?

Possible issues:

With users who install their own applications, determining the migration path for those systems is much more difficult. The earlier section "Applications" discusses standard applications with the assumption that someone in IT is responsible for testing and installing those applications. If users can install their own applications, however, there's no way to know what might really be installed on each workstation.

If a user relies on a nonstandard application for part of his or her occupational function, you'll be expected to make sure that he or she can still function under the new environment. On the other hand, the OS upgrade may provide a good catalyst for removing nonstandard applications from the environment. Keep in mind that if the user needs a nonstandard application after the upgrade, you may need to have the original installation media on hand.

You may want to consider managing application installations using a software distribution service, such as Microsoft's SMS 2.0, or the Windows 2000 Software Installation and Maintenance component available through Windows 2000 Server. For more information on the Windows 2000 Software Installation and Maintenance component and how it could help with the distribution and management of software in your environment, see Chapter 8, "Application Management and Software Installation."

Disk Quotas

Questions:

- Is there a limit to the amount of local file space the user can use?
- Is there a limit to the amount of network file space the user can use?

Possible issues:

If your local systems have no disk quotas, you'll have no way of evaluating the total possible amount of network space needed to facilitate user data migration. In addition, if you want to implement local disk quotas after implementing Windows 2000, the existing user data might already exceed the space you intend to allocate. Disk quotas are beneficial; they encourage users to perform regular file maintenance. Often, users neglect to go through periodically and clean out old files. As a result, local data storage requirements grow and grow, until the local drive is entirely out of space. This is a big problem if you use software distribution, such as Microsoft's SMS or the Windows 2000 Software Installation and Maintenance feature.

Scripts

Questions:

- Do you currently use logon scripts?
- Will they run on Windows 2000?
- Do you need to add OS-specific logic?
- Do your scripts use environment variables?

Possible issues:

Logon scripts are often used to map drives, install updates, patch the registry, map printers, and perform other, similar tasks. Needed variables, commands executed, and local file locations may be different on Windows 2000 Professional clients than on older operating systems. Because the logon script is often an integral part of overall network security, you must ensure that all scripts are able to perform required tasks.

Windows 2000 Professional increases the available types of scripts. There are now four actions that can call a script (listed here in order of execution):

- Computer startup
- User logon
- User logoff
- Computer shutdown

In addition, Windows 2000 contains native support for using batch files, Windows Scripting Host scripts, or executable files for each of these actions. As a result, you can accomplish much more than the native support for down-level client scripts would allow. This enhanced script support makes it worthwhile to consider re-creating logon scripts altogether, to enhance and streamline the logon and logoff processes.

Local File Systems

Questions:

- What's the current file system?
- Do you use FAT, FAT32, NTFS, or some other standard?

Possible issues:

Fortunately, Windows 2000 can read FAT, FAT32, and NTFS drives. This covers file system standards for all older Microsoft operating systems, so reading and writing data shouldn't be an issue unless your data is on a non–Microsoft, non–FAT file system.

Older client operating systems, however, had certain limitations to the partition size of the system drive. For example, if you're installing Windows 2000 on a machine that once had Windows 95 installed on a FAT drive, the existing partitioning scheme may have only 2GB FAT partitions. With a full install of Windows 2000, Office 2000, and a couple of additional applications, you're likely to hit that 2GB limit fairly fast. If you're installing to a machine that once had Windows NT installed to a FAT partition, the existing partition won't be greater than 4GB (NTFS didn't have this 4GB limitation).

Regardless of the current file system, you should consider converting to NTFS with the installation of Windows 2000. In the latest version of NTFS, you have more granular file-level security (more auditable events and a greater number of available permissions), the addition of the Encrypted File System for local file protection, more detailed file information, and better disk space utilization for large partitions than with earlier FAT, FAT32, or NTFS file systems.

Upgrading Versus Clean Install

Microsoft put forth considerable effort developing an end-user–friendly installation process for Windows 2000. Based in part on user feedback, Windows 2000 Professional integrates an extensible upgrade procedure for upgrading Windows 95, Windows 98, and Windows NT Workstation 4.0 clients. This section will help you determine whether upgrades are a viable option in your environment, by examining the ups and downs of the Windows 2000 upgrade process and exploring the benefits and risks compared with the clean install process.

In most cases, you should plan for a clean install. Even in a straightforward, well-tested environment, OS upgrades can—and often do—go wrong. A clean install makes certain that your systems are starting from the same baseline configuration. You're less likely to have leftover files and registry entries hiding on your systems from older operating systems and unused or partially uninstalled applications. As a result, you remove one level of complexity when troubleshooting workstation problems.

For many developers, it's not uncommon to voluntarily reinstall operating systems from the ground up a couple of times a year, just to make sure that such leftovers don't cause conflicts with other parts of the system. I'm not suggesting a periodic OS

Converting Drives to NTFS V5

To convert a FAT or FAT32 drive to NTFS under Windows 2000 Professional, type the following command at the command prompt:

```
CONVERT <drive> /FS:NTFS
```

where *<drive>* specifies the drive letter (followed by a colon), mount point, or volume name of the drive to be converted.

Conversion is irreversible. Under Windows 2000, drives can't be converted from NTFS to FAT or from FAT to FAT32.

NTFS V4 volumes (from Windows NT 4.0) will be converted automatically to NTFS V5 volumes when locally mounted under Windows 2000. This could potentially lead to unintended upgrades of NTFS-formatted removable media, such as Iomega Jaz cartridges or removable hard drives.

If you dual-boot between Windows NT 4.0 and Windows 2000, you must have Windows NT 4.0 Service Pack 4 or greater installed before installing Windows 2000. If not, you won't be able to access your local NTFS drives under Windows NT 4.0.

refresh for your users, but the rollout of Windows 2000 Professional would be a perfect opportunity to enforce a one-time full-system refresh, resulting in the removal of old files and settings.

In some environments, upgrades might make sense over clean installs. The success or failure of such a decision depends primarily on the existing environment. The following section addresses the evaluation of your current environment. At the end of this section is a migration method worksheet. This worksheet should help you evaluate the complexity of your current environment, and assist you in the selection of an upgrade or a clean install.

Fixing Applications That Will Run, But Won't Install

Some applications may run fine if installed under Windows NT 4.0 and upgraded to Windows 2000, even though those same applications may not install under Windows 2000. If you run into this problem, one possible reason is that the installation routine is making a call to `GetVersionEx`—an API call to check the version of an OS—looking for a value equal to `4`, rather than greater than or equal to `4`. In other cases, the installation routine may handle the greater than or equal to `4` issue, but may then be looking for a specific service pack that wouldn't be required under Windows 2000.

You may be able to get past this problem without resorting to installing Windows NT 4.0, installing the application, and upgrading to Windows 2000. In the \Support folder of the Windows 2000 Professional CD is an application named APCOMPAT.EXE, an application compatibility tool. Through the Application Compatibility interface, you can run an application on Windows 2000, but report a different OS version to any version-checking calls (see Figure 2.1).

The Application Compatibility tool lets you bypass version checking to install applications on Windows 2000 that—except for the installation routine—might otherwise be compatible. In the example in Figure 2.1, the Application Compatibility tool will execute D:\SETUP.EXE, returning Windows NT 4.0 Service Pack 4 as the current OS.

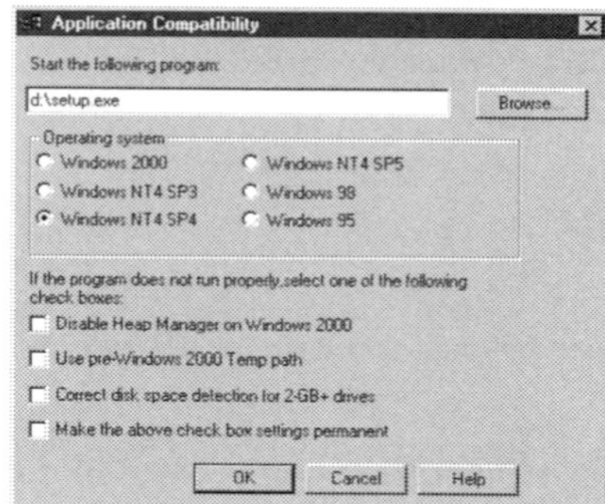

Figure 2.1 The Application Compatibility tool.

Evaluating Your Options

So is it realistic to even consider upgrades in your environment? You should have reviewed your desktop standards in the preceding sections; use some of that information now to determine the feasibility of upgrading. Most of the following subsections match those from the earlier "Reviewing the Current Desktop Standards" section, in order to provide an easy way to relate the evaluation of your current standards to your Windows 2000 installation options. The complexity of your current environment is a direct factor in determining the ease of upgrading users.

Hardware

One of the first components to evaluate is the existing desktop hardware. Obviously, any machine that doesn't meet the minimum requirements for your organization will need to be replaced or upgraded before it can run Windows 2000. If a majority of machines in the environment will need replacing, it would be better to use a clean install process for all of them, rather than spending resources developing and maintaining both a clean install routine and an upgrade routine.

If peripherals in your organization are incompatible with Windows 2000, you may need to remove the offending devices *before* upgrading to minimize the potential for resource conflicts and errors during the installation routine. Use the uninstall program included with the software for a given device (if such a routine is available). Be sure to remove the device drivers from the current system, or you're likely to see error messages during the upgrade. (To check whether your hardware is compatible with Windows 2000 Professional, you can use Microsoft's online Hardware Compatibility List, at `http://www.microsoft.com/hcl`.)

Desktop Operating System

Which operating systems are on the machines you're hoping to upgrade? First of all, they need to be running Windows 95, Windows 98, Windows NT Workstation 3.51, or Windows NT Workstation 4.0 clients, or you'll have to do a clean install. Next, it's much easier to develop an upgrade path if you have a single-client environment, rather than mixed clients. Finally, keep in mind that Windows NT Workstation 4.0 is the easiest client OS to upgrade, since the registry and file structures are the most similar to those of Windows 2000. Windows NT Workstation 3.51 and Windows 98 are the next easiest. Upgrading from Windows NT Workstation 3.51 has the same benefits as upgrading from Windows NT Workstation 4.0 in that the registry and file structure are similar, but 3.51 is more likely to have older, incompatible hardware and software than 4.0. Windows 98 is Microsoft's most recent pre–Windows 2000 operating system release, and many device drivers written to the WDM should be usable on Windows 2000. Windows 95, the oldest of the supported upgradeable operating systems, is the most likely to cause issues.

Desktop Security

Windows 95 and Windows 98 have user-level restrictions; the only variants in local user security come from the use of policy files. Windows NT Workstation 4.0 has both user-level restrictions and policy files. Do you consider your environment to be highly restrictive, somewhat restrictive, or not restrictive at all? The more restrictive your environment, the better chance that upgrades will work for your clients. In a restrictive environment, the users shouldn't be able to modify their machines without your knowledge. As a result, you'll be able to test upgrades on systems truly representative of your environment, which allows automation of the upgrade process to handle any exceptions or issues with your standard platform.

Local User Data Storage

To protect local user data—which includes such files as word processing and desktop publishing documents, spreadsheets, presentations, image files, project-management files, custom programs, local email archives, and more—you might consider including a data backup procedure in your OS migration, regardless of whether you opt to upgrade or perform clean installs. With enforced standards in place, an automated routine to copy files to a network location, install Windows 2000, and copy files back down to the local user data storage location is within the realm of possibility. If no standards exist, or there are only suggested guidelines, the user data may actually be safer if you upgrade rather than clean install. Upgrades don't usually touch non-OS files on the local drives; the files will be right where they were when the upgrade completes—unless, of course, something goes wrong during the upgrade process.

Is the BIOS Up to Date?

A final note on hardware: Be sure to update to a current BIOS on all devices before upgrading. Windows 2000 is much more BIOS-sensitive than previous Microsoft operating systems. More than 75% of the errors I've encountered when installing or upgrading machines to Windows 2000 have been resolved through BIOS updates.

Real-World Example

In a prior job, I was responsible for upgrading the desktop operating systems of eight different call centers from Windows 95 to Windows NT Workstation 4.0. Each call center agent needed an identical desktop with only two applications: one for email and one for terminal screen data entry. Supervisors at each of these locations needed the same two applications as well as Microsoft Office. In this instance, there was no upgrade path from Windows 95 to Windows NT Workstation 4.0, so we had no choice but to perform a clean install.

If I were to return to that company today to upgrade the call centers from Windows NT Workstation 4.0 to Windows 2000 Professional, I would suggest an upgrade over a clean install, because the software platforms are very similar across the entire environment. In my current occupation, I use both applications the call center agents had needed—oddly enough, on nearly identical hardware—and both applications are compatible with Windows 2000. Testing the existing applications would require little effort, and running the upgrade against one agent machine and one supervisor machine should present the same issues as would be encountered on 98% of the other machines.

Applications

Is there a standardized suite of applications across your environment? If not, are the applications standardized across groups? With applications, there are two primary complexity relationships. First, the more applications you have on a single system, the more difficult it will be to upgrade that system. Second, the more variable the standard software environment across user types, the more flexible the upgrade routine needs to be.

Application Installation

If users can install software on their own machines, you have no way of knowing what applications might be on each system. Without knowing what applications are installed, you won't know whether the resulting system will be compatible with Windows 2000. On the other hand, if you tightly control the software installation process, you should have an idea how the machines in your environment are configured, and you'll be able to test the upgrade process on representative systems. If this is the case, you can integrate workarounds or uninstall procedures into the upgrade process to fix troubled applications before issues develop.

Migration Method Worksheet

Use the worksheets in Tables 2.1 and 2.2 when deciding whether an upgrade path exists for a group of users. Table 2.1 presents the key factors to consider, but you should adjust the points associated with each category depending on the standard deviations within your own environment. Use your own judgment on the complexity threshold; my personal limits are at the bottom.

Using information presented in this chapter, follow these steps:

1. Evaluate your environment for each of the categories on the worksheet.
2. Select the value best describing each aspect of your environment.
3. Total the points.
4. Compare the result to the complexity threshold listed in Table 2.2.

An asterisk (*) in the Points column denotes a *critical point*. Don't consider any environment as a candidate for upgrade if it meets the criteria marked as a critical point. Unless a way exists to correct the variable responsible for the critical point classification before the rollout, the only solution for environments falling into these categories is to develop a clean install.

Table 2.1 **Migration Method Worksheet**

Category	Points	Item
Hardware	0	All devices on HCL.
	5	Most devices on HCL.
	*	No devices on HCL.
Client Operating System	0	All Windows NT Workstation 4.0.
	10	Mixed 95/98/NT clients, >75% NT Workstation 4.0.
	20	Mixed 95/98/NT clients, <75% NT Workstation 4.0.
	25	All 95/98 clients.
	*	Clients other than 95/98/NT.
Security	0	Highly restrictive, policies and user security groups.
	15	Somewhat restrictive; user security groups, no policies.
	25	Minimally restrictive; policies, no user security groups.
	*	Not restrictive; no policies or user security groups.
Local User Data Storage	0	Enforced standard exists.
	25	Suggested guidelines exist.
	50	No standards or guidelines.
Applications	0	Microsoft Office 2000 and/or Web-based applications only, across entire environment.
	10	Few applications, common across environment.
	30	Many applications, common across environment.
	20	Few groups of few applications, standardized within each of a number of job functions.
	40	Many groups of few applications, standardized within each of a number of job functions.
	*	No application standards, or many groups of many applications.
Application Installation	0	Tightly controlled with centralized responsibility; users can't install their own applications.
	20	Somewhat controlled with distributed responsibility; users can't install their own applications; responsibility is defined on a group-by-group basis.
	*	No control; users can install their own applications.
TOTAL POINTS		

Table 2.2 **Complexity Threshold**

Total Points	Conclusion
0–15	Upgrade possible with minimal customization, minimal technician interaction.
15–30	Upgrade possible, but expect a few bumps. Single upgrade process may work for a majority of clients. Medium level of technician interaction required.
30–50	Upgrade may work for a majority of the environment, with a mid-to-high level of technician interaction. May need to develop both an upgrade process and a clean install process. A single clean install process may be the best option.
50–75	Upgrade may work for a small portion of the environment, with a high level of technician interaction. Must develop a clean install path as well, as it's likely to be the best option for the majority of clients.
>75, in any category	Upgrade is not a realistic option. You should plan to develop a clean install process.

Developing the Standard Desktop

What will the standard Windows 2000 Professional desktop look like for your environment? Obviously, this component will be different for everyone. The following sections provide some examples and suggestions to consider when developing your standards for hardware requirements, OS configuration, and application installation and management. This section focuses more on guidelines and development theory than on implementation; implementation techniques are covered in later chapters.

Hardware Requirements

The first step is to select a standard supported hardware configuration. Chapter 1, "Why Upgrade?" lists the minimum requirements for Windows 2000 Professional, along with some additional recommendations on where a realistic hardware baseline should begin. For your environment, you need to evaluate Windows 2000 Professional with all of your standard applications loaded to determine your own baseline hardware configuration. Certain areas of your business may have heftier requirements, such as departments running AutoCAD or custom-built, memory-intensive in-house applications. You may want to determine a separate minimum hardware requirement for departments in these areas of the business. Consider piloting Windows 2000 in a few departments in your organization to get a more accurate assessment of hardware needs.

After selecting a standard hardware platform, determine the percentage of systems in your environment that already meet the minimum requirements. Systems that fall below the baseline will need hardware upgrades before they can run Windows 2000. Whether you replace the entire machine or upgrade only deficient components depends on how hardware refresh works in your organization. If you will be upgrading machines, carefully consider your hardware selection. More powerful hardware, although appearing more expensive in the short run, is more likely to be usable for a longer period of time than less expensive hardware that simply meets the current minimum requirements.

Hardware refresh cycles refer to the maximum amount of time a piece of hardware is allowed to operate in a given environment. Common refresh cycles are periods from 24 to 36 months. If your company has a 30-month hardware refresh cycle, no workstations in your environment should be more than 2½ years old. If you plan to do a gradual rollout of Windows 2000, you may be able to work in a majority of the operating system refresh with an existing hardware refresh cycle. If you have no hardware refresh plan in place and a majority of your existing hardware falls below the selected baseline, you should consider integrating the rollout of Windows 2000 with a workstation upgrade.

OS Configuration

Most of the configuration components in the operating system can be installed with scripts and subsequently controlled through group policy objects. Whether the initial OS configuration is implemented through an image file or a scripted install, much of the configuration will be easy to standardize and modify through the use of group policy objects.

For the most part, it's in your best interest to install the fewest components required to provide users with functional workstations. This goes for services as well as Windows components. If you don't want users playing Solitaire or running OpenGL screensavers at 100% CPU utilization, don't rely solely on corporate policy; if your employee guidelines restrict such things, remove the files before distributing the standard image. Keep in mind that if your current corporate policy doesn't explicitly restrict such games and entertainment, you should always get management buy-in before implementing such changes. And remember—your CEO might really like playing Minesweeper.

Following are some general suggestions for creating baseline OS images:

- Remove unnecessary components up front.
- Configure a networked and a stand-alone hardware profile for portable systems, and disable the network cards in the stand-alone profile. This often saves three to five minutes at logon.
- Don't use dynamic volumes on your images. Stick to the basics; you can always upgrade them later, as long as the partitions were initially created under Windows 2000. If they weren't, you must have a free 1MB partition at the end of each physical drive to upgrade to dynamic volumes.

- ACPI (Advanced Configuration and Power Interface) is your friend. If your current systems use APM, a clean install is the only way to enable ACPI. For portable computer users, it's worth the extra effort.
- Extra network components just cause extra network traffic. Disable or remove unnecessary network protocols and services. The Windows 2000 default protocol is TCP/IP; in fact, a Windows 2000 network won't run without it. There's no need for NetBEUI unless down-level clients absolutely can't run with TCP/IP.
- If much of your environment uses hardware that is at or only slightly above the minimum requirements, turn off unnecessary GUI enhancements such as drop shadows on cursors or menus that fade in and out; such "enhancements" come at the cost of processing cycles and increased memory overhead.
- Use NTFS. Not only do you benefit from enhanced local file security, but with today's large-capacity hard drives you'll actually be able to store more files than with FAT or FAT32. Converting a full 2GB partition can recover 300MB or more of slack space.
- Don't install unnecessary services. The average user shouldn't be running a Web page from the office, so there's no need to install Internet Information Services on his box.

Ultimately, your goal in developing the baseline Windows 2000 Professional image should be to create a single streamlined, flexible initial configuration usable on the majority of workstations in your environment. It's much easier to add components to a minimum number of systems after the fact than to remove unnecessary components on a large portion of the environment.

Standard Applications

Standard applications can be grouped into two categories: enterprise-wide applications and department-specific applications. Enterprise-wide applications are the programs installed on every computer in your organization, regardless of the computer's ultimate function. Common enterprise-wide applications include the following:

- An office suite such as Microsoft Office, containing the company-standard word processing program, spreadsheet program, and presentation manager.
- A standardized Web browser such as Internet Explorer or Netscape Navigator, with any needed plug-ins or security certificates installed and configured.
- A virus scanner, such as Norton AntiVirus or McAfee VirusScan.
- File compression and expansion utilities such as WinZip and WinRAR.
- A personal information management (PIM) application suite such as Microsoft Outlook or Lotus Notes, containing email, scheduling, and business contact information.
- Company-specific standard applications such as time and attendance trackers or terminal emulators.

Enterprise-wide applications can be integrated into the core operating-system image installation procedure, since they'll go on every machine in the company. Alternatively, you could use group policy objects to assign enterprise-wide applications through a software installation policy at the domain level. See Chapter 8 for more details on managing software installation with group policy objects.

Departmental applications, on the other hand, are found only in specific organizational units within the company. A single user could belong to multiple organizational units, requiring software common to multiple groups. You shouldn't integrate department-specific applications into your baseline system image; if you do, you'll have to pay for software licenses for every application on every machine in your enterprise-wide environment. In addition, it's generally in your best interest as a system administrator to give users only as much software as you absolutely must. The simpler your base configuration, the easier it will be to manage and maintain end-user workstations.

Departmental applications could include the following:

- Financial management packages such as Quicken for accounts receivable, accounts payable, and payroll departments.
- Software authoring packages such as PowerBuilder or Microsoft Visual Studios for software development departments.
- HTML authoring packages such as Macromedia DreamWeaver or Microsoft FrontPage for Internet/intranet developers.
- Résumé-management applications for human resources staff.
- Computer-aided drafting (CAD) applications such as AutoCAD or MicroStation for architects, landscape designers, and mechanical and electrical designers.
- Project-management programs such as Microsoft Project or Netmosphere for project managers.

With department-specific applications, rather than building separate system images for each department in your environment, you can use the Windows Installer service to install departmentalized applications on top of the standard enterprise image. Chapter 8 provides technical guidance on group-based software distribution, as well as configuration management via group policy objects and the Software Installation and Maintenance component of IntelliMirror.

Once you've developed a detailed plan for your standard desktop—from the hardware requirements down to the details of application configurations—you'll be ready to design your deployment and management structure for Windows 2000 Professional. The remainder of this book will lead you through the technical processes involved in the development of these critical components.

> **Group Policy Objects and the Active Directory**
>
> Be sure to look at Chapter 6, "Group Policy Objects," to see how the Active Directory enables management of OS and application settings for both users and computers across the enterprise.

3

Deployment Options

This chapter covers:

- Deployment methods available with Windows 2000
- Deploying Windows 2000 Professional using the Windows 2000 Server Remote Installation Services (RIS)
- Cloning systems with disk-imaging utilities and SYSPREP
- Cloning systems with RIPREP
- Deploying Windows 2000 Professional over Microsoft Systems Management Server 2.0 (SMS)

After reading this chapter, you should be able to do the following:

- Create a distribution share point
- Prepare a system for disk imaging, image the system, and apply the image to a new machine
- Understand the infrastructure requirements for deployment over Remote Installation Services
- Understand the limitations of system imaging and determine which hardware differences require separate images
- Select viable deployment methods that will work in your environment

In addition to the improved manual setup program provided with Windows 2000 Professional, Microsoft has provided a number of enhanced technologies to allow for easier wide-scale deployment. This chapter explores and compares the various deployment solutions, and details the creation of distribution share points, distributable disk images, and Remote Installation Services (RIS) images. Throughout the chapter are a number of exercises for you to try. These exercises have been designed to guide you through the various deployment mechanisms.

A number of methods are available for installing and deploying Windows 2000. These include the following options:

- **CD install.** Install Windows 2000 using a Windows 2000 CD. This process can be interactive, or it can be automated by creating an answer file.
- **Distribution share point.** Install over the network from a file server share. This process can be interactive, or it can be automated using an answer file.
- **Remote Installation Services (RIS).** A more sophisticated method of deploying Windows 2000 Professional by booting from a NIC card ROM or ROM emulator disk.
- **SYSPREP and disk-copying tools.** Use a disk image to deploy an identical software image to a large number of systems.
- **Systems Management Server (SMS).** Can be used to deploy Windows 2000, but only as an upgrade for existing Windows 9x/NT clients. SMS can't be used to do a clean install of Windows 2000.

A Brief Comparison of Installation Methods

Table 3.1 presents a comparison of the features and drawbacks for various installation methods for Windows 2000 Professional. This is a very generalized, high-level overview. Much of the complexity and development time involved in a successful implementation of the various methods is dependent on both the existing environment and the desired resulting environment.

For example, for my current customer, I plan to use a SYSPREP image. The hardware and base application requirements are very similar. There is a large and continually expanding number of computers in the environment. The existing environment is widely variant, but the target environment will be highly managed. We have a sufficient quantity of developer resources available.

On the other hand, if I were rolling Windows 2000 Professional internally at a small technology consulting firm with fewer than 100 employees, most of whom were technical, and my target environment was to be unmanaged, I might elect to simply create a network share and have the users upgrade their own machines from the network.

Table 3.1 **Installation Method Comparison**

	Manual Install	**Unattended Install**	**RIS**	**RIPREP Image**	**SYSPREP Image**	**Upgrade via SMS 2.0**
Clean install or upgrade	Either	Either	Clean only	Clean only	Clean only	Upgrade only
User/tech interaction level	Clean:High Upgrade:Low	Low	Low	Low	Med Low with SYSPREP.INF	Low
Development effort	Low	High	Med	Med-High	Med-High	Med-High
Hardware considerations (other than meeting minimum configuration requirements)	None	None	NIC must support PXE[1]	NIC must support PXE and hardware must be similar[2]	Hardware must be similar[2]	None
Distribution method	CD, DSP[3]	CD, DSP	Network via PXE	Network via PXE	CD, DSP, pre-loaded hard drive	Network via SMS
Difficulty of modifying/ maintaining after initial creation	Low	Med; change via Setup Manager Wizard	Med; modify answer file	High; must reconfigure and re-image master	High; must reconfigure and re-image master	High; must modify deployment package
Installation time[4] (1=slowest, 6=fastest)	Clean: 1 Upgrade: 5	2	2	3	6	4

[1]PXE, the Pre-boot Execution Environment, is a network protocol allowing a machine to boot from a network card and attach to a Windows 2000 Remote Installation Services server.

[2]Similar hardware means same HAL, same number of processors, same ACPI capability (enabled or disabled), and same drive controller device driver.

[3]DSP (distribution share point) is a network file share.

[4]See Table 3.2 for details.

CD-ROM Installation

Unlike Windows NT Workstation 4.0, which required a manual install when booted from the installation CD-ROM, Windows 2000 Professional setup can be run in unattended mode when booted from the original source CD-ROM. This type of install has the following dependencies:

- The computer must be able to boot from the CD-ROM drive. You may need to enable this option in your BIOS.
- The answer file must be on a floppy disk. The format is similar to that of an UNATTEND.TXT file (Chapter 4, "Answer Files and the Setup Manager Wizard," contains more information on the creation of the UNATTEND.TXT

file), but instead of UNATTEND.TXT, the file must be named WINNT.SIF. Insert the floppy disk in drive A: as soon as the computer starts to boot from the CD. If the computer supports a configurable boot sequence and you're booting from CD-ROM before booting from floppy disk, you can insert the floppy disk at the same time that you insert the Windows 2000 Professional installation CD.

The main difference between an UNATTEND.TXT file and WINNT.SIF is that the latter must contain a `[Data]` section. The `[Data]` section must be present in the WINNT.SIF file when performing an unattended install by booting from the Windows 2000 Professional installation CD. The `[Data]` section of the WINNT.SIF file should appear as follows:

```
Data
AutoPartition = "1"
MSDOSInitiated = "0"
UnattendedInstall = "yes"
```

`AutoPartition` enables Windows 2000 to select a partition on which to install. If this option isn't set, the installation will stop in the text mode setup and wait for the user to select an installation partition. `MSDOSInitiated` tells the setup routine that an unattended setup is being run directly from the installation CD. If your setup is failing at the beginning of the GUI-mode setup, make sure that this value is set to `"0"` (zero)—we are initiating the install directly from the CD, not from DOS. `UnattendedInstall` informs the setup engine that the install is running in unattended mode.

You can specify one additional optional setting in the `[Data]` section: `UseBIOSToBoot`. By default, `UseBIOSToBoot` is set to `"0"` (zero). This directs the setup routine to use the miniport driver if a SCSI drive controller is detected. If your computer has both SCSI and IDE controllers, setting `UseBIOSToBoot = "1"` will tell the setup routine to use `"multi"` instead of `"scsi"`. Think of the appearance of the ARC (Advanced RISC Computing) paths in the BOOT.INI file of Windows 2000 and Windows NT 4.0; `"MULTI()"` indicates that Windows 2000 should rely on interrupt 13 BIOS calls to load system files, and `"SCSI()"` indicates that Windows 2000 must load a boot device driver before it will be able to access the boot partition.

In an all-IDE system, `multi` works for up to four drives on a dual-channel controller (two on the primary channel, two on the secondary channel). In an all-SCSI system, `multi` works for the first two drives of the first SCSI controller. In a system with both IDE and SCSI, `multi` works only for the IDE drives on the first controller.

Distribution Share Points

For anyone who has ever performed a wide-scale deployment of Windows NT 4.0, the concepts and processes behind the *distribution share point* installation method should be familiar. The same basic process applies to Windows 2000 Professional. And as with Windows NT 4.0, you can also deploy Windows 2000 Server (any edition) using the distribution share point method.

Depending on the number of systems you need to install and the amount of development time you're willing to spend, installation via distribution share point can be as simple as creating a folder on the server, copying the i386 folder to this new folder, and sharing the new folder. After setting up this shared folder, install Windows 2000 by booting your target system, connecting to the share, and running WINNT.EXE (if you're booting with a DOS boot disk) or WINNT32.EXE (if you're booting to Windows 95, 98, or NT). As in the CD install method discussed earlier, you need to manually answer all the questions in the Windows 2000 Setup Manager Wizard.

This is perhaps the lowest-effort distribution method next to using the Windows 2000 Professional installation CD. The clean install isn't automated in any way; the person performing the install must answer all questions presented by the Windows 2000 Setup Manager Wizard. This method of installation takes the longest because you install over the network and wait on user input. The upgrade process is a bit faster, and nearly completely automated, because it takes many of the required answers and the configuration information from the operating system being upgraded.

With more development effort, installation via distribution share point can be automated to the point that running a batch file installs and configures Windows 2000 Professional, answers questions via an UNATTEND.TXT file and a uniqueness database file, and automatically logs on as the administrator upon the first boot to install applications, all without a single keystroke of user interaction. (For more on the uniqueness database file, see Chapter 4.)

Options for WINNT and WINNT32

For a complete list of the parameters supported by WINNT and WINNT32, open a command prompt window and run the command **winnt /?** or **winnt32 /?** from the i386 folder of the Windows 2000 source files. Note that WINNT32.EXE offers more options.

WINNT Syntax

```
WINNT [/s:sourcepath] [/u:path\answerfile] [/udf:id[,UDF]] [/t:driveletter]
[/r:folder] [/rx:folder] [/e:command] [/a]
```

Use the WINNT command when installing Windows 2000 from a DOS boot disk or 16-bit DOS/Windows machine. WINNT can't be used to upgrade an existing Windows installation.

Optional WINNT Command Parameters

Parameter	Description
/s:*sourcepath*	Source of the Windows 2000 installation files. The location must be a full path, including either a drive letter or UNC name. If you're doing an unattended install, you must specify the source path.
/u:*path\answerfile*	Specifies the location of your answer file. You must include the complete path to the answer file. If you're doing an unattended install, this option is required. Using /u also requires the /s:*sourcepath* parameter.

continues

Optional WINNT Command Parameters Continued

Parameter	Description
/udf:*id* [,*UDF*]	Points to a specific identifier in the uniqueness database file (UDF). A UDF file can be used to override values in an answer file, allowing a single answer file to be used for multiple configurations that vary only slightly. The ID determines which section of the UDF should replace values in the answer file. If no UDF is specified, Setup prompts you to insert a disk that contains a $UNIQUE$.UDB file.
/t:*driveletter*	Specifies the drive on which to store temporary install files and install Windows 2000. This is an optional parameter; if unspecified, Setup attempts to locate a drive with sufficient free space.
/r:*folder*	Specifies an optional folder to be installed. The folder won't be deleted at the end of the setup procedure. The folder is created under the WINNT directory of the system drive. You can specify multiple `/r` entries.
/rx:*folder*	Specifies an optional folder to be copied. The folder is created under the WINNT directory of the system drive, and deleted after the GUI portion of the setup procedure. You can specify multiple `/rx` entries.
/e:*command*	Runs the specified command at the end of GUI-mode setup. You can specify multiple `/e` entries.
/a	Enables Windows Accessibility options.

WINNT32 Syntax

```
WINNT32 [/s:sourcepath] [/unattend[num][:answerfile]] [/udf:id[,UDF]] [/tempdrive:drive]
[/copydir:folder] [/copysource:folder] [/cmd:command] [/debug[level]:[filename]]
[/syspart:drive] [/m:folder] [/makelocalsource] [/noreboot]
[/checkupgradeonly]
[/cmdcons]
```

Run WINNT32 from Windows 95, Windows 98, Windows NT 3.51, Windows NT 4.0, or a previous installation of Windows 2000 to install or upgrade Windows 2000. You can't run WINNT32 from a DOS boot disk or other operating system not listed in this section.

Optional WINNT32 Command Parameters

Parameter	Description
/s:*sourcepath*	Source of the Windows 2000 installation files. The location must be a full path, including either a drive letter or UNC name. If you're doing an unattended install, you must specify the source path. If you specify multiple /s switches, Setup copies installation files from multiple sources.

Parameter	Description
/unattend[*num*][:*answerfile*]	Specifying /`unattend` alone upgrades to Windows 2000 in unattended mode. All user settings are taken from the previous installation, so no user intervention is required during setup. This runs the same as running WINNT32 from Windows Explorer and selecting Upgrade from the first screen of the Windows 2000 Setup Wizard. Specifying an answer file runs a fresh install (rather than an upgrade) in unattended mode. You must specify the full path to *`answerfile`*. This option also requires the /`s:`*`sourcepath`* parameter. Specifying an integer for `[`*`num`*`]` directs the Windows 2000 Setup Wizard to pause for `[`*`num`*`]` seconds after the file copy before restarting your computer. This switch works only on Windows NT or Windows 2000.
/udf:*id* [,*UDF*]	Points to a specific identifier in the uniqueness database file (UDF). A UDF file can be used to override values in an answer file, allowing a single answer file to be used for multiple configurations that vary only slightly. The ID determines which section of the UDF should replace values in the answer file. If no UDF is specified, Setup prompts you to insert a disk that contains a $UNIQUE$.UDB file.
/tempdrive:*drive*	Specifies the drive on which to store temporary install files and install Windows 2000. This is an optional parameter; if unspecified, Setup attempts to locate a drive with sufficient free space.
/copydir:*folder*	Specifies an optional folder to be installed. The folder is created under the WINNT directory of the system drive and is not deleted at the end of the setup procedure. You can specify multiple /`copydir` entries.
/copysource:*folder*	Specifies an optional folder to be copied. The folder is created under the WINNT directory of the system drive and deleted after the GUI portion of the setup procedure. You can specify multiple /`copysource` entries.
/cmd:*command*	Runs the specified command at the end of GUI-mode setup, just before the final reboot. You can specify multiple /`cmd` parameters, but in my experience, a better choice is to use /`cmd` to call a batch file containing the commands from a temporary directory specified in a /`copysource` switch.

continues

Optional WINNT32 Command Parameters Continued

Parameter	Description
/debug[*level*]:[*filename*]	Specifying `/debug` with no additional information creates a debug level 2 log titled WINNT32.LOG under the WINNT directory. You can change the debug level and log filename by specifying the additional information. For example, `/debug4:C:\Win2Ks.log` sets the debug level to 4 and saves the file in the Win2Ks.log file at the root of drive C:. Debug levels are as follows: 0: Severe errors 1: Errors 2: Warnings 3: Information 4: Detailed debugging information Each level includes the levels below it. Reference the system log in the Event Viewer to get an idea of events that fall into the various categories.
/syspart:*drive*	Tells the setup engine to copy setup startup files to a hard disk, mark the disk as active, and then stop. You would then remove the drive referenced in the command and install the disk in a different computer. When you boot the new computer, it automatically starts with the next phase of the setup. If you use `/syspart`, you must specify the `/tempdrive` parameter as well. The `/syspart` option works only if the install is initiated under Windows NT or Windows 2000. Windows 9x systems can't handle this switch.
/m:*folder*	Specifies an alternate location for setup files. Any files in this location will be used to replace original Windows 2000 installation files. For example, if you want to include a customized version of NOTEPAD.EX_, you put your version in the folder specified after the `/m` switch. When Setup looks for NOTEPAD.EX_, it uses your version rather than the standard included version. You must specify the full path to the folder, including either a drive letter or a UNC name.
/makelocalsource	This option forces Setup to copy all installation source files to the local hard disk. Use `/makelocalsource` when installing from a device that won't be available later in the installation, such as when installing from a network share or when using the `/syspart` option and Ghost to copy the initial text-mode setup files.

continues

Parameter	Description
/noreboot	Prevents Setup from automatically restarting the computer after the file-copy phase of WINNT32.
/checkupgradeonly	This parameter directs Setup to check whether the computer can be upgraded to Windows 2000. It doesn't install Windows 2000, nor should you specify any additional parameters with this command. For Windows 95 or Windows 98 upgrades, this option creates a report named UPGRADE.TXT in the Windows installation folder. For Windows NT 3.51 or 4.0 upgrades, this option creates a report named WINNT32.LOG in the NT installation folder.
/cmdcons	This option is only for use after a completed install of Windows 2000. You shouldn't specify any additional parameters with this command. Running `WINNT32 /cmdcons` from an installed Windows 2000 machine installs the Windows 2000 Recovery Console, a DOS-like command-line interface to Windows 2000 to use in emergency recovery and repair procedures.

With a distribution share point, the source files for Windows 2000 Professional are on a network share. Because these files are remote to the target system, you need a network boot disk to attach to the network and start WINNT.EXE.

Manual Install

Exercise 3.1 walks through the creation of a manual install procedure that runs from a distribution share point. To perform this exercise, you need two computers, a server onto which you will copy the shared installation files, and the target system onto which you will load Windows 2000.

Exercise 3.1 **Manual Install over Distribution Share Point**

Step 1 Select a server with enough free space to copy the entire i386 folder from the Windows 2000 Professional CD (approximately 350MB).

Step 2 Create a share on the server and copy the contents of the Windows 2000 Professional\i386 folder into the share. You may want to set read-only permissions on the share, so users don't inadvertently delete or modify files.

continues

Creating a Network Boot Disk

Windows NT Server 4.0 included a utility, the *Network Client Administrator* (*NCA*), to facilitate creation of the network boot disk. This utility isn't included in Windows 2000. For network cards compatible with both Windows 2000 and the old Windows NT 4.0 Network Client Administrator, you could use the NCA utility to create a network client boot disk. If the Windows NT 4.0 NCA doesn't support your network card, follow the directions in the manufacturer's documentation to create a DOS network boot disk.

Exercise 3.1 **Continued**

Step 3 Create a DOS network boot disk and boot your target workstation using this disk.

Step 4 Connect to the network share created in step 2.

Step 5 From the network share, run WINNT.EXE. This will start the Windows 2000 installation process. Monitor the install and enter answers manually for all the prompts.

To upgrade Windows 95, Windows 98, or Windows NT Workstation 4.0 machines to Windows 2000 Professional over a distribution share point, you should first perform steps 1 and 2. Then boot your current system and connect to the network as normal. Finally, run WINNT32.EXE from the network share created in step 2 to start the Windows 2000 installation program.

Exercise 3.1 represents a baseline installation of Windows 2000. To reduce the time required, you can make use of the unattended install feature, in effect to pre-answer all the questions you had to answer manually in Exercise 3.1. The following section describes this process.

Unattended Install

Exercise 3.2 outlines the process to allow a basic unattended install procedure to run from a distribution share point. Creating this basic unattended install process using the distribution share point requires a lower development effort than any other automated install procedure when installing only the operating system. By using the unattended install option, you can automate answering questions asked by the setup program, which will (minimally) reduce the time required to complete a system installation. In addition, the install takes place over the network, so the file copy portion of the install takes longer than it would from a CD-based install.

Exercise 3.2 **Automated Install over Distribution Share Point**

Step 1 Select a server with enough free space to copy the entire i386 folder from the Windows 2000 Professional CD (approximately 350MB).

Step 2 Create a share on the server and copy the contents of the Windows 2000 Professional\i386 folder into the share. You may want to set read-only permissions on the share, so users don't inadvertently delete or modify files.

Step 3 Create an UNATTEND.TXT file to answer all questions required in the install (see Chapter 4). Save this file to the share point of your installation files.

Step 4 Create a DOS network boot disk and boot the target workstation using this disk.

Step 5 Map drive Z: to the server and share name created in step 2. Make Z:\ the current working directory.

Step 6 From drive Z:, run the command **WINNT.EXE /s:Z:\ /u:UNATTEND.TXT** from the command line. If the UNATTEND.TXT file was created properly, the install will complete without prompting the user for any information.

Enhancing the Distribution Share Point Installation Process

To integrate application installation and configuration with the distribution share point method, you need to create a number of additional files and folders under the i386 directory share. With Windows NT Workstation 4.0, these additional components had to be created manually. With Windows 2000 Professional, many of the complex customization aspects of an unattended install can be generated automatically through the Setup Manager Wizard. These enhancements are explained in detail in Chapter 4.

Remote Installation Services (RIS)

This section covers some benefits and drawbacks to RIS compared to other installation methods, and outlines some of the basic infrastructure requirements. Technical implementation detail is provided in Chapter 5, "Remote Installation Services (RIS)."

While the distribution share point requires only a network share accessible via bootable floppy disk, Remote Installation Services requires the following server services on the network:

- DHCP
- TCP/IP
- Active Directory
- Remote Install Server
- DNS

In addition to meeting the base hardware requirements for Windows 2000 Professional, the client must have a network interface card that either supports PXE (Pre-boot Execution Environment) v0.99c or greater, or is compatible with the remote boot floppy.

Installing Windows 2000 Professional using RIS is a bit faster than similarly configured distribution share point installations. The primary benefit is in the client connection process. With a NIC that supports PXE, there's no need to create a network boot disk. The client can be configured through the BIOS to boot to the NIC. This network boot process takes less time to boot than a DOS-based network boot disk, and there's no need to worry about duplicate IP addresses or duplicate client names. When the client boots, a DHCP server assigns the IP configuration information, and the client attaches to the network and queries DNS for an Active Directory controller.

> **Create Your Own Setup Answer File**
>
> The Setup Manager Wizard, located in the Windows 2000 Server\Support\Tools\DEPLOY.CAB file, is the easiest tool you can use to create the UNATTEND.TXT file. Of course, you can create this file manually using your favorite text editor (such as Notepad). A very simple template UNATTEND.TXT file is included on the Windows 2000 Professional installation CD. You can find it at `<drive letter>:\i386\unattend.txt`. The full syntax for the UNATTEND.TXT file can be found in the UNATTEND.DOC file located in the DEPLOY.CAB file mentioned above.

The Active Directory controller then points the client to an assigned Remote Installation Services server. The client uses TFTP, the Trivial File Transfer Protocol, to copy the install files from the RIS server to the client and install the OS.

In the base configuration, RIS is designed to install only Windows 2000 Professional—there's no support for installing Windows 2000 Server or for installing applications. The Windows Installer would be needed to handle application installs. However, an enhancement to the Remote Installation Services functionality known as the *Remote Installation Preparation Wizard*, or *RIPREP*, allows for the installation and configuration of Windows 2000 Professional and any needed applications over RIS. RIPREP takes what is essentially a differential snapshot of files and registry settings added to a representative machine after the initial load of the OS, and applies the same changes to subsequent machines, utilizing the same network transfer technology as RIS. This feature is discussed in the later section "Creating RIPREP Images for Remote Installation Services," and the process is outlined in detail in Chapter 5.

System Cloning

If all systems in your environment are similar, *system cloning*—the process of creating a master system, duplicating the files, and distributing the resulting system image to multiple machines—might be your best option for deployment. Two types of system cloning are available with Windows 2000 Professional: third-party disk images and RIPREP images. Disk cloning via third-party utilities and SYSPREP is the fastest deployment method, often cutting installation time from a number of hours down to just 10–15 minutes, including additional applications. The major downside to either type of system cloning is that all target systems must have fairly similar hardware configurations.

Note that the term *third-party utilities* doesn't necessarily refer to software. A number of hardware disk cloning solutions are also available.

Creating Disk Images with Third-Party Utilities and SYSPREP

With Windows NT Workstation 4.0, *ghost images*, named after the third-party utility used to create and deploy system snapshots, were a favored method for wide-scale OS deployments. Unfortunately, Microsoft didn't support ghost images because the software couldn't handle the workstation's unique security identifier (SID).

Regardless of the security identifier concern, customers wanted to be able to use disk images, so Microsoft developed the SYSPREP utility (for a very brief time, it was called SYSIMAGE) for Windows NT Workstation 4.0. SYSPREP rolled back an installation to allow users to re-accept license agreements, specify new administrative passwords, and regenerate the computer's SID. An administrator could set up and configure Windows NT Workstation 4.0, run SYSPREP, use a third-party disk imaging tool to create a disk image, and then copy it to other *identically configured* machines—all without losing the ability to be supported by Microsoft.

Windows 2000 Professional includes an enhanced version of SYSPREP. With Windows 2000, the hardware on cloned systems doesn't have to be identical—within certain constraints. A single SYSPREP-prepared disk image can be applied to a variety of systems, as long as the systems use the same Hardware Abstraction Layer (HAL) and disk controller. Basically, this means that

- The systems must all have the same number of processors.
- The systems must all either have ACPI (Advanced Configuration and Power Interface) enabled, or all have ACPI disabled.
- The systems must use hard disk controllers that can use a common driver, such as a generic IDE controller.

At first glance, these restrictions may sound fairly limiting, but the system will re-detect all other hardware components, including video cards, network interface cards, PC cards (PCMCIA), modems, removable media drives, and more.

Disk-Image–Based Install

Exercise 3.3 covers the creation of a disk-image–based system clone. Later in this chapter, Exercise 3.4 takes you through applying that image to a new machine.

Exercise 3.3 **Creating a Disk-Image–Based Install**

This exercise takes approximately five hours to complete. The bulk of this time is consumed by the manual installation of Windows 2000 Professional and the additional applications.

Step 1 Install Windows 2000 Professional on a representative machine. This machine must use the same HAL, the same hard disk controller, the same number of processors, and the same power management technology as the systems on which you will be applying it. You can use any of the other distribution methods (such as an UNATTEND.TXT file on a distribution share point) for your initial install, or you can perform the installation manually.

Step 2 Create a local user account using Local Computers and Groups, and add it to the local administrators group. You'll need this logon ID later in the process.

Step 3 Log on using the default local administrator account (username "administrator"), set all OS configuration options, install and configure any services, and make any needed changes to the registry. If desired, copy any required shortcuts or documents to the desktop.

Step 4 Install and configure third-party applications such as virus protection, office suites, or WinZip.

continues

Where to Find the SYSPREP Files

The files needed to run SYSPREP—SYSPREP.EXE and SETUPCL.EXE—are located in a CAB file in the following location on the Windows 2000 Professional and Server CDs:

<*CD-ROM drive letter*>`\SUPPORT\TOOLS\DEPLOY.CAB`

You can extract the files using Windows Explorer. This CAB file also contains a help file, DEPTOOL.CHM, which gives details on to how to use SYSPREP.

Exercise 3.3 **Continued**

Step 5 Set the default home page, add any items to the Favorites folder, and configure links in Internet Explorer.

Step 6 Right-click the Internet Explorer icon and select Properties from the pop-up menu. On the General tab, click Delete Files and Clear History to clean up unnecessary temporary IE files.

Step 7 Log off as administrator, and log on as the account created in step 2.

Step 8 Copy the Administrator profile folder to the Default User profile folder. Now new users will be presented with the same desktop settings and program groups as were present under the Administrator account. When possible, you should manage your user's settings through group policy objects in the Active Directory, but this step ensures that locally created user accounts have any needed shortcuts or settings.

Step 9 Create a SYSPREP folder on the root of your system volume (for example, C:\SYSPREP) and then extract the SYSPREP.EXE and SETUPCL.EXE files from the <*CD-ROM*>:\SUPPORT\TOOLS\ DEPLOY.CAB file on the Windows 2000 Professional CD to the SYSPREP folder. Copy your customized SYSPREP.INF file into this folder as well, if you have created one. (See Chapter 4 for information about customizing the SYSPREP.INF file.)

Step 10 Clean up any temporary folders or unneeded files.

Step 11 If your computer is joined to a domain, remove it from the domain and join a local workgroup. This is required before SYSPREP will run. When asked to reboot, select No. You'll have to reboot after the next step.

Step 12 Run a disk check and a disk defrag on your local disk. This reduces the potential for problems with the disk imaging process.

Step 13 Reboot.

Step 14 Log on as the local administrator account.

Step 15 Delete the administrative account created in step 2.

This process may seem pointless—create an account, copy some files, and then remove the account—but you can't copy the profile if you don't have another account with administrative rights. You have to be logged out of a profile to copy it over.

Step 16 Clear the Event Viewer log files.

Step 17 Make a note of the amount of used drive space on your system. You'll need this information to determine the disk space requirements when creating the image file.

Step 18 Set the password on the Administrator account to blank. This allows SYSPREP to accept a new administrator password during the mini-setup wizard portion of the install. If you specify a non-blank password, the password will be applied to the Administrator account for all imaged systems. Entering a different password in the mini-setup wizard or specifying a different password in the SYSPREP.INF file won't override a non-blank password built into the image.

Step 19 Open a DOS command prompt.

Step 20 Click Start, Settings, Taskbar and Start menu, click the Advanced tab, and then click the Clear button. This erases command history, recently accessed files, and Internet Explorer history.

Step 21 From the DOS window opened in step 19, change folders to the SYSPREP folder and run the following command:

```
SYSPREP -PNP
```

Note: Although you could run this command from Windows Explorer, the command would then be the only entry in the command history list under the Administrator account on every imaged machine.

Step 22 If the system is ACPI- or APM-compliant, it will shut down automatically after SYSPREP completes. If it's not compliant with one of these power management specifications, you'll get a message notifying you when it's safe to shut down the computer.

WARNING: Don't boot again from the hard drive until after you've imaged the system. Booting from the hard drive will run the setup wizard, apply a new SID, and prepare the system to run Windows 2000. If you boot, you'll have to run SYSPREP again before imaging the system.

Step 23 Create an image of the drive using the third-party utility of your choice, such as Norton Ghost or PowerQuest Drive Image. For this process, you'll need to either boot to a DOS network boot disk and connect to a share with as much free space as noted in step 17, or install a blank second hard drive in the system, formatted with FAT, on which you can save the image. Rather than using software-based disk duplication utilities, you could use a hardware solution to duplicate a number of disks at once. If you're using hardware-based disk duplication, the primary drive of the PC would be used as your master disk.

You have now completed the process for imaging a Windows 2000 system. Exercise 3.4 (next section) applies the image you just created to a new workstation.

Command-Line Switches for SYSPREP

Switch	Description
-quiet	Don't display confirmation messages.
-nosidgen	Don't generate a new SID at reboot. Avoid using this option when creating an image for multiple machines; it should only be used if you want to pre-stage machines and roll back the mini-setup wizard after the install to allow the user to customize the available options.
-pnp	Redetect all hardware on reboot. Use this option on any image that will be applied to multiple machines.
-reboot	Reboot the machine after SYSPREP completes. By default, SYSPREP shuts down the machine.

Distributing the Image

Once you've created an image, how will you go about distributing that image? You have a few options:

- CD-ROM
- Pre-imaged hard drives
- Network share
- Network multicasting

By putting the image onto a CD, you can install the image with a simple CD boot disk. In fact, using a program such as Goldhawk's CDRWIN or Adaptec's CD Creator Deluxe, you can make the CD bootable, so the user won't even need an additional boot disk. If the CD mastering software is capable of creating bootable media, the process should be explained in the product documentation. Of course, if the client systems aren't equipped with a CD-ROM, this isn't the recommended installation solution. A CD is much faster than a network-based method, but not quite as fast as a pre-imaged hard drive. CD burners and write-once media are fairly inexpensive, but the media isn't reusable. If you burn a batch of disks and need to change the image file, you'll have to track down all the CDs to keep users from installing old images on their machines. With unsecured distributable physical media such as a CD, there's also the risk that unauthorized users may install the Windows 2000 image on their machines.

Pre-imaged hard drives are the fastest method of installing an image. Pre-imaging a drive can be as simple as installing a secondary drive in a machine and using Norton Ghost or PowerQuest to make a disk-to-disk image. In addition, there are multiple-disk duplication systems, such as the Image MASSter from Intelligent Computer Solutions (`http://www.ics-iq.com`). These devices duplicate the data from a master drive to multiple hard drives at the same time. The downside to this method is the requirement to physically remove and install hard drives on machines. This could be a very expensive solution if you're buying new hard drives for every system, but that cost can be reduced if you recycle the old drives being replaced by the pre-imaged drives.

With a network share, the workstation to be cloned has to boot up and attach to the network, and then the image file must be transferred over the network. Network shares can be the slowest method of drive imaging. However, if the disk-imaging program allows high compression (both Ghost and Drive Image have compression capability), the transfer is often faster than with an uncompressed image—even with decompression calculations—because less data is coming over the network wire. A major advantage of this method is that the image is stored at a single management point, so image updates are easy to manage. User access can be controlled through standard network account security, so unauthorized installations aren't as big a risk.

One possibly significant disadvantage of a network share install is the requirement to provide DOS network boot disks to connect the clients to the network. Depending on the variations in network cards in the environment, this can be difficult or, in some cases, impossible to manage. There are also network bandwidth considerations—copying a 2GB file over the network to 300 simultaneous users is pretty much guaranteed to cause some bottlenecks. Often, network share installs must be performed after hours, and with a maximum number of simultaneous client downloads.

Network multicasting is similar to the network share install in most aspects, with one major difference. With multicasting, you can load a number of users at the same time, but with network traffic only slightly greater than the traffic generated when loading a single client. Both Ghost and Drive Image have multicast servers and clients available. If you're pre-staging a large number of workstations in a network lab, multicasting may be the way to go.

Exercise 3.4 **Applying a Disk-Image–Based Install**

This exercise takes approximately 20–30 minutes to complete if you're applying the image from local source media (such as a CD or disk-to-disk copy). It will take longer if you're copying the image down from a location on the network.

Step 1 Apply the disk image created in Exercise 3.3 to a new hard drive. The application method will depend on both the software used to create the image and the media on which the image file is located. In my experience, installing from a bootable CD image usually takes 10–20 minutes; downloading from a network share usually adds an additional 20–30 minutes to the process—but your mileage may vary.

Step 2 Boot to the newly imaged drive. (Note that the system used to create the master image will start at this point on the first boot to the system drive.)

Step 3 Unless specified in the SYSPREP.INF file, you must now enter the 25-character Windows 2000 product key for your new installation.

Step 4 The machine will detect new plug and play devices. This process takes approximately 3–5 minutes.

Step 5 Answer the questions posed by the mini-setup wizard. You only need to answer questions not handled by the SYSPREP.INF file. (See Chapter 4 for information on creating and configuring the SYSPREP.INF file.) In many cases, this step can be completely automated; you won't need to answer any questions. Even with no SYSPREP.INF file, answering all questions posed by the mini-setup wizard can be completed in around five minutes.

Without a SYSPREP.INF file, the mini-setup wizard asks the user to do the following:

1. Accept the EULA. A Welcome screen may pop up before this screen; setup will continue automatically after about five seconds. If SYSPREP was run with the `-PNP` switch, plug-and-play detection runs after accepting the EULA.
2. Specify regional settings for system or user locale and keyboard layout.
3. Personalize the software by entering the user's name and organization.
4. Enter the 25-character product key.
5. Specify a computer name and administrator account password.

continues

Exercise 3.4 **Continued**

6. If the system has a modem installed, you'll be prompted to enter TAPI settings information.
7. Specify the current date and time, and select the proper time zone.
8. Select network protocols, clients, and services, and configure related settings.
9. Select a domain or workgroup.

Step 6 Reboot the system as directed at the end of the setup wizard.

Step 7 Windows 2000 presents the Welcome screen for the Network Identification Wizard. Click Next to start the wizard, or Cancel to log on as the local administrator and manually complete additional network user configuration. If you're operating in Workgroup mode, the wizard can add a new local user account to any of the existing local security groups, such as the Power Users, Users, or Administrators groups. If you're participating in a domain, this wizard can add a single existing domain user account to any of the existing local security groups. Note that specifying a domain during the setup wizard from step 5 will have already added the Domain Users group to the local Users group, and the Domain Admins group to the local Administrators group.

Unless the SYSPREP.INF file contains additional commands for post-install scripts or program configuration, you should be able to log on normally after the reboot. The C:\SYSPREP folder and all files contained therein are automatically deleted at the end of the install process.

Use a Single SYSPREP Image with Multiple SYSPREP.INF Files

To provide separate SYSPREP.INF files for multiple users, you don't have to build multiple images. SYSPREP on Windows 2000 Professional gives you the option of using a SYSPREP.INF file from a floppy disk. To use this function, apply the image file to the system drive, reboot, and insert the floppy disk containing the SYSPREP.INF file into the floppy drive when the Windows 2000 Professional boot menu appears. This method will override any SYSPREP.INF file stored as part of the image. This feature can also keep you from having to rebuild a system image if you need to modify an existing SYSPREP.INF file.

In my office, we use Dell Computers exclusively, including desktops, workstations, servers, and portables. I've successfully applied a single image created on a Dell Latitude CP notebook computer (single processor, IDE drives, ACPI enabled) to the following types of Dell machines:

- Latitude CP notebook
- Latitude CPi notebook
- Optiplex GX1 desktop
- Optiplex GXa desktop
- Precision 210 workstation

In the past, installing to these different machine types would have required different images. I've also applied the image to a number of differently configured systems within each of these groups. With Windows 2000 Professional and SYSPREP, I can now maintain a single image that applies to all of these differently configured machines.

Creating RIPREP Images for Remote Installation Services

Remote Installation Services (RIS) contains a function similar to disk duplication known as *RIPREP* (covered in greater detail in Chapter 5). RIPREP allows for a differential application of system configurations and components beyond the default RIS configuration, using the same mechanisms utilized by a RIS server.

A RIPREP image is essentially a folder containing every file and folder needed for a complete system. The files in a RIPREP image are all separate and can all be viewed, opened, copied, or deleted through Windows Explorer. A SYSPREP image, on the other hand, is a single image file that contains all files needed for a system. The only way to view individual files within that image file is through a special utility provided by the vendor of the disk duplication tool.

RIPREP images have the same hardware difference limitations as SYSPREP images. Target machines must use the same HAL, the same hard disk controller, the same number of processors, and the same power management technology as the system used to create the master image. RIPREP installs take longer than SYSPREP images because RIS performs a complete unattended install on a machine before applying the differences, including disk partitioning and formatting, and both the text portion and the GUI portion of the Windows setup program.

RIPREP only supports single-drive, single-partition systems. The target drive must be the same size as or larger than the source drive. If the default image needs two partitions on the first drive, SYSPREP and disk duplication could be used to do unattended installs, but RIPREP wouldn't pick up or apply changes outside the system partition.

The basic flow of a RIPREP install is as follows:

1. Install Remote Installation Services on a Windows 2000 server.
2. Create the default Windows 2000 Professional load image.
3. Modify or create the RISTNDRD.SIF file. This file has the same function as the UNATTEND.TXT file on an unattended install. The RISTNDRD file is in the \Setup\<*language*>\Images\<*image folder*>\I386\Templates subfolder of the Remote Installation Services folder.
4. Install a representative system using the basic RIS image.
5. Configure the OS and install additional applications as needed.
6. Run the Remote Installation Preparation (RIPREP) wizard on the fully configured Windows 2000 Professional machine. The executable, RIPREP.EXE, is under the \Admin\i386 folder of the Remote Installation Services share.
7. The RIPREP wizard creates a new image option on the RIS server.

Using SYSPREP Images Over a Network

A new feature in Norton Ghost 6.0 Enterprise Edition allows a Windows 2000 RIS server to store and distribute a standard Ghost image file. In this way, SYSPREP-prepared disk images can be applied over the network in the same way as standard RIS or RIPREP images.

8. Connect a new client to RIS and select the new image.
9. The base RIS install is applied, and then configuration changes and third-party applications are layered onto the install.
10. A mini-setup wizard runs, similar to the SYSPREP mini-setup wizard.
11. The system reboots and is ready for use.

Systems Management Server (SMS)

Microsoft's *Systems Management Server* (*SMS*) can be used to deploy Windows 2000 Professional on computers in your environment that are already running operating systems with an SMS client. SMS can't install Windows 2000 on a new computer that has no operating system installed. SMS also can't perform a clean install, only an upgrade from one of the Windows 2000 upgradeable down-level clients. Because of this limitation, I personally haven't installed Windows 2000 via an SMS package outside of a testing environment. I do, however, use SMS in pre-deployment preparation activities—such as gathering hardware inventories and reporting application profiles—and in post-deployment software management and system monitoring.

For more information about SMS 2.0 terms, concepts, and best-practices, consult the *Systems Management Server 2.0 Administrator's Guide*.

Pre-Deployment Preparation with SMS

SMS can assist you in many pre-deployment preparations, even if you decide not to use SMS to install Windows 2000 Professional. In perhaps one of the most important functions, SMS can be used to collect configuration information about workstations in the environment. After inventorying system hardware, you can query SMS to determine which systems are properly configured to receive Windows 2000 Professional. In this way, you can better gauge the cost of hardware upgrades associated with converting existing systems to Windows 2000.

Another pre-deployment preparatory step could be the distribution of Windows 2000 Professional source files to various servers in your organization. Even if you want to use UNATTEND.TXT files in conjunction with distribution share points rather than installing to clients via SMS, you could push the files required for an unattended install out to network file servers via SMS 2.0. The biggest benefit of SMS for this plan is the capacity to utilize SMS senders.

SMS *senders* can copy files over a wide range of network protocols and link types while providing a more intelligent file transfer method than standard network file copies. Senders can be configured to cap their bandwidth utilization so they won't bog down the entire network. In addition, they can use different bandwidth caps, depending on the time of day. For example, if most of your users go home by 5:00 p.m., the sender can be configured to increase the bandwidth it's using for file copying after that time. If a sender loses connection during a transfer, the sender can resume the transfer where it left off, rather than starting the file copy from the beginning.

Deploying the Operating System

If you want to use SMS 2.0 to distribute Windows 2000 Professional, you first need to create an SMS *package*. The package contains the source files and information required for SMS to complete the distribution process. SMS 2.0 includes a predefined package for a basic configuration of Windows 2000 Professional. You can use this package as a starting point for your customized distribution package. Exercise 3.5 walks you through the basic steps to create a Windows 2000 Professional SMS package. This exercise assumes that you've already set up a Microsoft Systems Management Server 2.0 infrastructure in your environment, and installed the client on the workstations you'll be upgrading via SMS.

Exercise 3.5 **Deploying Windows 2000 Professional with SMS 2.0**

Step 1 Begin by creating an unattended install over distribution share point as described in Exercise 3.2.

Step 2 On the SMS 2.0 server, open the SMS Administrator console.

Step 3 Right-click the Packages item and select New, Package from Definition. This starts the Package Definition Wizard.

Step 4 Select Windows 2000 Professional from the Package Definition screen of the wizard.

Step 5 On the Source Files screen, select Create a Compressed Version of the Source.

Step 6 On the Source Directory screen of the wizard, enter the location of the distribution share point. Click Next.

Step 7 Click Finish to complete the Package Definition Wizard.

Step 8 Under the newly created Windows 2000 Professional package, select Programs. From the right window of the management console, select the automated upgrade option applicable for your environment. Set the command line to call the WINNT32 executable with the options needed to call your version of the Windows 2000 install (such as WINNT32 /unattend:<*unattend file*>).

Step 9 Add any desired descriptive text to the Comments field for your program. Set the Estimated Disk Space and Estimated Run Time values under the Requirements tab to the appropriate values for your package.

Step 10 On the Environment tab, set the Program Can Run option to Whether or Not a User Is Logged On. Close the properties window.

Step 11 Right-click the Windows 2000 Professional package and select Properties from the pop-up menu. On the Reporting tab, set Version to **5.0**. Set Name to **Windows NT** and Publisher to **Microsoft**.

Step 12 Give permission to the proper user accounts under the Access Accounts option for the Windows 2000 Professional package.

Step 13 Create an SMS Advertisement to computers you want to upgrade. You can schedule the program to run at a specific time, or you can allow users to run the program independently of assignments and kick off the upgrade from the SMS client of the computer to which the program has been assigned.

You have now prepared and assigned a Systems Management Server deployment of Windows 2000 Professional. All that remains is to confirm the successful distribution of the package and test the resulting system.

Time Comparison for Different Installation Methods

Table 3.2 presents total installation time requirements for various distribution methods across the major components of a Windows 2000 installation, based on testing done by the author during the writing of this book. These numbers will vary—often by quite a great deal—depending on the environment, network bandwidth, client machine configuration, and the amount of user data to back up and restore.

For testing, I used an isolated network with 100 Mbps connections, minimal constant simulated load, and a dedicated server.

The client machines were configured with identical hardware. The same additional software was installed in each case—an automated install of Office 2000, WinZip, Norton AntiVirus, and a small number of additional custom applications.

The total installation footprint was approximately 1.3GB, excluding the virtual memory paging file. Operating system configuration settings were identical, and the user data folder contained 800MB of various document and program files.

Table 3.2 **Installation Method Time Comparison (in minutes)**

<table>
<tr><th></th><th colspan="7">Distribution Method</th></tr>
<tr><th>Component</th><th>Manual Network Install</th><th>Unattended Network Install</th><th>RIS</th><th>RIPREP Image</th><th>SYSPREP Image from CD</th><th>Upgrade from CD</th><th>Upgrade via SMS 2.0</th></tr>
<tr><td>Data backup</td><td>30</td><td>30</td><td>30</td><td>30</td><td>30</td><td>30</td><td>30</td></tr>
<tr><td>Partition and format</td><td>10</td><td>10</td><td>10</td><td>10</td><td rowspan="5">30</td><td>N/A</td><td>N/A</td></tr>
<tr><td>OS install</td><td>150</td><td>120</td><td>120</td><td rowspan="4">150</td><td rowspan="4">90</td><td rowspan="4">150</td></tr>
<tr><td>OS configure</td><td>30</td><td>—</td><td>—</td></tr>
<tr><td>Application install</td><td>60</td><td>60</td><td>60</td></tr>
<tr><td>Application configure</td><td>15</td><td>15</td><td>15</td></tr>
<tr><td>Data restore</td><td>30</td><td>30</td><td>30</td><td>30</td><td>30</td><td></td><td></td></tr>
<tr><td>Total (HH:MM)</td><td>05:25</td><td>04:25</td><td>04:25</td><td>03:40</td><td>01:30</td><td>02:00</td><td>03:00</td></tr>
</table>

Note that data backup—although highly recommended—is not necessarily required when upgrading from CD or over SMS. Data restore under these methods won't be required unless the upgrade doesn't complete properly.

This data doesn't suggest always using SYSPREP and never using a manual network install; installation time is simply one component among many to consider when developing a Windows 2000 Professional deployment solution. Each deployment mechanism has its own strengths and weaknesses; each requires different development considerations and different resources. Some solutions may not be feasible in some environments. Hopefully, this book will help you to recognize and sufficiently address the additional elements involved in developing the deployment solution best suited for your environment.

4

Answer Files and the Setup Manager Wizard

THIS CHAPTER COVERS:

- Creating an answer file and a uniqueness database file to facilitate unattended installs
- Selecting the proper type of answer file for a specific installation mechanism
- Enhancing the unattended install process through the extended features of the Setup Manager Wizard
- Installing additional applications through the unattended install process
- Debugging the unattended install process

After reading this chapter, you should be able to do the following:

- Create a complete unattended install process using the Setup Manager Wizard
- Modify an existing answer file for use with a different installation mechanism
- Create a uniqueness database file to provide machine-level customization of the answer file
- Install Windows 2000 Professional and additional applications with near-zero user interaction

With Windows NT 4.0, creating an unattended install process was a difficult, time-consuming procedure involving a great deal of manual development effort. The setup tools developed for Windows 2000 strive to reduce this effort by providing more options for installation mechanisms, as well as easier means through which those mechanisms can be customized and utilized. The Windows 2000 Setup Manager Wizard is one of the most important tools in taking advantage of these new technologies.

This chapter takes an in-depth look at using answer files and the Windows 2000 Setup Manager Wizard to enable customized unattended installs of Windows 2000. We'll walk through creating an unattended process from scratch, and look at some of the other Windows 2000 install technologies that take advantage of the files generated by the Setup Manager Wizard. For readers familiar with the Windows NT 4.0 unattended install process, we'll briefly examine porting the NT 4.0 setup procedure over to Windows 2000.

Answer Files in Windows 2000

The hinge pin of an effective unattended install process is the *answer file*. The answer file contains the values needed by the setup tools to complete an install without requiring user interaction. The answer file's name and contents will vary, depending on the purpose of the answer file, but the basic format of all answer files is the same:

```
; Any line preceded by a semicolon is treated as a comment.
; It is a good idea to put versioning information at the top
; of your answer file.

; UNATTEND.TXT file for Windows 2000 Professional
; Written January 1, 2000, by Jeffrey A. Ferris
; Version 1.0

[Section1]
key1 = value1
; Values containing spaces should be enclosed in double quotes.
key2 = "value 2"
key3 = value3

[Section2]
key1 = "value 1"
key2 = value2
key3 = value3
```

There are four primary types of answer files and one companion file, outlined in the following sections.

UNATTEND.TXT

The most widely recognized unattended install file is UNATTEND.TXT. This file is used when performing an unattended install from a distribution share point. When running the install from DOS or a DOS boot disk, this is the command line to kick off an unattended install:

```
WINNT /S:<SourcePath> /U:<Path\UNATTEND.TXT>
```

When running the install from Windows 95, Windows 98, Windows NT, or Windows 2000, use this command line:

```
WINNT32 /S:<SourcePath> /UNATTEND:<Path\UNATTEND.TXT>
```

Note that in either scenario, the UNATTEND.TXT file can have any filename, so long as you specify the name correctly after the `/U:` or `/UNATTEND:` switch.

WINNT.SIF

When using an answer file to install from the Windows 2000 Installation CD, the file should be located on a floppy disk to be inserted into drive A: after the computer begins to boot from the CD-ROM. For this type of install, the file *must* be named WINNT.SIF.

The format of the WINNT.SIF file is nearly identical to that of a standard UNATTEND.TXT file, with one important addition—the `[Data]` section. The options under the `[Data]` section are described in detail in Chapter 3, "Deployment Options," in the section "CD-ROM Installation." Just as a quick recap, the `[Data]` section of the WINNT.SIF file should appear as follows:

```
[Data]
AutoPartition = "1"
MsDosInitiated = "0"
UnattendedInstall = "yes"
```

Converting an existing UNATTEND.TXT file to a WINNT.SIF file is simple; just add the `[Data]` section, rename the file, and copy it to a floppy disk. Keep in mind that the WINNT.SIF file can't do all the same things as the standard unattended process. Because the OEM directory—a directory structure used with distribution share points to distribute extra files, such as drivers and application install files—doesn't exist on the Windows 2000 Professional Installation CD, installation components relying on the OEM directory structure won't run, but all the answers and component configuration information should work the same.

The OEM Folder

When performing an unattended install from a distribution share point or from a SYSPREP image, you can use an optional OEM folder to facilitate the inclusion of files not included with the basic distribution of Windows 2000. When using the

> **Don't Try to Upgrade with Boot from CD**
>
> The install method of booting to the Windows 2000 CD can only be used to perform a clean install. You can't upgrade an existing OS installation by booting from the installation CD.

OEM folder with a distribution share point (DSP) based installation on an i386-based platform, the folder should be created as a subfolder under the i386 folder containing all of the base Windows 2000 source files. When using the OEM folder with a SYSPREP installation, the folder should be created as a subfolder under %systemdrive%\SYSPREP.

A number of special files and folders are recognized under the OEM structure. Figure 4.1 shows the OEM folder structure.

The following list describes the folders:

- **OEM**

  The root of the OEM hierarchy. This folder contains all files and folders not included on the Windows 2000 Installation CD. Additional files under the root OEM folder can be used during GUI-mode setup, but will be deleted after the GUI-mode setup completes.

  In the example in Figure 4.1, logo.bmp, Backgrnd.bmp, cmdlines.txt, reg.exe, and $$Rename.txt are all included under the OEM folder. The two bitmap files are used as backgrounds during the GUI-mode setup, and would be specified under the `[OEM_Ads]` section of the answer file. The cmdlines.txt file is automatically processed as a batch file at the end of GUI-mode setup.

- **$$**

  Files and folders under the $$ folder are copied to the Windows 2000 installation root (%windir%). For example, if you install Windows 2000 in C:\WINNT, the files and folders under $$ will be copied to matching locations under C:\WINNT.

  If you want to copy files into existing Windows 2000 installation directories, you must duplicate the applicable folder structure under this folder. For example, to copy files to the `\WINNT\Help` or `\WINNT\System32` directories, you would create a `System32` and a `Help` subfolder under the $$ folder.

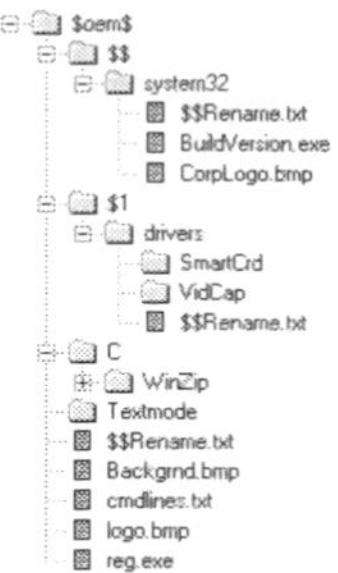

Figure 4.1 Contents of the OEM folder.

- **System32**

  Since this folder is under the $$ folder, anything under this directory will be copied to the `%windir%\System32` directory. In Figure 4.1, BuildVersion.exe and CorpLogo.bmp are both copied into the System32 directory. CorpLogo.bmp is the default background assigned through group policy, and BuildVersion.exe is a custom-developed application I use in my images to display the string contained in the `HKLM\System\Setup\OemDuplicatorString` registry key.

- **$1**

  Setup translates the $1 subfolder into the %systemdrive% environment variable. For example, if you install Windows 2000 to C:\WINNT, anything under this folder will be copied down to matching locations on the C:\ drive.

- **Drivers**

  Plug and play drivers not included with the default Windows 2000 installation source should be included in separate subfolders under this directory. In the sample structure in Figure 4.1, there is a driver directory for a `SmartCrd` device and a `VidCap` device. The Drivers folder replaces the Display and Net folders used under NT 4.0.

- **C**

  Any subfolders under OEM consisting of a single letter are interpreted as drive letters. Files and subfolders contained within these <*drive letter*> subfolders are copied to corresponding locations on the volume matching the subdirectory name.

  For example, in Figure 4.1, the `WinZip` program directory and all files within it will be copied to the `C:\WinZip` folder. If your system has two drives, a C:\ and a D:\ drive, you could specify a folder called \OEM\D into which you would place files you wanted to copy to the D:\ drive.

- **Textmode**

  The Textmode directory contains driver files to be used during text-mode setup, such as OEM-provided HALs and disk controllers. Any files and folders provided under this directory should be specified in the `[OEMBootFiles]` section of the answer file.

- **CMDLINES.TXT**

  This file is automatically processed as a batch file at the end of GUI-mode setup. The file contains DOS-style commands, one per line, in the same format as one would enter those commands directly from the command prompt.

  Commands specified in this file are not executed as a user; instead, they run under the same security context as the Windows 2000 setup process.

- **$$RENAME.TXT**

  This is a special type of text file that should be included in the root of any folder that contains files or subfolders with long filenames. This file instructs Setup to convert certain short filenames to long filenames.

  The basic format of this file is simple. Specify a section name as the File Directory where the files or subfolders will be located. Entries under the section are in the format `shortfilename = "long filename"`, like this:

  ```
  [File Directory]
  ShortName1 = "Long Filename 1"
  ShortName2 = "Long Filename 2"
  ```

  For example, the $$Rename.txt file under the System32 directory in Figure 4.1 would appear as follows:

  ```
  [\winnt\system32]
  CORPLOGO.BMP = "Corporate Logo.bmp"
  BUILDV~1.EXE = "BuildVersion.exe"
  ```

  This will rename the CorpLogo.bmp file to Corporate Logo.bmp, and the BuildVersion.exe program, which Setup would have converted to a short filename of BUILDV~1.exe, will retain its associated long filename. If you use the Windows 2000 Setup Manager Wizard to generate answer files and create the OEM folder structure, the wizard will automatically create $$RENAME.TXT files when they're needed.

SYSPREP.INF

To deploy disk images, you can use SYSPREP in conjunction with a third-party disk duplication product such as Norton Ghost or PowerQuest Drive Image (refer to the section "System Cloning" in Chapter 3 for details). You must prepare Windows 2000 for imaging by running SYSPREP. After you run SYSPREP, you can use the disk imaging system to create an image, and install this image on other clone systems. When these cloned systems are rebooted, a mini-setup program is invoked. The SYSPREP.INF file is an optional answer file you can add to the SYSPREP folder prior to running SYSPREP.EXE. This file *must* be named SYSPREP.INF. The SYSPREP.INF file answers the questions posed by a lightweight version of the Setup Manager Wizard. This enables you to customize the individual Windows 2000 Professional machines based on a single SYSPREP image. Note that when the cloned system has completed the setup, the SYSPREP folder is deleted.

There is one drawback to this approach, which is that if you need to change your SYSPREP.INF file, you have to re-image the whole machine. With Windows 2000, however, you also can update SYSPREP.INF. Copy SYSPREP.INF to a floppy disk and insert the floppy as soon as the Windows 2000 boot menu appears. The install engine picks up the SYSPREP.INF file from the floppy disk, ignoring the file built into the image. This is similar to the WINNT.SIF approach discussed earlier.

Converting an existing UNATTEND.TXT–style answer file to SYSPREP.INF can be as simple as renaming the file. A SYSPREP install runs from a disk image, however, so your customization limitations exist within the files contained on the system image.

SYSPREP answer files support a limited set of the sections and keys available in other types of answer files (see Appendix B, "Complete Answer File Syntax," for the complete set). The sections and keys supported by SYSPREP are as follows:

- `[Unattended]`

  The following keys are supported:

  - `ExtendOemPartition`
  - `InstallFilesPath`
  - `KeepPageFile`
  - `OemPnPDriversPath`
  - `OemSkipEula`
  - `UpdateHAL`
  - `UpdateUPHAL`
- `[Oem_Ads]`

  All keys are supported.
- `[GuiUnattended]`

  The following keys are supported:

  - `AdminPassword`
  - `AutoLogon`
  - `AutoLogonAccountCreation`
  - `AutoLogonCount`
  - `OEMDuplicatorString`
  - `OEMSkipRegional`
  - `OEMSkipWelcome`
  - `TimeZone`
- `[UserData]`

  All keys are supported.
- `[LicenseFilePrintData]`

  (Server only.) All keys are supported.
- `[GuiRunOnce]`

  RunOnce command keys are supported.
- `[Display]`

  All keys are supported.

- `[RegionalSettings]`

  All keys are supported if language files are available.
- `[TapiLocation]`

  All keys are supported if a modem is installed.
- `[Networking]`

  This section should be specified, but no keys are required.
- `[Identification]`

  All keys are supported.

REMBOOT.SIF

When using Remote Installation Services (RIS), REMBOOT.SIF answer files can be used to create RIS-based installs with different configuration options. These files are identical in format to the standard UNATTEND.TXT files mentioned earlier, with the three additional sections `[Data]`, `[RemoteInstall]`, and `[OSChooser]` (for descriptions and alternate values for each of these sections, see Appendix B):

```
[Data]
AutoPartition=1
MsDosInitiated="1"
UnattendedInstall="Yes"
floppyless="1"
OriSrc="\\%SERVERNAME%\RemInst\%INSTALLPATH%"
OriTyp="4"
LocalSourceOnCD=1

[RemoteInstall]
Repartition=Yes

[OSChooser]
Description="Windows Professional - Standard Installation Sample"
Help="This will install Windows Professional in a standard configuration."
LaunchFile="%INSTALLPATH%\%MACHINETYPE%\templates\startrom.com"
ImageType=Flat
```

The Windows 2000 Setup Manager Wizard generates these sections automatically when you select the Remote Installation Services option as the type of answer file you want to generate.

To convert an existing UNATTEND.TXT file to a REMBOOT.SIF, you must add the `[Data]`, `[RemoteInstall]`, and `[OSChooser]` sections. You can add these sections with any text editor, such as Notepad. After modifying the answer file, change its filename to REMBOOT.SIF. To save this file as the install used with the default image created during the installation of RIS, it would actually need to be named

RISTNDRD.SIF. The default location for this file, where `R:\` is the Remote Installation Services volume, is as follows:

```
R:\RemoteInstall\Setup\English\Images\win2000.pro\i386\templates\ristndrd.sif
```

See Chapter 5, "Remote Installation Services (RIS)," for more information on configuring the RIS server to use the file in conjunction with a RIS image.

$UNIQUE$.UDB

When creating an answer file to use on multiple machines, you might have noticed a potential inconvenience. To apply the answer file to multiple machines, you must edit the file for each machine, changing elements such as the computer name, username, and product ID. To get around this problem, we have the $UNIQUE$.UDB file. The $UNIQUE$.UDB file is different from the types of answer files discussed to this point. This file is a *uniqueness database file* (*UDF*), and is used to override values in an existing answer file. This feature allows one answer file together with one UDF companion file to be used for multiple similar configurations, while still allowing granular customization and personalization on a system-by-system basis.

The Setup Manager Wizard can automatically create a UDF. The UDF is called with the `/UDF:id,[UDF]` switch when running WINNT or WINNT32, where *`id`* specifies the section of the UDF to apply to the specific machine you're installing. (See Chapter 3 for details on WINNT and WINNT32 syntax.) *`UDF`* specifies the path and filename to the uniqueness database file. *`UDF`* is an optional parameter; if no *`UDF`* is specified, the wizard prompts you to insert a disk containing a $UNIQUE$.UDB file. If specified after the `/UDF` switch, the filename can be anything you want. If not specified, the file must be located at A:\$UNIQUE$.UDB.

The format of the UDF is as follows (lines preceded by semicolons are comment lines):

```
[UniqueIds]
; Required section.  List the unique IDs (computer names)
; of the individual computers in this section. These are
; the IDs called after the /UDF:id switch when running Setup.
    WKS01=UserData
    WKS02=UserData, GUIUnattended, Identification
    WKS03=UserData

[WKS01:UserData]
    ComputerName=WKS01

[WKS02:UserData]
    ComputerName=WKS02

[WKS02:GUIUnattended]
    TimeZone=21
```

```
[WKS02:Identification]
    JoinDomain=W2Kdomain2

[WKS03:UserData]
    FullName="Lab Computer"
    ComputerName=WKS03
```

In the preceding example, the UDF provides customized answers for three unique machine names—WKS01, WKS02, and WKS03—as listed in the `[UniqueIds]` section. All three have customized `UserData` sections. The `UserData` section *must* be specified unless you're automatically generating computer names. For WKS02, the `GUIUnattended` and `Identification` sections are also customized. For keys not specified in customized UDF sections, the default value specified in the answer file will be used.

Is the Server Accessible?

When using the `/s:`*`sourcepath`* switch for multiple source locations, the first specified server must be accessible or setup will fail.

`/syspart` Versus SYSPREP

I often use the `/syspart` command in conjunction with Ghost to speed the initial process of partitioning, formatting, and copying the install files to the drive. This switch directs Setup to copy required files, mark the partition as active, and then stop. Setup will continue after the next reboot. Before rebooting, I image the drive and apply the image to other systems. The machines to which the image is applied will start running at the beginning of the setup procedure, but they'll already be partitioned and formatted, and they'll already have all the setup source files copied over.

With this method, I can use a single image on widely varied hardware platforms, overriding the few limitations of SYSPREP. It's slower than using SYSPREP on similar hardware, but much faster than manually partitioning and formatting, then running WINNT from the beginning.

Creating and Modifying Answer Files

The deployment tools provided with NT 4.0 did little more than create a template answer file to handle common questions and install standard hardware through the normal Windows setup routine. Customizing the installation of the various Windows components required manually editing answer files and creating the OEM folder structure to hold any additional files and folders needed in the distribution. The most reliable tool for modifying the answer files was the Windows Notepad application. In Windows 2000—both Server and Professional—Microsoft addresses these weaknesses by including a much-improved Windows 2000 Setup Manager Wizard.

Using the Setup Manager Wizard

The Setup Manager Wizard not only creates the answer file required for an unattended install, it can also create the uniqueness database file (UDF), the directory and share point for the Windows 2000 files, customization settings for Internet Explorer, updated or additional drivers for plug and play hardware devices to be used during setup, and the temporary files and folders needed to install third-party applications.

The syntax of the answer file for Windows 2000 covers the installation and configuration of nearly every component of Windows 2000, from network protocols to Solitaire. The Setup Manager Wizard doesn't handle all aspects of configuration (such as which accessories are installed), but it handles the most common—and most complex—functions of the answer file.

The Setup Manager Wizard is in the same location on any version of the Windows 2000 Installation CD: in the DEPLOY.CAB file under the <*CD-ROM*>:\SUPPORT\TOOLS directory. Extract the contents of this CAB file to a new directory with Windows Explorer. After extracting the contents, run the SETUPMGR.EXE file to start the wizard. Exercise 4.1 walks through the creation of a distribution share point unattended install using the Windows 2000 Setup Manager Wizard.

Exercise 4.1 **Creating a Distribution Share Point Unattended Install with the Setup Manager Wizard**

Completion time: 45-60 minutes.

Requirements: Windows 2000 Professional CD, network share point with approximately 500MB of free space

Step 1 Extract SETUPMGR.EXE and SETUPMGX.DLL to a local directory from the \SUPPORT\TOOLS\DEPLOY.CAB file on the Windows 2000 CD-ROM. Run SETUPMGR.EXE, and the Welcome to Windows 2000 Setup Manager Wizard screen appears. Click Next.

Step 2 On the New or Existing Answer File screen, select Create a New Answer File and click Next.

Step 3 The Product to Install screen appears. For this exercise, we'll create a Windows 2000 unattended install file. Select the Windows 2000 Unattended option and click Next.

Note: Although this exercise follows the path of the Windows 2000 unattended install, the SYSPREP install and Remote Installation Services options follow a nearly identical process.

Step 4 On the Platform screen, select Windows 2000 Professional and click Next.

Step 5 The next screen is User Interaction Level (see Figure 4.2). This screen allows you to specify the amount of information that the user is expected to provide during the installation. The Fully Automated option answers all questions without user interaction, provided that the answer file is complete and accurate. The Description section at the bottom of the screen describes the function of the selected option. Select the Fully Automated option and click Next.

Step 6 On the License Agreement screen, read the terms of the License Agreement. Keep in mind that you're accepting the license agreement for every user and every PC that will be using the UNATTEND.TXT file you're creating. Accept the terms of the license agreement and click Next.

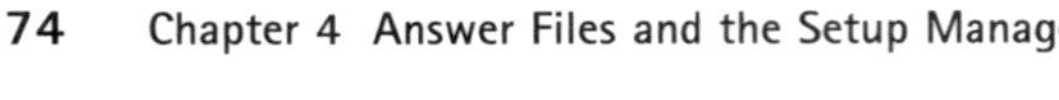

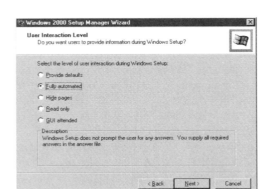

Figure 4.2 Selecting the user interaction level.

Step 7 The Customize the Software screen allows you to specify the default name and organization for the installation. In Fully Automated mode, you can't move on until you enter a value for at least the Name field. If you don't fill in both of these values, the install will halt at the GUI install screen where this information is normally requested. For this exercise, use your company name for both spaces, or use your department name for Name and your company name for Organization. Click Next.

Step 8 Figure 4.3 shows the next screen, Computer Names. Here you can enter multiple computer names and generate a uniqueness database file in addition to the answer file. If you enter only one computer name in this screen, the Setup Manager Wizard doesn't generate the UDF. You can also elect to generate computer names automatically, based on organization name. With this option, Setup will create computer names by appending a random number to the end of the organization name. In this way, a single answer file can be used on multiple systems without requiring a UDF to assign unique computer names. Optionally, you can populate this field by creating a text file with one computer name per line. You import the names by clicking the Import button and selecting the text file.

We'll generate a UDF along with our answer file for the computer names WKS001 through WKS005, as shown in the figure. For each name, enter the name in the Computer Name field, and then click Add. Click Next when the list is complete.

Step 9 On the Administrator Password screen, you can specify the password for the local administrator account. For this exercise, enter **wksadmin** in both blanks. Keep in mind that the password is case-sensitive, and will be stored in plain text in the resulting UNATTEND.TXT file.

Select the option When the Computer Starts, Automatically Log on as Administrator. Configuring these options causes Windows to log on as the local administrator account the first time it comes up after the install has completed. This is useful for executing RunOnce commands at the level of the local administrator. After the install completes and the auto logon executes, the machine will need to be shut down or restarted to prevent it from continuing to auto logon as administrator. The administrator is unable to simply log out until the system has been completely rebooted. Set the Number of Times to Auto Logon option to **1** and then click Next.

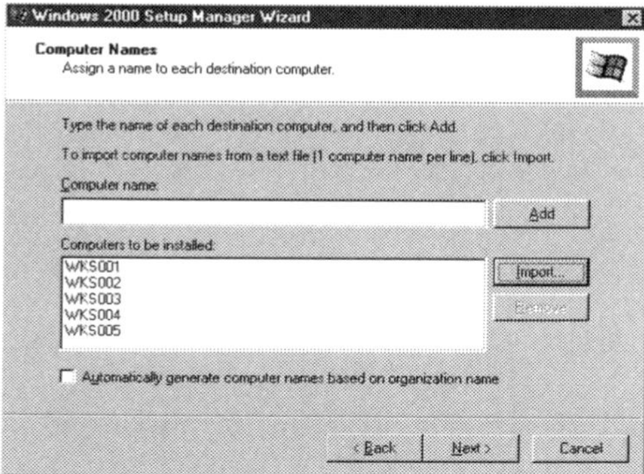

Figure 4.3 Adding multiple computer names automatically generates a uniqueness database file.

Step 10 At the Display Settings screen, leave everything set to Windows Default, and click Next.

Step 11 On the Network Settings screen, you can specify the network settings for your automated install. If you're running TCP/IP with DHCP in a Microsoft Windows client/server environment, you can select Typical Settings. If you have special client configuration requirements in your network environment, such as static IP addressing, select the Custom Settings option. Selecting Custom Settings displays the standard Windows 2000 Network Control Panel. Fill in the options just as you would if setting up a stand-alone Windows 2000 Professional client machine. The Setup Manager Wizard will transfer the settings information to the answer file. For this exercise, we'll assume typical settings. Select the Typical Settings option and click Next.

Step 12 The Workgroup or Domain screen appears next (see Figure 4.4). Here you can specify whether this machine should participate in a workgroup or a domain. For this exercise, we'll add the machine to the W2KDOMAIN domain. You should substitute a valid domain name for your network here, or install to a workgroup if you have no Windows NT domains available. If you want to participate in a domain, you must either pre-create your computer accounts, or specify a domain user account with permission to add new accounts on the lower portion of this screen. In the figure, the user account named WKSInstall is used to join this system to the domain. You should enter an existing user account with permission to create new computer accounts in the domain specified on the top portion of this screen. Fill in the options as they apply to your environment and click Next.

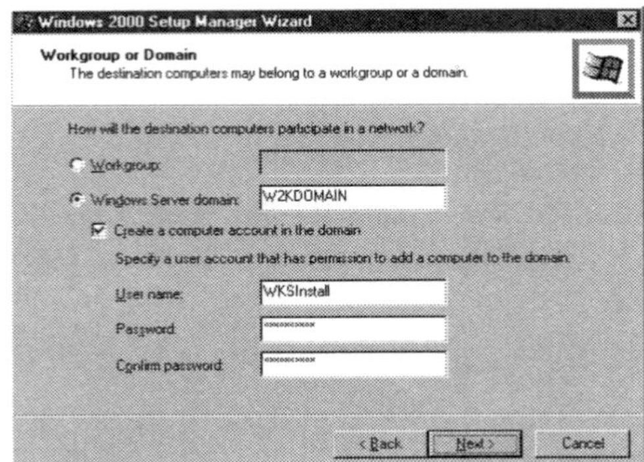

Figure 4.4 Specifying the workgroup or domain network environment.

Step 13 The Time Zone screen opens. If you have machines in multiple time zones, you can take care of those by modifying the uniqueness database file after the Setup Manager Wizard has completed. The Time Zone index values you would need to manually edit this entry are listed in Appendix B. Fortunately, this Wizard provides a drop-down box from which to select your time zone. Do so, and click Next.

Step 14 The Additional Settings screen allows you to specify additional settings such as the folder into which you want to install Windows 2000. If you select No at this screen, you can skip to step 23. The resulting answer file will facilitate a basic install.

To display the additional settings, select the Yes, Edit the Additional Settings option, and click Next.

Step 15 The next screen is for Telephony configuration. Complete this section based on your specific location, and click Next to continue.

Step 16 On the Regional Settings screen, select Use the Default Regional Settings for the Windows Version You Are Installing and click Next.

Step 17 Click Next on the Languages screen. There's no need to specify additional languages for this exercise.

Step 18 The Browser and Shell Settings screen has three options (see Figure 4.5). In the second part of this book, we'll use the Active Directory group policy objects to configure settings for Internet Explorer. The second option on this screen enables you to specify an automatic configuration file (usually AUTOCONFIG.INS) as either a URL or a local file. The third option allows you to manually specify the proxy settings, the default home page, and a selection of default favorites.

For this exercise, select the first option, Use Default Internet Explorer Settings, and click Next.

Step 19 On the Installation Folder screen, you select the installation folder for Windows 2000 Professional. Select the Windows 2000 default, A Folder Named Winnt, and then click Next.

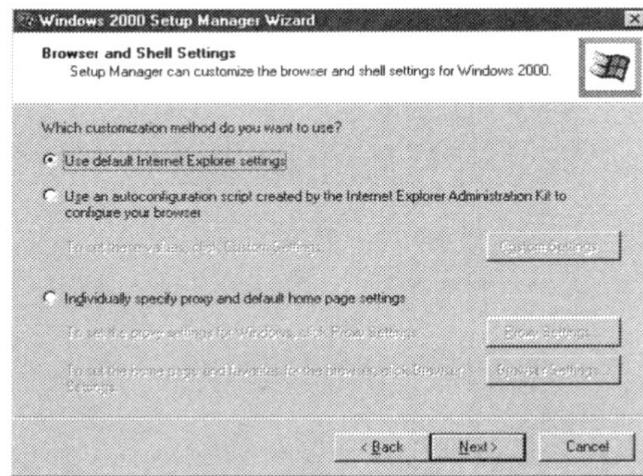

Figure 4.5 Configuring the browser and shell settings.

Note: When installing software, especially operating systems, it's usually best to go with the default directory—in step 19, WINNT—because documentation on bug fixes, program installation, and system configuration usually references files using their default folder locations.

Step 20 Use the Install Printers screen to add any network printers you want to install. These selections will be converted to RunOnce commands when added to the answer file. For purposes of this exercise, add two printers, \\printsvr\color and \\printsvr\laser. You can substitute these for actual servers and print shares applicable to your environment. When you're finished adding printers, click Next.

Step 21 The Run Once screen enables you to specify commands to run the first time a user logs onto a new machine. As Figure 4.6 shows, the settings from the Install Printers screen are converted to RunOnce commands. Ultimately, these commands will be imported into the RunOnce registry key during the unattended install process. Add the following additional command in the Command to Run box, as shown in the figure:

```
reg import settings.reg
```

Click Next to continue.

Step 22 With the options on the Distribution Folder screen, the Setup Manager Wizard can automatically create your Windows 2000 Professional distribution folder. Select the option Yes, Create or Modify a Distribution Folder and click Next.

Modifying the Registry from the Command Line

Exercise 4.1, step 21 uses the REG command to import a registry file from the command line. REG.EXE is a command-line registry utility included with the Windows 2000 Support Tools. It's located in the \Support\Tools directory of the Windows 2000 installation CD. REG.EXE can be extracted from the SUPPORT.CAB file, or installed with the rest of the support tools by running SETUP.EXE in this directory.

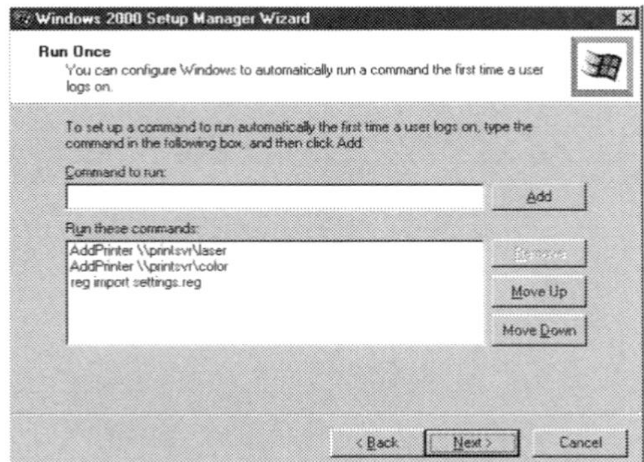

Figure 4.6 The completed Run Once screen.

Note: If you want to create an unattended install file to use when booting from the distribution CD-ROM, select No, This Answer File Will Be Used to Install from a CD, skip to step 29, and name the file WINNT.SIF. Using this option adds the necessary `[Data]` section.

Step 23 The Distribution Folder Name screen is next. Select the option to create a new distribution folder, select a distribution folder on a drive with approximately 500MB of free space, and share the folder as the default Win2000dist. Then click Next.

Step 24 On the Additional Mass Storage Drivers screen, you can specify additional drivers. Assuming that you're using standard hardware, you shouldn't need to worry about additional drivers. Click Next.

Step 25 The Hardware Abstraction Layer screen appears, on which you can select a different HAL. Click Next to use the Windows 2000 Professional default HAL, or if your PC vendor provided a replacement HAL, select that HAL here. Don't specify a replacement HAL unless instructed to do so by the PC vendor.

Step 26 The Additional Commands screen appears (see Figure 4.7). Commands entered on this screen appear in the CMDLINES.TXT file, and are executed at the end of GUI-mode setup, but before the final reboot. By placing commands here rather than the `[GuiRunOnce]` section, the commands will run under the security context of the Setup program. Commands entered in the `[GuiRunOnce]` run under the security context of the first user to log on. Add the three commands shown in the figure and then click Next.

Step 27 The OEM Branding screen enables you to enter the path and filename to a logo and background file to use during the unattended install. If you specify these files, point to their current locations—Setup will automatically copy them to the proper directories during the install. For this exercise, enter **D:\LOGO.BMP** and **D:\BACKGRND.BMP** in their respective text boxes and then click Next.

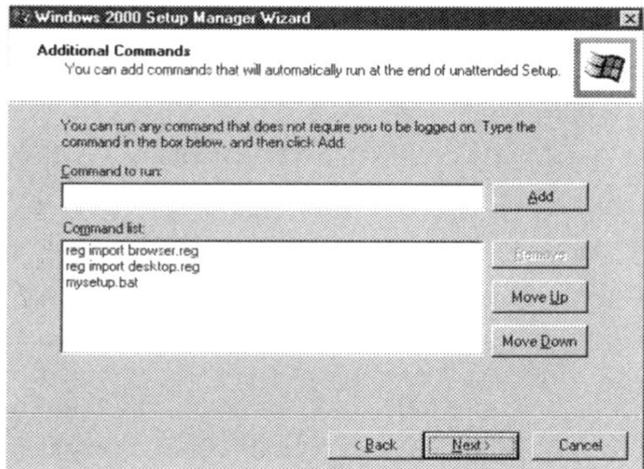

Figure 4.7 The completed Additional Commands screen.

Step 28 The Additional Files or Folders screen (see Figure 4.8) is perhaps one of the nicest additions to the Windows 2000 Professional Setup Manager Wizard. In the past, adding additional files to support your unattended install was not easy. The Additional Files or Folders screen provides a simple GUI interface to specify additional files and folders and their intended locations on the destination computers. From this screen, you can specify files and folders for each of the following locations:

- System drive
- Windows folder
- System32 directory

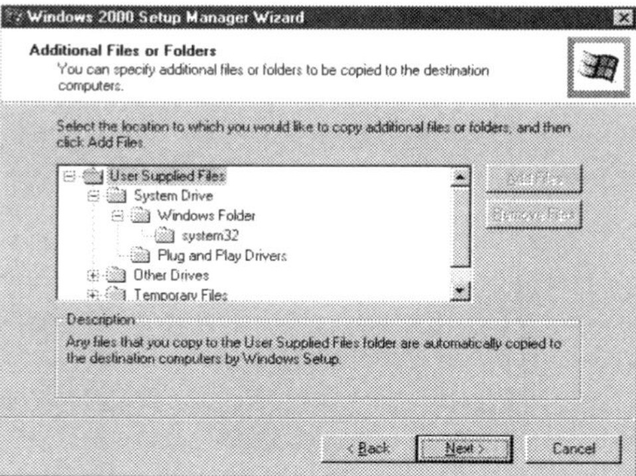

Figure 4.8 Adding files and folders to create on the destination computer.

- Plug and play drivers folder, used during setup to install additional plug and play devices not included with the Windows 2000 distribution media
- Any standard local drive or subfolders therein
- A temporary directory deleted at the end of GUI-mode setup

To add files or folders to any of these locations, simply select the destination, click the Add Files button, and browse to the file or folder you want to add.

At this step, you would add the supporting files for any commands added in previous steps, such as the REG.EXE executable, SETTINGS.REG, BROWSER.REG, DESKTOP.REG, and MYSETUP.BAT files specified in steps 21 and 26. You should add these files to the Temporary Files location. Note that we haven't actually created these files in this exercise. The REG.EXE file is part of the Windows 2000 Support Tools, included on the Windows 2000 distribution CD under \SUPPORT\TOOLS\SUPPORT.CAB. The registry files are just settings exported from various points in the registry, and the MYSETUP.BAT file would contain any extra commands to run during setup. Figure 4.9 shows sample contents for these files.

Additional applications, document files, and directory structures can be created under the Other Drives folder. If you create directories containing files or folders with long filenames, Setup Manager Wizard will automatically generate the $$RENAME.TXT file needed by Setup to map long filenames to the standard 8.3 names recognized by DOS.

When you're finished adding files and folders, click Next.

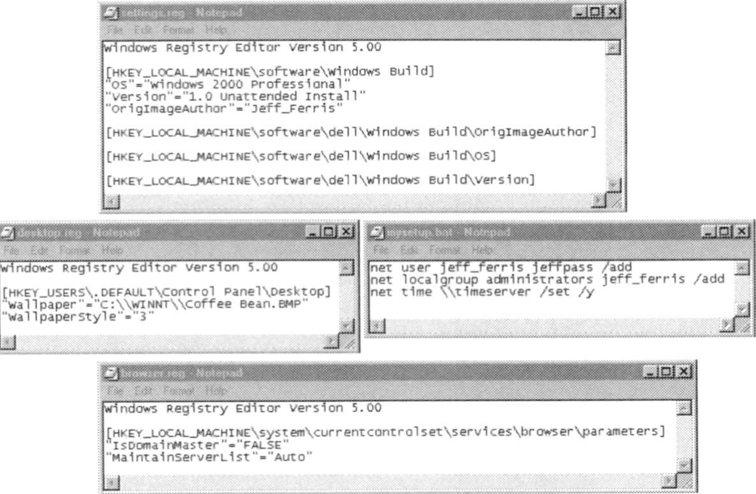

Figure 4.9 Contents of the MYSETUP.BAT, SETTINGS.REG, BROWSER.REG, and DESKTOP.REG files.

Step 29 On the Answer File Name screen, you can specify the full path and filename of the answer file to be generated by the Setup Manager Wizard. You should save the file in the same location as the distribution share point as specified in step 23, which is the default. Click Next.

Step 30 The Location of Setup Files screen that appears next requests the location of the Windows 2000 Professional setup files. You'll need the Windows 2000 Professional CD at this point. Select Copy the Files from CD and click Next. The Setup Manager Wizard will copy the files from the CD to the distribution share point. When this copy is complete, the Setup Manager Wizard will move to the next screen automatically.

Step 31 Figure 4.10 shows the final screen of the Setup Manager Wizard. You can see from the wizard the names of the answer files created. In this case, we have the following names:

- UNATTEND.TXT, the unattended install answer file
- UNATTEND.UDF, the uniqueness database file
- UNATTEND.BAT, a batch file to kick off the unattended install process from a 32-bit Windows client.

Click Finish to close the wizard.

Now that you've created an answer file, a UDF, a batch file, and a distribution share point, applying your image is a simple process. Attach your client PCs to the share point—alternatively, you could copy the entire share point to a CD-ROM or other form of local media—and run this command:

```
UNATTEND <COMPUTERNAME>
```

where *COMPUTERNAME* is one of the five workstation names defined in Step 8 of Exercise 4.1. That's all there is to it! Assuming that your file was properly created, the machines should install without any extra prompting.

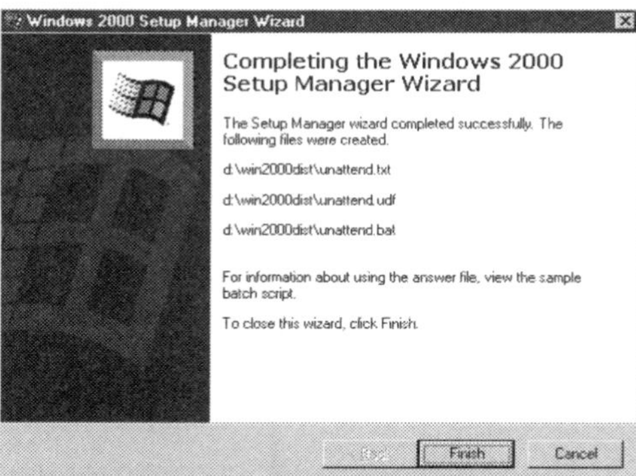

Figure 4.10 The final screen of the Windows 2000 Setup Manager Wizard.

Note: Even though you've completely automated the install process, with file copying, plug and play detection, and other machine installation tasks, the unattended install could still take an hour or two per machine.

Debugging the Answer File

Having now created your answer file and the supporting files, you can test them by installing Windows 2000 on a computer. In most cases, if you followed the steps in Exercise 4.1, you should see a successful automated install. If the unattended install hangs at the first screen, or the resulting system configuration isn't quite what you'd expected, there's a good chance that you need to improve your answer file. Some errors can actually cause the install process to stop, requiring a restart of the install. The two most common errors that result in a system lock are keys without values and values without quotation marks.

The following example shows an answer file section that we'll use to illustrate some critical errors you might see in an answer file:

```
[section]
key1=
key2=*
key3=value
key4
key 5=value
key6=value with spaces
key7="value with spaces"
```

In this example, key2, key3, and key7 are valid, but the other keys could cause critical errors. In key1, there's no value after the equal sign. For blank values, you must use an asterisk (*), as shown in key2. Key4 is invalid because there's no equal sign or value. Spaces aren't allowed in the key portion, so key5 would be invalid even if enclosed in quotes. Values with spaces, such as key6, must be enclosed in quotes, as in key7, or they'll cause failures.

Non-critical errors in answer files are errors that allow the install process to complete, but either stop and wait for user input at some point or incorrectly configure a Windows 2000 option. These types of errors usually result from incorrect values associated with a key, or a required section or key that has been missed altogether. These types of errors are the most common, and debugging them is, unfortunately, usually a matter of trial and error. The following list shows some of the more common things to look for:

- Yes/No values answered with 1 or 0
- 1 or 0 values answered with Yes/No
- Incorrect table lookup, such as time zone or regional settings values
- Missing answer file section
- Missing key within a section

- Key located in incorrect section
- Misspelled key or section name
- Duplicate keys or sections

Converting an NT 4.0 Answer File for Use with Windows 2000

The unattended setup files for Windows 2000 Professional are very similar to those for Windows NT Workstation 4.0, which makes the task of converting them easier. Although an undocumented—and possibly unsupported—feature, the Windows 2000 Setup Manager Wizard can actually convert your old Windows NT Workstation 4.0 answer files.

The process is similar to that of creating a new answer file, but when you start the Setup Manager Wizard, you select the option Modify an Existing File at the initial screen, rather than the option to create a new file. Specify the path and filename to an existing Windows NT 4.0 answer file in the text box. You'll get this error message:

```
The file <path>\Unattend.txt was not created by the Setup Manager Wizard. Would you
like to overwrite it anyway?
```

Select Yes to allow modifications to the file. As you step through the wizard, sections answered by your Windows NT 4.0 answer file will already be complete. Missing sections can be filled in through the standard wizard interface.

The time zone settings and regional settings will definitely need to be reconfigured, as they now use index values rather than text strings. You'll also need to add a current serial number to the product ID string. There are a number of enhancements to the Windows 2000 customization levels available with the answer file, so don't settle for simply converting your existing answer files. Look at the other options available with Windows 2000 (see Appendix B); you might be surprised how much you can customize just by using the answer file.

Is Your Setup Manager Wizard the Current Version?

In pre-release versions of the Setup Manager Wizard, the RunOnce commands that were supposed to add printers neglected to enclose themselves in quotation marks. As a result, the install process would hang as soon as it was initiated. If you're having problems with your answer file, make certain that you're using the latest release version of the Setup Manager Wizard, and double-check your RunOnce section to make sure that the values are enclosed in quotes.

Unattended Application Install

While it is my recommendation to use the Windows Installer service for installation of all of your core applications, there are often reasons why such a solution is not a viable option. It's possible to integrate application installation with Windows 2000 Professional unattended installs. Two ways of accomplishing this task are the SYSDIFF utility and the ScriptIt utility.

SYSDIFF

Many people who have done unattended installs in the past are familiar with the SYSDIFF tool. While I wouldn't recommend using SYSDIFF for complex applications like an office suite or an antivirus application, it's often a useful tool for the installation of small utilities, such as WinZip or the Windows 2000 Support Tools. SYSDIFF is included with the Windows NT 4.0 and the Windows 2000 Resource Kits.

For those who may be unfamiliar with SYSDIFF, the premise is simple. First, install a clean image of your operating system and use SYSDIFF to take a system state snapshot. Next, make configuration changes, install applications, and take a differential snapshot, which wraps all registry changes and file changes into a difference package. Finally, apply the difference package to other clean OS images. In theory, all changed files and configuration settings are applied to the new computer, and it will look just like the one that was manually configured.

In my experience, it's never that easy.

More often, you must install a clean system, take a snapshot, make configuration changes, and take a differential. Then reinstall to a clean system, take a snapshot, install your first application, and take a differential. Reinstall again to a clean system, snapshot, install your second application, and take a differential. . . and so on, reinstalling your system with each new application to ensure clean SYSDIFF packages. Even then, the order in which you apply SYSDIFF packages could produce configuration issues, file conflicts, and the like.

ScriptIt

Before ScriptIt, I would spend hours with an application installation package, creating a customized Visual Basic executable to emulate a technician, using SendKeys to answer questions in the installation routines. After awhile, I wrote my own Visual Basic scripting engine, to accept text files and parse out information to send to various application windows, automating third-party application installs by sending keystrokes on a window-by-window basis. My application paled by comparison to Microsoft's ScriptIt.

ScriptIt is a simple utility, available for free from Microsoft's Web site at the following URL (it relocates now and again, so you may need to use the Search option on Microsoft's Web site—just search for ScriptIt):

```
http://www.microsoft.com/NTServer/nts/deployment/custguide/scriptit3.asp
```

ScriptIt can send keystrokes to application windows, answering questions with standard answers, just like a technician sitting at the machine supervising the install. To this end, it's more accurate and much more consistent than SYSDIFF. To use ScriptIt with an unattended install, follow these steps:

1. Create a directory named ScriptIt.
2. Add the ScriptIt executable and any script files you've created. Generally, you should write one script file per application you want to install, rather than kicking off all of your applications with a single script file.

3. Add subdirectories of the installation programs for the applications you want to install using ScriptIt.
4. Add the entire ScriptIt directory, including all files and subfolders, to your unattended install by specifying its location on a local drive through the Setup Manager Wizard (see Exercise 4.1, step 28 for information on how to add the directory to your install).
5. Then just add the commands to call ScriptIt to a batch file called via the RunOnce command, such as the MYSETUP.BAT specified in Exercise 4.1. At the end of the batch file, be sure to delete the ScriptIt subdirectory.

Here's a sample ScriptIt script for installing WinZip (`http://www.winzip.com`) version 7.0SR1:

```
[SCRIPT]
REM Unattended script to install WINZIP 7.0SR1
REM Available from http://www.winzip.com
RUN="c:\scriptit\winzip\winzip70.exe"
WinZip 7.0 (SR-1) Setup=!S
WinZip Setup=~
WinZip Setup+Thank you=!n
License Agreement=!Y
WinZip Setup+Select=!c!n
WinZip Setup+Click=!e!n
WinZip Setup+Thank you={tab}~
```

To use this file, you would save it as WINZIP7.SIT (or any other filename; the application is not even extension-specific), and call this command line from the MYSETUP.BAT file:

```
C:\SCRIPTIT\SCRIPTIT C:\SCRIPTIT\WINZIP7.SIT
```

See the documentation included with the utility for more information on creating scripted installs with ScriptIt. There are more sample scripts at the end of the ScriptIt white paper.

5 Remote Installation Services (RIS)

This chapter covers:

- What exactly *is* Remote Installation Services (RIS)?
- Architectural requirements for using RIS
- Installing the RIS server component
- Creating RIS installs for Windows 2000 Professional
- Identifying workstation requirements to install Windows 2000 Professional via RIS
- Enhancing the Remote Installation Services process

After reading this chapter, you should be able to do the following:

- Install and configure the server component for Remote Installation Services
- Configure supporting services to enable RIS in your environment
- Create an image of a fully configured system using RIPREP
- Create a complete unattended install process using Remote Installation Services

After designing a standardized system image for a new operating system (OS), one of the more complicated logistics hurdles in rolling out the new OS is selecting the distribution method. Depending on the number of workstations in your environment, physically distributing installation media (such as SYSPREP images burned to

CD-ROM) could require an exceptional amount of effort, especially when modifications to the image are needed. On the other hand, *distribution share point* (*DSP*) installs require creating and distributing custom network boot disks for each type of network card in your environment—and if you've ever done an unattended install of Windows NT Workstation 4.0 via network DSP, I'm sure you've run into the problem of duplicate computer names when people copy the network boot disk without changing the NETBIOS name in the PROTOCOL.INI file.

The *Remote Installation Services* (*RIS*) component of Windows 2000 addresses some of these issues. This chapter provides an introduction to RIS, explaining what RIS is and describing some of the benefits of RIS as they apply to the unattended install process. I examine additional network services that must be in place before implementing RIS in your environment, and walk through the installation of the RIS server component. Later sections also walk through the creation and distribution of basic and advanced RIS images, including important functions such as access control, pre-staging, and image storage considerations.

What Is RIS?

Remote Installation Services (*RIS*) is one of the change and configuration management features included with Windows 2000. RIS is an optional Windows 2000 service that enables you to set up new client computers remotely, without the need to physically visit each client machine. Specifically, you can install operating systems on remote boot-enabled client computers by connecting the computer to the network, starting the client computer, and logging on with a valid user account.

By installing a RIS server in your environment, you're providing a potentially diskless boot (booting with no boot floppy or CD—although the system still requires a hard disk) as well as a fully automated, network-based mechanism for deploying Windows 2000 Professional.

Installing Windows 2000 Professional using RIS is similar to installing with the network-based distribution share point (DSP) unattended install method. All files are transferred across the network to the local system, and the standard Windows 2000 Setup process runs in unattended mode, including text-mode and GUI-mode setup. RIS-based installs are only slightly faster than similarly configured DSP-based installs; the speed difference results from changes in the network client connection method. With RIS, there is no longer the same need for a customized network client boot disk as there is with a DSP-based network install. Instead, a RIS-based install uses *PXE* (*Pre-boot Execution Environment*) to connect to the network. With any PXE-compliant network card, the user can actually boot directly from the network card—with no additional drivers or configuration steps—to initiate an OS install. For many systems without a PXE-enabled network card, a simple boot disk with a PXE emulator can simplify the process of attaching to the network.

PXE is a technology standard that provides a mechanism for connecting to the network and executing program code by booting directly from a network interface card (NIC).

A workstation with a PXE-enabled NIC must first be configured in the computer's BIOS to boot to the network. When the machine is powered on, the user can press the F12 key to boot to the PXE. PXE sends out a DHCP discovery packet. If a DHCP server responds, the client requests an IP address for itself as well as the IP address of a RIS server. After the client receives this information, it contacts the RIS server, using the *Boot Information Negotiation Layer* (*BINL*). BINL provides the location and filename of the bootstrap image to the client. Under Windows 2000, this image is the executable for the Windows 2000 Client Installation Wizard. The client then uses the Trivial File Transfer Protocol (TFTP) to download and execute the Client Installation Wizard.

PXE Emulator Disk

PXE is required when installing systems using RIS; you can't connect using a standard network client boot disk. If the NIC doesn't have on-board support for PXE, Windows 2000 provides a PXE ROM emulator to allow a workstation to take advantage of the PXE connection process by booting to a floppy disk. See the later section "PXE Boot Disk" for more information.

Once the client has successfully downloaded and executed the Client Installation Wizard, someone must log onto the client. After a successful user logon, RIS checks the Active Directory to see whether the machine account has been pre-staged. If so, RIS takes client configuration information from the Active Directory and starts the installation of Windows 2000. If the client hasn't been pre-staged, the Client Installation Wizard prompts the user to select an image, and then runs a complete unattended install of Windows 2000 Professional.

RIS is closely related to the IntelliMirror technology suite (see Chapter 7, "IntelliMirror"). RIS provides fast workstation OS recovery in the event of a critical system failure. In a tightly managed environment and coupled with the IntelliMirror technologies (which restore applications, user data, and user settings), a user could immediately and automatically completely recover his or her system, even if the local machine had been irrevocably destroyed.

Architecture Requirements

Aside from the Windows 2000 server running the Remote Installation Services server components, RIS is dependent on the proper implementation of these additional technologies:

- **TCP/IP-based network.** TCP/IP is the basic networking requirement for a Windows 2000 domain.
- **DHCP.** The Dynamic Host Configuration Protocol service must assign TCP/IP configuration information to RIS clients, or the clients won't be able to access the RIS server.

- **DNS.** A Windows 2000–compliant Domain Name System service is required so the RIS server will be able to find the Active Directory controller.
- **Active Directory.** The Active Directory provides client authorization and configuration information to the RIS server during the client install process.

DNS must be updated to a version compliant with the Windows 2000 DDNS (Dynamic Domain Name System) requirements, which includes support for the following standards:

- **RFC 2052.** The *service location resource record* (*SRV RR*), sometimes referred to as a service record. Support for SRV records is mandatory—if your DNS server doesn't handle these resource records, you can't use it in conjunction with Active Directory.
- **RFC 2136.** The Dynamic Update protocol (support for dynamic update isn't required, but is strongly recommended).

The Windows NT Server 4.0 DNS Service *is not* compliant with these requirements and won't support RIS. If you're using Windows NT Server 4.0 DNS, you must upgrade at least one DNS server to Windows 2000 before you can utilize RIS. If you're using BIND, versions 8.1.2 and above support the required protocols.

Microsoft recommends using the DNS server built into Windows 2000 unless you have a good business reason for not doing so. If you use the Windows 2000 DNS service, you can take advantage of Active Directory–integrated zones, which can improve replication of DNS data.

The service location resource record is the DNS component that tells any Active Directory–aware DNS client where to find an Active Directory domain controller. Active Directory then tells the client where to find a Remote Installation Services server. The Dynamic Update standard allows the client to register in DNS, so the RIS server will know how to find and address the client.

Remote Installation Services can't be used in a legacy Windows NT Server 4.0 domain environment because the service relies on the Windows 2000 Active Directory for a number of functions. The domain environment can be either mixed-mode or native mode, as long as Active Directory is present. The server running RIS must participate in the Active Directory—in other words, it must be a domain controller or a member server of an Active Directory domain—in which the target client machines participate. After installing the RIS server, you must authorize the server in the Active Directory in the same way you would authorize a DHCP server. This prevents unauthorized individuals from setting up RIS servers on the network.

BIND 8 Releases Prior to 8.1.2

Earlier versions of BIND 8 support the additional required standards, but any BIND 8 release prior to 8.1.2 is subject to a denial-of-service security vulnerability, explained in detail in the CERT advisory CA-98.05 (`http://www.cert.org/advisories/CA-98.05.bind_problems.html`).

From a network perspective, RIS doesn't use multicasting, so it would put about as much draw on your bandwidth as copying around a gigabyte of data to as many clients as are simultaneously initiating RIS installs. Fortunately, the RIS client isn't pulling data over the network during the entire install process—only during the normal file copy process of a standard Windows 2000 Professional setup. Staggering the initialization of the RIS clients might help ease the hit on the RIS server.

Authorizing a DHCP/RIS Server

To allow a DHCP or RIS server to service network clients, you must first authorize the server providing the service in the Active Directory. It can be a bit confusing, because the authorization dialogs never mention RIS—all appear to handle only DHCP authorization. But you must go through the same steps for either service, regardless of what the dialogs say. To authorize a DHCP or RIS server, follow these steps:

1. Start the DHCP management console from the Administrative Tools menu.
2. Select the DHCP node. From the Action menu, select Manage Authorized Servers.
3. In the Manage Authorized Servers dialog box, click the Authorize button.
4. In the Authorize DHCP Server dialog box, enter the IP address or the computer name of the DHCP or RIS server and click OK. Even though this dialog doesn't mention RIS, you can authorize RIS servers or DHCP servers from this box.
5. The server name and IP address should now appear in the Authorized DHCP Servers list. Select the Close button to close the Manage Authorized Servers dialog.

Setting Up RIS

Before installing RIS, make sure that the basic server hardware requirements are sufficiently covered. The minimum recommended configuration for a Remote Installation Services server is as follows:

- 200 MHz Pentium-class processor or greater
- 128MB RAM—more if you use the same server for additional functions (DHCP, DNS, Active Directory)
- 2GB volume dedicated to the operating system files, per the minimum installation requirements for Windows 2000 Server
- 2GB volume for the Remote Installation Services server's folder tree; Microsoft recommends using physically separate drives for the system volume and the volume used for RIS
- 10 Mbps network adapter card (100 Mbps network adapter recommended)

Keep in mind that these hardware requirements are the minimum recommendation. If you provide only the 2GB minimum for the volume used for the RIS directory tree, this will provide space for very few images of Windows 2000 Professional. The space required by an image will vary, depending on the level of customization and the size and number of other applications that are installed through RIS. Due to the functions of the *Single Instance Store* (*SIS*) service, accurately gauging the space required for storage of multiple images isn't an easy task (see the later section "Single Instance Store (SIS)" for details on SIS). For planning purposes, with minimal additional software installations, assume an average requirement of an additional 500MB per image. If your images are very similar in configuration and application inclusion, the physical storage space required for each additional image could be less than 50MB per image.

If you'll be installing multiple clients using RIS, you'll need a somewhat heftier configuration. Suppose you expect to simultaneously load 20–40 machines from a RIS server during peak times. The server will contain five different images loaded with Office 2000, a few other standard application packages at an average of 50MB each, and a custom line-of-business application that varies on each image. From my experience with this configuration scenario, I would recommend the following hardware:

- Pentium II 300 MHz processor or greater
- 256MB RAM
- 4GB SCSI drive dedicated to OS files, with hardware mirroring
- 10GB hardware-based SCSI RAID5 array dedicated to the Remote Installation Services images
- Dual 100 Mbps NICs

It's quite likely that you'll maintain a high number of client connections on your RIS server only during the initial rollout period. After an initial rollout, your RIS server may only be needed intermittently throughout the week—for occasional reloads, new hires, and employee relocations requiring new images. At this point, the RIS servers could easily be adapted to double as file-and-print servers. Considering this, you may want to select hardware that approximates your current environment's requirements for file and print servers. If you choose to implement RIS servers with multiple tasks, I highly recommend dedicating a drive or partition to RIS—and *only* RIS. Use another partition, or preferably use a separate physical device altogether, to store other types of data.

Installing and Configuring the Service

You install Remote Installation Services on a Windows 2000 server just as you would install any other server component. You can select Remote Installation Services as an optional component during the initial OS install (either an attended install or via an

> **RIS and Groveling**
>
> The entire RIS partition is subject to the SIS groveling service as explained in the "Single Instance Store (SIS)" section, later in this chapter. As such, the RIS partition shouldn't be used for other functions, such as installations of application software.
>
> **RIS and Active Directory**
>
> Your RIS server must be a member of an Active Directory domain (either a domain controller or a member server). It can't be a stand-alone server.

unattended install), or, if you want to add RIS to an existing server, by using the Add/Remove Windows Components screen in the Add/Remove Programs applet in Control Panel to select the Remote Installation Services component. After you click Next, the RIS files are copied from the CD.

Note: The RIS install process described in this section assumes that you have already installed and configured the DHCP, DNS, and Active Directory services in your environment.

Now that you've installed RIS on your server, you must configure the service. Fortunately, a simple wizard walks you through the initial configuration. Run RISETUP by using the Start, Run command. The first screen after the Welcome screen requests a drive and folder location for the RIS server service main folder. RIS requires that you format this drive as NTFS. You should select a folder on a volume that will be dedicated to RIS. You can't select the same volume on which your system files are located. Preferably, the RIS volume should be on a dedicated physical disk to reduce system performance degradation associated with the RIS disk activity.

After selecting the RIS file location, RISETUP asks whether to enable the service at the end of setup. By default, RIS won't service client requests at the end of setup unless you check the box on this Initial Remote Install Server Settings screen. If you're installing RIS in a production environment, stick with the default selection and manually enable RIS when you've completed the creation of the client images; you wouldn't want RIS installing clients until you've properly configured the client images. If you choose to configure the server to respond to client computers on completion of the wizard, you can select the Do Not Respond to Unknown Client Computers option to prevent computers without accounts in the Active Directory from receiving an image. If you select this option, you must pre-stage the Active Directory, creating the computer account in the Active Directory. See the later section "Adding RIS Managed Computer Accounts to the Active Directory" for more information on pre-staging.

The next screen requests the Windows 2000 Professional installation files. You can either enter a network location or insert the Windows 2000 Professional CD in the CD-ROM and point to the i386 folder on the CD-ROM drive. Note that you can only use RIS with Windows 2000 Professional.

After you point to the Windows 2000 Professional source files, the next screen requests a Windows installation image folder name. This is the folder where the server will store the Windows 2000 Professional image files. The folder will be created as a subfolder under the RIS server service main folder. (Figure 5.1 shows the complete RIS folder structure.) After selecting a subfolder, name and describe the install you're creating. This descriptive name and help text will be displayed during the text-based Client Installation Wizard, which the user will see when installing a machine using RIS.

RIS and Windows 2000 Server

RIS doesn't support remote installs of Windows 2000 Server. You can only use RIS to deploy Windows 2000 Professional.

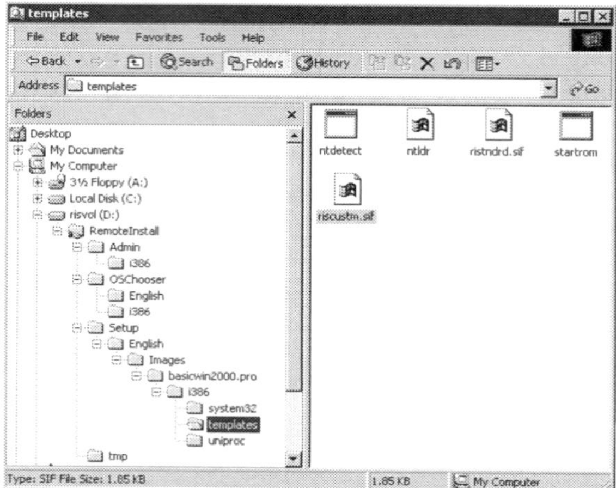

Figure 5.1 The complete RIS folder structure, with added RISCUSTM.SIF customized RIS answer file.

The final screen of the wizard summarizes and confirms the options you've selected throughout the process of the wizard. Once you've confirmed or corrected any necessary entries, click Finish, and the initial RIS server installation and configuration will be complete.

Authorizing the DHCP Service

If you install RIS and DHCP on the same server, the DHCP service *must* be authorized in the Active Directory before either service will be permitted to respond to client requests.

Creating the Basic Image

Once the RISETUP wizard has completed, the files needed to create a basic image are present and available on the RIS server. This image uses a generic default answer file, which pretty much guarantees it won't match your corporate standard. You can create a custom remote install answer file through the Setup Manager Wizard (see Chapter 4, "Answer Files and the Setup Manager Wizard"), and associate that answer file with the existing default CD image installation installed on the RIS server by following the steps outlined in Exercise 5.1.

Exercise 5.1 **Associating the Default RIS Answer File to the Basic Image**

After setting up the RIS service and copying over the basic Windows 2000 files needed for a RIS-based install, you still must associate an answer file with the installation files before RIS will be able to service client installation requests. This exercise walks through associating a default answer file with the Windows 2000 Professional setup files to create a basic unattended RIS install image. This exercise assumes that you have installed and configured the

RIS service as described in the earlier section "Installing and Configuring the Service." In addition, you should create a customized REMBOOT.SIF answer file for use with RIS by following the guidelines in the "Using the Setup Manager Wizard" section of Chapter 4. Save the REMBOOT.SIF file to a known location.

Step 1 Open the Active Directory Users and Computers management console.

Step 2 Find the computer account associated with the RIS server. Right-click the computer account and select Properties from the pop-up menu.

Step 3 Select the Remote Install tab. Click the Advanced Settings button and select the Images tab.

Step 4 Click the Add button. In the resulting Add wizard, select the first option, Associate a New Answer File to an Existing Image, and click Next.

Step 5 In the Unattended Setup Answer File Source window, select An Alternate Location and click Next.

Step 6 On the Location of Answer File screen, enter the full path to the REMBOOT.SIF file in the Path text box and click Next.

Step 7 Select the default image from the list. If you selected all of the defaults during the initial RISETUP wizard, the default image will be win2000.pro. Click Next.

Step 8 The Friendly Description and Help Text page lets you change description and help text associated with the image you're creating. The description is presented to the user during the Client Installation Wizard in the list of images that can be installed. The help text shows up in the Help field of the Client Installation Wizard when the image description is selected. Make any desired changes to this information and click Next.

Step 9 The Review Settings box displays summary information before creating the answer file. Review the information and then click Finish. Assuming a default RIS install of the English language Windows 2000 Professional installation source files on an Intel platform, this will be the location for the answer file:

```
\\<RISServer>\<RISShare>\Setup\English\
➥Images\win2000.pro\i386\Templates\REMBOOT.sif
```

Step 10 The configured image should now show up under the Images tab.

RIS Default Configuration

Assuming that you select the default options during the setup and configuration of RIS, you may be interested in a few of the default file locations for various files associated with RIS-based installs. All the files and folders listed below are off of the \\<*RIS Server*>\<*RIS Share*> UNC, the share created during the initial setup of RIS. In the paths, <*architecture*> refers to the processor architecture (for example, i386), and <*language*> is the default language of the source install (for example, English):

- **\Admin\<*architecture*>:** Location of RIPREP.EXE and RBFG.EXE files.
- **\OSChooser:** Location of default *.OSC files used by the Client Installation Wizard. Language-specific client screens are under <*language*> subfolders, and

platform-specific boot files used to run the OSCHOOSER boot loader are under <*architecture*> subfolders.

- **\Setup\<*language*>\Images\:** Subfolders containing source files for both CD-based and RIPREP-based image can be found under this location.

Important files and folders under the \\<*RIS Server*>\<*RIS Share*>\Setup\<*language*>\Images\<*image*>\<*architecture*> subfolder are as follows:

- \: Source files for Windows 2000 Professional.
- **\RI*.SIF:** Sample templates created during RIS setup. RINORPRT.SIF is a default install with no repartitioning, RISTNDRD.SIF is a default install with repartitioning.
- **\Templates**: The STARTROM.COM and NTDETECT.COM boot files used to initialize the OSCHOOSER boot loader are in this folder, as are any additional customized templates associated with the \\<*RIS Server*>\<*RIS Share*>\Setup\<*language*>\Images\<*image*>\<*architecture*> folder. Additional templates can be associated with a folder as described in Exercise 5.1.

The following code listing is the text of the sample RIS answer file, RISTNDRD.SIF:

```
[data]
floppyless = "1"
msdosinitiated = "1"
OriSrc = "\\%SERVERNAME%\RemInst\%INSTALLPATH%\%MACHINETYPE%"
OriTyp = "4"
LocalSourceOnCD = 1

[SetupData]
OsLoadOptions = "/noguiboot /fastdetect"
SetupSourceDevice = "\Device\LanmanRedirector\%SERVERNAME%\RemInst\%INSTALLPATH%"

[Unattended]
OemPreinstall = no
NoWaitAfterTextMode = 0
FileSystem = LeaveAlone
ExtendOEMPartition = 0
ConfirmHardware = no
NtUpgrade = no
Win31Upgrade = no
TargetPath = \WINNT
OverwriteOemFilesOnUpgrade = no
OemSkipEula = yes
InstallFilesPath = "\\%SERVERNAME%\RemInst\%INSTALLPATH%\%MACHINETYPE%"

[UserData]
FullName = "%USERFIRSTNAME% %USERLASTNAME%"
OrgName = "%ORGNAME%"
ComputerName = %MACHINENAME%
```

```
[GuiUnattended]
OemSkipWelcome = 1
OemSkipRegional = 1
TimeZone = %TIMEZONE%
AdminPassword = "*"

[LicenseFilePrintData]
AutoMode = PerSeat

[Display]
ConfigureAtLogon = 0
BitsPerPel = 8
XResolution = 640
YResolution = 480
VRefresh = 60
AutoConfirm = 1

[Networking]
ProcessPageSections=Yes

[Identification]
JoinDomain = %MACHINEDOMAIN%
CreateComputerAccountInDomain = No
DoOldStyleDomainJoin = Yes

[NetProtocols]
MS_TCPIP=params.MS_TCPIP

[params.MS_TCPIP]
; transport: TC (TCP/IP Protocol)
InfID=MS_TCPIP
DHCP=Yes

[NetClients]
MS_MSClient=params.MS_MSClient

[params.MS_MSClient]
InfID=MS_MSClient

[NetServices]
MS_Server=params.MS_Server

[params.MS_Server]
; service: SRV (Server)
InfID=MS_Server
BroadcastsToLanman2Clients = No

[ServicesSection]

[RemoteInstall]
Repartition = Yes
UseWholeDisk = Yes
```

```
[OSChooser]
Description ="Microsoft Windows 2000 Professional"
Help ="Automatically installs Windows Professional without prompting the user
➥for input..."
LaunchFile = "%INSTALLPATH%\%MACHINETYPE%\templates\startrom.com"
ImageType =Flat
Version="5.0"
```

Adding RIS Managed Computer Accounts to the Active Directory

If you choose to configure the server to respond only to authorized clients, you must add accounts for authorized computers to the Active Directory before the users will be able to install their systems. This isn't as simple as creating a normal computer account. You must know the GUID (Global Unique Identifier) for the computers.

The GUID is a 128-bit (32 hex characters) unique identification number, and it should be available either in the BIOS or on the initial screen visible when booting via PXE. Some vendors provide the GUID associated with a system on the outside of the box or on a spreadsheet or floppy disk included with a new system. If a machine doesn't have a GUID, you can calculate it by prefixing the MAC address with enough zeroes to create an address of exactly 32 characters.

If the GUID can't be ascertained through one of these methods, Microsoft's suggested GUID discovery routine is to use a packet sniffer such as Network Monitor to monitor the machine during the PXE boot sequence and read the GUID from the DHCP discover packet. If it looks like you'll have to go through that kind of trouble, my recommendation is to forget about pre-populating the computer accounts and open the RIS server to all clients. If you don't trust your users to select the proper image, send a workstation technician to initiate the RIS connection. It will take quite a bit less time and effort than sniffing network packets.

After you obtain a GUID for the machines in your network, you need to add a managed client computer account for each computer, by following these steps:

1. Open the Active Directory Users and Computers management console.
2. Add a new computer account in the desired organizational unit (OU), enter the computer name as you would for any other computer account, and click Next.
3. The next screen provides a check box labeled This Is a Managed Computer (see Figure 5.2). Select this option to enable the GUID entry box, and enter the GUID for the PC you want to add. Notice that the Next button isn't active unless you've entered the correct number of characters for a GUID. This doesn't guarantee validity of your GUID, but it does provide minimal error checking.
4. The next screen enables you to select a specific RIS server to service a request from the managed client. This allows rudimentary selective load balancing and location-based installation services.

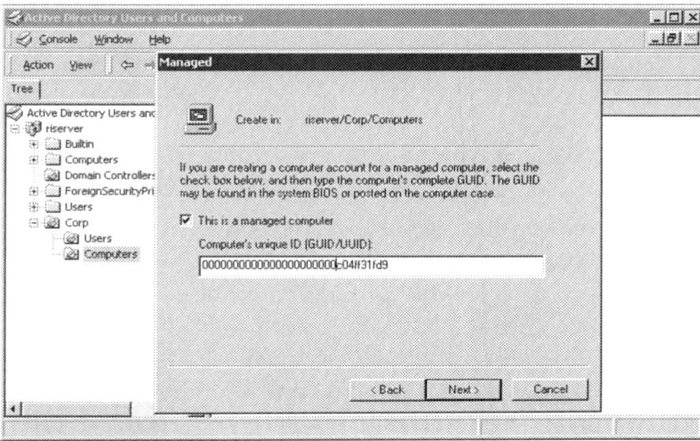

Figure 5.2 Configure a managed computer by entering a properly formatted GUID. In this case, the GUID is the MAC address prefixed by zeroes.

When the client machine with the associated GUID connects, you have pre-staged the computer account in the Active Directory. The client will be forced to comply with the information in the Active Directory; the end user doesn't need to worry about assigning the correct computer name, choosing the correct organizational unit, or specifying the correct RIS server.

Workstation Hardware Requirements

Obviously, workstations must meet the minimum hardware requirements for Windows 2000 Professional. With RIS, it's more important than ever to ensure the latest BIOS revision, for both the PC and the NIC. In terms of hard disk space, installation via RIS requires a drive with around 200MB more than the image footprint plus the swap file. In general, try to stick with 2GB or greater, depending on application and local data storage requirements. RIS can configure only a single drive, single partition in the client system.

RIS will install to the first physical hard disk. If you want to have a specific partition size, you can pre-partition the drives before running a RIS install. Otherwise, to extend a RIS-based install over the entire first physical disk, add the key and value to the `[Unattended]` section of your remote install *.SIF file. In addition, create a `[RemoteInstall]` section, with the key and value `Repartition="Yes"`. This will delete all partitions on the first drive and create one partition formatted as NTFS.

> **RIS Is a Clean Install, Not an Upgrade!**
>
> *Warning:* FDISK and format are an automatic, integrated component with a RIS install. Any data present on the system will be lost at install.

PXE (Pre-boot Execution Environment) Boot Support

To use RIS, a client workstation must contain a PXE DHCP-based boot ROM (version .99c or greater) embedded on the NIC, or a NIC compatible with the PXE boot floppy. Notebook computers are often unable to take advantage of RIS, as booting via PXE would require enabling the PC Card services before the system boots, and few PC Card NICs are capable of this type of operation. To use RIS with a notebook computer, you may need to dock the notebook in a docking station with an internal NIC.

Just having a PXE-compliant NIC ROM might not be enough—your PC BIOS must also support booting from a network card. You can select the option to boot to the NIC from the same place in your BIOS where you would configure the machine to boot from floppy disk, fixed disk, or CD-ROM. If your PC BIOS doesn't provide an option to boot from the network, you won't be able to utilize an on-board PXE ROM.

Although the requirements of RIS call for a PXE boot ROM version .99c or greater, I seem to have the best luck with version .99L and above. If you have an out-of-date PXE ROM, it may be flash-upgradeable. Otherwise, if the PXE boot floppy supports your model of network card, just use the boot floppy instead of booting to the PXE ROM.

PXE Boot Disk

If your network card doesn't contain a boot ROM or your PC doesn't support booting to the network, you may still be able to use RIS. 3COM provides a utility with the Remote Installation Services called the *Remote Boot Floppy Generator* (*RBFG*). After installing RIS, you can start the Remote Boot Floppy Generator on the RIS server, under %systemroot%\SYSTEM32\REMINST\RBFG.EXE. The following list shows the NICs supported by the remote boot floppy:

- 3Com 3C900B-Combo
- 3Com 3C900B-FL
- 3Com 3C900B-TPC
- 3Com 3C900B-TPO
- 3Com 3C900-Combo
- 3Com 3C900-TPO
- 3Com 3C905B-Combo
- 3Com 3C905B-FX
- 3Com 3C905B-TX
- 3Com 3C905C-TX
- 3Com 3C905-T4
- 3Com 3C905-TX
- AMD PCnet Adapters

- Compaq NetFlex 100
- Compaq NetFlex 110
- Compaq NetFlex 3
- DEC DE450
- DEC DE500
- HP DeskDirect 10/100 TX
- Intel Pro 10+
- Intel Pro 100+
- Intel Pro 100B
- SMC 8432
- SMC 9332
- SMC 9432

Note that this list may change. A current version is always included within the RBFG.EXE; click the Adapter List button.

As Figure 5.3 shows, RBFG is a very straightforward application. Simply run the executable, insert a floppy disk in the drive, and click the Create Disk button. To use the remote boot floppy with a supported NIC, configure the boot order on target workstations to boot to the floppy drive. No additional configuration is required on the floppy disk. You can copy and distribute the remote boot floppy to any number of clients. Because it uses DHCP and doesn't require a NetBIOS name, you shouldn't run into issues of duplicate machine names or duplicate IP addresses, as often happens with a normal DOS network client boot disk.

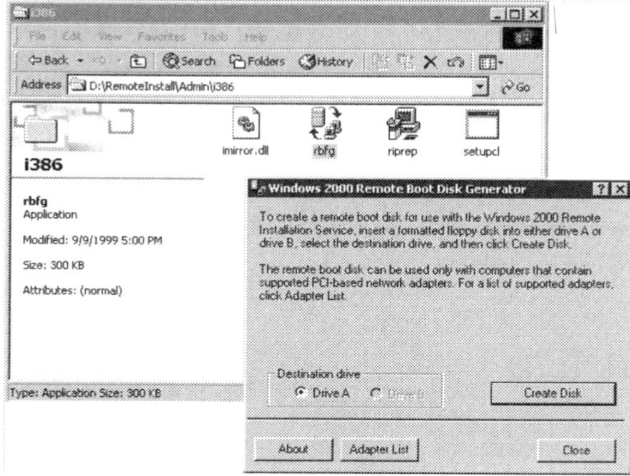

Figure 5.3 The location and complete interface to the Remote Boot Floppy Generator (RBFG).

Installing a Workstation

Before attempting to install a workstation, you must grant the Logon as a Batch Job user right to any user account that will be used to install a workstation via RIS. Your best option is to assign the right either to the Authenticated Users group or to a custom global group, such as RIS Users, containing the user accounts of all RIS users.

Once you've granted the Logon as a Batch Job right, you must either create computer accounts for target computers, or delegate RIS users the ability to create computer accounts in the required computer containers. To do this, right-click the destination container for computer accounts in the Active Directory Users and Computers management console, select Delegate from the pop-up menu, and use the Delegation Wizard to configure RIS users with the right to join computers to the domain.

Now set the target client workstation BIOS to boot from the network card—from the floppy drive if you're using the remote boot floppy—and reboot the PC. During the initial boot sequence, you'll be prompted to press F12 to boot from the network. At this point, the network boot process will automatically contact a DHCP server, assign DNS and IP address information, query the DNS for an Active Directory controller, query the Active Directory for the location of a RIS server set up to service the given client, and download the Client Installation Wizard from the RIS server.

Installing the client is now just a matter of logging on and using the Client Installation Wizard. If the client has been pre-staged, the install kicks off with all required screens answered, and the client will download required setup files via TFTP (Trivial File Transfer Protocol) to complete the install.

Granting the Logon as a Batch Job User Right

This procedure assumes that RIS is running on a member server in your Active Directory domain.

1. From the RIS server, start a new MMC. Click Start, Run, and type **mmc** in the Run box.
2. Select Add/Remove Snap-in from the Console menu. On the Standalone tab, click the Add button.
3. Select Group Policy from the resulting dialog box. Click OK, and make sure that the group policy is for managing the local computer.
4. Navigate to Computer Configuration\Windows Settings\Security Settings\Local Policies\User Rights Assignment, and double-click the Logon as a Batch Job right.
5. Add the group containing the user accounts for users that need permission to set up RIS clients.

Advanced RIS

Previous sections walked through the basic installation of Windows 2000 Professional, with configuration customization provided strictly via the remote boot answer files. RIS enables you to install Windows 2000, but only customized within the limitations of the answer file customization options. Fortunately, RIS includes a mechanism by which to image a machine—including all application installations, OS configuration settings, and application preferences—up to a RIS server. That image can then be applied to additional machines with similar hardware. This process, mentioned briefly in earlier chapters, is called *Remote Installation Preparation* or *RIPREP*.

RIPREP Wizard

RIPREP images are similar in function to—but quite different in format from—SYSPREP images, which were discussed in the section "Creating Disk Images with Third-Party Utilities and SYSPREP" in Chapter 3, "Deployment Options." A RIPREP image is an image of a fully configured system, held in a distribution folder containing all files and folders needed for a completely configured install procedure. The files in a RIPREP image are all separate, and could all be viewed, opened, copied, or deleted through Windows Explorer. (However, modifying files that are used in a RIPREP image is generally a very bad idea, as modifications could potentially affect important application dependencies elsewhere in the RIPREP image.) A SYSPREP image, on the other hand, is a single physical image file that contains all files needed for a system. The only way to view individual files within that image file is through a special utility provided by the vendor of the disk duplication tool.

RIPREP images have the same hardware difference limitations as SYSPREP images. Target machines must use the same HAL, the same hard disk controller, the same number of processors, and the same power management technology (ACPI or non-ACPI) as the system used to create the master image.

Without defining the `Repartition` keys in a RIPREP image answer file, RIPREP-based image target machines will have system partitions of exactly the same size as the master image (see the earlier section "Workstation Hardware Requirements" for details on the `Repartition` answer file entries). So if you take a RIPREP image of a 2GB system and apply it to a 6GB hard drive, you end up with a 2GB system partition and 4GB of unpartitioned space. Including the `Repartition` keys ensures that the system drive will format and utilize the additional space.

An even bigger drive-related limitation occurs when applying an image to a *smaller* hard drive. If you make a RIPREP image of a 3GB drive and try to apply it to a 2GB drive, the install will fail, even if the data doesn't require all the space available on the drive. When the RIS client image is selected under the Client Installation Wizard, Setup checks the partition size of the target drive against the partition size from the master system. If the target partition is smaller, the Client Installation Wizard displays an error message, and the RIS image isn't installed. The target drive must be greater than or equal to the size of the source drive. This problem can occur with even a single megabyte of difference in the partitions.

RIPREP and Partitions

Warning: RIPREP only works on single-drive, single-partition systems. The target drive must be the same size as or larger than the source drive. RIPREP won't pick up or apply changes outside the system partition.

I once built a RIPREP image using a machine pulled from a batch shipment of identically configured hardware, but the 4GB drives were made by different manufacturers. The drive metrics of the system I used created a partition of just a megabyte or so larger than a handful of the other client machines. The RIPREP image wouldn't install to the machines with the smaller drives, even though the image only used 1.6GB of space. To prevent running into this type of scenario, your best bet is to manually configure a smaller partition on the machine you intend to use for your master image, and set the `Repartition` key equal to `"no"` in the answer file. After building your initial machine, don't forget to set the `Repartition` key back to `"yes"`.

Assuming an existing RIS server and base RIS image, the basic flow behind creating and applying a RIPREP install is as follows:

1. Install a representative system using the basic RIS image.
2. Configure the OS and install additional applications.
3. Run the RIPREP wizard on the fully configured Windows 2000 Professional machine from the Admin folder of the RIS server (\\<*RIS Server*>\<*RIS Share*>\Admin).
4. Follow the steps of the RIPREP wizard. The RIPREP wizard is very similar to the initial RISETUP wizard used to create the initial image:

   4a. From the client machine you want to image, connect to the RIS server's Admin folder and run the RIPREP executable.

   4b. After the introductory wizard screen, you'll be prompted for the server name. By default, the text box will contain the name of the RIS server from which you're running RIPREP (see Figure 5.4).

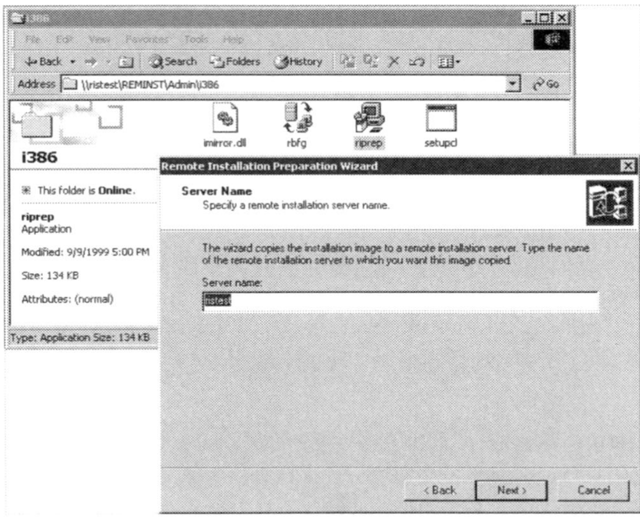

Figure 5.4 As the UNC name shows, the pre-populated server name matches the source server for the RIPREP executable.

4c. Enter the name of the subfolder where you want to create the RIPREP files. This folder will be located at the same level as the base image folder (refer to the basicwin2000.pro folder in Figure 5.1).

4d. Enter a friendly description and help text.

4e. If any services or programs are running, Windows 2000 displays a window with the program, service, or process names. Close any listed programs, stop any listed services, and kill any listed processes before continuing.

4f. You'll get an opportunity to review your answers for the wizard. If everything is correct, click Next to initiate the RIPREP image upload.

RIPREP creates the new image option on the RIS server. After it completes, you need to reboot the master workstation and answer the mini-setup wizard. After the mini-setup wizard completes, you can make additional changes or add applications, and then rerun RIPREP to create additional images.

5. Connect a new client via RIS, answer all the questions, and select the new image.
6. The disk is partitioned and formatted. Installation files are copied to the local machine, including all additional non-OS files from the master image.
7. The base RIS Windows 2000 Professional install is applied. Configuration changes, new files, registry entries, third-party applications, and application settings are all layered onto the install.
8. An attended mini-setup wizard runs, similar to the SYSPREP mini-setup wizard.
9. The system reboots and is ready for use.

Customizing Existing Images

You can customize existing CD-based installs simply by modifying the associated answer file (*.SIF). For RIPREP images, the files are stored as individual source files. Although it's possible to read, modify, or delete the files in place, you should avoid doing so, as you may accidentally modify or delete a file that's critical to the proper operation of something on the system. If you need to change something in a RIPREP image, the best method is to apply the existing image to a client, make any required changes, and rerun the RIPREP wizard from the RIS server's Admin folder to upload the new, updated image to the RIS server.

You can still modify the *.SIF file associated with a RIPREP-based install, but you'll only be able to modify options that can be configured via the answer file. The RIPREP answer file, named RISETUP.SIF by default, will be located under the i386\Templates subfolder of the folder created for the RIPREP image.

Single Instance Store (SIS)

The *Single Instance Store* (*SIS*) service is a file-storage enhancement automatically installed to the server along with the Remote Installation Services. Duplicate files are removed from the RIS volume by the SIS groveler, which replaces duplicate files with file links pointing to a common data store containing the original instance of a given file. This process reduces duplicate data on the RIS volume, so common files in RIPREP images are only taking up disk space for the initial instance of an original file. SIS can't be installed separately from RIS, nor is there any type of user interface to manipulate or configure the SIS feature.

The SIS groveler periodically scans the disk, looking at filenames, dates, and sizes, making sure to get all original files. If you have two identically named files with the same file date and file size, SIS compares the contents of the files to make sure that they're identical before adding the instance to the file store. If identical, both files are replaced by links into the Single Instance Store, and the original file is renamed with a 128-bit GUID and stored in the common store. SIS tracks the number of links to any files in the data store so the system can delete original files when they're no longer required. When there's sufficient space on the RIS partition, the SIS groveler will only perform linking operations during relatively idle times. After reaching a certain free-disk-space threshold, the SIS groveler becomes somewhat more aggressive, scanning drives as files are copied.

File links on the RIS volume still appear as individual files; the link file even appears to occupy the same amount of disk space as the original file. In reality, the file link only occupies a single cluster of physical disk space. When SIS file links are accessed, the link file points to the location of the original file in the common store, and the file is retrieved and manipulated accordingly.

Why Dedicate a Volume to RIS?

If you save additional files to the RIS volume—meaning files not required for RIS or RIPREP images—the SIS Groveling Agent still processes the files. This is why it's important to dedicate an entire drive to the Remote Installation Services file store. Files that change frequently are not recommended for storage on a SIS volume.

Tips, Tricks, and Suggestions for Using RIS

The following sections provide some tips and tricks gleaned from my personal trials and tribulations with the Windows 2000 Remote Installation Services.

Customize OSCHOOSER Screens with OSCML

The OSCHOOSER screens are the text screens displayed to the user during the Client Installation Wizard. These screens are formatted in OSCML, an OSCHOOSER-customized version of text-only Hypertext Markup Language (HTML), based somewhat on a subset of HTML 2.0. The files have an *.OSC extension, and can be found on the Remote Installation Services volume. Use the File Search feature of Windows 2000 to find the *.OSC files. Much like HTML, you can edit the OSCML files in any text editor, such as Windows Notepad. Edit the *.OSC files to present any desired additional information to your end users. For example, you could add support information to the Welcome screen, so that individuals running the Client Installation Wizard would know who to call for support issues.

Limit RIS Options with NTFS Permissions

If you have a large number of install images, it could be confusing for end users to select their own images from the full list of available options. To limit the images that can be selected by a user, use NTFS security on the associated *.SIF answer file. If you set file permissions such that a user can read only one of the image files, he or she won't even see the image selection screen of the OSCHOOSER, but instead will be taken straight from logon to the RIS confirmation screen. To prevent an image from showing in the selection list, simply remove or deny the read permission for the appropriate user groups.

Preset the Description and Help Text of a RIS Image in the Answer File

When creating a custom *.SIF file to import into a CD- or RIPREP-based load, you can preset the name and description of your answer-file–based image by including the following keys:

```
[OSChooser]
    Description="Windows Professional - Custom Sales Load"
    Help="This RIS image installs a workstation with the corporate standard
    ➥Sales load."
    LaunchFile="%INSTALLPATH%\%MACHINETYPE%\templates\startrom.com"
    ImageType=Flat
```

The same keys will allow you to rename or change the description for an existing load without going through the RIS configuration tab of the computer account properties screen for your RIS server in the Active Directory.

Minimize Use of RIPREP

If you decide to implement Remote Installation Services, you'll have the greatest success—and the greatest flexibility—by utilizing only the CD-based RIS install modified by answer files. Lock down or configure OS settings through group policy objects, and manage the software installations for your various user groups by leveraging the Windows Installer. The CD-based RIS install is more flexible, as any image can be applied to any hardware. RIPREP images, on the other hand, still have dependencies on hardware. The second half of this book explains what you need to know to manage software and configuration settings through the Active Directory.

You may wonder why you would want to use RIS at all, when it would require less effort to set up a distribution share point–based install. While RIS and DSP installs are nearly the same, there are a few differences from the client end. When using a DSP-based install, you can't install Windows 2000 without booting to a different OS and connecting to the network. In addition, with a DSP-based install you must manually partition and format the disk before running Setup. RIS gets around both of these issues. A RIS client can boot and connect to an installation server without an OS and without a network client. Partitioning and formatting of the system disk occur as part of the RIS install.

Choose Servers Carefully

When running at peak capacity—for example, during the initial stages of a rollout where multiple clients connect simultaneously—RIS puts quite a strain on a server's network bandwidth and disk transfer. You shouldn't install any non-redundant, time-sensitive services on your RIS box. Except in a testing environment, I don't even recommend running DHCP and RIS on the same machine. Never run RIS in a production environment on an Active Directory domain controller. The high traffic load from the RIS client installs could potentially affect the ability of the domain controller to authenticate clients. If you're combining server functions, RIS is well suited for coexistence on a file-and-print server, so long as the RIS partition is separate from the file share partitions.

Services Installed by RIS

The following services are installed and used by Remote Installation Services:

- **Boot Information Negotiation Layer (BINL).** Provides the ability to install Windows 2000 Professional on PXE remote-boot–enabled client computers. This is the part of RIS that negotiates the handling of the OSCHOOSER executable on the client, initializing the Client Installation Wizard.
- **Trivial FTP Daemon (TFPT, or Trivial File Transfer Protocol).** Implements the Trivial FTP Internet standard, which transfers files without the requirement of a username or password. This server protocol passes both the Client Installation Wizard *.OSC menus and the Windows 2000 Professional source files from the server to the client.
- **Single Instance Store Groveler (SIS)**: Scans Single Instance Store volumes—in this case, the RIS volume—for duplicate files, and points duplicates files to one data storage point, conserving disk space.

II

Managing and Maintaining the Desktop

6

Group Policy Objects

THIS CHAPTER COVERS:

- Overview of group policy
- Creating group policy objects (GPOs)
- Managing end users with group policy objects
- Optimizing group policy objects
- Assigning logon/logoff and startup/shutdown scripts with group policy objects
- Selecting locations for and controlling access to group policy objects

After reading this chapter, you should be able to do the following:

- Create new group policy objects for sites, domains, or organizational units
- Select optimal locations and security settings for group policy objects
- Control machine configuration and user settings through group policy objects
- Create scripts to run at user logon/logoff and workstation startup/shutdown
- Develop an effective group policy object hierarchy for your Windows 2000 domain

Group policy is the cornerstone technology behind management and workstation security in a Windows 2000 environment. Group policy objects—which consist of collections of group policy settings—can be used for, among other objectives, deploying and managing software, controlling user privileges, providing logon/logoff and startup/shutdown scripts, and redirecting and synchronizing local folders to the network. Ultimately, these features give an IT department a great deal of control over the desktop environment, driving down the cost of user support and reducing total cost of ownership (TCO) associated with maintaining workstations.

> This chapter assumes a basic knowledge of the function and structure behind the Active Directory. In addition, you should be familiar and comfortable with the Microsoft Management Console (MMC). I don't spend much time discussing the design of the Active Directory domain, but I offer some suggestions on organizational units based on various security distribution concepts. This chapter looks at both GPO design theory and implementation, focusing on the features that help with desktop management.
>
> At last count, there were more than 560 group policy settings available. This chapter doesn't go into detail on every available setting—that level of information is available through the Windows 2000 Server Resource Kit and the Explain tab of the individual policies. But I do explore some of the details of the more interesting policies from the workstation management and security aspects, and look at the differences between local group policies and Active Directory group policies.

Introduction to Group Policy

Group policy objects (*GPO*s) enable granular management of sites, domains, organizational units (collectively referred to as Active Directory *containers*), and local computers. Despite the name, a group policy object can't be applied directly to a group or user. Group and user permissions—similar to NTFS file and folder permissions—can be assigned to restrict which users within a site, domain, or organizational unit receive the effects of a group policy object.

Group Policy Terminology

A number of terms surrounding group policy can be rather confusing if you aren't sure how they're related. The following list describes the major terms:

- *Group policy* refers to the overall technologies that enable the policy-based management of Windows 2000.
- *Group policy settings* describe the actual settings applied to the user's desktop. You change the group policy settings with the Group Policy Editor.

- The *Group Policy Editor* (*GPE*) is an MMC snap-in accessed through the Group Policy tab of an applicable Active Directory container used for modifying group policy configuration settings. The Group Policy Editor can also be opened directly via the Add/Remove Snap-in menu option in the MMC, which will allow editing of the local group policy object.
- A *group policy object* (*GPO*) is a collection of group policy settings, assigned a *global unique identifier* (*GUID*) and stored in the Active Directory. A GPO can be applied to sites, domains, or organizational units (SDOUs). In addition, each computer has one local GPO, stored in %windir%\system32\GroupPolicy, which affects only settings specific to that local machine.
- A *group policy container* (*GPC*) is an object in the Active Directory that maintains version numbering, status information, and policy information. For policies to apply, the GPC must be in sync with the associated group policy template.
- *Group policy templates* (*GPTs*) store policy information, and are located on any domain controller under the folder \\<*Machine_Name*>\SYSVOL\<*Domain_Name*>\Policies. The group policy template folders are named with global unique identifiers. In each GPT folder is a GPT.INI file containing a version number. If you define administrative templates (*.ADM files) for a GPO, they're stored in the GPT folder under an ADM subfolder. Startup and shutdown scripts are stored in the Machine\Scripts subfolder. Logon and logoff scripts are stored in the User\Scripts subfolder.

Don't Manually Edit Group Policy Template Files

Warning: These files and folders are created and maintained automatically when group policy objects are created or edited through the Group Policy Editor. You should never attempt to manually edit the files and folders contained within a GPT.

Group Policy and Containers

The default locations for users and computers in a newly created Active Directory domain are the *Users container* and the *Computers container*, respectively. These containers, as well as the *Builtin container* for default security groups, are not organizational units. Therefore, you can't apply a group policy object to these containers. The only GPOs that will apply to objects in the Users or Computers container are those filtering down from the *Site* or *Domain* level containers. Throughout this chapter, when I refer to containers, I am referring only to sites, domains, and organizational units (SDOUs) for which GPOs can be applied.

Group Policy and the Default Active Directory Containers

You can't apply a group policy object directly to the Users, Computers, or Builtin default Active Directory containers; they're special containers, not organizational units (OUs). Domain Controllers, another default Active Directory container, is an organizational unit container; therefore, you can apply group policy objects to the Domain Controllers container.

Group Policy Objects Versus NT 4.0 Policies

Although similar in some ways to policies enabled through the policy templates of Windows NT 4.0 environments, group policy objects are much more advanced. Group policy settings are more granular, and they provide many more functions than simple registry modification. One of the more notable features is the correction of the tattooing effect inherent with Windows NT 4.0 policies. Basically, applying a policy in NT 4.0 permanently overwrote the user's local settings. If the administrator removed an NT 4.0 policy after it had already been applied to a user's machine, the settings from the policy would remain in place until overridden by a new policy. This made backing out of incorrect policies an administrative nightmare. With Windows 2000 environments in the default configuration, removing a group policy object returns the machine or user to the prior state of configuration.

Local Computer Policy Objects

In addition to centralized administration of group policy objects applied to Active Directory containers, each server or workstation can have local policy settings applied through a *local computer policy* object. Local computer policy, as the name suggests, can be used to manage the security policy that applies to local user accounts, local groups, and the local machine settings. Local computer policy can be used on any machine, regardless of domain membership. If a domain user logs onto a machine with local computer policy defined, the local computer policy settings will apply for any group policy settings not otherwise defined by Active Directory group policy objects. The local computer policy is stored in the %windir%\system32\GroupPolicy folder on the applicable local machine. Note that you should not attempt to modify the local computer policy from this location; you should use the Group Policy MMC snap-in.

Group Policy Objects and the Active Directory

Active Directory group policy objects are stored in the Active Directory. Computer management through an Active Directory GPO requires a machine to participate in the Active Directory. Computer settings can be applied to a computer account joined to a domain even if the user only authenticates as a user in the local machine's security database. For group policy objects at the SDOU levels to be applied to user settings, the user must be logged onto the Active Directory. Although Windows NT 4.0 clients and Windows 9x clients can be made Active Directory aware, they can't take advantage of Active Directory management features such as group policy. Older-style policies, such as NTCONFIG.POL, can still be stored in the NETLOGON share for use by any down-level clients.

Group policy objects follow a hierarchical structure similar to the Active Directory. By default, they're applied in a top-down approach, meaning that the site GPO applies first, then the domain GPO, followed by the organizational unit GPO. Multiple GPOs can be assigned to a single container, and a single GPO can be linked to multiple containers. GPOs can be applied or denied based on group membership, which provides a mechanism for further granulating the applicable scope of a group policy object.

The Group Policy Editor

When you want to create or modify a group policy object, you must use the Group Policy Editor (GPE). The GPE, which is accessed through the Microsoft Management Console (MMC), provides a complete environment for viewing and modifying group policy objects, including context-sensitive help and in-depth explanations for each policy. How you start the Group Policy Editor depends on where you'll be creating or editing a GPO, as shown in the following table.

To Manage This . . .	Do This . . .
Site GPO	Use the Active Directory Sites and Services console.
Domain or organizational unit GPO	Use the Active Directory Users and Computers Console.
Local computer policy	Add the Group Policy console snap-in to a new MMC, and specify the focus for the snap-in as the local computer.

Local Computer Policy

Let's take a look at the Local Computer Policy console. Since the console doesn't exist by default, we'll have to create it. Follow these steps:

1. Click Start, Run. From the Run box, start a blank MMC by running the **mmc** command.
2. Select Add/Remove Snap-in from the Console menu.
3. Click Add in the Add/Remove Snap-in window.
4. Select Group Policy from the Snap-in column of the Add/Remove Standalone Snap-in window, and click Add.
5. Ensure that the group policy object focus is set to Local Computer, and click Finish.
6. Close the Add Standalone Snap-in window, and click OK in the Add/Remove Snap-in window.

You should now see a console window with a Local Computer Policy console document under the Console Root, as shown in Figure 6.1. You can customize and save this console if you want. If you save the console in the default folder, it will show up under the Administrative Tools program group.

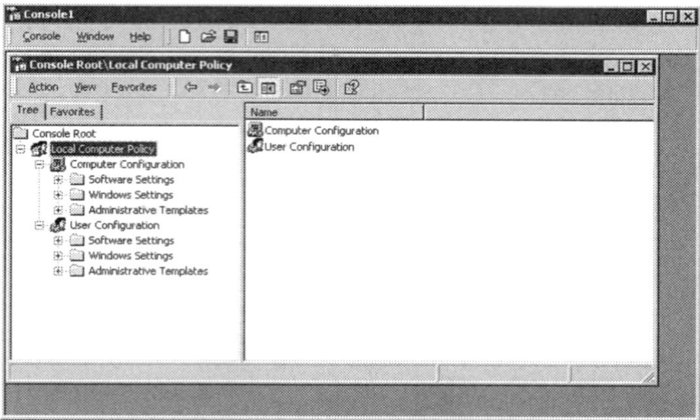

Figure 6.1 The Local Computer Policy console.

Take a few minutes to explore the Local Computer Policy console. Notice that the Software Settings nodes for both Computer Configuration and User Configuration provide no additional functions. These nodes are used only in conjunction with Active Directory group policy objects to distribute and manage software installations. In all cases, any policies set at the domain level will override policies set on the local machine.

Computer Configuration Node

Under Computer Configuration\Windows Settings\Scripts, you can set the startup and shutdown scripts that execute during the startup and shutdown of the machine. These scripts operate independently of any user logon.

The Computer Configuration\Windows Settings\Security Settings contains four nodes:

- **Account Policies.** Location of the password policy and account lockout policy. In NT 4.0, these options were configured through the User Manager's Account Policy menu.
- **Local Policies.** Under Local Policies, you can configure Auditing, User Rights Assignments, and Security Options. The Auditing node allows you to set flags for success and failure audits of various Windows 2000 activities. The results of the success and failure audits appear in the Security section under the Event Viewer. User Rights Assignments contains the basic and advanced user rights that used to be available through the NT 4.0 User Manager, with some additional options specific to Windows 2000. For example, the Logon Locally, Logon as a Service, and Logon as a Batch Job policy settings are available under this node. Security Options contains a variety of policies to further enhance the security of your local workstation. Policies set in the Active Directory will override the local computer policy settings.

- **Public Key Policies.** This node contains a single subnode, Encrypted Data Recovery Agents, which holds the security certificates for encrypted data-recovery agents. The user accounts associated with the security certificates under this section are able to decrypt files stored in the Encrypted File System (EFS) in case the owner of the encrypted files is unavailable or unwilling to decrypt those files.
- **IP Security Policies on Local Machine.** This node lets you create and select policies for IPSec communication. Right-click the node and select Create IP Security Policy to start the IPSec Wizard. There are three existing policies that may be adequate for most users.

Under Computer Configuration\Administrative Templates are administrative policies for managing template-based software configurations. These settings are controlled through *.ADM files similar to those of Windows NT 4.0 policy templates. Any template files added to this section are automatically added to the Administrative Templates node of the User Configuration counterpart. Enabled policy template files are stored under %systemroot%\System32\GroupPolicy\ADM. By default, you'll have a policy for Internet Explorer (INETRES.ADM) and the System policy (SYSTEM.ADM). These policy templates are described in more detail in the "Administrative Templates" section, later in this chapter.

User Configuration Node

The User Configuration node has some of the same options as the Computer Configuration node, but the settings apply to the local user accounts rather than the local machine settings. For example, under User Settings\Scripts, you can select scripts to execute at user logon and user logoff. Note that it's possible to select multiple scripts for each event. There's a Security Settings node under User Configuration as well, but it contains only a Public Keys Policy node, identical in function to the same node under Computer Settings.

Under User Configuration\Administrative Templates, you'll find the administrative policies for management of template-based software configuration, which apply to the user configuration as defined in the *.ADM template file.

In addition to the Scripts and Security Settings nodes found under the Computer Configuration\Windows Settings branch, there are two additional nodes under the User Configuration\Windows Settings branch. The first, Remote Installation Services, isn't functional as a local computer policy. The other, Internet Explorer Maintenance, can be used to set local user policy for Internet Explorer configuration options, including the following settings:

- **Browser User Interface.** Customize the default browser title, the Internet Explorer logo and logo animation, or the toolbar button configuration.
- **Connection.** Connection settings, automatic browser configuration settings, proxy settings, and the user agent string.

- **URLs.** Pre-configure Favorites and links; set important URLs such as the home, search, and support pages; and specify settings for channels.
- **Security.** Settings for Authenticode, security zones, and content ratings.
- **Programs.** Specify the applications used for the HTML editor, email client, newsgroup client, Internet calling, calendar, or contact list.

An interesting feature tied to the Internet Explorer Maintenance node is the Preference Mode option. Preference mode allows you to specify the initial settings for Internet Explorer via group policy, but the user can manually change any of the default settings with his or her preferences. For example, using preference mode, you could provide a default home page and a collection of default Favorites. Each user would receive those defaults the first time he or she logged on to the Active Directory. The user could then specify the home page or reorganize or delete the default Favorites. These preferred settings would be maintained for future sessions. Be careful, though; the settings will revert to the GPO settings whenever any part of the policy is modified. Taking that into consideration, it's good practice to specify preference settings in a group policy object that's separate from policy settings that may require frequent edits.

By contrast, creating a group policy for Internet Explorer without enabling preference mode means that the user will receive any configuration options specified in the group policy, regardless of what the user specifies. The user can change the home page, but it will revert to the GPO setting with the next refresh of the policy object.

You enable preference mode by right-clicking the Internet Explorer Maintenance node and selecting Preference Mode from the pop-up menu. You can't switch back and forth between preference mode and non-preference mode. Any settings entered under one option must be cleared and re-entered if you change modes.

Active Directory Group Policy

Although the basic layout is similar, the Active Directory management level provides quite a few more policies than are available at the level of the local computer. This section compares the local computer group policy (described previously) to the Computer Policy section of a group policy object applied to an organizational unit.

Note: Keep in mind that even though the examples throughout this section reference an organizational unit, the same concepts apply for any Active Directory–based group policy object, whether applied to a site, a domain, or an organizational unit.

First, we need to get into the Group Policy Editor. For this, we must create a new policy:

1. Run the Active Directory Users and Computers console from the Administrative Tools program group. If you're on an Active Directory controller, this console will exist by default. If you're running the console from a member server or a Windows 2000 Professional machine, you must first install the Administrative Tools by running the ADMINPAK.MSI file, found in the i386 folder of any Windows 2000 Server CD.

2. Right-click any organizational unit in your Active Directory and select Properties from the pop-up menu.
3. Select the Group Policy tab and click the New button. You can name the new group policy anything you want. Double-click the new policy, or select the policy and click the Edit button.

You should now have a Group Policy Editor console with a Computer Configuration node and a User Configuration node. Unlike the corresponding nodes from the local computer policy options, the Software Settings nodes for both Computer Configuration and User Configuration contain a Software Installation node. Right-click either of these nodes to add a new software installation package. This feature is described in more detail in Chapter 8, "Application Management and Software Installation."

All the options listed under the local Computer Configuration settings (described previously) are applicable to the Active Directory Computer Configuration, but there are a few additional nodes, described in the following sections.

Computer Configuration Node

Under Computer Configuration\Windows Settings\Security Settings are the following additional nodes:

- **Event Log.** Use this node to set default settings for the event logs to machines for which this policy will apply. With this policy, you can specify a maximum log size, restrict access to the logs, and set the overwrite actions for the logs, among other tasks.
- **Restricted Groups.** This policy restricts group membership for security groups to specified user accounts. If you configure this policy, specified groups can only contain individuals listed in the Members column, and the group can only be a member of other groups specified in the Member Of column. Any variance from this configuration will be corrected on each refresh of the policy. This prevents unauthorized user accounts from being added to privileged or secure user groups.
- **System Services.** With this policy, you can specify the default service startup mode for any of the Windows 2000 services. Additional services can be configured only if present on the box from which you're configuring the policy object. For example, with this policy, you could configure the Secondary Logon Service (used by the RunAs command) to Disabled, preventing the service from running on any machines with accounts in this organizational unit.
- **Registry.** With the Registry policy, you can set user and group permissions on individual keys and values in the registries of all machines with accounts in this organizational unit. Use this key to prevent users from changing registry values, either directly or programmatically. You can also override default settings and give a user permission to change a registry setting to which he or she would not otherwise have access.

- **File System.** Similar to the Registry policy, with this setting you can set user and group permissions on individual files and folders in the file systems of all machines with accounts in this organizational unit. For example, you can deny file access permission to certain groups of users for a specified local folder on the hard drive of any PC, give another group the ability to read but not modify the files in the folder, and give yet another group read and write access to the folder. This setting applies to the same folder on every PC, without requiring the administrator to set local NTFS permissions for every workstation.

The Computer Configuration\Administrative Templates node functions the same as in its local computer policy counterpart; the only difference is the scope. Options in this node apply to all computer accounts in the site, domain, or organizational unit, whereas options in the local policy apply only to the source computer. The default templates for administrative template files are SYSTEM.ADM and INETRES.ADM.

User Configuration Node

As with the Computer Configuration node, the Active Directory User Configuration node has many of the same options as the local User Configuration node. In this case, however, the settings apply to the user accounts stored within the organizational unit. The only policy differences between the Active Directory and the local User Configuration branches are the Remote Installation Services and Folder Redirection nodes. The Remote Installation Services node lets you specify which options will be available through the RIS Client Installation Wizard, based on user account membership in the applicable container. Folder Redirection allows for universal or security-group–based redirection of the following items:

- Application data
- Desktop
- My Documents/My Pictures
- Start menu

When implementing Folder Redirection policies, you can choose to copy existing data stored in the current folder locations to the locations specified by the policy. In addition, if you ever remove the policies, you have the option of leaving the data where it is or copying it back to the previous location. Folder redirection is a component of the IntelliMirror technology suite. IntelliMirror is discussed in detail in the next chapter.

Defining the Functions of a Group Policy Object

What settings will you control with a single group policy object? For example, you could create a single GPO to do any of the following:

- Manage only computer accounts.
- Manage only user accounts.

- Handle software installation for all managed software packages used across your enterprise, or create separate group policy objects for each package you want to install.
- Control every policy setting in one location, or create multiple individual group policy objects, each responsible for a limited set of policy settings.

More group policy objects could translate to more time required at logon. Each GPO that applies to a computer account will be downloaded during the computer's startup. Each GPO that applies to a user account will be downloaded at user logon, as well as periodically throughout the day. In addition, fewer GPOs make it easier to debug and troubleshoot the GPO as well as simplifying future maintenance.

If you'll have many group policy objects, each managing a granular setting, it would be wise to apply them at the closest possible levels to the applicable accounts. If you'll have few GPOs managing many settings, it might work better to apply the GPOs at the domain level, and filter based on group membership (filtering is discussed in the later section "Filtering by Group Membership").

Managing Group Policies

With Active Directory group policy objects, you can associate multiple group policies to a single container. In addition, because user and computer accounts generally exist within organizational units, and an OU can belong to a parent OU, it's quite possible to have multiple GPOs applied via a multilevel hierarchy of containers. With the multiple levels of containers added to the cumulative inheritance for the majority of policies, it can be confusing trying to figure out which policies apply to which objects.

As the following sections show, managing multiple levels of group policies can be very complex. It's important to document your configuration and closely monitor any modifications to the GPOs in your environment. I recommend a stringent change-control process and tight restrictions on any delegated authority to manage GPOs.

Inheritance, Blocking Inheritance, and Preventing Override

First, it's important to realize that GPO inheritance is cumulative by default, with only two exceptions. IP security policies and user rights are not cumulative; instead, the last policy to configure any of these settings will be the effective policy. For example, if a group policy object is created to configure IP security policy at the organizational unit level, the domain level, and the site level, only the settings configured by the organizational unit level policy will be applied.

In other cases, group policy settings are cumulative, with the closest policy settings (such as the immediate organizational unit policy) overriding any conflicts from more distant ones (such as a parent OU, domain, or site). For example, if you configure Audit Policy settings at the organizational unit level, the domain level, and the site level, all policies will be applied, with conflicting policies using options defined at the OU level. This is a default behavior; it can be overridden, and policy inheritance can be blocked at any level. In cases where multiple GPOs are applied to a single container, the GPOs are applied from the bottom up, as listed on the Group Policy tab. Objects higher in the list have higher priority.

You can prevent a group policy from being overridden by selecting No Override in the link options. Follow these steps:

1. Navigate through the Active Directory to the container with the organizational unit you want to configure.
2. Open the properties page for the container and select the Group Policy tab.
3. In the group policy object's Links window, right-click the applicable group policy and select No Override from the pop-up menu.

With this option, child containers and other conflicting policies won't be able to override the policies in the selected GPO. Most often, you'll want to apply the No Override option to critical policies at the site or domain level, since the setting prevents child containers from overriding policies higher up in the Active Directory structure.

With the complexity involved in maintaining your group policy hierarchy, it's quite possible to set the No Override at multiple levels in your Active Directory. In this case, the highest order GPO will take precedence over the lower order GPOs. For example, a site policy marked No Override would override a domain policy marked No Override.

To block policy inheritance altogether—that is, to prevent any GPO from a higher-order Active Directory container from applying to the current container—access the properties on the container you want to manage, select the Group Policy tab, and select the option Block Policy Inheritance. For example, selecting this option in an organizational unit would block the effects of GPOs from any parent OUs, from the parent domain, and from the parent site; selecting this option at the domain level prevents inheritance of any site GPOs.

Now, to further complicate things, what would happen if you applied No Override to a GPO, and a container further down the hierarchy was set to Block Policy Inheritance? The No Override option takes precedence over the Block Policy Inheritance option, so the policy marked No Override will be applied.

Linking

A group policy object can be linked to multiple sites, domains, or organizational units (SDOUs). To create a link to an existing GPO, follow these steps:

1. Go to the Group Policy tab of the properties page for the Active Directory container you want to link.
2. Click the Add button and navigate to the container that currently holds the GPO you're looking for. If the GPO isn't linked to any container, look on the All tab.
3. Select the GPO and click OK. The GPO should now appear in the group policy object's Links box.

Keep in mind that modifying the linked GPO in one container modifies the GPO for all containers to which the policy is linked. Before modifying any GPO, make sure that you won't be negatively affecting any other containers. To see other containers to which a GPO is linked, follow these steps:

1. Select any instance of the GPO from the group policy object tab of a container's properties page.
2. Right-click and select Properties from the pop-up menu.
3. Select the Links tab in the resulting dialog box.
4. Select the applicable domain and click the Find Now button. Any SDOUs showing up in the linked list don't include child SDOUs that might be receiving the policy through inheritance.

Filtering by Group Membership

Although you might think it from the name, group policy objects can't be applied to security groups. They do, however, have an associated *Access Control List (ACL)*, allowing for security management similar to that of NTFS files and folders. Security settings are available by clicking the Security tab of the properties page for a group policy object. Figure 6.2 shows the default security settings for a group policy object:

- Authenticated Users allows Read and Apply permissions. To apply a group policy, a group must have at least the Read and Apply permissions.
- CREATOR OWNER has no permissions configured.
- Domain Admins, Enterprise Admins, and SYSTEM all allow Read, Write, Create All Child Objects, and Delete All Child Objects.

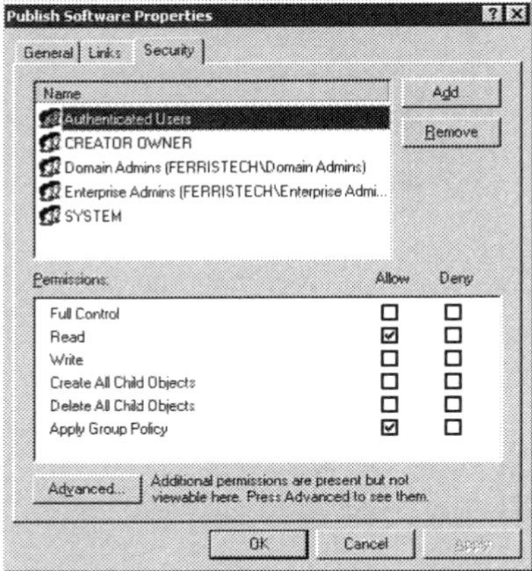

Figure 6.2 The default group policy object security permissions. To receive a group policy, the user must have both Read and Apply Group Policy permissions.

By default, group policy objects are not applied directly to the Administrators, Domain Administrators, or Enterprise Administrators groups. Unfortunately, they are applied to the Authenticated Users group, so policies may apply anyway. To prevent administrators from receiving group policy settings, consider either denying the Apply Group Policy permission to the administrative groups, or removing the Authenticated Users from the GPO Access Control List and replacing them with Domain Users, and then removing your administrative accounts from the Domain Users group. If you do this, you may need secondary accounts for users with administrative privileges in your domain—a recommended security practice anyway. The RunAs command keeps administrators from needing to log off and log back on as a privileged account when they need to perform administrative tasks.

RunAs: Running Commands with Alternate Account Credentials

The RunAs command allows a logged-on user to execute a command or run a program under the security context of a different user account. For example, domain administrators can be logged on with a standard user account, but still run the Active Directory Users and Computers console under the context of the Domain Administrator account. There are three ways to use RunAs. The first is the command-line utility, which can run from the DOS prompt or from the Start, Run command:

```
RUNAS "/u:<domain>\<PrivilegedUserID>" "<command>"
```

The second method of using RunAs is to hold the left Shift key and right-click a shortcut in the Program bar, then select Run As from the pop-up menu. Figure 6.3 shows the resulting dialog.

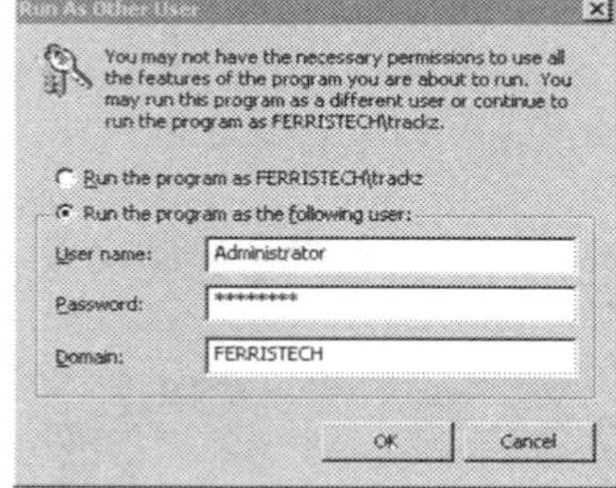

Figure 6.3 Selecting and running Active Directory Users and Computers as a different user. Enter the user account, domain, and password for the privileged account under which you will run the specified command.

The final method is to enable the Run as Different User option on a shortcut for an application. Right-click a shortcut to an application and select Properties from the pop-up menu. On the Shortcut Properties page, select the Shortcut tab, and enable the Run as Different User option, as shown in Figure 6.4.

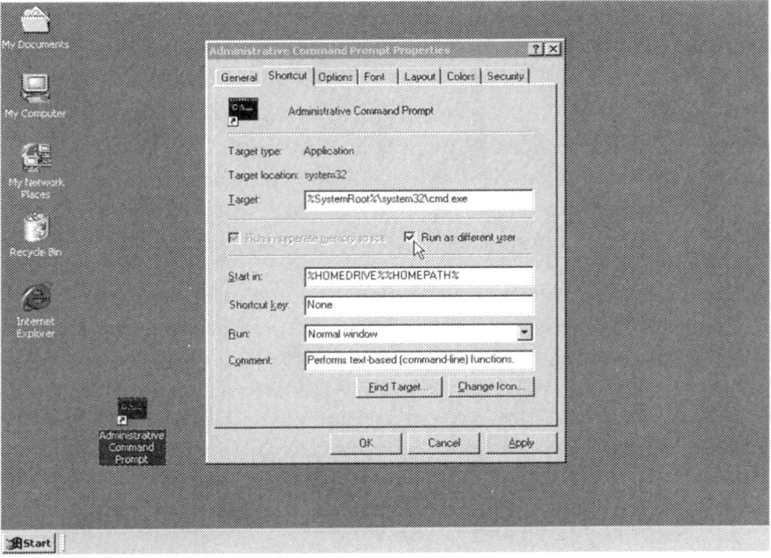

Figure 6.4 Enabling the Run as Different User option in the properties of a shortcut will prompt for a secondary username and password any time the application is executed using the configured shortcut.

To determine which accounts do or don't receive a GPO based on the security group, there are two main mechanisms for filtering. The first is to grant everyone permission to the policy, then apply a Deny permission to a group of users who shouldn't receive the policy. With this method, you can leave the Authenticated Users group permissions untouched. Follow these steps:

1. Create a security group—for this example, we'll call it DenyMyGPO—and add the group to the ACL for the GPO.
2. Under the permissions for the DenyMyGPO group, deny the Read and Apply Group Policy permissions.

Users or computers added to the DenyMyGPO group in this example won't receive the selected GPO. As with file system security, denied permissions always override granted permissions.

The second filtering mechanism is to grant read access only to those users who should receive a policy, and to specify no permissions—but don't deny permissions—for anyone else. To do this, follow these steps:

1. First remove the Authenticated Users from the ACL for the group policy object. Now, no users will receive the GPO; at the same time, no one is denied access if it's specifically granted through group membership, as would happen if you granted the Deny permission.

2. Add the users who should receive the policy to a security group—for this example, call the group AllowMyGPO—and add the group to the ACL for the GPO.
3. Under permissions for the AllowMyGPO group, allow the Read and Apply Group Policy permissions. Now only accounts added to the AllowMyGPO group will now receive this GPO—assuming, of course, that the account also falls within the Active Directory hierarchy that would lead to application of the group policy object in question.

Deny Permission Versus Removing Permissions

Note the distinction between granting the Deny permission and removing permissions. The Deny permission, as in file security, always overrides specifically granted permissions. By removing permissions, an account still has access to an object if granted through another security group. If you assign the Deny permission, and then assign the Allow permission through group membership, the Deny will override the Allow, and the group policy won't be applied. Using the Deny method can cause a lot more work in the long run.

Filtering group policy objects based on group membership doesn't allow you to apply a GPO to a security group. It simply filters the application of a GPO, based on security groups, for accounts that would have received the group policy based on the account's location in the Active Directory.

Example: Filtering GPOs by Security Group Membership

Suppose you have a CORP domain with two child organizational units, MarketingOU and SalesOU. In addition, you have three security groups: MarketingGroup, SalesGroup, and OtherGroup. Your Marketing organizational unit has a group policy object named MarketingGPO, your Sales organizational unit has a GPO named SalesGPO. All user accounts in the MarketingGPO are in MarketingGroup, and all user accounts in SalesGPO are in SalesGroup.

Jim's user account is in the MarketingOU organizational unit, and is a member of the MarketingGroup security group, but he sometimes helps out the Sales department, so you want Jim's user account to receive the policy settings from both the SalesGPO and the MarketingGPO group policy objects.

You decide to add Jim's user account to the OtherGroup security group, and allow the Read and Apply permissions to the SalesGPO group policy object for OtherGroup. Unfortunately, Jim won't see the effects of the SalesGPO policy settings. Because his account wouldn't normally receive the GPO from the other organizational unit, adding filtering for his account will have no effect.

Although there are many ways to solve this problem, I'll give you two possible approaches here:

- First, you could link the SalesGPO and MarketingGPO group policy objects to the CORP domain and remove their links to their respective organizational units. Remove the Authenticated Users group from the default ACL for both GPOs. Add the MarketingGroup to the MarketingGPO ACL, and allow the

Read and Apply Group Policy permissions. Add the SalesGroup to the SalesGPO ACL, and allow the Read and Apply Group Policy permissions. Now, members of MarketingGroup will receive the settings in MarketingGPO, and members of SalesGroup will receive settings from SalesGPO. Add Jim to the SalesGroup, and he'll receive settings from the MarketingGPO and from the SalesGPO. If there are conflicting policies, the settings that will apply to Jim's account will be from the group policy object highest in the GPO list under CORP.

- The second approach is somewhat more complicated. Since Jim is in the MarketingOU and needs access to the SalesGPO, you could link the SalesGPO to the MarketingOU. Move the MarketingGPO to the top of the group policy object's Links list, so that the MarketingGPO policy settings will take precedence over the SalesGPO policy settings. Now, in the ACL for SalesGPO, remove the Authenticated Users group, and add both the MarketingGroup and OtherGroup. Allow the Read and Apply Group Policy permissions to both groups, and add Jim's user account to OtherGroup. Since you linked the GPO, security modifications under the SalesOU apply to the GPO in any other container where it's used—this is why you had to explicitly add the MarketingGroup permissions; otherwise, members of the SalesOU would no longer have received the policy settings. Jim—and any other members of OtherGroup under the MarketingOU—will now receive the SalesGPO, in addition to other GPOs assigned to the MarketingOU.

Deleting, Unlinking, and Disabling Policy Objects

If you're retiring a group policy object, it may be better to disable the object for any containers in which you no longer want it, rather than outright deletion. Once you delete a GPO, the only way to restore it is by manually re-creating it. You can disable a GPO by right-clicking it in an Active Directory container and selecting Disable from the pop-up menu. This will only disable the policy for the current container; if the GPO is linked to multiple containers, it will need to be disabled or unlinked in each one. When you decide to delete a GPO, you have two options. You can either unlink the GPO from a specific container, or you can remove the link and permanently delete the GPO.

Administrative Templates

Administrative templates are similar to the *.ADM policy template files used for all Windows NT 4.0 registry-based policy settings. Administrative templates can be added or removed under the Computer Configuration or the User Configuration nodes by right-clicking Administrative Templates and selecting Add/Remove Templates from the pop-up menu. The administrative templates are still based on plain-text files with an *.ADM extension, just as in Windows NT 4.0. Windows 2000 templates, however, are quite a bit more detailed.

Deleting Versus Unlinking

Never permanently delete a GPO unless you're sure you no longer need it. Simply unlink the GPO from all containers. GPO deletion is a permanent action.

My Preferred GPO Model

From a management and maintenance standpoint, I prefer to create a small number of common GPOs for the domain level, with any required exceptions handled by organizational units and group-based filtering. In the Active Directory environment for which I'm responsible, I have no site GPOs. That way, I can manage all of my GPOs through the Active Directory Users and Computers console. At the domain level, I've defined the following GPOs:

- **Default Computer Settings.** Contains only settings to the Computer Configuration node. The User Configuration settings are disabled in the group policy object properties.
- **Default User Settings.** Contains only settings to the User Configuration node. The Computer Configuration settings are disabled in the group policy object properties.
- **Standard Software.** Contains software installation policies for the common application set required by all users.

I've also added three security groups to the directory—NoDefaultComputer, NoDefaultUser, and NoStandardSW. Each of these groups has been configured with the Deny Read and Deny Apply permissions in their associated group policy object. If ever I need to prevent a user from receiving policy settings associated with one of the standard GPOs, I can simply add his or her account to the associated security group.

Further down the line, I've divided the Active Directory into two upper-level organizational units, one for user accounts and one for computer accounts. The computer accounts are broken out into departmentalized OUs, since the computers are more likely to stay in the same department than the users. User accounts are divided into OUs based on their authoritative roles (User, Manager, Director, Administrative Assistant), since those roles change less frequently than the departments to which a user reports. There is at least one security group per department, and user accounts are members of groups based on their departments.

For each departmental OU under the computer accounts OU, I create a departmentalized Software Installation policy, assigning the packages in the Computer Configuration settings node and disabling the User Configuration settings.

Administrators have separate privileged accounts, residing in a special Administrative OU. No policies are applied to members of the Administrative OU.

Additional policy settings are on an as-needed basis; most functions are successfully manageable at the domain level.

This model was originally geared toward a mid-sized proof-of-concept domain of about 7,500 objects. With larger environments, such intricacies as delegated management tasks could ultimately drive a more detailed organizational unit structure than the one outlined in this example.

For an Active Directory group policy object, the templates are stored in the *.ADM subfolder of the group policy template (GPT). These GPTs are located in the Sysvol share on domain controllers and are replicated using File Replication Service. For the local GPO, the active *.ADM files can be found in %systemroot%\System32\GroupPolicy\ADM. Additional *.ADM files for both local and Active Directory GPOs are stored under the %systemroot%\System32\INF folder. You should never add, move, or delete files directly through the file manager; instead, use the Administrative Templates node of the GPO you want to edit. Policies should only modify registry settings stored in `HKEY_LOCAL_MACHINE` and `HKEY_LOCAL_USER` hives under either the `\Software\Policies` or `\Software\Microsoft\Windows\CurrentVersion\Policies` keys. Of course, this means that managing other software settings through custom *.ADM files requires the software to use these locations in the registry for configuration options.

By default, you'll have enabled policy templates for Internet Explorer (INETRES.ADM) and the System policy (SYSTEM.ADM). INETRES.ADM is used to define policies available under the Windows Components\Internet Explorer nodes. The SYSTEM.ADM policy template contains the policy groups displayed in Figures 6.5 and 6.6.

You can add *.ADM files from Windows NT 4.0 registry-based policy files, but since they weren't written to the same specifications as a GPO-based template, they may cause undesired tattooing of the registry—the default behavior of NT 4.0 policies. By default, these types of policy files won't be applied to client machines. To override the default setting and enable registry-based policy processing, you must enable the policy through the Computer Configuration\Administrative Templates\System\Group Policy\Registry Policy Processing policy.

Figure 6.5 SYSTEM.ADM policy groups from the Computer Configuration\Administrative Templates node.

Figure 6.6 SYSTEM.ADM policy groups from the User Configuration\Administrative Templates node.

Setting Scripts Through Group Policy

In Windows NT 4.0 domains, you could specify a logon script for any user account through the User Manager. With a Windows 2000 Active Directory domain, you can still specify a logon script in the properties for each user account, but group policy objects allow for some additional flexibility. Now, through group policy settings, you can create scripts to execute for any or all of these four events (in order):

- Computer startup
- User logon
- User logoff
- Computer shutdown

Multiple scripts can be associated with each event through a single GPO. If scripts are executed synchronously (the default), they'll execute in order from the top of the list to the bottom. If they're executed asynchronously, all scripts will run at the same time. In addition, because an object can have multiple group policy objects applied, the object could inherit multiple scripts from a number of GPOs.

Only Windows 2000 clients will execute the GPO-based scripts. Under Windows 2000, you can run any of the following file types as scripts:

- Batch files (*.BAT)
- Command files (*.CMD, same format as batch files)
- Executable files (*.EXE and *.COM)
- Windows scripting host files (VBScript or JScript)

When adding a new script, you can specify parameters to pass to the script via the resulting Add Script dialog box.

No scripts will execute if the user only locks the workstation, suspends to RAM (Standby mode), or suspends to disk (Hibernate mode) without ever restarting the machine or logging out and logging back on.

Logon/Logoff Scripts

Logon/logoff scripts apply to user accounts. The scripts are stored as part of the group policy object, located under the User\Scripts subfolder of the group policy template. Note that you should not edit the scripts directly from this location; rather, you should use the Show Files button in the script's property window. Logon scripts are executed at user logon. Common uses for logon scripts assigned through group policy objects include mapping global or OU-specific drives and printers, forcing the initialization of a required application for a group of users, or loading a Web browser pointed to a predetermined location.

Obviously, logoff scripts are executed as the user logs off. Logoff scripts could be used to clean up temporary files, clear the recently accessed files list, or send a notification message to a time and attendance program.

Startup/Shutdown Scripts

Startup/shutdown scripts apply to the computer accounts. These scripts are stored as part of the associated group policy object, and can be found under the Machine\Scripts subfolder of the group policy template. Note that you should not edit the scripts directly from this location; rather, you should use the Show Files button on the script's policy property window.

Startup scripts are executed before the user is presented with the option to log on. Common uses for startup scripts include updating virus protection, checking for network connectivity, mapping drives specific to the computer's needs, or running inventory software. Shutdown scripts execute after the user has been logged out, but before the computer shuts down or restarts. Common uses for shutdown scripts include cleaning up temporary files, running a disk check, or kicking off a backup routine for locally stored files.

Group Policy Tools, Tips, and Tricks

This section outlines some tips, tricks, "gotcha's," and tools to assist you in your implementation of group policy objects.

Improve Performance by Disabling Unused Portions of the GPO

By default, all computer policies must be applied before the logon screen is available. After logon, all user policies must be applied before the user can interact with the desktop. Therefore, the more policies that apply to an object, the longer it may take for the startup and logon processes to complete.

Each policy file has both a Computer Configuration section and a User Configuration section, even though you may not choose to configure policies under both sections in a single policy. If you choose to configure policies under only one of the two sections for a GPO, you can improve the download time for that GPO by disabling the unused section of the policy:

1. Select the GPO from any container to which it applies, and click the Properties button.
2. On the General tab, select Disable Computer Configuration Settings if the GPO applies only to user account policies. Select Disable User Configuration Settings if the GPO applies only to computer account policies.

Even local computer policy has a Properties box under the Action menu in which you can disable user configuration settings or disable computer configuration settings.

The default behavior of a Windows 2000 client is to download only group policy objects that have been changed. GPOs are cached in the local registry and tracked via version number to minimize startup time needed for downloading multiple GPOs.

The client determines whether to download a new copy of a GPO by comparing the version information of the Active Directory–based GPO to the locally cached copy. I don't recommend modifying this behavior, as transferring complete images of every applicable policy file at every logon is sure to cause problems for your network bandwidth.

Search the Group Policy Explanations

There are over 560 group policy settings available under Windows 2000. Windows 2000 makes the descriptions for each policy setting readily available, which is great for a better understanding of the individual policies—many of which are new in Windows 2000. For most policy settings, especially those in the default set of Administrative Template policies, you can double-click the policy and select the Explain tab to see a full description (often a page or more) for the function and application of the selected policy.

In case the Explain tab isn't good enough and you'd like a fully searchable set of policy explanations, the Windows 2000 Resource Kit includes a group policy reference in the form of an HTML help file named GP.CHM. This help file mirrors the structure of the Active Directory group policies, and provides the full context of the Explain tabs—often with additional information and context-sensitive links—in the standard, searchable Windows help file format.

Standard GUIDs for Group Policy Extensions

Policies are applied to the client machines through client-side group policy extensions. These extensions show up as registry keys under this key:

```
HKLM\Software\Microsoft\Windows NT\CurrentVersion\Winlogon\GPExtensions
```

The key names appear as GUIDs for the associated policies, and the (Default) string value contains the friendly name for each extension. These are the common extensions:

- Folder Redirection: `{25537BA6-77A8-11D2-9B6C-0000F8080861}`
- Microsoft Disk Quota: `{3610eda5-77ef-11d2-8dc5-00c04fa31a66}`
- Scripts: `{42B5FAAE-6536-11d2-AE5A-0000F87571E3}`
- Security: `{827D319E-6EAC-11D2-A4EA-00C04F79F83A}`
- IE Branding: `{A2E30F80-D7DE-11d2-BBDE-00C04F86AE3B}`
- EFS Recovery: `{B1BE8D72-6EAC-11D2-A4EA-00C04F79F83A}`
- Application Management: `{c6dc5466-785a-11d2-84d0-00c04fb169f7}`
- IPSEC: `{e437bc1c-aa7d-11d2-a382-00c04f991e27}`

These extensions are what ultimately manage the application of group policy objects on the client side. A corresponding extension key is maintained in the

`\Software\Microsoft\Windows\CurrentVersion\Group Policy\History` keys of both the `HKEY_LOCAL_MACHINE` and the `HKEY_CURRENT_USER` hives. The History key contains version information for each GPO to determine whether it's necessary to download a policy file at logon. If the version information matches up, the system can use GPO information already cached on the client.

Resultant Set of Policies (RSoP)

With all the inheritance, blocking, and multiple-GPO capability available with Active Directory group policy, large numbers of GPOs and deep Active Directory management structures can make it difficult to determine the final results that a collection of policies may have on a user or computer. This is where a Resultant Set of Policies (RSoP) tool becomes useful. Microsoft is expected to ship a graphical RSoP utility in mid- to late 2000, but I have yet to see it. In the meantime, here are a couple of third-party vendors who provide RSoP utilities:

- Trusted Enterprise Manager 3.0, from Master Design & Development, Inc. (`http://www.mddinc.com`)
- FAZAM 2000, from Full Armor (`http://www.fullarmor.com`)

Utilities for Group Policy Objects

The following table describes a few additional utilities that may help you in your GPO management endeavors.

Utility	Description
GPRESULT.EXE	Command-line Resource Kit utility for group policy results. This tool doesn't provide a Resultant Set of Policies; rather, it displays general information about group policy and Active Directory membership for the computer and user account under which the utility is executed.
GPOTOOL.EXE	Command-line Resource Kit utility to execute a consistency check on the group policy containers and the group policy templates. This utility can also create or delete a GPO from the command line, making it useful for scripting.
Event Viewer	The Windows 2000 Event Viewer reports error conditions for GPOs.

Mixed-Mode Domains

If you're in a mixed-mode domain environment with some of your domains converted to Windows 2000 and some remaining Windows NT 4.0, pay close attention to the policy implications for Windows 2000 clients. Group policy objects can only be used on Windows 2000 clients. On the other hand, Windows NT 4.0 policy files could apply to both Windows NT 4.0 clients and Windows 2000 clients, so if your NT 4.0 domain utilized policy files, you could inadvertently apply the policies to Windows 2000 clients.

Suppose you were running a single master domain under NT 4.0. The single master domain model calls for a single trusted domain containing all user accounts, with computer accounts in trusting resource domains. You use NT 4.0–style policies in each domain. You upgrade your client workstations to Windows 2000 Professional. Now, if you upgrade your account domain to Windows 2000 and leave the resource domains as NT 4.0, users will receive user settings through GPOs, but computer accounts—which are still in the NT 4.0 resource domains—will inherit the old Windows NT 4.0 policies for machine settings. On the other hand, if you upgrade your resource domains to Windows 2000 and leave the master accounts domain untouched, computer accounts will receive machine settings through GPOs, and user settings will inherit the old Windows NT 4.0–style policies for user settings.

So how would I recommend implementing a mixed-mode environment? It depends. If you currently use an NT 4.0 domain with no policies, I would start by upgrading your mobile users to Windows 2000 Professional; they'll see the most immediate benefit. From there, upgrade your domain controllers—and your domain security model—to Windows 2000. After you've given it some time to settle, convert your domain to Native mode. Filter through upgrades for the rest of your environment—the desktop computers, the member servers, etc.—as the final step in your migration.

On the other hand, if you have already implemented a number of management policies in an existing Windows NT 4.0 domain, I'd recommend upgrading your domain to Windows 2000. Again, give it some time to settle, then convert your domain to Native mode. Your legacy policies should still work just fine with the down-level clients. Review the Windows 2000 policy options, and translate your down-level policies into Windows 2000 GPOs. Upgrade the member servers and workstations after getting your policies configured. I wouldn't recommend applying the existing NT 4.0 policy files to Windows 2000 clients; it can be rather difficult to recover from the tattooing effect the Windows NT 4.0 policies will have on the Windows 2000 machines.

Group policy is perhaps one of the most beneficial technologies included with Windows 2000. With NT 4.0 domains, policies provided an extremely limited level of registry-based workstation management. The available policies were vague, and configuring multiple groups of users with different management options was difficult and time-consuming. Windows 2000 addresses these limitations, providing a highly granulated, detailed, well-documented, and distributable management infrastructure. With group policy objects, the desktop management functions can be managed through a centralized interface. By properly implementing group policy technologies, an IT organization should see reduced costs associated with issues such as software distribution, workstation management, and domain security.

7 IntelliMirror

THIS CHAPTER COVERS:

- What is IntelliMirror?
- Benefits of IntelliMirror
- Implementing IntelliMirror
- Where IntelliMirror fits in the Windows 2000 Change and Configuration Management model
- Technologies that complement IntelliMirror

After reading this chapter, you should be able to do the following:

- Understand the technical benefits of IntelliMirror
- Configure IntelliMirror components via Active Directory group policy objects
- Enable access to cached network files for mobile users who have disconnected from the network
- Implement an IntelliMirror solution, including User Data Management, User Settings Management, and automatic installation of user software

One of the big buzzwords attached to the Windows 2000 Change and Configuration Management features is *IntelliMirror*. IntelliMirror is a Microsoft marketing term for a suite of standard Windows 2000 technologies—the Active Directory, group policy objects, Windows Installer, User Data Management, User Settings Management, and offline network shares—that, when used together, facilitate automatic data recovery, "follow-me" user configuration, and a complete roaming user-managed environment.

This chapter examines the technologies that form IntelliMirror, breaking apart each component and explaining how to implement the management and recoverability features in your environment to reduce Total Cost of Ownership (TCO) for the user's desktop machines. The chapter concludes with a selection of implementation tips, including some storage and bandwidth considerations that accompany the IntelliMirror technology suite.

Overview of IntelliMirror

IntelliMirror describes a suite of components that, when enabled, create a managed, cohesive, and consistent environment for your end users. Regardless of where a user logs on, that user will see his or her configuration preferences, personal data files, and authorized applications. For mobile users, interaction with the machine is identical whether the user is connected or disconnected from the network; although stored on network file servers, files are still available when the user is not physically connected to the network. The features of IntelliMirror make it an ideal technology for these type of environments:

- Many users need access to a small number of shared computers.
- Users are not assigned to specific machines.
- User-specific data, settings, and applications should be available to the user from any workstation.
- Users are not always connected to the network.
- Fast recovery of damaged or lost systems is desired.
- All user data and configuration settings are to be stored on the network, but should still be available when the network is down.

The technologies associated with IntelliMirror work only in a Windows 2000 environment. User accounts must be hosted on a Windows 2000 Active Directory domain, and clients must be running Windows 2000 as the desktop operating system. IntelliMirror will function in a mixed-domain environment where computer accounts are hosted on a Windows NT Server 4.0 domain and user accounts are located in a Windows 2000 Active Directory, but you can't apply group policy objects to the machine accounts until they're migrated into the Windows 2000 domain.

Windows 95, Windows 98, and Windows NT 4.0 workstations can't utilize any of the recoverability and configuration-management features of IntelliMirror.

A measurable reduction in TCO is therefore dependent on a large percentage of the environment running Windows 2000 client machines. While there are Active Directory clients for Windows 95, Windows 98, and Windows NT 4.0, the software only makes the down-level operating system aware of the Active Directory. The older OSes can't use features such as software assignment and group policy.

IntelliMirror Components

The IntelliMirror technology suite consists of three separate technological concepts:

- Software Installation and Maintenance
- User Settings Management
- User Data Management

The IntelliMirror components, which can be used together or individually depending on your needs, are enabled through the use of these Windows 2000 technologies:

- Active Directory
- Disk Quotas
- Folder Redirection
- Group Policy
- Offline Files
- Roaming User Profiles
- Synchronization Manager
- Windows Installer

Remote Installation Services (RIS), while an important part of the Windows 2000 Change and Configuration Management model, is not a component of the IntelliMirror technology suite. RIS and IntelliMirror combine to provide the automated system-recovery features described as Windows 2000 Change and Configuration Management. Figure 7.1 depicts the relationship of these four components of the Change and Configuration Management model.

Remote Installation Services can be used to install or restore the base OS image. Software Installation and Maintenance then loads user- and group-specific applications on the machine. The User Data Management feature replicates the user's My Documents folder down to a local cache, and User Settings Management restores all user-selected application configuration preferences.

Software Installation and Maintenance

The Software Installation and Maintenance component (described in detail in Chapter 8, "Application Management and Software Installation,") enables user- or machine-based application installation, configuration, and maintenance. Through the combined use of the Windows Installer, the Active Directory, and group policy objects, you can configure applications to be assigned or published to user or computer accounts. The scope for a software installation policy is set via group policy object, so software installation can be applied at the site, domain, or organizational unit level, and filtered based on group membership.

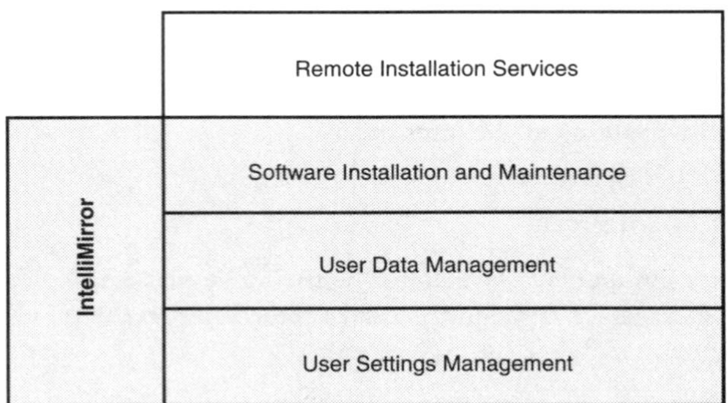

Figure 7.1 The Windows 2000 Change and Configuration Management model.

There are two ways to use Software Installation and Maintenance to distribute applications to the desktop. Applications can be published or assigned. Applications that are *published* in the Active Directory will be available to users through the Add New Programs option on the Add/Remove Programs applet in the Control Panel. Applications can only be published to users, not to computers. Since published applications are not automatically distributed to the workstations, users can decide for themselves whether they need to install applications that have been published.

The other installation option, *assigned* applications, causes software to install automatically for applicable user or computer accounts. Application assignment is typically used to install required software packages without user intervention. If an application is assigned to a computer account, the software will install on the next reboot of the computer. If an application is assigned to a user, the administrator can select a few installation options. One option is to configure the package to install automatically during the user's next logon. The other option is to have the system install the package the first time the user accesses the associated application by running the application from the program menu.

Associating Extensions with Applications

Applications that are assigned or published can be configured to install automatically if a user attempts to open a file with an extension associated to the application through the Active Directory software installation policy. This can minimize the number of times a user sees the familiar Open With dialog that pops up whenever the user attempts to open a document with an unrecognized extension.

Software Installation and Maintenance doesn't install software using standard setup executables; instead, the application install options must support the Windows Installer. These installation programs appear as *.MSI files. Older applications, obviously, won't include *.MSI packages; these standards didn't exist until recently. Office 2000 is an example of an application that includes an *.MSI installation option. All Windows 2000 Service Packs, which use Windows Installer Patch (*.MSP) files instead of *.MSI files, will also be installable via the Windows Installer.

For applications that don't include pre-made Windows Installer packages, there are two options. First, the installation can be repackaged with a third-party utility to create a self-contained *.MSI file. These repackaged files can be either published or assigned. The second option is to create a *.ZAP file (explained in Chapter 8) to kick off the default setup routine for the application. Application installs using *.ZAP files cannot be assigned—they can only be published. In addition, *.ZAP installations can't install using elevated privileges; they must install at the same security level as the associated user. Finally, *.ZAP files are not self-healing; the only way to repair a damaged *.ZAP-based application installation is to reinstall the entire application.

Slipstreaming Service Packs

In the past, any time a new application was installed, the latest service pack had to be re-applied. With Windows 2000, this will not be necessary. Service Packs will "slipstream" over older Windows 2000 installation files, and components won't be allowed to install down-level versions. This provides greater system integrity, which hopefully translates to higher uptime.

SMS and Software Installation and Maintenance Don't Mix

Warning: If you use Microsoft Systems Management Server (SMS) for software deployment, you *should not* use the Windows 2000 IntelliMirror Software Installation and Maintenance in parallel. More information on Software Installation and Maintenance versus SMS is provided at the end of Chapter 8.

User Data Management

User Data Management—enabled by a combination of the Offline Files and Folder Redirection technologies—allows data to follow the user, regardless of whether the user's PC is connected to the network or disconnected and operating in stand-alone mode. Although this feature doesn't require the machine to participate in an Active Directory domain, User Data Management will *not* work for a machine that's used strictly in a disconnected environment; the machine must occasionally be connected to the network to allow the system to synchronize offline data. The Synchronization Manager controls synchronization behavior for offline files, offline folders, and offline Web pages.

Offline Files

With the Offline Files component of User Data Management, files and folders that are critical for a user can be configured to be available offline. This can include an individual data file, a complete data share, or an entire program folder, but cannot work for database files (*.MDB) or Outlook message stores (*.PST, *.OST). If the user's system is then disconnected from the network, the user will have access to the offline files using the same security permissions and file attributes as if the system were still connected.

Access to offline files is initiated exactly as if the user were still online. If the user had a drive mapping to the server and share name, that drive letter would be available to access the offline files. If the files were accessed using the UNC (\\<*server*>\<*share*>), then the UNC would still point to the locally cached versions of the files.

When the user is online, modifications to files that have been made available offline will apply to the file on the network. The updated file will then be synchronized to the locally cached version of the file. If the user is offline, modifications to Offline Files affect the locally cached file, and will be synchronized with the network file the next time the network is available.

Synchronization can be fully automated except for instances when both the local copy and the network copy of a file have been modified. In these instances, the Synchronization Manager will prompt the user with the option to save the local copy to the network, replace the local copy with the network version, or keep both versions by saving the local copy with a different filename.

Synchronization Manager also controls the timing of offline file synchronization. You can open the Synchronization Manager from the Synchronize shortcut in the Accessories folder under Programs on the Start menu. You can configure the Synchronization Manager to synchronize offline files at logon, at logoff, at scheduled times, or after the computer has been idle for a specified amount of time. Different options can be set for each network connection defined on the local system, and you can specify different behaviors for each share or Web page configured to be available offline. When synchronizing, or when the Offline Files feature generates a status message, Synchronization Manager displays a small icon that looks like a computer and monitor in the taskbar. Important messages will pop up in "thought bubbles" above this status icon.

Offline Files features can be configured locally on a user-by-user basis on a specific machine, or for groups of users through Active Directory group policy objects. If configured locally on a per-user basis, the user only needs access to an available network share on a server that uses the Server Message Block (SMB) protocol for file and print sharing. SMB is supported for Windows 95, Windows 98, Windows NT 4.0, and Windows 2000 network shares.

How to Tell Whether Files Are Available Offline

Files and folders that are available offline can be easily identified by the presence of an offline file icon overlay. This overlay appears as two small blue arrows—one pointing up, and one pointing down—contained in a small white square in the lower-left corner of the icon. If a network file has no icon overlay, it's not available offline.

SMB and NetWare Don't Mix

Warning: SMB is not used on a Novell NetWare file and print server. Therefore, Offline Files won't work for files hosted by a NetWare server.

For Windows 2000 Server or Professional shared folders, Offline Files can be configured on the share itself. The Sharing tab of a Windows 2000 shared folder properties page has a Caching button at the bottom. With this option, you can enable or disable caching for the folder. If you decide to allow caching of files in the share, you have three additional configuration options:

- **Automatic Caching for Documents:** Files that have been opened are automatically made available when working offline. This is the recommended setting for folders containing required user documents. If the user is online, the server version of the file is always used with this setting. Using the server version of the file requires the system to use proper network file-sharing behaviors. For example, if a user is online and accessing files that have been made available offline, the online versions of the files will be used.
- **Automatic Caching for Programs:** Any files that are executed, read, or referenced are automatically made available when working offline. This is the recommended setting for read-only data shares and network application shares. Since this setting is generally used for read-only data shares, this setting doesn't guarantee adherence to network file-sharing behaviors when the user is online. For example, if a user is online and accessing files made available offline, the offline versions of the files will be used (as long as the offline version is in sync with the online version), rather than accessing the files over the network.
- **Manual Caching for Documents:** Any files or folders needed offline must be made available manually from the users' workstations by right-clicking the object and selecting Make Available Offline from the pop-up menu. This is the recommended setting for folders containing user documents that may be needed offline. If the user is online, the server version of the file is always used with this setting. Using the server version of the file requires the system to use proper network file-sharing behaviors.

Folder Redirection

The Folder Redirection component of User Data Management allows the administrator to redirect certain special folders to specific local folders or network shares locations. From the local machine, only the My Documents special folder can be redirected. To do so, right-click the My Documents icon on the desktop and enter a new location on the Target tab.

If you are using group policy objects in an Active Directory environment, Folder Redirection can be enabled via policy settings for any of the following special folders:

- Application Data
- Desktop
- My Documents
- My Pictures
- Start Menu

User Data Management Implementation Examples

To enable User Data Management through group policy objects, the user must have an account in the Active Directory. Exercise 7.1 walks through setting up a group policy object in the Active Directory to redirect the My Documents special folder to a network location. In the process, any files in the existing local My Documents locations will be relocated automatically to the corresponding user's network share My Documents location. Finally, we'll make the My Documents special folder available to the users offline, ensuring data availability when the network is not available, such as during network outages or when a portable computer user disconnects his or her computer from the internal network.

Exercise 7.1 **Enabling User Data Management**

Time Required: 30 minutes

Requirements: Windows 2000 Active Directory domain, Windows 2000 client machine, Windows 2000 file and print server

This exercise uses the Group Policy Editor through the Active Directory Users and Computers snap-in for the MMC to configure a group policy object that demonstrates the Windows 2000 User Data Management features. As always, you should not perform this exercise in a production environment. You will need Domain Admin rights to perform this exercise.

There are two parts to this exercise. Part 1 creates the default share location for user documents and enables automatic caching for user documents on the share. Part 2 creates the group policy to redirect the users' My Documents folders.

Part 1. Creating a file share with file caching enabled:

Step 1 On the Windows 2000 file and print server, referenced in this exercise as <*FileServer*>, select the drive where you want to store the network My Document shares.

Step 2 On the drive selected in step 1, create a folder named **UserDocs**.

Step 3 Right-click the UserDocs folder and select Sharing from the pop-up menu.

Step 4 Share the UserDocs folder as **UserDocs$**.

Step 5 At the bottom of the Sharing tab, click the Caching button.

Step 6 Select the option Allow Caching of Files in This Shared Folder.

Step 7 In the Setting drop-down box, select Automatic Caching for Documents. Click OK and close the folder properties dialog.

Part 2. Creating the group policy object for My Document redirection:

Step 1 In the Active Directory Users and Computers management console, select the domain or organizational unit containing the users for whom you want to enable User Data Management. You may want to create a special OU and add some fictional users to test the steps outlined in this section of the exercise.

Step 2 Start the Group Policy Editor for the selected Active Directory container by right-clicking the container and selecting Properties from the pop-up menu. Select the Group Policy tab from the resulting dialog.

Step 3 Click New to create a new group policy object. Change the name of the new GPO to **Roaming My Documents** and double-click the new policy to open the editor.

Step 4 Under User Configuration\Windows Settings\Folder Redirection, right-click the My Documents node and select Properties from the pop-up menu.

Step 5 Select the Target tab. Under the Setting option, select Basic - Redirect Everyone's Folder to the Same Location.

Step 6 Under the Target folder location, enter `\\`*`<FileServer>`*`\UserDocs$\%username%` as the desired location.

Step 7 Under the Settings tab, check the option Grant the User Exclusive Rights to My Documents. It should be selected by default. This ensures proper NTFS permissions on the network folders used to store the user's network cache of the My Documents folder. The user and local system will both be granted full control for the folder specified in step 6.

Step 8 Confirm the selection of the option Move the Contents of My Documents to the New Location. This option will automatically move any existing data in the current My Documents folder up to the new network My Documents location on the first application of the new group policy object.

Step 9 Under the Policy Removal box, confirm the selection of the option Leave the Folder in the New Location When Policy Is Removed, to prevent the redirected folder from automatically reverting to the original My Documents location if the policy is removed.

Step 10 Under My Pictures Preferences, decide whether you want to include the My Pictures subfolder in the redirected My Documents location.

Step 11 Click OK and close the Group Policy Editor.

Step 12 Close the Active Directory Users and Computers console.

From your Windows 2000 Professional workstation, log on as a user under the same container for which you configured a group policy object. When you view the properties of the My Documents folder, the Target tab should point to the location specified in Part 2, step 6. Save a few files in the My Documents folder. Log off the computer and then remove the network cable. Log back on—the computer should use cached logon information—and open the My Documents folder. If everything is configured properly, you should still have access to the files on the network My Documents share, even though the network cable is not attached.

Folder redirection targets under group policy objects for User Data Management can be set to one of three values under the Setting drop-down of the policy's Target tab, as shown in Figure 7.2 (refer to Exercise 7.1, Part 2, for directions on finding this screen). These are the possible values:

- **Basic - Redirect Everyone's Folder to the Same Location.** Policy-based redirection with this setting redirects the specified folder to the same location for all users.

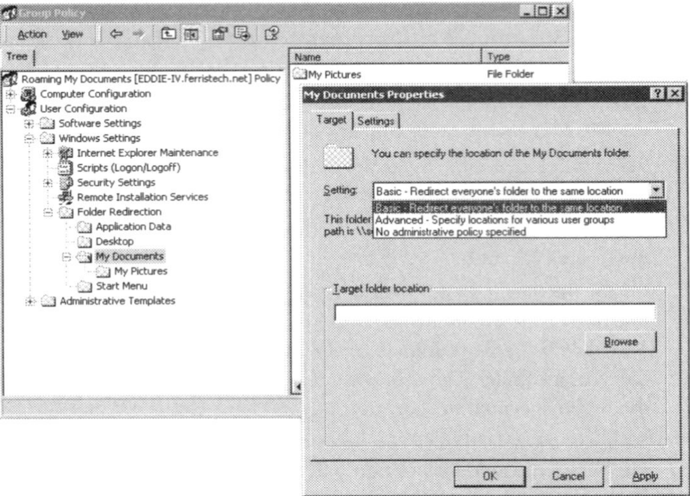

Figure 7.2 Selecting one of the three options available with a Folder Redirection policy.

- **Advanced - Specify Locations for Various User Groups.** This value presents a dialog enabling an administrator to redirect one of the special folders based on security group membership. After selecting this value, click the Add button to select a security group. Enter the Universal Naming Convention (UNC) for the redirect location for each associated security group.
- **No Administrative Policy Specified.** With this option selected, the GPO will not redirect the location of the associated special folder. This is the default value for all folder redirection policies.

Exercise 7.1 walked through the creation of a Basic folder redirection policy. The GPO used this setting to redirect all instances of the My Documents folder to \\<*server*>\UserDocs$\%username%. This policy would create a subfolder under the UserDocs$ share for each user to whom the policy applied. When the subfolders are created, the %username% variable will expand to the unique user logon name assigned to each user. For an example of the Advanced folder redirection policy, see Exercise 7.2.

Exercise 7.2 **Converting Basic Folder Redirection to Advanced Folder Redirection**

Time Required: 20 minutes

Requirements: Windows 2000 Active Directory domain, Windows 2000 client machine, two Windows 2000 file and print servers

This exercise assumes the completion of Exercise 7.1. For a simple example of the Advanced folder redirection option, suppose you have been directed to modify the behavior of the My

Documents folder redirection to separate storage locations based on user groups. In this case, we'll use two file servers; the My Documents folder for managers will be located on a separate server from the My Documents folder for non-managers.

Note: Why use two file servers here rather than one file server and two shares? Using two file servers is more realistic for many organizations than separate shares on the same server (for example, because of separate building locations). Otherwise, the shares could just as easily be located under the same root.

First, follow the steps outlined in Exercise 7.1, Part 1 for both of the file and print servers. For this exercise, the server used for file storage of managers' files will be referenced as *<MgmtServer>*. The server used for file storage of non-management files will be referenced as *<EmpServer>*.

Step 1 Create two global security groups in your domain, called **Management** and **Employees**.

Step 2 Add all managers' user accounts to the Management group. (You may need to create some fictional user accounts to populate this group, such as MGT1 and MGT2.)

Step 3 Add all non-management employees' user accounts to the Employees group. (You may need to create some fictional user accounts to populate this group, such as EMP1 and EMP2.)

Step 4 Open the Group Policy Editor for the Roaming My Documents group policy object that was created in Exercise 7.1.

Step 5 Under User Configuration\Windows Settings\Folder Redirection, right-click the My Documents node and select Properties from the pop-up menu.

Step 6 Select the Target tab. Under the Setting option, change the selection to Advanced - Specify Locations for Various User Groups.

Step 7 Click the Add button. In the Security Group Membership field, select the Management group from the browse list. Specify the Target Folder Location of `\\<MgmtServer>\UserDocs$\%username%` and click OK.

Step 8 Click the Add button. In the Security Group Membership field, select the Employees group from the browse list. Specify the Target Folder Location of `\\<EmpServer>\UserDocs$\%username%` and click OK. The policy should now look like Figure 7.3.

Step 9 Click OK on the Folder Redirection policy and then close the Group Policy Editor.

Step 10 Close the Active Directory Users and Computers console.

After completing the steps above, the Roaming My Documents GPO will use a single folder redirection policy to specify different file storage locations for the My Documents folders of managers and non-managers.

Redirection Based on Location

The Advanced folder redirection policy setting is an excellent mechanism for location-based selection of network file servers. Add the users to security groups associated with their office locations, and point the My Documents target for each security group to a file and print server in the same physical location.

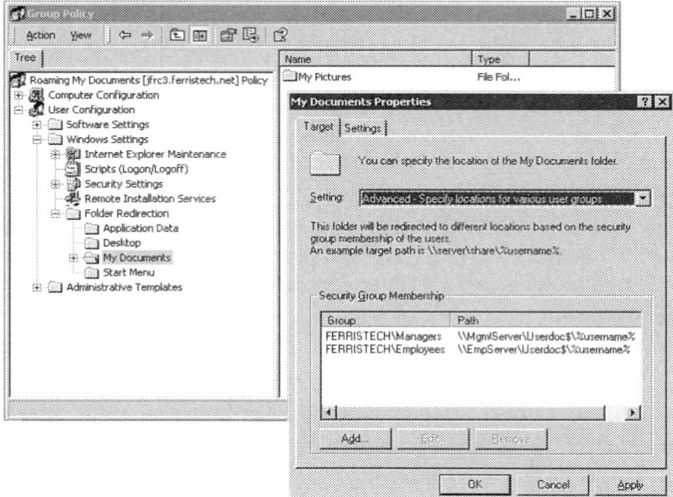

Figure 7.3 After you complete step 8, the Advanced Folder Redirection policy should look like this.

User Settings Management

User Settings Management—essentially an enhanced implementation of the Roaming User Profile technology from Windows NT 4.0—enables the user-specific configuration settings to follow the user from computer to computer. This includes application settings, OS options, custom dictionaries, Internet Explorer Favorites, cookie files, and other user-specific configuration elements. For Windows 2000 to handle roaming user settings correctly, applications must separate user-state and machine-state configuration settings properly.

Roaming user profiles are configured through the Active Directory Users and Computers interface, under the Profile tab of the user account properties. For roaming user profiles to work, the profile must be stored on a network file share. A common practice is to create a Profile$ share on file and print servers to serve as a central location for storing roaming user profiles. For example, specifying a profile path of \\<*FileServer*>\Profile$\%username% (where <*FileServer*> is the machine name of your file and print server) for each user will automatically create a %username% folder for the user's profile upon closing the User Account Properties window.

Enabling Roaming User Profiles

For an example of enabling roaming user profiles, let's assume we're creating roaming profiles for two users, Amy O'Brien and Leslie Boyd. In this environment, user accounts are made using the first name plus the last initial, so the user accounts for our two users are AmyO and LeslieB. The file server is named FileServ01, and the data share is Profile$.

After finding the user accounts under the Active Directory Users and Computers Management console, right-click one of the accounts to bring up the properties page. On the Profile tab, in the Profile Path box, enter this string:

\\FileServ01\Profile$\%username%

Repeat the above process to set the profile folder for the other user. You can now close the Active Directory Users and Computers Management console. The next time one of the users logs on, a subfolder with his or her username will be created under the \\FileServ01\Profile$ data share. The default user profile will be created under this subfolder. Changes made during the user session will be saved up to the network when the user logs off.

Copying Local Profiles to Roaming Profiles

If a user already has a local profile, an administrator could copy the profile from the associated local machine up to the network location by following these steps:

1. Log onto the local machine with an account with administrative privileges on the machine and full control to the user's roaming profile destination. You can't be logged on with the user account you want to move, even if the user has administrative rights.
2. Right-click the My Computer icon on the desktop and select Properties from the pop-up menu.
3. Select the User Profiles tab from the properties dialog.
4. Highlight the source user profile and click the Copy To button.
5. In the Copy To dialog, enter the UNC to the user's network profile destination in the Copy Profile To box.
6. Make sure that the Permitted to Use box reflects the domain user account of the associated user.
7. Click OK.

This process will set NTFS permissions in addition to copying the selected user profile up to the network location. This could take a long time, depending on the amount of user data contained within the profile.

Profile Storage on the Local Workstation

When a user with a roaming profile logs on to a Windows 2000 Professional workstation, his or her profile is copied from the network share down to the local profile storage location on the workstation. This occurs after the user has logged on but before the desktop is available, ensuring proper application of user configuration options and group policy settings.

The profile location—the same for both local profiles and cached roaming profiles—depends on the process used to load the Windows 2000 machine. If the machine was created using a clean install process, or by using an upgrade from a

Windows 95 or a Windows 98 machine with profiles disabled, the profiles will be stored at this location:

%systemdrive%\Documents and Settings\%username%

If the machine was created by upgrading a Windows 95 or Windows 98 machine with profiles enabled, or by upgrading a Windows NT 3.51 or a Windows NT 4.0 machine, the profiles will be stored at this location:

%systemroot%\Profiles\%username%

Changing the location of the profiles folder after Windows 2000 has been installed is neither supported nor recommended. The only way to relocate the profiles folder is during setup through the use of an unattended install answer file. The key, `profilesdir`, is under the `GUIUnattended` section. The value is the new location for the profiles folder. For example, to store profiles under the C:\Settings folder, where C: is the default system drive, the answer file would need to contain the following:

```
[GUIUnattended]
profilesdir="%systemdrive%\Settings"
```

Useful Windows 2000 Environment Variables

The following list contains some of the more common environment variables used when referencing paths in Windows 2000. These environment variables can be used in most batch files, scripts, and policy settings to allow Windows 2000 to find special drives and folders without requiring an administrator to set up separate policies or scripts for differently configured systems or different users.

%logonserver%	Translates to the UNC-format server name (\\<*server*>) of the machine that authenticated the current user's logon information.
%systemdrive%	Translates to the volume letter of the drive on which Windows 2000 was installed. If Windows 2000 is installed to the default location on a system with a single drive, this environment variable would equate to C:\.
%systemroot%	Translates to the install location of Windows 2000. If Windows 2000 is installed to the default location on a system with a single drive, this environment variable would equate to C:\WINNT.
%username%	Translates to the user account name of the associated user. This variable is often entered as a path in the user manager, used in logon scripts, or referenced in batch files.
%userprofile%	Environment variable that translates to the path of the current user's local profile.

What happens if a machine has a local user account with the same name as an account on the domain with a roaming profile? For the most common example, consider the Administrator account. Each local machine has a local account named Administrator. In addition, each domain has an account named Administrator. If you first log onto the machine using the local Administrator account, the profile will be stored under the Administrator profile subfolder. When you then log on with the domain Administrator account from the MyDomain domain, the profile subfolder will be Administrator.MYDOMAIN.

If you used the domain account for the first logon, the domain Administrator profile subfolder will be Administrator. A subsequent logon using the local account on a computer named MyWin2K will be stored under the profile subfolder Administrator.MYWIN2K.

Important Profile-Management Group Policy Settings

Two important profile-related group policies are available to help manage roaming user profiles. Both can be found in any Active Directory group policy object under User Configuration\Administrative Templates\System\Logon/Logoff. The policies are as follows:

- Limit Profile Size
- Exclude Directories in Roaming Profile

The first policy, Limit Profile Size, enables an administrator to set a maximum profile size for the users' profile storage. If this policy is not set, the user quotas could potentially grow until they've used all the free space on the server. Options within this policy, illustrated in Figure 7.4, allow the administrator to configure a custom message to display to a user who exceeds his or her profile storage limit. Through the same policy, the message can be made to display repeatedly within a set interval of minutes. In addition, this policy has an option to include the registry utilization (used for application configuration settings) in the disk space utilization calculation. The user can't log off until his or her profile is back within the constraints of the quota.

The second policy, Exclude Directories in Roaming Profile, lets administrators select folders that will *not* be replicated to the server when the user logs off; instead, these files remain on the local PC where they were created. New and independent instances of these folders will exist on every PC where a user logs on. By default, the following folders are not replicated:

- Temporary Internet Files
- Temp
- History
- Local Settings

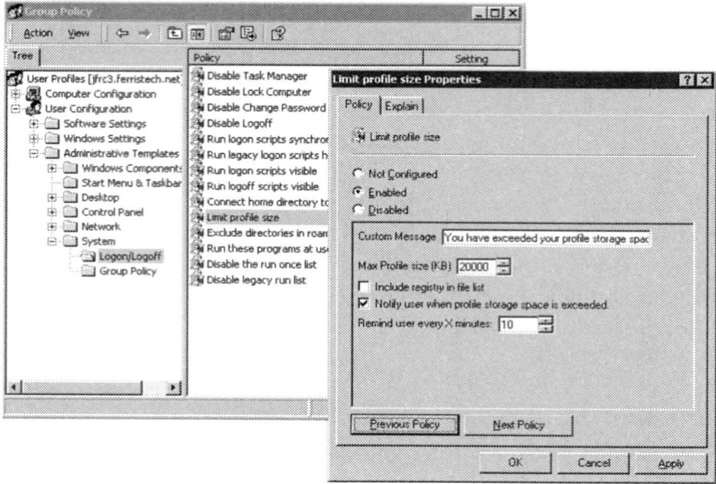

Figure 7.4 With the policy shown here, users are limited to 20MB profiles and the registry is not used in calculating the size utilization. If a user violates the quota, a pop-up message appears, advising the user to reduce his or her disk usage. This message will repeat every 10 minutes until the profile size is reduced to under 20MB.

Avoiding Unwanted Profiles

If you have a group of users for whom you don't want to store any profiles, either roaming or local, simply add their user accounts to the Domain Guests group. Windows 2000 will automatically delete the profile for any user account in a guest group when that user logs off a machine.

You can't enable the replication of the default excluded folders with this policy. You can, however, select additional folders that should *not* be replicated, as shown in Figure 7.5. If you choose not to configure this policy, the default subfolders will still be excluded from the roaming profile replication. Enter multiple subfolders by separating them with a semicolon. All entries should be entered as if the profile were the root folder.

Implementation Tips

Moving all of your user data, user configuration, and software installation tasks to the network is certain to affect your requirements on the back end. While these features are not particularly processor- or memory-intensive, they do have noticeable impact on network bandwidth (see the next section), drive utilization, and network storage (discussed together in the later section "Data Storage Considerations").

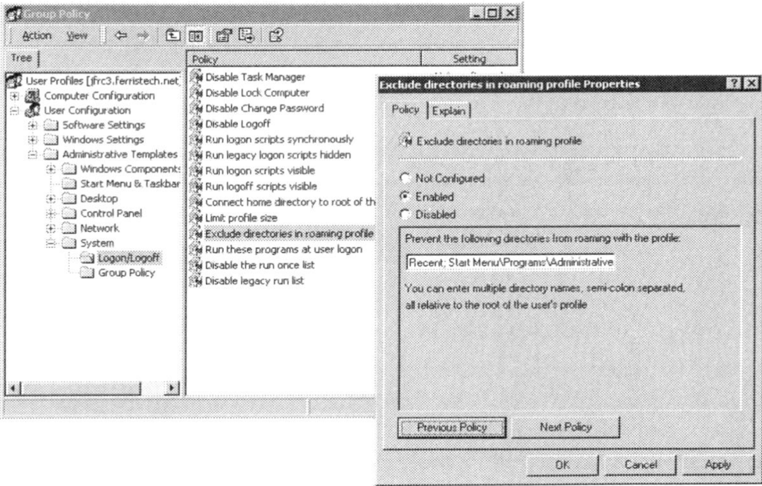

Figure 7.5 In this example, the policy has been configured to prevent the Recent and the Start Menu\Programs\Administrative Tools folders from being replicated from machine to machine.

Network Bandwidth Considerations

In most environments, network bandwidth utilization will experience three peak usage periods. The first peak occurs in the morning as the majority of users log on, installing new software packages and replicating profiles and documents from the servers down to the workstations. The second peak occurs around lunchtime. The final peak occurs as users log off for the day, when profiles are replicated back up to the network and offline documents are synchronized as the user logs off.

Let's return to the lunchtime peak. What might lead to a peak during the lunch hour? Many users log off before leaving for lunch, and log back on after returning. Either activity causes profile and document replication traffic. An additional and perhaps unexpected contributor to the lunchtime rush is the Synchronization Manager. By default, offline files are automatically synchronized after 15 minutes of idle time, and if the system remains idle, the process is repeated hourly.

Depending on the number of changed files between a file share and a workstation cache, this synchronization can generate a sizable amount of activity throughout the lunch hour. Fortunately, files that haven't changed are not replicated, so replication traffic for individual user shares is minimized; however, widely-accessed cached network shares can be another matter. If a single public cached network share is accessed by 500 people, and 10% of those people add or modify a file in the public share, a possible 25,000 documents (the 50 changed documents would be replicated to each of the 500 workstations) may need to be synchronized across the environment to reach all the users. Even if files receive only minor modifications, the changed files are transferred in their entirety. With larger environments and large document sizes, associated data traffic could potentially reach a fairly high level.

> **Determining Peak Periods**
> These peak periods won't apply to all environments. The best way to determine the peak usage in your environment is through the use of performance-monitoring software, such as Performance Monitor, included with Windows 2000.
>
> Performance analysis concepts for Windows 2000 Server are similar to those of Windows NT Server 4.0. For some suggested guidelines on performance analysis, see the Microsoft TechNet presentation "Performance Analysis and Optimization of Windows NT 4.0" at the following address:
>
> `http://www.microsoft.com/TechNet/events/agenda/perform.asp`

Data Storage Considerations

Network storage and drive utilization both fall under the category of data storage considerations. Because file servers are perhaps the most critical element of IntelliMirror, disk space utilization on the file servers could be much greater than with previous operating systems. Drive utilization could potentially experience the same peaks as network bandwidth utilization. As such, storage devices must be geared toward greater demand. Use large, fast, reliable, and dedicated storage devices for roaming user profile shares, roaming user document shares, and software installation share points.

Storage area networks (*SANs*) and/or *Network Attached Storage* (*NAS*) solutions are well-suited for IntelliMirror environments. A SAN is a specialized network of interconnected, high-speed, high-capacity data storage devices that combines the various data storage devices into a single accessible high-capacity storage resource for an enterprise network. A NAS is a specialized platform-independent storage appliance that provides instant "plug and play"–type network storage, simply by connecting a NAS appliance to your network.

Depending on the number of users in your environment, network storage requirements could become rather excessive. While User Settings Management can be limited with a policy setting, User Data Management is another matter. To limit space used by User Data Management, consider implementing *disk quotas*.

To enable a disk quota, follow these steps:

1. Start the Computer Management MMC for the applicable file server.
2. Under the Storage\Disk Management node, select the volume on which the root share for the redirected folder is located.
3. Right-click the volume and select Properties from the pop-up menu.
4. Click the Quota tab and select the Enable Quota Management option.
5. Configure the desired quota settings.
6. Use the Quota Entries button to select users for whom the quota should apply.

You also can configure quota settings directly from Windows Explorer. Simply open My Computer, right-click the applicable volume, and select Properties from the pop-up menu. Select the Quota tab and configure the desired quota settings.

You can't configure quota entries based on group membership. Unfortunately, you must add each individual user account to any quota entries. In addition, quotas can't be configured at the folder level; they can only be set on a per-volume basis, limiting disk space utilization for any folders or shares across the entire volume.

If you're preventing users from saving data to their local machines, be sure to provide plenty of storage space. You may want to consider technologies such as a *storage* area network (SAN) for mass network storage solutions, and *hierarchical storage management (HSM)* with *remote storage service (RSS)* to move seldom-accessed data to less expensive storage mediums. Refer to the "Remote Storage" topic in the Windows 2000 Server help file for more information on these technologies.

Disaster Recovery Considerations

Since all critical user data is now potentially stored on the network, don't overlook the importance of a disaster recovery plan. Disaster recovery preparations should include a minimum of regular data backups and protection from viruses. Data backups should include—at the very least—a combination of weekly full backups, nightly incremental backups, off-site archival of mission-critical backup sets, and redundant data storage mechanisms (for example, RAID sets).

In addition to regularly scheduled backups, antivirus software for Windows 2000 Server should be installed on all file servers and updated regularly. With the increase in virus activity throughout 1999, a number of companies experienced massive and costly data loss. With multiple users storing all critical data on a single server, it's important to protect the servers from such threats.

Protecting server-based storage from viruses will also require protecting client workstations with frequently updated antivirus software. Virus activity on a client computer can actually destroy server-based files without alerting the server's antivirus software. For example, the ExploreZip Trojan Horse virus from June, 1999, would search local and network drives for data files with .H, .C, .DOC, .XLS, .PPT, .ASM, or .CPP extensions, and attempt to delete any files it found. If a client machine were to become infected with the ExploreZip virus, the network-stored files would be deleted from the local machines. The server-based antivirus application may not detect the virus, because the code is actually executing on the client system.

Data Redundancy

For unique data, such as user settings and documents, redundancy and on-the-fly data protection—RAID 5, for example—is a must.

For software installation shares, you may have redundant data images distributed among a number of servers. If so, localized redundancy is not as important a consideration.

8

Application Management and Software Installation

THIS CHAPTER COVERS:

- How Application Management fits in with the Windows 2000 Change and Configuration Management model
- The difference between assigning and publishing applications
- The Application Management features of Windows 2000 that assist in the reduction of TCO
- How Windows 2000 Software Installation and Maintenance compares to SMS 2.0

After reading this chapter, you should be able to do the following:

- Publish applications in the Active Directory for users to select and install from the Add/Remove Programs applet
- Assign applications to users or computers in an install-on-demand configuration
- Configure Software Installation and Maintenance policies to upgrade or remove applications
- Select SMS or Windows 2000 Software Install services based on the needs of your environment

Managing and supporting software in a corporate environment without a centralized point of management can be a costly and time-consuming exercise. In an environment without centralized software distribution, users may not be able to install software on their own workstations. As such, any time new software is needed, or any time existing software needs to be reinstalled or upgraded, someone with administrative rights must physically interact with the machine. Some environments have attempted to remedy this situation by configuring all users with local administrative rights, so users will be able to install any software at any time. Obviously, this is not a preferred environment; it would be impossible to maintain a consistently managed desktop. The Software Installation and Maintenance features of Windows 2000 address these concerns.

Software Installation and Maintenance enables you to configure group policy objects for installing, removing, upgrading, and managing software for users and computers across sites, domains, and organizational units (SDOU). These applications can be configured to install only when needed. By assigning applications to a user, the applications can "follow" the user through your environment to any system where the user logs on. This chapter discusses the features of Software Installation and Maintenance that help reduce Total Cost of Ownership (TCO) and administrative overhead associated with application management.

Introduction to the Software Installation and Maintenance Features

The idea of centralized software management is not new. Products such as Microsoft's SMS, Tivoli's Application Management Suite, and Computer Associates' Unicenter TNG have provided some software management capabilities for a number of years. But Windows 2000 Software Installation and Maintenance is the first application-management package built in as a core feature of the network operating system (OS).

Integrating Software Installation and Maintenance services with the core OS provides certain features not yet available with existing third-party solutions. Windows 2000 Software Installation and Maintenance is fully integrated with the Active Directory. Without Active Directory, there is no way to use Software Installation and Maintenance services. Application management is enabled and controlled via group policy objects (GPOs). Using GPOs means that Software Installation and Maintenance policies will be aware of sites, domains, and organizational units within your Active Directory. From the client end, Software Installation and Maintenance requires the Windows Installer on a Windows 2000 client workstation or server that is participating in the Active Directory.

Software Installation and Maintenance is considered a part of the IntelliMirror technology suite. The IntelliMirror features, which enable applications, documents, and settings to follow a user from machine to machine, are described in detail in Chapter 7, "IntelliMirror." The Software Installation services fit in with the Windows 2000 Change and Configuration Management model as shown in Figure 8.1. The

Software Installation and Maintenance component of IntelliMirror provides two important functions:

- **Application availability**: Applications follow users from machine to machine, so users never have to be without their critical applications when roaming within the environment.
- **System recoverability**: If a user's workstation is damaged and needs to be replaced, Remote Installation Services can reinstall the operating system, Software Installation and Maintenance can then reinstall the user's software, User Settings Management recovers the user-specific application settings, and User Data Management can restore the user's important data files. These features help reduce TCO associated with recovering from unexpected machine failures.

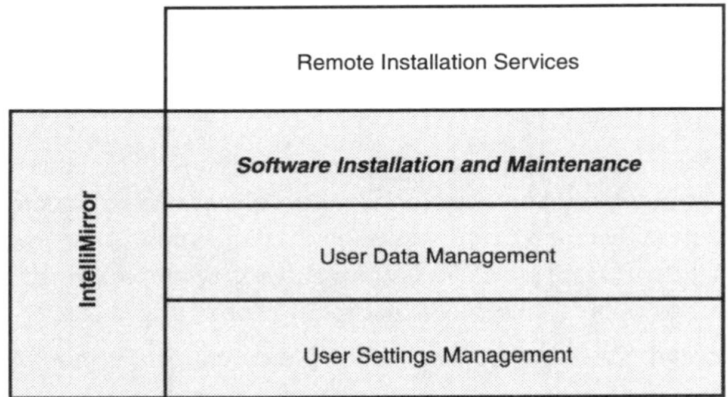

Figure 8.1 Software Installation and Maintenance is an integral part of the Windows 2000 Change and Configuration Management model.

The scope of the Software Installation and Maintenance policy is managed as with any other group policy object. (See Chapter 6, "Group Policy Objects," for more detail on defining the scope for a GPO.) Software Installation and Maintenance enables user- or machine-based application installation and configuration. Through the combined use of the Windows Installer, the Active Directory, and group policy objects, you can configure applications to be assigned or published to user or computer accounts.

A key issue for administrators is that Windows 2000 Software Installation and Maintenance is absolutely dependent on Windows 2000 technologies. Down-level clients, such as Windows NT 4.0 and Windows 9x, don't include these technologies, and are therefore unable to take advantage of Software Installation and Maintenance. For an environment with a large number of down-level clients, software management must be handled with a third-party application.

Microsoft provides Active Directory clients for both Windows 9x (on the Windows 2000 CD under the \clients\win9x folder) and Windows NT 4.0 (included with Service Pack 7). The down-level AD client provides site awareness, *Active Directory*

Services Interface (*ADSI*) compatibility, searching capability, enhanced authentication via NTLMv2, and access to directory information (such as user property pages) in the Active Directory. It doesn't provide support for Kerberos authentication, group policy objects, or IntelliMirror technologies. The Windows Installer is installed on down-level clients along with Office 2000, and can be installed as a stand-alone application. But even with the AD client and the Windows Installer technologies installed, the down-level clients can't take advantage of the Windows 2000 Software Installation and Maintenance feature.

Before getting into the technical implementation details of Software Installation and Maintenance, it's important to have a high-level picture of how the process flows:

1. The administrator selects an application package to deploy, copies the installation files to a file server, and configures a Software Installation policy in an Active Directory GPO. The application package can be published to users or assigned to users or computers. (For a comparison of published applications versus assigned applications, see the later section "Installing and Managing Applications.")
2. The applicable user or computer logs onto the Active Directory. If the application was assigned, the Software Installation policy is downloaded and processed immediately. If the application was published, the application won't install until the user selects it from the Add/Remove Programs applet in the Control Panel, or attempts to open a document that requires the application.
3. Once initiated, the Software Installation policy tells the Windows Installer service on the client machine to run an installation package from the share point defined in the policy. The files required by the application package must have the proper file and share permissions applied so that the applicable user or computer can read and execute the package over the network.
4. The application setup process runs on the client machine. Depending on the features of the application package and the options selected in the Software Installation policy, this could occur with or without user interaction. The entire application may not be installed at this stage; often, subsequent utilization of features or optional application components will require additional access to the application's setup files.

Setting Up Software Installation and Maintenance

Setting up Software Installation and Maintenance is a relatively straightforward process. Because all required services and components are built into Windows 2000, there's no need to install any additional software services on the client or server side. There are, however, a few basic Windows 2000 infrastructure requirements.

As mentioned earlier, Software Installation and Maintenance won't function without the Active Directory. Active Directory enables the creation and assignment of the group policy objects needed to implement Software Installation and Maintenance policies. The later section "Installing and Managing Applications" walks through the creation of these policies. Because the clients must be able to install the software over the network, you'll need an available file server in addition to an Active Directory controller. Note that in very small networks or testing environments, it's acceptable to use a file share on the Active Directory controller; just remember to use a Universal Naming Convention (UNC) path rather than a local path when creating Software Installation and Maintenance policies.

Setting Up a Software Distribution Server

Applications installed via Software Installation and Maintenance require the setup files to be available from a network share location. Even if you're setting up your software installation policy from the same server that will host the application files, you must address the file location by using a UNC path. You can't point to a drive letter—whether a local or a mapped network drive—or client machines won't know where to find application setup files.

Make sure that the share permissions and NTFS permissions for the source files allow proper security permissions for the required user groups. For the software installation share point, users should need only the Read and Execute NTFS permission.

Note: When restricting access to a file share, the preferred practice is to set permissions through NTFS File and Folder security, and leave the Sharing security set to Full Control. This minimizes the potential for resource permission conflicts, and ensures that all users have the same access to files whether they access them over the network or (for some reason) are logged on from the local file server console.

I recommend creating a centralized share point, such as *<FileServer>*\Software$, under which individual application installation folders will be located. Put each application in its own subfolder, even if the install is only a single *.MSI file. Doing so will make the share point cleaner to manage. In addition, all application folders can be viewed in alphabetical order. With mixed files and folders in the installation share point, all folders would be listed first, and single file installs would be listed at the end. Problems would arise if two setup programs used the same name (for example, SETUP.MSI), because you could accidentally overwrite a file needed for a different software installation policy.

Note: Don't count solely on group policy objects to prevent users from installing their own applications; mirror NTFS permissions after GPO filters to prevent unauthorized users from finding the installation source files. In other words, if you restrict a group of users from installing a software package through Software Installation and Maintenance policies because you don't want them installing the software, be sure to set NTFS permissions on the installation file(s) as well, to prevent users from browsing the network shares and manually running the application setup program.

Depending on the size of your environment, you may want to further break down the top level of the file share folder into application groups. For example, Figure 8.2 shows a departmentalized folder structure. Common applications required for all users are under the COMMON.REQ folder. Common applications that are optional according to the user's preferences are under COMMON.OPT. Applications specific to departments or functions are under the additional subfolders. NTFS folder-level permissions are applied to prevent file access from unauthorized users.

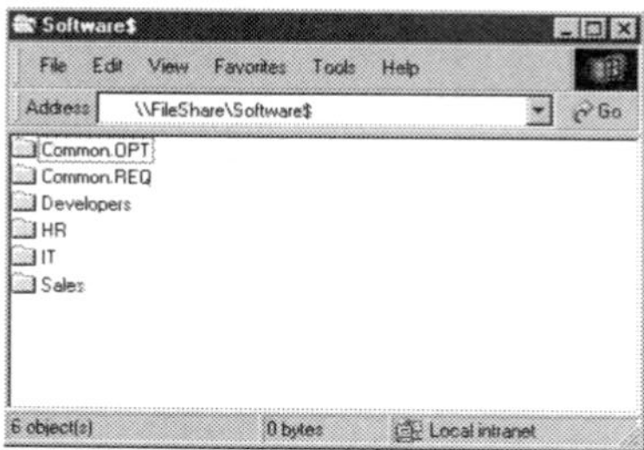

Figure 8.2 In this sample folder structure for the application installation share point, application subfolders have been departmentalized.

Software Installation and Maintenance Client Considerations

Using Windows 2000 Software Installation and Maintenance requires a Windows 2000 client machine. As stated previously, down-level clients won't work with the Software Installation and Maintenance feature, even though they may be able to utilize the Windows Installer and interact with the Active Directory. The client can be running Windows 2000 Professional or any member of the Windows 2000 Server family. Since Software Installation and Maintenance is dependent on both Active Directory and group policy objects, the target client machine must be a member of an Active Directory domain (if software will be assigned to computer accounts), and the user account must be a member of the Active Directory (if software will be assigned or published to user accounts).

Load Balancing with DFS

To increase the availability and accessibility of the application installation share in large or distributed corporate environments, look into implementing *DFS*, the *Distributed File System*. DFS provides a mechanism by which administrators can create a single logical share location that includes multiple physical file servers with redundant replicated content. DFS is site aware and can automatically load-balance client access to DFS file shares.

For more information on implementing DFS under Windows 2000, see the Windows 2000 Server Help or point your Web browser to this address:

`http://www.microsoft.com/windows2000/library/howitworks/fileandprint/dfsnew.asp`

There is no special client-side software or configuration change needed to enable Windows 2000 Software Installation and Maintenance on client machines. The Windows Installer service—the basic service required to use Software Installation and Maintenance—is installed and enabled by default. This service must be running to take advantage of the Windows 2000 Software Installation and Maintenance features.

Educating the Users

Whatever software installation method you may have used in the past—whether users could install their own software, a client service installed the software after hours, or users called technicians for software installs—don't overlook the importance of educating users on the new method for finding and installing applications. These are the main points of concern of which users should be aware:

- Applications published in the Active Directory are available for installation through the Add/Remove Programs applet of the Control Panel.
- Applications that have been installed through normal means, such as from CD media or a file share, may first be uninstalled when accessed through the Add/Remove Programs applet.
- An application installed under one user account via Software Installation and Maintenance won't be accessible automatically by other users logging onto the same system. For example, if an application is published and must be installed through the Add/Remove Programs Control Panel applet, all local users who want to use the application must install the application through the Control Panel, even if those users are logging onto a system on which a previous user had already installed the software.
- If applications have been assigned to the computer, it may take the computer a longer time before displaying the logon screen. There's nothing wrong with the system; don't reboot when the boot process seems to be running too long.
- If applications have been assigned to a user, it may take a longer time from the point at which the user enters his or her logon information until the system displays the desktop. Fortunately, Windows 2000 displays status information between logging on and displaying the desktop. Depending on the amount of software being installed, this status information may not change for an extended period of time. There's nothing wrong with the system; don't reboot when the logon process seems to be running too long.
- Occasionally, when opening a document for which application software hasn't been installed, or utilizing a software feature for the first time, the Windows Installer window may pop up, and the application or document may seem unresponsive. This is normal behavior while the Windows Installer installs the application or feature. It may occur multiple times, depending on the application or application features being accessed.

Installing and Managing Applications

The primary use of Software Installation and Maintenance is to allow applications to install on a user's workstation without needing to send out a technician or grant administrative rights to a user. Many applications can be installed with no user interaction. Distributing software with Software Installation and Maintenance helps reduce TCO associated with traditional application installation processes. There are three ways to use the Software Installation and Maintenance service to distribute applications to the desktop. Applications can be

- Published to a user
- Assigned to a computer
- Assigned to a user

The following sections describe these three methods.

Publishing Application Packages

Applications that are published in the Active Directory will be available to users through the Add New Programs option in the Add/Remove Programs applet in the Control Panel. Published applications are not distributed automatically to the workstations, so users can decide for themselves whether—and when—they need to install applications that have been published.

Applications that can be published include both Windows Installer packages (*.MSI files) and ZAW (Zero Administration for Windows) application packages (*.ZAP files). A ZAP file is a plain-text file describing certain installation parameters for an application utilizing a standard setup executable. ZAP files are the less flexible of the two options. Install routines utilizing a ZAP file must be installable in the security context of the logged-on user, whereas MSI files can install with elevated privileges. This means that MSI-based installs can be configured to run as the local administrator, regardless of the security permissions of the logged-on user. ZAP file installations, however, will only be successful if they could normally be run with the privileges of the logged-on user.

Exercise 8.1 walks through creating a GPO to publish the Windows 2000 Administration Tools (ADMINPAK.MSI) to an organizational unit (OU).

Exercise 8.1 **Publish an Application**

Time Required: 30 minutes

Requirements: Windows 2000 Active Directory domain, Windows 2000 client machine, Windows 2000 file and print server, Windows 2000 Server installation CD

This exercise uses the Group Policy Editor through the Active Directory Users and Computers snap-in for the MMC to configure a group policy object to publish the Windows 2000 Administration Tools to an Administrators organizational unit (OU).

Before beginning this exercise, select a file share location for the software you will be distributing. For purposes of this exercise, I'll refer to this share location as \\<*FileServer*>\Software$. In the \\<*FileServer*>\Software$ share, create a subfolder named AdminTools. Copy the ADMINPAK.MSI file from the i386 folder of your Windows 2000 Server CD into the AdminTools folder. The complete path to this file should be \\<*FileServer*>\Software$\AdminTools\Adminpak.msi.

Step 1 In the Active Directory Users and Computers snap-in, create an OU named **Administrators**. Create a user account, **ADMIN1**, in the Administrators OU.

Step 2 Right-click the Administrators OU and select Properties from the pop-up menu. Select the Group Policy tab and click New to create a new GPO. Name the new GPO **Software Distribution**.

Step 3 Double-click the Software Distribution GPO to open the Group Policy Editor.

Step 4 Expand the User Configuration\Software Settings node. You should see Software Installation.

Step 5 Right-click Software Installation, point to New, and then click Package from the New submenu as shown in Figure 8.3.

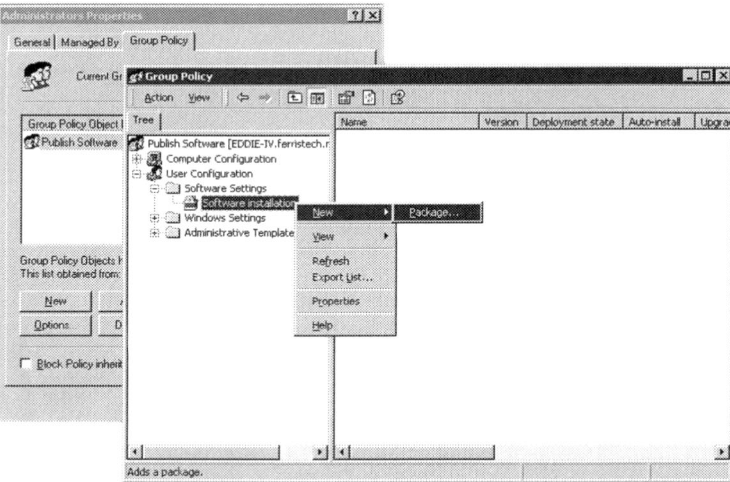

Figure 8.3 Adding a new Software Installation package.

Step 6 When the Open With dialog box appears, enter the full path to the Administrative Tools in the File Name box (\\<*FileServer*>\Software$\AdminTools\Adminpak.msi).

Step 7 The Deploy Software dialog box opens (see Figure 8.4). Select Published as the deployment method and click OK.

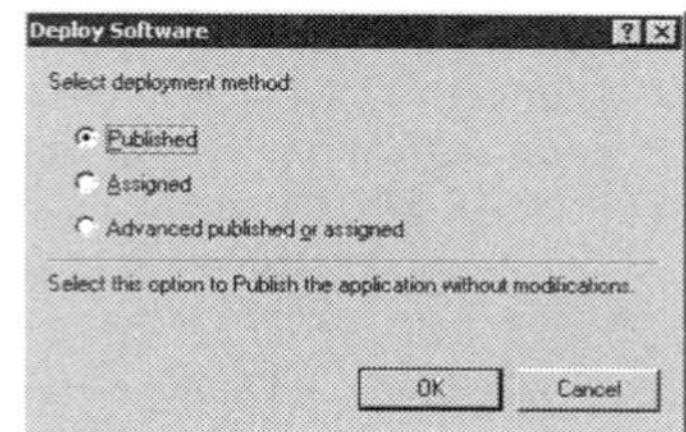

Figure 8.4 Select the type of application deployment from this box.

Step 8 The Windows 2000 Administration Tools package should now show up under the application list for the Software Installation policy. You can close the Group Policy Editor and the Active Directory Users and Computers console.

To see the effects of the new published software policy, log onto a client machine as ADMIN1. In the Add/Remove Programs applet of the Control Panel, you should see Windows 2000 Administration Tools listed under the Add New Programs option.

Assigning Application Packages

With assigned applications, application software is automatically installed for applicable user or computer accounts. Application assignment is typically used to install required software packages without prompting or interaction from the end user.

If an application is assigned to a computer account, the software will install on the next reboot of the computer. If an application is assigned to a user, the system creates shortcuts on the user's desktop or program menu, and the package installs the first time the user opens the application's shortcut. It's generally best to assign an application to a user account rather than a computer account. Applications assigned to computers are installed by default; applications assigned to users are only installed when first executed. If an application assigned to a user is never accessed, the application takes up no space on the local hard drive. In addition, assigning an application to a large number of computers will distribute the package during the next startup of the computer. If a package is distributed during off-hours, and the users all boot their systems in the morning, the application must install to all the systems at the same time, rather than installing on an as-requested basis.

Applications cannot be assigned unless their installation routines are built to take advantage of the Windows Installer. These files will have an .MSI extension. You can't use application assignment for executable files (such as SETUP.EXE) or *.ZAP files. Exercise 8.2 walks through converting a published software installation package into an assigned software installation package.

Exercise 8.2 **Assign an Application**

Time Required: 10 minutes

Requirements: Completion of Exercise 8.1

This exercise uses the Group Policy Editor through the Active Directory Users and Computers snap-in for the MMC to reconfigure the Windows 2000 Administration Tools as an assigned installation package, rather than a published installation package.

Step 1 In the Active Directory Users and Computers snap-in, select the Administrators organizational unit created in Exercise 8.1.

Step 2 Right-click the Administrators OU and select Properties from the pop-up menu. Select the Group Policy tab and double-click the Software Distribution policy to open the Group Policy Editor.

Step 3 Expand the User Configuration\Software Settings node. Select the Software Installation policy.

Step 4 In the right-side panel, right-click the Windows 2000 Administration Tools package. Select Assign from the pop-up menu.

You have now converted the Windows 2000 Administration Tools from a published application to an assigned application. To see the effects of the assigned software policy, log onto a client machine as ADMIN1. Under Start, Programs, there should be an Administrative Tools group containing links for all of the tools from the AdminPak.MSI file. Clicking one of the icons will start the Windows Installer service, install the Windows 2000 Administration Tools, and start the tool you selected from the program group.

Rather than converting the published package, you could also create the initial package as an assigned application by following all the steps in Exercise 8.1, but selecting Assigned rather than Published as the deployment method in step 7 (refer to Figure 8.4).

Converting an assigned package to a published package works the same way as in this exercise—simply right-click the assigned package and select Publish from the pop-up menu.

Document Association

By default, applications that are assigned or published are configured to install automatically if a user attempts to open a file with an extension associated to the application through the Active Directory software installation policy. This can minimize the number of times the familiar Open With dialog box pops up when a user attempts to open a document with an unrecognized extension. If you want to disable this behavior for a particular software package, deselect the option Auto-Install This Application by File Extension Activation on the Deployment tab of the package's properties page.

Software Installation Default Properties

The default behavior when creating new Software Installation packages can be modified on a per-policy basis by right-clicking the Software Installation policy from the Software Settings node of either the Computer Configuration or User Configuration section. Select Properties from the pop-up menu to display the general properties used for all software distribution packages created under the current GPO. There are three tabs in the resulting dialog box:

- General
- File Extensions
- Categories

Only the configuration options set under Categories are static throughout the domain. Options on both the General tab and the File Extensions tab are specific to the policy being modified.

The General tab lets you set certain defaults to use in the creation of all new software installation packages. As Figure 8.5 shows, the default package share location, behavior when creating a new package, installation interface options, and uninstall management option can all be configured through this interface. You may want to use the General tab to configure defaults when adding a large number of similarly configured applications to your environment. For example, if you will be publishing a number of applications from the same share and want all of them to use the basic user interface, make those settings on the General tab to minimize the configuration changes necessary for each package.

For Software Installation packages created under the policy in Figure 8.5, the following settings apply:

- The package creation wizard will look for *.MSI files in the \\<*FileServer*>\Software$ share.
- New packages will always display the Deploy Software dialog box.

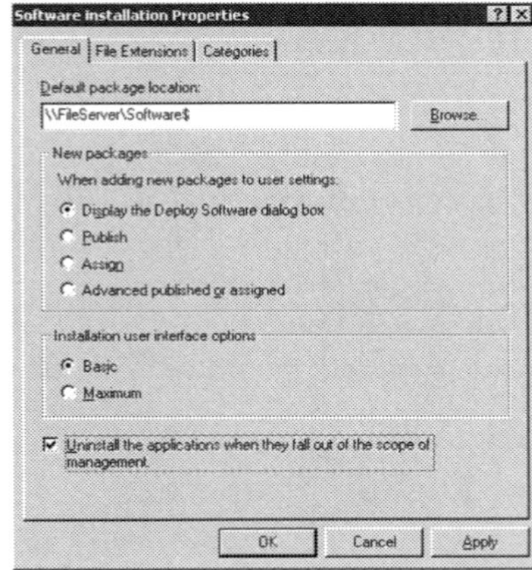

Figure 8.5 Creating a policy for software installation.

- Packages will be configured to use the basic user interface initially.
- Applications are configured by default to uninstall when they fall outside the scope of the GPO.

The File Extensions tab configures the preferred application to install when a user triggers a software installation package by starting a document with an extension recognized by the Windows Installer service, but not recognized by the user's local machine. For example, suppose you publish Office 2000 in the Active Directory, but a user hasn't yet installed the package on his or her machine. If the user attempts to open a Microsoft Word document (*.DOC), but the file is not recognized by the machine, the local Windows Installer service will check the Active Directory to see whether any published or assigned applications recognize the *.DOC extension. If so, and if the user has been granted access permission to the policy and the install share, Microsoft Office will install to the machine, and the Word document will open in Microsoft Word.

The Categories tab enables you to add, delete, or modify existing categories available for the packages distributed using the Software Installation and Maintenance feature. These categories show up under the Add/Remove Programs applet of the Control Panel, as shown in Figure 8.6.

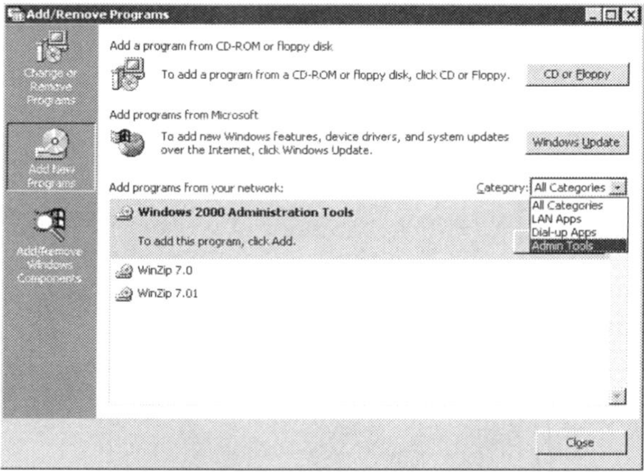

Figure 8.6 The Add New Programs panel displays available software packages. The Categories option lists the categories defined in the Properties panel of the Software Installation policy.

Individual Application Package Properties

Regardless of the initial method used to deploy an application, packages created under the Software Installation policy of the Active Directory all have a common Properties dialog box. You can't view this dialog box until you've created a software installation package. The earlier Exercises 8.1 and 8.2 walk through the creation of such packages for deployment of the Windows 2000 Administration Tools. After completing Exercise 8.2, the Windows 2000 Administration Tools Properties dialog box contains six tabs:

- General
- Deployment
- Upgrades
- Categories
- Modifications
- Security

General Options

The General tab, as the name implies, contains general product and support information. The only configurable option on this tab is the name of the deployment package. This is the name that will appear in the Add/Remove Programs applet of the Control Panel. This tab also displays general read-only information about the selected package (such as publisher, version number, and support information) as contained within the MSI or ZAP file used to create the package.

Deployment Options

The Deployment tab, shown in Figure 8.7, allows you to configure the deployment settings for the selected package. From this tab, you can configure a package to install via the published or assigned method, to auto-install when a document with an associated extension is activated, to uninstall when the GPO no longer applies to an associated computer or user account, to display or conceal the package in the Add/Remove Programs applet, and/or to install using a Basic or Maximum amount of user interaction.

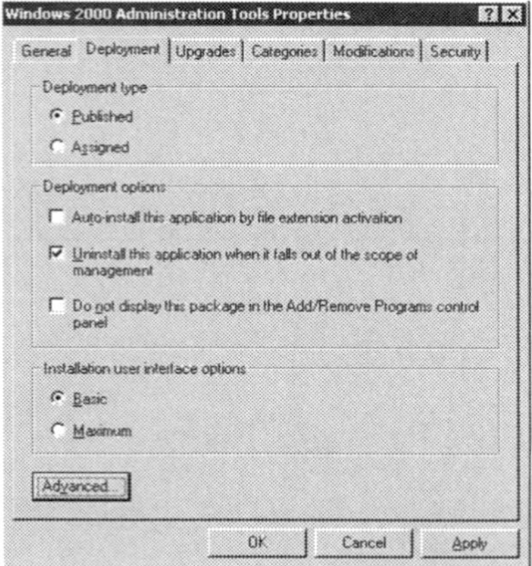

Figure 8.7 Deployment options.

In the example in Figure 8.7, the Windows 2000 Administration Tools software installation package, the package has been configured with the following settings:

- Published deployment type.
- The package will not install by file extension activation, but will be displayed in the Add/Remove Programs Control Panel.
- When the related GPO no longer applies to a user, the package will be removed automatically.
- Setting the user interface option to Basic ensures that installation of this package will require the minimum amount of user interaction.

Most of the options on the Deployment tab are fairly self-explanatory; the two that warrant additional clarification are the option to uninstall the application when it falls out of the scope of management, and the installation user interface options.

The option to uninstall an application when it falls out of the scope of management controls the behavior of the application package when it no longer applies to a user or computer account. For example, consider two organizational units, SalesOU and MarketingOU. SalesOU includes a software installation package for an application through which a member of the sales staff can view detailed customer order information. Since no one outside of the sales staff should have access to this information, the package is configured to uninstall when it falls outside the scope of management. Tim is a member of the sales staff, and his user account is in the SalesOU. Tim received the sales application through Software Installation and Maintenance. Tim leaves Sales to work in Marketing, so his user account is moved from SalesOU to MarketingOU, meaning he is no longer within the scope of management for any GPOs defined at the SalesOU level. The sales application will automatically be uninstalled the next time group policy is refreshed for Tim's account.

The Installation User Interface options contain the Basic and Maximum selections. Selecting Basic causes the application to display only the installation progress dialog box while installing. The user can't interact with the installation in any way. The Maximum option displays all installation messages, screens, and progress dialog boxes throughout the installation. Some applications will only work with the Basic option. Microsoft Office 2000, for example, can't be configured to use the Maximum user interface option, or the install will fail. Whether an application supports Basic and/or Maximum installation options depends on the behaviors enabled in the setup package.

Notice also the Advanced button on the Deployment tab. With this option, you can configure the selected package with the following two options:

- Ignore Language for Region-Specific Applications.
- Remove Any Prior Installations of the Same Software if the Package Was Not Installed by Group Policy.

The Advanced options also display the product code (as a GUID), and the deployment count for the package.

Upgrades Options

The Upgrades tab displays packages that the selected package will upgrade, as well as other packages within the same GPO that will upgrade the selected package. If the package will be used to upgrade existing applications, the option Required Upgrade for Existing Packages can be enabled to force the package to upgrade existing installations.

Categories Options

The Categories tab lets you select categories under which a package will appear in the Add/Remove Programs applet of the Control Panel. The left pane displays available categories for the package; the right pane displays categories assigned to the selected package.

You can't create new categories from this screen. To modify the categories list, right-click the Software Installation policy from the Software Settings node of either the Computer Configuration or User Configuration section. Select Properties from the pop-up menu. This displays the general properties used for all software distribution packages created under the current GPO. The Categories tab allows you to add, delete, or modify existing categories available for the packages throughout the domain.

Modifications Options

A *transform* (recognizable by its .MST extension) is a Microsoft Installer file used to customize an *.MSI-based install package. Transforms are usually either included with an application or created through an installer utility customized for the given application. For example, you can set the default installation options for Microsoft Office 2000 by creating a transform using the Custom Installation Wizard included with the Office 2000 Resource Kit (information about the Office 2000 Resource Kit is available at `http://www.microsoft.com/office/ork/2000/default.htm`). Transforms that have been applied to a package appear on the Modifications tab. When creating an install package the first time, all transforms must be entered through the Advanced Published or Assigned package setup before clicking OK.

> **Apply Transforms Before Completing the Package**
>
> *Warning:* Once an application has been published or assigned, transforms cannot be added or deleted, and their order of application cannot be modified, without creating an upgrade package or removing and re-creating the package.

Security Options

The Security tab is the standard object permissions interface (similar in appearance to the NTFS permissions interface) that appears on Windows 2000 directory objects. From this window, you can configure security groups or individual users to have Read, Write, or Full Control permissions to the package being configured. If the Read permission is denied for a group of users, the package won't be installable through the Windows Installer service.

Upgrading an Application

Upgrading an application package with a new application package is facilitated by configuration options set on the Upgrades tab of the package's Properties dialog box, as described earlier. You should configure upgrade options through the newer package being used to upgrade an older package.

For example, suppose you deploy Microsoft Office, in a package named Microsoft Office 2000—Default. Now, if you use the Office 2000 Custom Installation Wizard from the Office 2000 Resource Kit to create a custom transform (*.MST) file, you could add a new package named Microsoft Office 2000—Customized. You may want to remove the default Office configuration in favor of the custom configured package. You would set this up through the Upgrades tab, like this:

1. Open the properties for Microsoft Office 2000—Customized.
2. Click Add on the Upgrades tab.
3. Select the current GPO or specify a different GPO containing the Microsoft Office 2000—Default policy.
4. Select the name of the package.
5. Specify whether you want to uninstall the existing package or simply upgrade over the existing package.

When you have completed the configuration, the Upgrades tab of the Microsoft Office 2000—Customized package properties would list Microsoft Office 2000—Default in the top box, labeled Packages That This Package Will Upgrade. The same tab on the Default version of the package will contain Microsoft Office 2000—Customized in the bottom box (Packages in the Current GPO That Will Upgrade This Package).

Using the same process, you can automatically deploy the upgrade of Office 2000 to the next major release version of Office (when available). This feature helps keep software up to date throughout the environment. Because of the ability to remove packages before upgrading, you can even use software installation policies to "upgrade" one product to an entirely new application. For example, let's say that Microsoft Works is your current office suite, and you want to upgrade to Microsoft Office 2000. If Works was deployed using a software installation policy, you could create a package for Microsoft Office 2000 and configure the package to upgrade Works by first removing the previous package. Even though Works can't be upgraded to Office through an in-place upgrade, the remove-then-install upgrade procedure can be used to accomplish the goal.

Removing a Deployed Package

Once a Windows Installer–ready application has been deployed through the Active Directory, whether assigned or published, removing the application from connected users and computers is a simple process:

1. Open the related group policy object and find the application in the Software Installation policy.

2. Right-click the application, select All Tasks from the pop-up menu, and select Remove from the submenu. The resulting dialog box gives you two options:
   - **Immediately Uninstall the Software from Users and Computers.** This option will remove the package from all connected users and computers to which the package has been deployed. Users who are roaming and not connected to the network will still be able to use the software until they connect to the Active Directory and the updated policy is applied. Computers that are not powered on will have the software uninstalled the next time they start up, and users who are not logged on will have the software removed at their next logon.
   - **Allow Users to Continue to Use the Software, But Prevent New Installations.** This option prevents new installations, but doesn't affect users who have already installed a published package. In addition, users won't be able to repair removed applications through the Add/Remove Programs applet.

ZAP files don't provide the same options. Because ZAP files don't take advantage of all features of the Windows Installer, removing an application deployed via a ZAP file presents only one option: Remove the Package But Leave the Application Installed Everywhere It Is Already Installed. Removing the application from user machines where it has been installed must be performed from the local machine's Add/Remove Programs applet in the Control Panel.

Preparing Applications for the Windows Installer

Windows 2000 Software Installation and Maintenance doesn't install software using standard setup executables; instead, the application install must support the Windows Installer. These installation programs appear as *.MSI files. Older applications, obviously, won't include *.MSI packages; the standards didn't exist until recently. Office 2000 is an example of an application that includes an *.MSI installation option. Modifications to the installs performed by *.MSI files are performed by Microsoft Installer Transform (*.MST) files, as described in the earlier section "Modifications Options."

All Windows 2000 Service Packs, patches, and related files will be installable via the Windows Installer in the form of Windows Installer Patches (*.MSP files). MSP files cannot be used to remove components or features, to change product codes, or to remove or change the names of shortcuts, files, or registry keys.

Even upgrades from Windows 2000 Beta 3 and Windows 2000 Release Candidates can be completed using a WINNT32.MSI file included with the Windows 2000 release code. It's expected that future major release upgrades of the core operating system will be able to utilize Windows Installer–based upgrade packages.

For applications that don't include any of the preceding Windows Installer–recognized installation packages, there are two options:

- The installation can be repackaged with a third-party utility to create a self-contained *.MSI file. These repackaged files can be either published or assigned. The Windows 2000 CD includes the WinINSTALL Limited Edition MSI repackager from Veritas software (see the next section for details).
- The second option is to create a *.ZAP file to kick off the default setup routine for the application. Application installs using *.ZAP files cannot be assigned, only published. ZAP-based installations are not self-healing; the only way to repair a damaged installation is to reinstall the entire package. In addition, ZAP installations cannot install using elevated privileges; they must install at the same security level as the associated user. Because a *.ZAP file kicks off the default install routine for an application, the application can only install without user intervention if the initial installation routine didn't require user intervention.

Repackaging an Application for Software Installation and Maintenance

To repackage a setup application for distribution with Software Installation and Maintenance, you must convert the existing installation to a Windows Installer–based installation. This requires the creation of an MSI file to replace any functions required to install the application. A number of third-party repackagers are available, including the following:

- InstallShield for Windows Installer from InstallShield (`http://www.installshield.com`)
- WinINSTALL from VERITAS (`http://www.veritas.com`)
- Wise for Windows Installer from Wise Solutions (`http://www.wisesolutions.com`)

A limited edition (LE) version of VERITAS WinINSTALL is included with Windows 2000, on the Windows 2000 installation CD-ROM under the folder named \VALUEADD\3RDPARTY\MGMT\WINSTLE. WinINSTALL LE repackages applications in a manner similar to that of the SYSDIFF utility (described near the end of Chapter 4, "Answer Files and the Setup Manager Wizard"). WinINSTALL LE first takes a snapshot of the system state, including files and registry settings. You then install an application, configure the application, and take another snapshot. The system state snapshots are compared, and the differences are wrapped into an MSI file that can then be assigned or published via the Windows 2000 Software Installation and Maintenance feature. Exercise 8.3 walks through creating a Windows Installer file to deploy WinZip.

Exercise 8.3 **Repackaging WinZip for Software Installation and Maintenance**

Time Required: 45 minutes

Requirements:

- WinZip setup files, available from `http://www.winzip.com`. Save the file as **C:\WZSetup.EXE**.
- WinINSTALL LE, available from the Windows 2000 installation CD, under \VALUEADD\3RDPARTY\MGMT\WINSTLE.
- Clean installation of Windows 2000 Professional without WinZip installed. It's important to complete this process on a system that has *never* had WinZip installed. For this exercise, you should use a Windows 2000 Professional machine with a single drive (C:\), with Windows 2000 installed in C:\WINNT.

This exercise uses the WinINSTALL LE repackager (from VERITAS Software Corporation) included with Windows 2000 to create an installation package for WinZip (from Nico Mak Computing, Inc.) that can be deployed using Software Installation and Maintenance.

Step 1 Install WinINSTALL LE on a clean install of Windows 2000 Professional by running the SWIADMLE.MSI file, which is located in the folder \VALUEADD\3RDPARTY\MGMT\WINSTLE\ on the Windows 2000 CD.

Step 2 Run the VERITAS Discover application from the VERITAS Software program group (Start, Programs, VERITAS Software, VERITAS Discover).

Step 3 The dialog boxes in the VERITAS Discover application walk you through the process of creating the initial system snapshot. Click Next on the introductory screen.

Step 4 The next screen prompts you for the name of the application and the path at which to create the MSI file. As illustrated in Figure 8.8, enter **WinZip** as the application name, and **C:\Packages\Winzip.MSI** for the path and filename. Click Next. If the C:\Packages folder doesn't exist, VERITAS Discover will prompt you to create it. Click Yes to create the destination path.

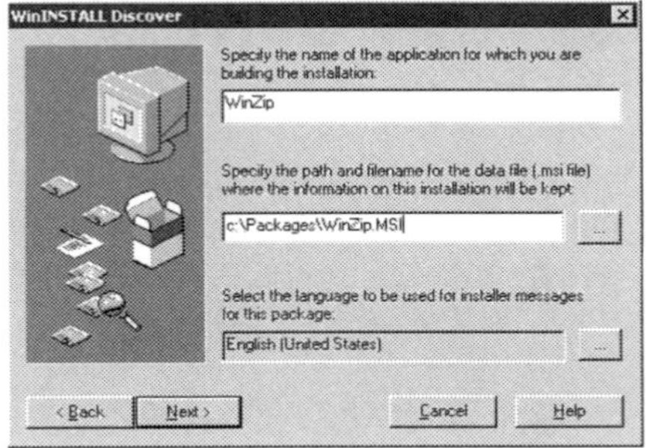

Figure 8.8 Creating the "Before" snapshot in VERITAS Discover: entering the application name and MSI path.

Step 5 The next screen prompts you to select a drive on which to store the temporary work files. Depending on the size of your installation, these files can grow to be quite large. Select `[-c-]` and click Next to continue.

Step 6 The next screen asks you to select drives to scan for changes. Select `[-c-]` from the Available Drives column and click the Add button to move drive C: to the Drives to Scan column. Click Next.

Step 7 On the next screen, select the folders that should *not* be scanned for changes. (Exclude any folders on drive C: that you're certain won't be modified by the application you're repackaging.) When you click Next, WinINSTALL LE Discover will scan and record information about your current system, including files, INI file settings, and registry entries.

Step 8 When scanning is complete, WinINSTALL displays a dialog box named Launch Application Setup Program. Click OK, and WinINSTALL will prompt for the location of a setup program. Enter **C:\WZSetup.EXE** to start the setup of WinZip.

Step 9 Install WinZip to C:\Program Files\WinZip. You can configure it with your preferences. When you're finished installing WinZip, rerun VERITAS Discover.

Step 10 The dialog box shown in Figure 8.9 should appear. Select Perform the 'After' Snapshot Now, and click Next. WinINSTALL LE Discover will scan and record changes between the previous system state and the current system state.

Step 11 When scanning is complete, watch for a dialog box named Conversion Successful, containing any messages generated during the snapshot process. Click OK. A message box will pop up to tell you the location of the final WinZip.MSI file.

The WinZip.MSI package should now be available in the C:\Packages folder. You can use this file to assign or publish a preconfigured WinZip installation via Software Distribution and Management.

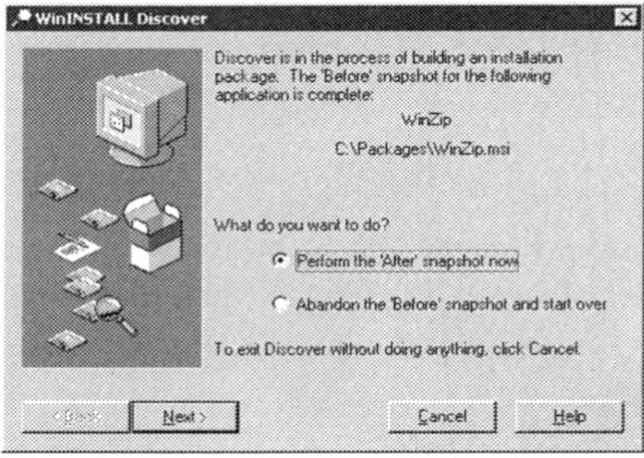

Figure 8.9 Creating the "After" snapshot in VERITAS Discover.

ZAP File Format

ZAP files are plain-text files; you can create a ZAP file using Notepad or your favorite plain-text editor. ZAP files are similar in format to *.INI files. Section headers are contained in brackets, and key/value pairs fall below the section headers. Comment lines are denoted by a leading semicolon (;). The section headers are `[Application]`, `[ext]`, `[CLSIDs]`, and `[progIDs]`. The `[Application]` header is the only one required; the other three are optional. Key/value pairs fall below each section header, in this format:

```
Key1=Value
Key2="Value with Spaces"
```

Notice that values containing spaces must be enclosed in quotation marks (").

Applications

Under the `[Application]` section are two required keys: `FriendlyName` and `SetupCommand`. `FriendlyName` is the name of the application that will appear under the Name column of the Software Installation policy. This value will also appear in the Add/Remove Programs applet of the Control Panel. `SetupCommand` is the command line needed to start the native application setup routine. The value of this key is usually `Setup.exe` or `Install.exe`. If specifying a full path, use a UNC name. (A better practice is to use a path relative to the location of the ZAP file, locating the ZAP file in the main folder of the application install source files.)

There are five optional keys under the `[Application]` section. None of these keys are required in a ZAP file, but they're often helpful in facilitating administration of multiple similar packages:

- `DisplayVersion`. The deployment package version number that will appear under the Software Installation policy and in the Add/Remove Programs applet of the Control Panel.
- `Publisher`. The name of the developer of the application. For example, if creating a ZAP file to install WinZip, the publisher would be Nico Mak Computing, Inc.
- `URL`. The URL points to a support page or informational page for the application. The value of this key will appear under the Software Installation policy information, and in the Add/Remove Programs applet of the Control Panel.
- `LCID`. This is the Language Code Identifier for the application. It specifies the default language code for a regionalized application.

Extensions

Under the optional extensions section, denoted by the section header `[ext]`, specify any file extensions that should make the application auto-install. The key is the file extension. You can precede it with a dot (.) or not; it won't affect the function. Any values after the equal sign (=) are ignored, but the equal sign is required. For example, an application used to open compressed archives may use any of the following lines:

```
.ZIP=
ARJ=
TAR="TAR compressed archive files"
Z=
```

Class Identifiers

Class identifiers, or CLSIDs, are a more specific method of associating a document type with an application than relying on the document extensions. Using the CLSIDs instead of document extensions, multiple document types with the same extensions could call separate ZAP files. Under the optional class identifiers section, marked by the section header `[CLSIDs]`, you can specify any class identifiers that should make the application auto-install. The key is the CLSID. The value is `LocalServer32`, `InprocServer32`, or `InprocHandler32`. Multiple values must be separated by commas. You can find CLSIDs by searching the Windows registry under the registry entry `HKEY_CLASSES_ROOT\CLSID`, but associating a CLSID with an application can be difficult. You'll need to install the application on a test machine and search the CLSID keys in the registry for references to the application name or installation path. The value following the CLSID key will be determined by subkeys from the CLSID. For example, the following would be a CLSID section for WinZip:

```
{E0D79300-84BE-11CE-9641-444553540000}=InProcServer32
{E0D79301-84BE-11CE-9641-444553540000}=InProcServer32
{E0D79302-84BE-11CE-9641-444553540000}=InProcServer32
```

Program Identifiers

Under the optional program identifiers section, marked by the section header `[progIDs]`, you can specify any program identifiers that should make the application auto-install. The key is the CLSID for the program identifier. The value is the ProgID. These values are located using the same method as to locate a CLSID. The ProgID will be listed as a subkey from the CLSID registry entry. Not all applications have ProgIDs. For example, a ProgID section for Word documents may look like this:

```
{00020900-0000-0000-C000-000000000046}=Word.Document.6
{00020906-0000-0000-C000-000000000046}=Word.Document.8
```

Sample ZAP File

The following is a sample ZAP file that could be used to install WinZip 7.0. This file and the related WinZip installation file (WZ7Setup.exe) would be located in the same folder off of the software distribution share point.

```
; #  WinZip Sample ZAP file  #

; Only APPLICATION section is required
[Application]
```

```
; Required keys
FriendlyName = "WinZip 7.0"
SetupCommand = WZ7Setup.exe

; Optional keys
DisplayVersion = 7.0
Publisher = "Nico Mak Computing, Inc."
URL = http://www.winzip.com

; The remaining sections are all optional

[ext]
; The following extensions will cause the WinZip
; package to auto-install.
.ZIP=
ARJ=
TAR="TAR compressed archive files"
Z=

[CLSIDs]
; The following CLSIDs will cause the WinZip package
; to auto-install.
{E0D79300-84BE-11CE-9641-444553540000}=InProcServer32
{E0D79301-84BE-11CE-9641-444553540000}=InProcServer32
{E0D79302-84BE-11CE-9641-444553540000}=InProcServer32

; End of WinZip Sample File
```

Repairing Applications

Another way the Software Installation and Maintenance feature of Windows 2000 helps reduce TCO is through automated application repair. Many applications created for use with the Windows Installer service (*.MSI files) and published or assigned through the Active Directory are able to automatically repair themselves if damaged or deleted in whole or in part.

If the machine shuts down incorrectly and corrupts important application folders in the process, or a program folder is inadvertently deleted during routine drive maintenance, the Software Installation and Maintenance feature prevents a technician from needing to physically visit the workstation. The applications can repair themselves automatically, instantly, and—most importantly—without any user interaction. In most cases, the user may never even realize there was a problem.

For example, if you install Microsoft Office 2000 by publishing the MSI file in the Active Directory, and then delete the WINWORD.EXE file from your local machine, the next time you try to open a Microsoft Word document the system will see that the file is missing and will reinstall it from the published deployment package in the Active Directory.

ZAP files don't auto-repair in the same way as MSI files. If a ZAP installation is corrupted, the application reruns the entire setup program rather than replacing only the missing files.

Windows File Protection

Anyone who has worked with Windows for a while is probably familiar with the problems surrounding improperly behaving application installs and DLL conflicts. Occasionally, an application installs a different version of a system DLL, and other applications fail to run correctly. This problem is often referred to as "DLL Hell." Although not a component of the Windows Installer service, Windows 2000 file protection is an important concept related to application management and repair.

Windows 2000 protects important system files—including DLL files, system executables, *.SYS files, ActiveX controls, critical system fonts, and more—from being overwritten by third-party applications. All files critical to the functions of Windows 2000 are protected, up to the limits of the file protection cache size. Windows 2000 Professional has a default file protection cache size of 50MB. Windows 2000 Server has a default file protection cache size of 4294967295MB. The default cache size can be modified through the Computer Configuration\Administrative Templates\System\Windows File Protection\Limit Windows File Protection cache size policy. Protected files have backup copies located in the %systemroot%\system32\dllcache folder. If a protected file is deleted, modified, renamed, or moved, the Windows File Protection feature restores a copy of the original file to the proper location.

You can't use Windows Explorer to browse to the %systemroot%\system32\dllcache folder unless you have configured your folder options to show hidden files and folders, and not hide protected operating system files—but typing **%systemroot%\system32\dllcache** in the Run box will open an Explorer window in the folder. To see Windows File Protection in action, go to your system root folder (usually C:\WINNT) and find the NOTEPAD.EXE file. You may need to click the Show Files line in the left column to see the Windows 2000 System Files. Highlight NOTEPAD.EXE and press the Delete key. The Confirm File Delete dialog box will ask if you're sure you want to delete Notepad. Click Yes. In less than five seconds, the NOTEPAD.EXE file will be restored automatically. In addition, the System Log of the Event Viewer will log an informational event (see Figure 8.10).

Now suppose that, for some reason, you *want* to modify or delete a file protected by Windows File Protection. For example, you want to replace NOTEPAD.EXE with your own version of a plain-text editor. If you modify the NOTEPAD.EXE file in the %systemroot%\system32\dllcache folder, you can delete the system file %systemroot%\NOTEPAD.EXE and it will be replaced by the modified version from the DLLCACHE folder. Keep in mind that changing files in this manner could cause system instability; the files are protected for a reason.

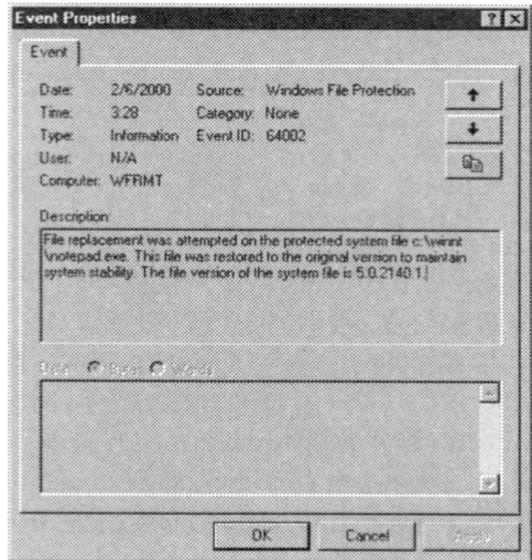

Figure 8.10 EventViewer system log entry for Windows file protection recovery of NOTEPAD.EXE.

Why would I tell you about a process that could make your system unstable? You may want to remove some files known to be non-critical, such as SOL.EXE (the Solitaire executable), but SOL.EXE is a protected file, so you wouldn't be able to delete it through Explorer. You must delete the file from the DLLCACHE folder. It can be rather frustrating to continually delete a file only to have it reappear seconds later. Of course, with optional Windows components such as Solitaire, the suggested removal method is to uninstall the application through the Add/Remove Programs applet of the Control Panel, under Add/Remove Windows Components. This removes the application without the headache of dealing with Windows file protection.

Software Installation and Maintenance Versus SMS 2.0

If you use Microsoft Systems Management Server (SMS) for software deployment, you should not use the Windows 2000 Software Installation and Maintenance feature for application distribution. SMS 2.0 can utilize the same *.MSI files as Windows 2000 Software Installation and Maintenance. The Windows Installer technology used by both products enables the elevated privilege application installation, package upgrade, software repair, and software removal features.

The only feature overlap between SMS 2.0 and Windows 2000 is in application deployment. SMS 2.0 provides additional features such as hardware inventory, software inventory, remote control of client machines, software metering, WAN-aware software distribution, and system monitoring. On the other hand, SMS is not yet OU aware. As such, SMS 2.0 can't take advantage of group policy objects and related Active Directory features; you must use SMS containers to organize and manage users and computers through SMS. SMS packages aren't available through the Add/Remove Programs applet of the Control Panel; instead, users must access the SMS client component for applications that are not installed automatically on their machines.

So when would you select the SMS 2.0 Software Distribution feature over the Windows 2000 Software Installation and Maintenance service? If your environment fits any of the following descriptions, your organization may be better served through the use of SMS 2.0:

- SMS 2.0 is currently deployed in your environment.
- Your organization needs the additional management features available through SMS 2.0.
- Your managed client environment includes machines running Windows-based operating systems other than Windows 2000.

For more information on Microsoft's Systems Management Server, see `http://www.microsoft.com/smsmgmt/default.asp`.

SMS 2.0 with Windows 2000 Clients

Before using SMS 2.0 in an environment with Windows 2000 clients, you'll need to apply SMS 2.0 Service Pack 2. Without the Service Pack, SMS 2.0 may not interact properly with Windows 2000.

9

Desktop Security

THIS CHAPTER COVERS:

- Basic concepts of desktop security
- Technologies included with Windows 2000 to enhance desktop security
- Analyzing the current desktop security settings
- Locking down the desktop

After reading this chapter, you should be able to do the following:

- Apply security templates to a Windows 2000 Professional system
- Customize the security templates included with Windows 2000 Professional
- Use the Security Configuration and Analysis MMC to apply or evaluate workstation security
- Integrate technologies such as group policy objects, NTFS security settings, and security policy templates to produce a highly managed desktop environment

Throughout the second section of this book, I've described technologies that can be used to manage applications on the desktop. This chapter discusses combining many of these technologies to implement security policies on workstations. These security policies can increase workstation and network security by defining, enhancing, or limiting user rights and user access to local and remote resources. Through this type of security control, you can create highly specialized desktop environments based on aspects such as user roles, computer functions, or user skill levels to enhance and customize the implementation of Windows 2000 Professional in a wide variety of environments.

The first part of this chapter discusses overall system security available through the security administration tools included with Windows 2000. This section focuses on the security policies and NTFS-based security permissions that can be applied through group policy objects to enforce a common set of security practices on all the systems running Windows 2000 Professional or Server in an environment. The second part of this chapter deals with desktop lockdown theory, such as usage profiles that warrant different degrees of desktop lockdown, locations of policies that you can use to implement various components of desktop lockdown, and some generic user classifications to help with the user-profiling process.

Security Administration Tools Included with Windows 2000

In the past, implementing NT security involved the creation of complex configuration policy files, under which security-related policies could be difficult to find. Applying registry or file security required complex scripts, using command-line tools such as CACLS that often needed to run as a local administrator to be effective. These types of policies and scripts were important to create, because the out-of-the-box configuration of Windows NT 4.0 was relatively insecure.

Under Windows 2000, administration and configuration of security settings has been dramatically improved. For example:

- With group policy objects, numerous security-related policy settings are available.
- NTFS permissions for files, folders, and registry keys are more granular.
- Administrative privileges can be delegated through the Active Directory to limited areas of control.
- Security templates can be applied to workstations and servers to control security-related local policy settings, registry permissions, file system permissions, local group membership, services that are allowed to run locally, local Event Log settings, and local account policies.

Two tools are included with Windows 2000 to ease administration and analysis of these types of security settings. The first is the Windows 2000 Security Configuration and Analysis tool—similar to the Security Configuration Manager included with Windows NT 4.0 Service Pack 4—which provides a single, organized reference point to view or configure the noted security enhancements. The second is security templates, which provide a way to apply standard sets of preconfigured security policies across a number of systems without needing to manually re-create all the policy settings for each machine. Combining security templates with Security Configuration and Analysis enables an administrator to generate a report comparing the settings contained in a security template file to the applicable settings of a given system. After generating reports, the administrator can easily determine which systems have potential security holes, and can apply system policies to reduce security vulnerabilities.

Security Templates

Security templates, which can be managed through the Security Templates snap-in of the Microsoft Management Console (MMC), organize existing Windows 2000 security configuration policies and settings into a single location to simplify management of these policies and settings. Security templates don't provide any security policies beyond those provided with standard group policy objects; the templates simply group security-related policy settings in a single, easily navigable location. Security templates are saved as plain-text *.INF files, which makes it easier to copy large sections of a template from one file to another by using a standard text editor. Security templates include settings for the following aspects of system security:

Security Policy Aspect	Example Settings in Policy
Account Policies	Passwords, account lockouts, Kerberos settings
Local Policies	User rights, auditing
Event Log	Logging for application, security, and system events
Registry	Security access permissions for registry keys, similar to NTFS security settings
Restricted Groups	Administration for local group membership
File System	NTFS permissions, access control for files and folders on NTFS formatted volumes
System Services	Security settings and startup modes for local services

Twelve standard security templates are included with Windows 2000. After selecting a security template, you can modify settings contained in the template and import the template into a group policy object for a site, domain, or organizational unit. Security templates can be imported into local computer policy objects as well, but only settings specified in the Local Policies and Account Policies sections will be applied.

Let's take a look at the Security Templates MMC now. Follow these steps:

1. Run the MMC.
2. Select Add/Remove Snap-in from the Console menu.
3. Click Add on the Standalone tab.
4. Select Security Templates from the list of available snap-ins, as shown in Figure 9.1. Click Add, then Close.

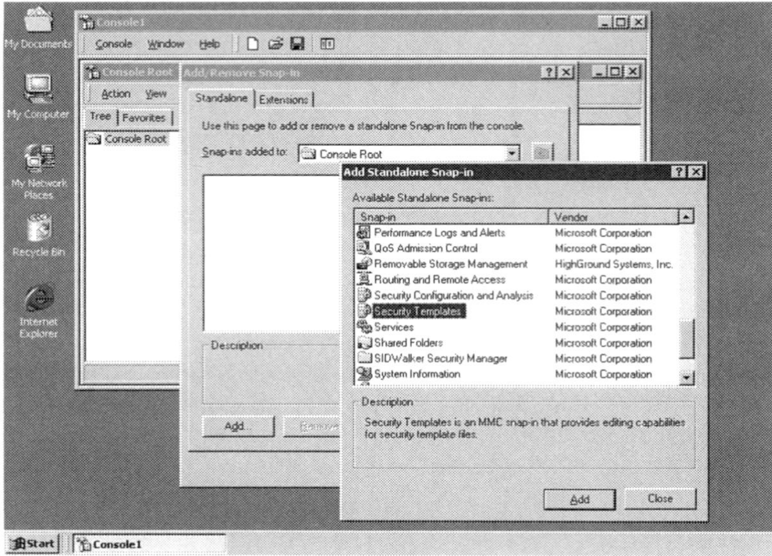

Figure 9.1 Adding the Security Templates snap-in.

The default template search path, %systemroot%\Security\Templates, is listed in the left pane under the Security Templates node. Twelve standard templates are included in this folder; when you select the template search path node, the included templates are described in the right pane, as shown in Figure 9.2. (In the left pane of Figure 9.2, I've expanded the basicdc security template to display the entire hierarchy of policy groupings available within a standard security template. Expanding any of the other templates yields an identical structure.)

The following table describes the policy templates available under Windows 2000 Professional:

Template	Description
basicdc	Restores default security settings to all areas of a Windows 2000 domain controller except for policies defined under the User Rights Assignment and Restricted Groups nodes.
basicsv	Restores default security settings to all areas of Windows 2000 Server except for policies defined under the User Rights Assignment and Restricted Groups nodes. You shouldn't use this policy on domain controllers; use basicdc instead.
basicwk	Restores default security settings to all areas of Windows 2000 Professional except for policies defined under the User Rights Assignment and Restricted Groups nodes.

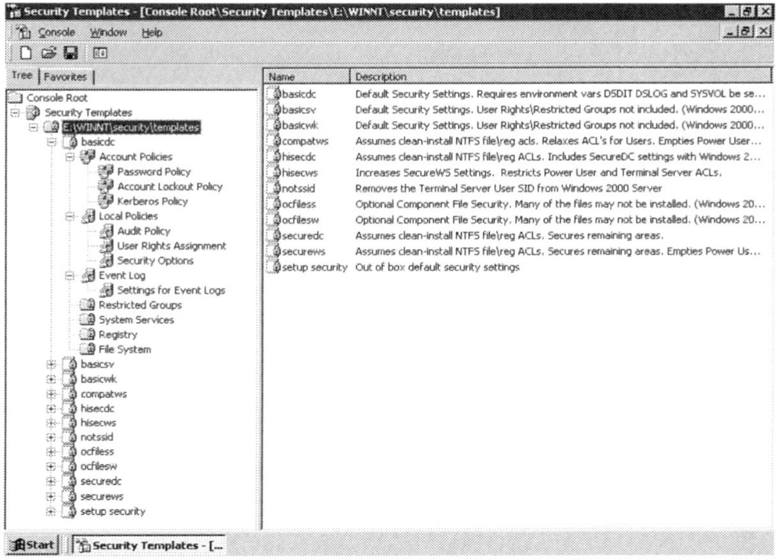

Figure 9.2 The Security Templates snap-in. The security templates are listed with their associated descriptions in the right pane.

Template	Description
compatws	This template, meant to be applied to Windows 2000 Professional machines, modifies the security settings of a workstation to increase application compatibility related to security for applications not certified to run on Windows 2000. This template gives the local Users group a security configuration somewhere between the Users and Power Users groups. The template lowers the security level required to access and/or modify certain files, folders, and registry keys that are commonly accessed by applications. The template doesn't grant the Users group the additional rights and privileges of the Power Users group, such as the ability to create local user accounts or the ability to stop and start local services. In addition, since this template is designed to minimize the need to add people to the Power Users group, all users and groups in the Power Users group will be removed.
hisecdc	*Warning:* If you apply this template, the target system will no longer be able to communicate with non–Windows 2000 machines. This template applies to Windows 2000 domain controllers. This policy configures high security for network components used

continues

Template	Description
	when communicating with other Windows 2000 machines. LAN Manager authentication will send only NTLMv2 responses. NTLM and LM requests are denied.
hisecws	*Warning:* If you apply this template, the target system will no longer be able to communicate with non–Windows 2000 machines. This template applies to Windows 2000 workstations. This policy configures high security for network components used when communicating with other Windows 2000 machines. LAN Manager authentication will send only NTLMv2 responses. NTLM and LM requests are denied. All accounts and groups in the local Power Users group will be removed from the group.
notssid	This security template, created for Windows 2000 Servers with Terminal Server installed, sets security on four registry keys and two folders to remove the Windows 2000 Terminal Server service account SID from those objects.
ocfiless	Sets file permissions on files associated with optional Windows 2000 Server components.
ocffilesw	Sets file permissions on files associated with optional Windows 2000 Professional components.
securedc	Applies Microsoft-recommended security settings for a Windows 2000 domain controller. File, folder, and registry key permissions are not modified.
securews	Applies Microsoft-recommended security settings for a Windows 2000 Professional client. File, folder, and registry key permissions are not modified. All accounts and groups in the local Power Users group will be removed from the group.
setup security	Restores out-of-the-box security configuration. Although this policy is included, I recommend using the applicable basic template (basicdc, basicsv, or basicwk) to apply more specific settings without overwriting user rights assignments.

Within each policy template, standard security-related policy settings are available for viewing and modifying. Any settings you modify through the Security Templates snap-in are modified only within the template; to apply the settings to a computer, the policy template must be imported to an applicable group policy object at the domain or organizational unit level, or applied to the local computer policy through the Security Configuration and Analysis tool or the SECEDIT command-line tool.

Security Configuration and Analysis Snap-in

The Security Configuration and Analysis snap-in is available from the MMC:

1. Run the MMC.
2. Select Add/Remove Snap-in from the Console menu.
3. Click Add on the Standalone tab.
4. Select Security Configuration and Analysis from the list of available stand-alone snap-ins (refer to Figure 9.1 in the preceding section). Click Add, then Close.

With the Security Configuration and Analysis snap-in, you can analyze and configure local system security from a graphical user interface, as shown in Figure 9.3. This is a good way to check the net effects of security templates imported into group policy objects. Exercise 9.1 demonstrates the use of the Security Configuration and Analysis tool to review the security configuration of a local workstation and to apply the settings from a security template file to the workstation.

Note: Be careful when you apply a security template to a workstation or server; if the policies aren't configured the way you want them, it may be difficult to roll back the changes.

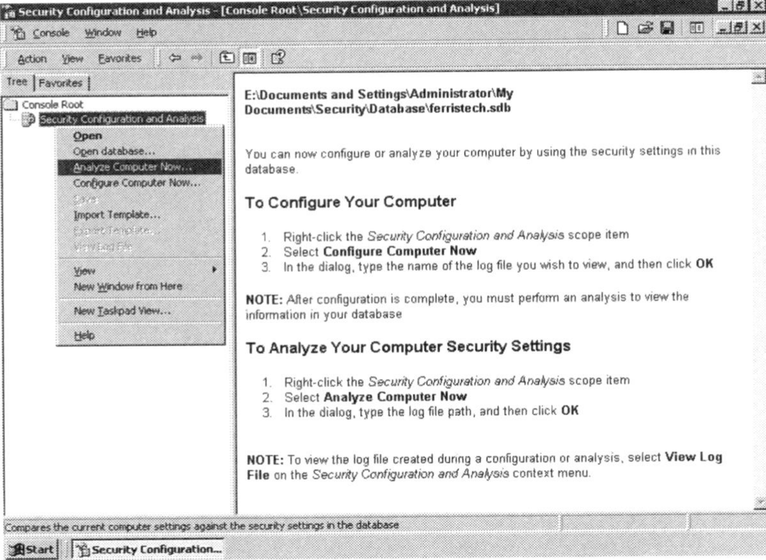

Figure 9.3 The Security Configuration and Analysis snap-in, after creating a new database and importing a template file. The menu in the left pane appears when you right-click the Security Configuration and Analysis node.

Exercise 9.1 **Analyzing Local Security with Security Configuration and Analysis**

Step 1	Open the MMC and add the Security Configuration and Analysis snap-in.
Step 2	Select the Security Configuration and Analysis node in the left pane (the console tree). The display in the right pane (the results pane) provides guidance for the basic operations of opening an existing database or creating a new database. Since this is the first time we've used this tool, let's create a new database.
Step 3	Right-click the Security Configuration and Analysis node and select Open Database from the pop-up menu.
Step 4	Select a save location and use the filename **MySecurity.SDB**. Click Open. Note that, since this will create a database file, you shouldn't select a folder on any server share that is enabled for Offline Files and currently offline; database files, such as *.MDB, *.SDB, and *.PST files, cannot be synchronized using the Offline Files technology.
Step 5	The Import Template window appears. Select a security template to which your current security should be compared. For this exercise, use the Setup Security.inf file. This will compare your current security settings with the out-of-the-box Windows 2000 security configuration. Click Open.
Step 6	Since we're analyzing current settings rather than applying the template settings, right-click the Security Configuration and Analysis node in the left pane and select Analyze Computer Now from the pop-up menu. Enter a save location for the error log and click OK. This log file will actually document quite a bit more than any errors that may be generated during the analysis. Additional information contained in the log file includes the results from each policy setting comparison, summary information for registry and file permission comparisons, service configuration, and local group membership analysis information. This log file is saved as plain text; you can view the contents in any text editor. The system will display an Analyzing System Security progress box while the system security analysis is generated. Be aware that this could take awhile.
Step 7	You can now expand the Security Configuration and Analysis node into the various security aspects that this process evaluates. Navigate through the various policies. A green check mark indicates that the local computer configuration matches the settings of the template; a red *x* shows that the configuration differs from the template, and no icon at all means that the setting isn't defined on either the template or the local computer. In Figure 9.4, only the Enforce Password History policy setting on the local computer differs from the configuration set in the template file. (Depending on the configuration of your local computer, you may receive different results than those displayed in Figure 9.4.)
Step 8	Select the Registry node in the left pane of the Security Configuration and Analysis snap-in. A summary table in the right pane displays the number of inconsistencies per hive evaluated.
Step 9	Select the File System node in the left pane. A summary table in the right pane displays the number of inconsistencies in file access permissions.
Step 10	Right-click the parent node for the Security Configuration and Analysis node in the left pane. Select View Log File from the pop-up menu. This displays the log file generated by the analysis engine in the right pane.

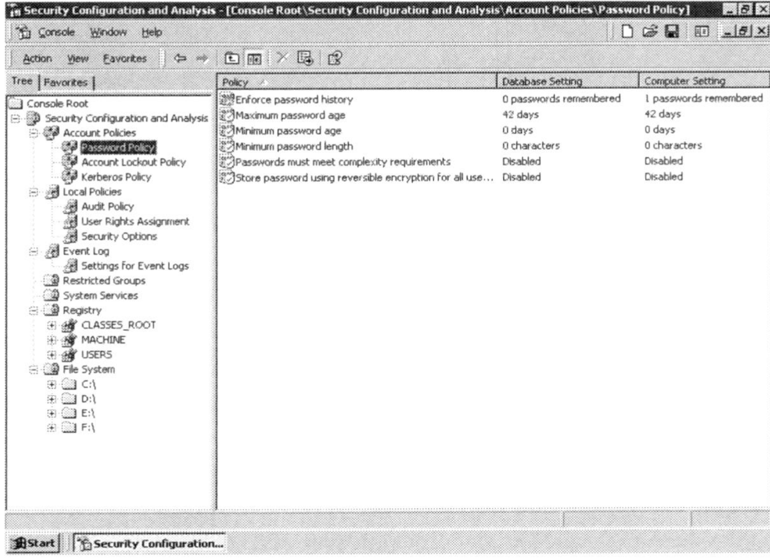

Figure 9.4 The Security Configuration and Analysis snap-in after running a system analysis. The Account Policies\Password Policy node is selected.

Feel free to explore the results from the security analysis. You can modify settings present in the database through this interface, but this doesn't change the values currently assigned to the computer. If you modify database settings and want to apply those settings to the local computer, right-click the Security Configuration and Analysis node and select Configure Computer Now from the pop-up menu.

If you want to save modified settings to the template file, make your changes and then right-click the Security Configuration and Analysis node. Click Save on the pop-up menu to save changes to the current template, or click Export Template to save changes to a new template. (Essentially, Export Template works like the Save As command.)

On reviewing the security settings, you may want to implement the settings in the current template file. This will update the local machine's security settings to the settings defined in the template. To perform this operation, right-click the Security Configuration and Analysis node and select Configure Computer Now from the pop-up menu. All settings defined in the Account Policies and Local Policies sections of the template will be applied to the local machine. Running this command on the local system won't override any security templates or policy settings that are specified on applicable domain-based group policy objects.

On the other hand, if you want to create a security template from the currently applied security settings of the local machine, you must use the SECEDIT command-line tool, as explained in the next section. Exporting the template from security settings of the local machine allows an administrator to clone security settings from one fully configured machine to an unconfigured system.

The SECEDIT Command-Line Tool

The SECEDIT command-line tool provides an easy way to script security analysis, security template application, and security template generation. SECEDIT.EXE can be called from a batch file, run from the task scheduler, or executed from the command line. SECEDIT is essentially a command-line version of the Security Configuration and Analysis tool. In addition to these functions, SECEDIT can be used to force an immediate refresh of machine or user policies.

To create a security template from the currently applied security settings for the Account Policies and Local Policies sections of the local machine and save them to the MySecurity.inf file in the default template location, the command would be as follows:

```
secedit /export /mergedPolicy /cfg %windir%\Security\Templates\MySecurity.inf
```

If you've created or modified your own security template file, you may want to validate the syntax of the template before using it for the basis of a system security analysis or applying the template to a local workstation. To validate the syntax of a security policy named MySecurity.inf in the default template location, use this command:

```
secedit /validate %windir%\Security\Templates\MySecurity.inf
```

To apply the security settings to a workstation from the MySecurity.inf security template from the default template location, use this command:

```
secedit /configure /db %windir%\security\database\secedit.sdb
➥/cfg %windir%\Security\Templates\MySecurity.inf
```

To analyze the current security settings against the out-of-the-box security settings, creating a new security database named MySecurity.sdb, the command would be as follows:

```
secedit /analyze /db %windir%\security\database\MySecurity.sdb
➥/cfg "%windir%\Security\Templates\setup security.inf
```

When changing security settings for group policy objects, the changes may not take effect until the local policy is refreshed at the workstation. This could take up to eight hours—the default policy refresh period. SECEDIT provides the ability to apply changes to the security policy to the local system immediately. To update security settings for the local computer, use this command:

```
secedit /refreshpolicy machine_policy /enforce
```

To force an update of the local user policy, use this command:

```
secedit /refreshpolicy user_policy /enforce
```

Help for SECEDIT.EXE

Type SECEDIT at the command line with no arguments to open the SECEDIT Windows Help file.

Desktop Lockdown

Desktop lockdown is the process of creating a centralized workstation management model by defining, limiting, or restricting the interactivity and customizable aspects of a workstation from an end-user perspective. It is regarded by many members of the technical user community as a mechanism of iron-fisted system administration, with little regard for the feelings of the individuals using the computers. For this reason, it's important to consider your current environment before implementing desktop lockdown policies. If your current desktop-management environment is wide open, with no restrictions on user customizations or user-installed programs, you shouldn't turn right around and implement locked down, non-customizable task stations. Along the same lines, highly technical users, especially developers and engineers, may spend considerable effort attempting to override your policies if they're too restrictive.

You must carefully consider your current environment, the various roles of users and computers in the environment, and the desired resultant environment when developing desktop lockdown policies. There are a number of valid reasons to consider implementing desktop lockdown policies:

- Limiting applications accessed by specific groups of end users or computers.
- Preventing a publicly-accessible task station from being used for unauthorized purposes.
- Restricting users from distractions such as Web surfing, Solitaire, or applications other than those required for their work.
- Reducing TCO and administrative overhead associated with workstation support, by preventing application installation or system modification by users not trained to perform such tasks.
- Providing users with a desktop environment that will make it easier for the users to perform their jobs.

Desktop lockdown can be used to restrict access to many components of Windows 2000 Professional. Following are some examples of the kinds of settings you can control:

- Drive and file access, including areas of the local storage devices where the user can and cannot save, modify, view, or delete data. Drives visible to the user can be displayed or hidden, and access to removable media devices can be enabled or disabled. Policies can prevent a user from setting preferences that would allow the user to view a hidden file system object, and NTFS permissions can be applied via security templates to granularly restrict operations granted or denied a user on individual files and folders.
- Components of the user interface the user can or cannot customize, such as display resolution, color scheme, background image, program group arrangement, default screen saver settings, sound scheme, and arrangement of the desktop. For security reasons, you may decide to force minimum idle time and password-protection options on the screen saver; these settings can enable a more secure environment by automatically locking idle workstations. Setting policies on the sound scheme can prevent users in close work quarters from disturbing each other by associating annoying sounds to common system events.

- Application control, including whether or not a user is allowed to install software, specific executables the user is allowed (or not allowed) to run, and application configuration and customization options.
- Operating system configuration settings, including Control Panel application access, network configuration or dial-up networking entries, installed printers, and performance options.

The later section "User Policies" discusses the location of the policies that enable management of these components.

Users with Special Needs

When defining a workstation lockdown policy, make sure that your policies accommodate users with special needs, whether those needs are technical or health-related. For example:

- Forcing a single color scheme and font size on the desktop could cause trouble for users with vision problems.
- Forcing everyone to use the same screen resolution could be detrimental to the departmental Webmaster's ability to create graphics.
- Disabling the Control Panel could prevent left-handed users from setting the mouse for left-handed use.

You have two options when dealing with such cases. You can either create default policies and exclude users with special needs from the policies, or you can leave such non-critical policies undefined for everyone. In the end, it really makes little difference in terms of administrative effort and TCO impact whether a user has permission to select a different color scheme.

Profiling Users

Before implementing any sort of desktop lockdown policy, you should *profile* the users. Profiling groups of users involves evaluating their job requirements, determining which applications they run, and determining their technical skill levels. In most organizations, I've found that most users can be grouped into three main classifications, which I call *limited-task users*, *average end users*, and *super users*. These classifications are based primarily on job requirements and functional technical skills.

Limited-Task Users

The limited-task user is the most restrictive user type of the three examples discussed in this chapter. The limited-task user may have access to a single application—or at least a very small number of applications. These users generally have very low technical skills. This profile is well-suited for situations such as the following:

- Call center agents
- Data entry personnel
- Users whose applications all run from a terminal emulator or Windows Terminal Server client

- Users who only use the computer to run a single application
- Computer used as a point-of-sale terminal
- Computer used as a public-access information kiosk
- Shared-access workstation used for a dedicated task by a large number of users, such as a time-and-attendance terminal or system-monitoring display.

The limited-task user profile is often restricted from any system modifications, including desktop preferences, program group arrangement, and Control Panel configuration settings. Only authorized applications will run on this profile; unauthorized software can't be installed or executed. The user accounts under this profile should be set no higher than the Guest or User access level.

Average End Users

The most common user profile is the average end user. These users generally use their computers for normal office functions, such as word processing, spreadsheets, email, and perhaps a selection of customized business applications. These users frequently have limited technical skills, relying on technical support staff for routine procedures such as software installation and basic system-configuration issues. This profile can often be applied to business support departments such as sales, marketing, finance, and human resources.

The average end user profile allows the user a greater level of control over the system configuration than the limited-task user profile. These users are generally permitted to set preferred desktop schemes, configure wallpaper, and select favorite screen savers—although, for security reasons, you may decide to force a particular configuration of the minimum idle time and password-protection requirement. Forcing these screen saver configuration options creates a more secure environment by automatically locking idle workstations. Depending on your environment, the access level for these users could be set at the User or Power User level.

Often, members under this profile are not allowed to install nonstandard software. Optional software packages for these users should be available through an automated distribution mechanism, such as SMS or Software Installation and Maintenance policies (see Chapter 8, "Application Management and Software Installation"). With this strategy, users still have some degree of choice over applications installed on their systems, but they won't need administrative access—or a visit from a support technician—to install those applications.

Super Users

Super users are the technicians, engineers, support desk staff, and other users with a high degree of technical competency. These users often have the skill level needed to provide their own technical support, frequently resolving their own technical issues without needing to call a help desk. Users falling under this classification are generally in the minority for most non–technology-related organizations. On the other hand, in technology consulting firms and technology-focused companies such as Microsoft, Dell, or IBM, a majority of users may fall under this category.

Note that "super users" as defined by this profile are *not* the same as the UNIX superusers, the root accounts with absolute administrative power over all aspects of the system. These users are limited to administrative control of their local machines. At the very least, they're members of the Power Users group, with permission to install personal applications from locally available sources. For example, any of the following might have the need for super user access:

- Remote users who may need administrative access to support themselves in the field
- Portable-computer users who may need to quickly reconfigure a system component or add a new hardware device on a PC Card slot to access needed resources
- System testers who frequently need to modify components on their machines that would otherwise be restricted

In many organizations, all users have access rights modeled after the super user profile. This environment often stems from political or corporate culture reasons. With proper user education, this type of setup may well prove beneficial to system supportability. For simple reconfiguration or system modification tasks that would otherwise require administrative access, users could be talked through those tasks by a technician over the phone, potentially saving the technician the need to physically visit the workstation.

User Policies

Once you've determined the user profiles and levels to which you would like to lock down the desktop environment for each profile, you're nearly to the finish line. All that remains is to create the group policy objects to implement the settings that will actually deliver the lockdown. (See Chapter 6, "Group Policy Objects.") So many policies and policy settings are available that I couldn't possibly discuss every one without adding hundreds of pages to this text. Fortunately, Microsoft provides an excellent digital reference for these settings in a Windows Help file format—the Group Policy Reference from the Windows 2000 Server Resource Kit—at the following address:

`http://www.microsoft.com/windows2000/library/resources/reskit/default.asp`

In addition, the policies themselves contain detailed descriptions on the Explain tab, which can be found by right-clicking any policy, selecting Properties from the pop-up menu, and selecting the Explain tab on the Properties window (see Figure 9.5). In addition to a description of the policy, the Explain tab often contains descriptions of the effect(s) the policy will have on the computer, descriptions of related technologies, and listings of similar or related policies.

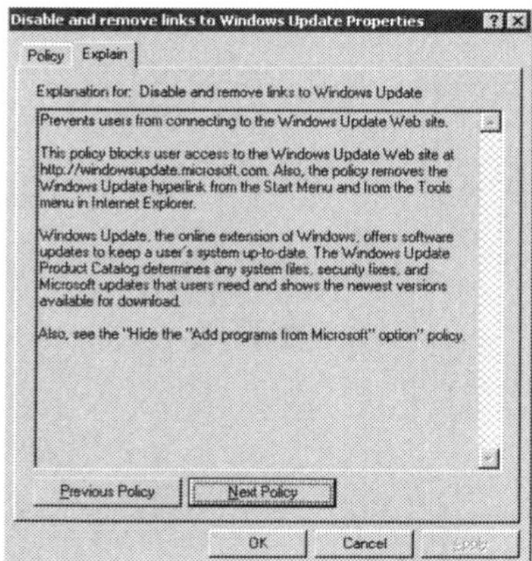

Figure 9.5 The Explain tab for the Disable and Remove Links to Windows Update policy.

The following sections list some common desktop-lockdown requirements with some of the policies needed to enable those elements. This information barely scratches the surface of the policies available under Windows 2000, but it will give you a starting point when evaluating the policies available for locking down the desktop.

Logon Security

Use these policies to display a message window after a user presses Ctrl+Alt+Del to log on, but before the user is able to enter a username or password:

Computer Configuration\Windows Settings\Security Settings\Local Policies\Security Options

- Message Text for Users Attempting to Log On
- Message Title for Users Attempting to Log On

These policies determine which groups or users have the right to log on locally:

Computer Configuration\Windows Settings\Security Settings\Local Policies\User Rights Assignment

- Log On Locally
- Deny Log On Locally

Forcibly disconnect a user when the user is connected beyond his or her allowed logon hours:

Computer Configuration\Windows Settings\Security Settings\Local Policies\Security Options

- Automatically Log Off Users When Logon Time Expires

Drive and File Access

With these policies, local drives can be displayed or hidden:
User Configuration\Administrative Templates\Windows Components\Windows Explorer

- Hide These Specified Drives in My Computer
- Prevent Access to Drives from My Computer

These policies control the behavior of removable media devices:
Computer Configuration\Windows Settings\Security Settings\Local Policies\Security Options

- Allowed to Eject Removable NTFS Media
- Restrict CD-ROM Access to Locally Logged-on User Only
- Restrict Floppy Access to Locally Logged-on User Only

Application Control

These policies specify executables that the user is allowed to run or prevented from running:
User Configuration\Administrative Templates\System

- Don't Run Specified Windows Applications
- Run Only Allowed Windows Applications

These policies control application installation:
User Configuration\Administrative Templates\Control Panel\Add/Remove Programs

- Disable Add/Remove Programs
- Hide Change or Remove Programs Page
- Hide Add New Programs Page
- Hide Add/Remove Windows Components Page
- Hide the "Add a Program from CD-ROM or Floppy Disk" Option
- Hide the "Add Programs from Microsoft" Option
- Hide the "Add Programs from Your Network" Option

Application-specific policies can be found under the User Configuration\Administrative Templates and Computer Configuration\Administrative Templates trees. Policy templates (*.ADM files) included with other policy-enabled applications can be added through these locations. The Windows Components hive for both areas contains settings for NetMeeting and Internet Explorer.

User Interface

Use these policies to control the appearance of the desktop:

User Configuration\Administrative Templates\Desktop

- Hide All Icons on Desktop
- Remove My Documents Icon from Desktop
- Hide My Network Places Icon on Desktop
- Hide Internet Explorer Icon on Desktop

These policies control display-configuration options:

User Configuration\Administrative Templates\Control Panel\Display

- Disable Display in Control Panel
- Disable Changing Wallpaper
- Hide Background Tab
- Hide Appearance Tab
- Hide Screen Saver tab

For control of the screen saver settings, use these policies:

User Configuration\Administrative Templates\Control Panel\Display

- No Screen Saver
- Screen Saver Executable Name
- Password Protect the Screen Saver

Operating System Configuration Settings

Control access to the registry with this policy:

User Configuration\Administrative Templates\System

- Disable Registry Editing Tools

Control access to the Control Panel applets with these policies:

User Configuration\Administrative Templates\Control Panel

- Disable Control Panel
- Show Only Specified Control Panel Applets
- Hide Specified Control Panel Applets

Control access to Dial-Up Networking with these policies:

User Configuration\Administrative Templates\Network\Network and Dial-up Connections

- Allow Access to Current User's RAS Connection Properties
- Enable Connecting and Disconnecting a RAS Connection

III
Reference

Common File Extensions

THE FOLLOWING TABLE CONTAINS FILE EXTENSIONS and their descriptions for files you might see in your environment. When building a process to back up user data, refer to this list for ideas on which file extensions to include (or exclude). This information is nowhere near complete—after all, there are better than 50,000 possible file extensions, just counting three-letter extensions and lower—but it's a good place to start. For updated file extension information, check the whatis.com Web site at `http://www.whatis.com`.

Extension	Description
A	Object code library
AAM	Authorware shocked file
AAS	Authorware shocked packet
ABF	Adobe binary screen font
ABK	CorelDRAW AutoBackup
ABS	Sometimes used to denote an abstract (as in an abstract or summary of a scientific paper)

continues

Extension	Description
ACE	Ace Archiver compression format
ACL	CorelDRAW 6 keyboard accelerator
ACM	Windows system directory file
ACP	Microsoft Office Assistant preview file
ACR	American College of Radiology file format
ACT	Microsoft Office Assistant actor file
ACV	OS/2 drivers that compress and decompress audio data
AD	After Dark screen saver
ADA	Ada source text (non-GNAT)
ADB	Ada source text body (GNAT); Appointment database used by HP 100LX organizer
ADD	OS/2 adapter drivers used in the boot process
ADF	Amiga disk file
ADI	AutoCAD device-independent binary plotter format
ADM	After Dark MultiModule screen saver; Windows NT policy template
ADP	Used by FaxWorks to do setup for fax modem interaction; Astound Dynamite file
ADR	After Dark Randomizer screen saver; Smart Address address book
ADS	Ada source text specification (GNAT)
AFM	Adobe font metrics
AF2,AF3	ABC Flowchart file
AI	Adobe Illustrator drawing
AIF, AIFF	Audio Interchange File, a sound format used by Silicon Graphics and Macintosh applications
AIFC	Compressed AIF
AIM	AOL Instant Messenger Launch
AIS	ACDSee Image Sequence file; Velvet Studio Instruments
AKW	Contains all A-keywords in the RoboHELP Help project Index Designer not associated with topics
ALAW	European telephony format audio
ALB	JASC Image Commander album
ALL	Arts & Letters Library
AMS	Velvet Studio music module (MOD) file; Extreme's Tracker module format
ANC	Canon Computer Pattern Maker file that's a selectable list of pattern colors
ANI	Animated cursor in a Microsoft Windows system
ANS	ANSI text file
ANT	SimAnt for Windows saved game file

Extension	Description
API	Application Programming Interface file; used by Adobe Acrobat
APR	Lotus Approach 97 file
APS	Microsoft Visual C++ file
ARC	LH ARC compressed archive
ARI	Aristotle audio file
ARJ	Robert Jung ARJ compressed archive
ART	Xara Studio drawing; Canon Crayola art file; Clip Art file format; another Ray Tracer format; used by AOL to designate files compressed using the Johnson-Grace compression algorithm
ASA	Microsoft Visual InterDev file
ASC	ASCII text; PGP armored encrypted file
ASD	Microsoft Word AutoSave; Microsoft Advanced Streaming Format (ASF) description file; opens with NSREX
ASE	Velvet Studio sample
ASF	Microsoft Advanced Streaming Format file
ASM	Assembler language source file; Pro/E assembly file
ASO	Astound Dynamite Objects
ASP	Active Server Page; ProComm Plus setup and connection script; Astound Presentation file
AST	Astound multimedia file; ClarisWorks "assistant" file
ASV	DataCAD Autosave file
ASX	Cheyenne Backup script; Microsoft Advanced Streaming Redirector file; video file
ATT	AT&T Group 4 bitmap
ATW	AnyTime Deluxe for Windows personal information manager file from Individual Software
AU	Sun/NeXT/DEC/UNIX sound file; Audio U-law (pronounced mu-law) file format
AVB	Computer Associates Inoculan Anti-Virus virus infected file
AVI	Microsoft Audio Video Interleave movie format
AVR	Audio Visual Research file format
AVS	Application Visualization System format
AWD	FaxView document
AWR	Telsis file extension format for digitally stored audio
A*xx*	ARJ compressed files from a multi-volume archive (*xx* = a number from 01 to 99)
A3L	Authorware 3.x library file
A4L	Authorware 4.x library file
A5L	Authorware 5.x library file
A3M, A4M	Unpackaged Authorware Macintosh file

continues

Extension	Description
A4P	Authorware file packaged without runtime
A3W, A4W, A5W	Unpackaged Authorware Windows file
BAK	Backup file
BAS	BASIC source code
BAT	Batch file
BDF	West Point Bridge Designer
BFC	Windows 95 Briefcase document
BG	Backgammon for Windows game
BGL	Scenery files from Microsoft Flight Simulator
BI	Binary file
BIF	GroupWise initialization file
BIFF	XLITE 3D file format
BIN	Binary file
BK, BK$	Sometimes used to denote backup versions
BKS	IBM BookManager Read bookshelf
BMK	Bookmark file
BMP	Windows or OS/2 bitmap
BM1	Apogee BioMenace data file
BOOK	Adobe FrameMaker Book
BOX	Mailbox in Lotus Notes
BPL	Borland Delphi 4 packed library
BQY	BrioQuery file
BRX	File for browsing an index of multimedia objects
BSC	MS Developer Studio browser information file
BSP	Quake map
BS1	Apogee Blake Stone data file
BS_	Microsoft Bookshelf Find menu shell extension
BTM	Batch file used by Norton Utilities
BUD	Backup disk for Quicken
BUN	CakeWalk Audio Bundle file (a MIDI program)
BW	SGI black-and-white image file
BWV	Business Wave file
BYU	Movie BYU format
B4	Helix Nuts and Bolts file
C	C code
C01	Typhoon wave files
CAB	Microsoft compressed cabinet file
CAD	Drafix CAD by Softdesk
CAL	CALS compressed bitmap; Calendar schedule data
CAM	Casio camera format
CAP	Compressed music file format
CAS	Comma-delimited ASCII file

Extension	Description
CAT	IntelliCharge categorization file used by Quicken
CB	Microsoft clean boot file
CBI	Column binary formatted file (used in IBM mainframe systems)
CC	Visual dBASE custom class file
CCA	cc:Mail file
CCB	Visual Basic Animated Button configuration
CCF	Multimedia Viewer configuration file used in OS/2
CCH	Corel Chart
CCM	Lotus cc:Mail box (for example, INBOX.CCM)
CCO	CyberChat data file
CCT	Macromedia Director Shockwave cast
CDA	CD audio track
CDF	Microsoft Channel Definition Format file
CDI	Phillips Compact Disc interactive format
CDM	Visual dBASE custom data module file
CDR	CorelDRAW drawing; Raw Audio-CD data
CDT	CorelDRAW template
CDX	CorelDRAW compressed drawing; Microsoft Visual FoxPro index
CEL	CIMFast Event Language file
CER	Certificate file (MIME x-x509-ca-cert)
CFB	Compton's Multimedia file
CFG	Configuration file
CFM	ColdFusion template files; Visual dBASE Windows customer form
CGI	Common gateway interface script file
CGM	Computer Graphics Metafile
CH	OS/2 configuration file
CHK	File fragments saved by Windows Disk Defragmenter or ScanDisk
CHM	Compiled HTML file
CHR	Character sets (font files)
CHP	Ventura Publisher chapter
CHT	ChartViewer file; Harvard Graphics vector file
CIF	Adaptec CD Creator CD image file
CIL	Clip Gallery download package
CIM	SimCity 200 file
CIN	OS/2 change control file that tracks changes to an INI file
CK1	iD/Apogee Commander Keen 1 data file
CK2	iD/Apogee Commander Keen 2 data file
CK3	iD/Apogee Commander Keen 3 data file

continues

Extension	Description
CK4	iD/Apogee Commander Keen 4 data file
CK5	iD/Apogee Commander Keen 5 data file
CK6	iD/Apogee Commander Keen 6 data file
CLASS	Java class
CLL	Crick Software Clicker file
CLP	Windows Clipboard file
CLS	Visual Basic class module
CMD	Command file for Windows NT, OS/2; DOS CP/M command file; dBASE II program file
CMF	Corel metafile
CMG	Chessmaster saved game
CMP	JPEG bitmap; Address document
CMV	Corel Move animation
CMX	Corel Presentation Exchange image
CNF	Configuration file used by Telnet, Windows, and other applications with varying internal formats
CNM	Windows application menu options and setup file
CNQ	Compuworks Design Shop file
CNT	Windows (or other) system content files for the Help index and other purposes
COB	trueSpace2 object
COD	Microsoft C compiler output as displayable machine language/assembler with original C as comments
COM	Command file (program)
CPD	Corel Print Office file (drawing)
CPD, CPE	Fax cover document
CPI	Microsoft MS-DOS code page information file
CPL	Control Panel extension; Corel color palette
CPO	Corel Print house file
CPP	C++ code
CPR	Corel Presents presentation
CPT	Corel Photo-Paint image
CPX	Corel Presentation Exchange compressed drawing
CRD	Windows Cardfile file
CRP	Corel Presents runtime presentation; Visual dBASE custom report file
CRT	Certificate file
CSC	Corel script
CSP	PC Emcee On-Screen image
CSS	Cascading Style Sheet file (MIME)
CST	Macromedia Director Cast file
CSV	Comma-separated values file

Extension	Description
CT	Scitex CT bitmap; Paint Shop Pro Graphic Editor
CTL	Used in general to mean a file containing control information; FaxWorks uses it to keep information about each fax sent and received
CUE	Microsoft Cue Cards data
CUR	Windows cursor
CUT	Dr Halo bitmap
CV	Corel Versions archive; Microsoft CodeView information screen
CWK	ClarisWorks data file
CWS	ClarisWorks template
CXT	Macromedia Director protected (not editable) Cast file
CXX	C++ source code file
DAT	Data file; WordPerfect merge data; used for some MPEG formats
DB	Borland's Paradox 7 tables
DBC	Microsoft Visual FoxPro database container file
DBF	dBASE file, a format originated by Ashton-Tate, but understood by Act!, Clipper, FoxPro, Arago, Wordtech, xBase, and similar database or database-related products; Enable database file (can be opened with Excel 97); Oracle 8.1.x tablespace file
DBX	DataBeam image; Microsoft Visual FoxPro table
DCM	DCM module format
DCR	Shockwave file
DCS	Desktop Color Separation file
DCT	Microsoft Visual FoxPro database container
DCU	Delphi compiled unit file
DCX	Microsoft Visual FoxPro database container; PCX-based fax image; macros
DC5	DataCAD drawing files
DDF	Btrieve or Xtrieve data definition file, which contains metadata describing a Btrieve or Xtrieve file
DDIF	Digital Equipment or Compaq format, used for storing images and their word processing documents
DEF	SmartWare II data file; C++ definition
DEFI	Oracle 7 de-install script
DEM	File with USGS standards for Digital Elevation Models
DER	Certificate file
DEWF	Macintosh SoundCap/SoundEdit recorded instrument format
DGN	Microstation95 CAD drawing file

continues

Extension	Description
DIB	Device-independent bitmap
DIC	Dictionary
DIF	Data Interchange Format spreadsheet
DIG	Digilink format; Sound Designer I audio file
DIR	Macromedia Director file
DIZ	Description file
DLG	C++ dialog script
DLL	Dynamic link library
DLS	Downloadable sound
DMD	Visual dBASE data module file
DMF	X-Trakker music module (MOD) file
DOC	FrameMaker or FrameBuilder document; WordStar document; WordPerfect document; Microsoft Word document; DisplayWrite document
DOT	Microsoft Word document template
DPL	Borland Delphi 3 packed library
DPR	Borland Delphi project header file
DRAW	Acorn's object-based vector image file
DRV	Driver
DRW	Micrografx Designer/Draw; Pro/E drawing file
DSF	Micrografx Designer v7.x
DSG	DOOM saved game
DSM	Dynamic Studio music module (MOD) file
DSP	Microsoft Developer Studio project
DSQ	Corel QUERY file
DST	Embroidery machines graphics file
DSW	Microsoft Developer Studio workspace
DTA	World Bank's STARS data file
DTD	SGML Document Type Definition (DTD) file
DTED	Digital terrain elevation data (geographic data format)
DTF	Symantec Q&A relational database data file
DTM	DigiTrakker module
DUN	Microsoft Dial-Up Networking export file
DV	Digital video file (MIME)
DWD	DiamondWare digitized file
DWG	AutoCAD drawing files; AutoCAD drawing, or older Generic CADD drawing format
DXF	Drawing Interchange (eXchange) format, a text representation of the binary DWG format; Data Exchange File
DXR	Macromedia Director protected (not editable) movie file
D64	Commodore 64 emulator disk image file
EDA	Ensoniq ASR disk image

Extension	Description
EDD	Element Definition Document (FrameMaker+ SGML documents)
EDE	Ensoniq EPS disk image
EDK	Ensoniq KT disk image
EDQ	Ensoniq SQ1/SQ2/KS32 disk image
EDS	Ensoniq SQ80 disk image
EDV	Ensoniq VFX-SD disk image
EFA	Ensoniq ASR file
EFE	Ensoniq EPS file
EFK	Ensoniq KT file
EFQ	Ensoniq SQ1/SQ2/KS32 file
EFS	Ensoniq SQ80 file
EFV	Ensoniq VFX-SD file
EMD	ABT Extended Module
EMF	Enhanced Windows Metafile
EML	Microsoft Outlook Express mail message (MIME RFC822)
ENC	Encore file
ENFF	Neutral File Format extension
EPHTML	Enhanced Perl-parsed HTML
EPS	Encapsulated PostScript image
EPSF	Encapsulated PostScript file
ER1	ERWin file
ERR	Stores the error messages that result when the RoboHELP Help Compiler attempts to compile the source files of a Help system
ERX	ERWin file
ESPS	ESPS audio file
EUI	Ensoniq ESP family compacted disk image
EVY	Envoy document
EWL	Microsoft Encarta document
EXC	Microsoft Word Exclusion Dictionary
EXE	Executable file (program)
F	FORTRAN file
F2R	Farandoyle linear module format
F3R	Farandoyle blocked linear module format
F77	FORTRAN file
F90	FORTRAN file
FAR	Farandole Composer music module (MOD) file
FAV	Microsoft Outlook navigation bar
FAX	Fax type image
FBK	Navison Financials Backup
FCD	Virtual CD-ROM

continues

Extension	Description
FDB	Navison Financials Database
FDF	Adobe Acrobat forms document file
FEM	CADRE Finite Element Mesh file
FFA, FFL, FFO, FFX	Microsoft Fast Find file
FFF	GUS PnP bank file format
FFT	Final Form Text (part of IBM's DCA)
FH3	Aldus Freehand 3 drawing
FIF	Fractal image file
FIG	A file format used by REND386/AVRIL
FITS	CCD camera image; Flexible Image Transport System
FLA	Macromedia Flash movie
FLC	Autodesk FLIC animation
FLF	Corel Paradox derived form; Navison Financials License file; OS/2 driver file
FLI	Autodesk FLIC animation
FLT	StarTrekker music module (MOD) file; file format used in MultiGen Inc.'s Open Flight; Corel filter
FM	Adobe FrameMaker Document
FMB	Oracle binary source code for form, version 4.0 and later
FML	File Mirror List (GetRight)
FMT	Oracle text format for form, version 4.0 and later; Microsoft Schedule+ print file
FMX	Oracle executable form, version 4.0 and later
FND	Microsoft Explorer saved search file (Find applet)
FNG	Font group file (Font Navigator)
FNK	FunkTracker module format
FOG	Fontographer font
FON	System font
FOR	FORTRAN file
FOT	Font-related file
FP	FileMaker Pro file
FP1	Flying Pigs for Windows data file
FP3	FileMaker Pro file
FPT	FileMaker Pro file; Microsoft FoxPro memo fields
FPX	FlashPix bitmap
FRM	Form; FrameMaker or FrameBuilder document; Oracle executable form, version 3.0 and earlier; Visual Basic form; WordPerfect Merge form; DataCAD Symbol Report file
FRT	Microsoft FoxPro report file
FRX	Visual Basic form stash file; Microsoft FoxPro report file

Extension	Description
FSF	f Print Audit Tool file format
FSL	Borland's Paradox 7 forms; Corel Paradox saved form
FSM	Farandoyle Sample format
FT	Lotus Notes full-text index
FTG	Full-text search group file resulting from using Find in the Windows Help system—can be erased; will be rebuilt when needed
FTS	Full-text search index file resulting from using Find in the Windows Help system
FW2	Framework II
FW3	Framework III file
FW4	Framework IV file
FXP	Microsoft FoxPro compiled source file
FZB	Casio FZ-1 Bank dump
FZF	Casio FZ-1 Full dump
FZV	Casio FZ-1 Voice dump
G721	Raw CCITT G.721 $bit ADPCM format data
G723	Raw CCITT G.723 3 or 5bit ADPCM format data
GAL	Corel Multimedia Manager album
GCD	Generic CADD drawing (later versions)
GCP	Ground Control Point file used in image processing of remote sensing data, often to form map projections—CHIPS (CopenHagen Image Processing System) uses these files
GDB	InterBase database file
GDM	Bells, whistles, and sound boards module format
GED	GEDCOM genealogical data file, a popular format for recording and exchanging genealogical data; Graphic Environment Document drawing
GEM	GEM metafile
GEN	Ventura-generated text file
GetRight	GetRight unfinished-download file
GFC	Patton&Patton Flowcharting 4 flowchart file
GFI, GFX	Genigraphics Graphics Link presentation
GHO	Norton Ghost disk image
GID	Windows 95 global index file (containing Help status)
GIF	CompuServe bitmap
GIM, GIX	Genigraphics Graphics Link presentation
GKH	Ensoniq EPS family disk image file
GKS	Gravis GripKey document
GL	Animation format
GNA	Genigraphics Graphics Link presentation

continues

Extension	Description
GNT	Generated Code, an executable code in a Micro Focus proprietary format
GNX	Genigraphics Graphics Link presentation
GRA	Microsoft Graph
GRD	Grid file used in image processing of remote sensing data, often to form map projections—CHIPS (CopenHagen Image Processing System) uses these files
GRF	Grapher (Golden Software) graph file
GRP	Program Manager Group
GSM	Raw GSM 6.10 audio stream; Raw "byte aligned" GSM 6.10 audio stream; US Robotics voice modems
GTK	Graoumftracker (old) music module (MOD) file
GT2	Graoumftracker (new) music module (MOD) file
GWX, GWZ	Genigraphics Graphics Link presentation
GZ	UNIX gzip compressed file
H	C program header
HCM	IBM HCM configuration file
HCOM	Sound Tools HCOM format
HCR	IBM HCD/HCM production configuration file
HDF	National Center for Supercomputing Applications (NCSA) geospatial Hierarchical Data Format file
HED	HighEdit document
HEL	Microsoft Hellbender saved game
HEX	Macintosh BinHex 2.0 file
HGL	HP Graphics Language drawing
HH	Map file, containing topic IDs and map numbers for each of the topics in a Help system—allows the running application to send the user the appropriate context-sensitive Help topic
HLP	Help file; DataCAD Windows Help file
HOG	LucasArts' Dark Forces WAD file
HPJ	Visual Basic Help project
HPP	C++ program header
HQX	Macintosh BinHex 4.0 file
HST	History file
HT	HyperTerminal
HTM, HTML	Hypertext document
HTT	Microsoft Hypertext Template
HTX	Extended HTML template
HXM	Descent2 HAM file extension
ICA	Citrix file
ICB	Targa bitmap

Extension	Description
ICC	Kodak printer format
ICL	Icon library file
ICM	Image Color Matching profile file
ICO	Windows icon
IDB	MSDev intermediate file
IDD	MIDI Instrument Definition
IDF	MIDI Instrument Definition (Windows 95 required file)
IDQ	Internet Data Query file
IDX	Microsoft FoxPro relational database index file; Symantec Q&A relational database index file; Microsoft Outlook Express file
IFF	Interchange Format File; Amiga ILBM
IGES	Initial Graphics Exchange Specification file
IGF	Inset Systems metafile
IIF	QuickBooks for Windows interchange file
ILBM	Bitmap graphic file
IMA	WinImage disk image file
IMG	GEM image
IMZ	WinImage compressed disk image file
INC	Assembler language or Active Server include file
INF	Information file
INI	Initialization file; MWave DSP synth's mwsynth.ini GM-setup; Gravis Ultrasound bank setup
INP	Oracle source code for form, version 3.0 and earlier
INRS	INRS-Telecommunications audio
INS	InstallShield install script; X-Internet sign-up file; Ensoniq EPS family instrument; Sample Cell/II MAC/PC instruments
INT	Intermediate Code, an executable code produced when a source program is syntax-checked
IOF	Findit document
IQY	Microsoft Internet Inquiry file
ISO	Lists the files on a CD-ROM; based on the ISO 9660 CD-ROM file system standard
ISP	X-Internet sign-up file
IST	Digital Tracker instrument file
ISU	InstallShield uninstall script
IT	Impulse Tracker music module (MOD) file
ITI	Impulse Tracker instrument
ITS	Impulse Tracker sample; Internet document set
IV	File format used in Open Inventor
IVD	Beyond 20/20 microdata dimension or variable-level file

continues

Extension	Description
IVP	Beyond 20/20 user subset profile file
IVT	Beyond 20/20 table or aggregate data file
IVX	Beyond 20/20 microdata directory file
IW	Idlewild screen saver
IWC	Install Watch document
J62	Ricoh camera format
JAR	Java ARchive file (a compressed file for applets and related files)
JAVA	Java source code
JBF	Paint Shop Pro image browser file
JFF, JFIF, JIF	JPEG file
JMP	SAS' JMPDiscovery chart-to-statistics file
JN1	Epic MegaGames' Jill of the Jungle data file
JPE, JPEG, JPG	JPEG graphic
JS	JavaScript source code
JSP	HTML page containing a reference to a Java servlet
JTF	JPEG bitmap
K25	Kurzweil 2500 sample
KAR	Karaoke MIDI file (text + MIDI)
KDC	Kodak Photo-Enhancer
KEY	DataCAD icon toolbar file
KFX	KoFax Group 4 image
KIZ	Kodak digital postcard file
KKW	Contains all K-keywords in the RoboHELP Help project Index Designer not associated with topics
KMP	Korg Trinity KeyMaP file
KQP	Konica camera native files
KR1	Kurzweil 2000 sample (multi-floppy)
KRZ	Kurzweil 2000 sample
KSF	Korg Trinity Sample File
KYE	Kye game data
LAB	Visual dBASE label file
LBM	Deluxe Paint bitmap
LBT, LBX	Microsoft FoxPro labels
LDB	Microsoft Access lock file
LDL	Corel Paradox delivered library
LEG	Legacy document
LES	Logitech Entertainment system game profiles (same as REG file)
LFT	3D Studio (DOS) loft file
LGO	Paintbrush logo file
LHA	Alternate file suffix for LZH

Extension	Description
LIB	Library
LIN	DataCAD line type file
LIS	Output file produced by a Structured Query Reporting (SQR) program
LLX	Laplink Exchange Agent
LNK	Windows shortcut file
LOG	Log file
LPD	Helix Nuts and Bolts file
LRC	Intel Video Phone file
LSL	Corel Paradox saved library
LSP	AutoLISP, CommonLISP, and other LISP language files
LST	List file
LU	ThoughtWing Library Unit file
LVL	Parallax Software's Miner Descent/D2 Level Extension
LWLO	Lightwave layered object file
LWOB	Lightwave object file
LWP	Lotus WordPro 96/97 file
LWSC	Lightwave scene file
LYR	DataCAD layer file
LZH	LH ARC compressed archive
LZS	Skyroads data file
M1V	MPEG-related file (MIME type "mpeg")
M3D	Corel Motion 3D animation
M3U	MPEG URL (MIME audio file)
MAC	MacPaint image
MAD	Microsoft Access module
MAF	Microsoft Access form
MAG	Graphics file format found in some Japanese files
MAGIC	Magic Mail Monitor configuration file
MAK	Visual Basic or Microsoft Visual C++ project
MAM	Microsoft Access macro
MAN	UNIX manual page output
MAP	Map file; Duke Nukem 3D WAD game file
MAQ	Microsoft Access query
MAR	Microsoft Access report
MAS	Lotus Freelance Graphics SmartMaster file
MAT	Microsoft Access table; 3D Studio MAX Material Library; Matlab variables binary file
MAUD	MAUD sample format
MAX	Kinetix's 3D Studio MAX file format for a 3D scene; Paperport file; OrCAD layout file

continues

Extension	Description
MAZ	Hover maze data; file format used by Division's dVS/dVISE
MB1	Apogee Monster Bash data file
MBOX	Berkeley Unix mailbox format
MBX	Microsoft Outlook saved email; Eudora mailboxes
MCC	Dialer10 calling card
MCP	Metrowerks CodeWarrior project file
MCR	DataCAD Keyboard macro file
MCW	Microsoft Word for Macintosh document
MDA	Microsoft Access add-in; Microsoft Access workgroup for version 2
MDB	Microsoft Access database
MDE	Microsoft Access MDE file
MDL	Digital Tracker music module (MOD) file; Quake model file
MDN	Microsoft Access blank database template
MDW	Microsoft Access workgroup
MDZ	Microsoft Access wizard template
MED	Music Editor, OctaMED music module (MOD) file
MER	Format for interchanging spreadsheet/database data; recognized by FileMaker, Excel, and others
MET	Presentation Manager metafile
MFG	Pro/ENGINEER manufacturing file
MGF	File in a Materials and Geometry Format
MHTM, MHTML	MHTML document (MIME)
MI	Miscellaneous
MIC	Microsoft Image Composer file
MID	MIDI music
MIF	Adobe FrameMaker Interchange Format
MIFF	Machine Independent Format File
MIM, MIME, MME	Multipart file in the Multi-Purpose Internet Mail Extensions (MIME) format, often created as the result of sending email with attachments in AOL; the files in a multipart MIM file can be "opened" (unarchived and separated into individual files) using WinZip or a similar program
MLI	File in 3D Studio's Material Library format
MMF	Meal Master Format, a recipe cataloging format; Microsoft Mail file
MMG	Beyond 20/20 table or aggregate data file
MMM	Microsoft Multimedia Movie

Extension	Description
MMP	Mindmapor MindManager file
MN2	Descent2 Mission File
MND, MNI	Mandelbrot for Windows
MNG	Multi-image Network Graphics
MNT, MNX	Microsoft FoxPro menus
MNU	Visual dBASE menu file; Intertel Systems Interact menu file
MOD	FastTracker, StarTrekker, Noise Tracker (etc.) music module file; Microsoft Multiplan spreadsheet; Amiga/PC tracker module
MOV	QuickTime for Windows movie
MP2	MPEG Audio Layer 2
MP3	MPEG Audio Layer 3 (AC3)
MPA	MPEG-related file (MIME type "mpeg")
MPE, MPEG, MPG	MPEG animation
MPP	Microsoft Project file; CAD drawing file format
MPR	Microsoft FoxPro menus (compiled)
MRI	MRI Scan
MSA	Magic Shadow Archive
MSDL	Manchester's Scene Description Language
MSG	Microsoft Mail message
MSI	Windows Installer package
MSN	Microsoft Network document; Descent Mission File
MSP	Microsoft Paint bitmap; Windows Installer patch file
MST	Windows Installer transform
MTM	MultiTracker music module (MOD) file
MUL	Ultima online
MUS	Music
MUS10	Mus10 audio
MVB	Microsoft Multimedia Viewer file
MWP	Lotus WordPro 97 SmartMaster file
NAN	Nanoscope file (Raw Grayscale)
NAP	NAP Metafile
NCB	Microsoft Developer Studio file
NCD	Norton Change Directory
NCF	NetWare Command File; Lotus Notes internal clipboard
NDO	3D low-polygon modeler, Nendo
netCDF	network Common Data Form
NFF	Neutral File Format
NFT	NetObject Fusion template file
NIL	Norton icon library file (EasyIcons-compatible)
NIST	NIST Sphere audio
NLB	Oracle 7 data

continues

Extension	Description
NLM	NetWare Loadable Module
NLS	National Language Support file used for localization (for example, by Uniscape)
NLU	Norton Live Update email trigger file
NOD	NetObject Fusion file
NSF	Lotus Notes database
NSO	NetObject Fusion document file
NST	Noise Tracker music module (MOD) file
NS2	Lotus Notes database (version 2)
NTF	Lotus Notes database template
NTX	CA-Clipper index file
NWC	Noteworthy Composer song file
NWS	Microsoft Outlook Express news message (MIME RFC822)
O01	Typhoon voice file
OBD	Microsoft Office binder
OBJ	Object file
OBZ	Microsoft Office Binder Wizard
OCX	Microsoft Object Linking and Embedding custom control
ODS	Microsoft Outlook Express mailbox file
OFF	3D mesh Object File Format
OFN	Microsoft Office FileNew file
OFT	Microsoft Outlook template
OKT	Oktalyzer music module (MOD) file
OLB	OLE object Library
OLE	OLE object
OOGL	Object-Oriented Graphics Library
OPL	Organiser Programming Language source file—Psion/Symbian
OPO	OPL output executable file
OPT	Microsoft Developer Studio file
OPX	OPL extension DLL
ORA	Oracle 7 configuration
ORC	Oracle 7 script
ORG	Lotus Organizer file
OR2	Lotus Organizer 2 file
OR3	Lotus Organizer 97 file
OSS	Microsoft Office search file
OST	Microsoft Exchange/Outlook offline file
OTL	Super NoteTab template file
OUT	C language output file
P3	Primavera Project Planner file

Extension	Description
P10	Tektronix Plot 10 drawing
P65	PageMaker 6.5 file
P7C	Digital ID file (MIME)
PAB	Microsoft Personal Address Book
PAC	SB Studio II package
PAK	Quake WAD file
PAL	Compressed file
PART	Go!Zilla partially downloaded file
PAS	Pascal source code
PAT	DataCAD Hatch pattern file; CorelDRAW pattern; Advanced Gravis Ultrasound/Forte tech; Patch
PBD	PowerBuilder dynamic library, an alternative to a native DLL
PBF	Turtle Beach's Pinnacle bank file
PBK	Microsoft Phonebook
PBL	PowerBuilder library used in the PowerBuilder development environment
PBM	Portable bitmap
PBR	PowerBuilder resource
PCD	Kodak Photo-CD image; P-Code compiled test scripts as in Microsoft Test and Microsoft Visual Test
PCE	Maps Eudora mailbox names to DOS filenames
PCL	Hewlett-Packard Printer Control Language file (printer-ready bitmap)
PCM	Audio file format; OKI MSM6376 synth chip PCM format
PCP	Symantec Live Update Pro file
PCS	PICS animation
PCT	Macintosh PICT drawing
PCX	ZSoft PC Paintbrush bitmap
PDB	3Com PalmPilot database file
PDD	Graphic image that can be opened with Paint Shop Pro and possibly other image software
PDF	Adobe Acrobat Portable Document Format file (displayable with a Web browser); Microsoft Systems Management Server Package Definition File; NetWare Printer Definition File
PDP	Brøderbund's Print Shop Deluxe file
PDQ	Patton & Patton Flowcharting PDQ Lite file
PDS	Photographic image file (origin not yet identified)
PF	Aladdin Systems Private Files encrypted file
PFA	Type 1 font (ASCII)
PFB	Type 1 font (binary)
PFC	PF Component

continues

Extension	Description
PFM	Printer Font Metrics
PGD	Pretty Good Privacy (PGP) virtual disk file
PGL	HP Plotter drawing
PGM	Portable Graymap (bitmap)
PGP	Pretty Good Privacy (PGP) encrypted file
PH	Temporary file generated by Microsoft Help Compiler
PHP, PHP3	HTML page that includes a PHP script
PHTML	HTML page that includes a PHP script; Perl-parsed HTML
PIC	PC Paint bitmap; Lotus picture; Macintosh PICT drawing
PICT	Macintosh PICT image file
PIF	Program Information File; IBM PIF drawing
PIG	LucasArts' Dark Forces WAD file
PIN	Epic Pinball data file
PIX	Inset Systems bitmap
PJ	MKS Source Integrity file
PJX, PJT	Microsoft Visual FoxPro Project
PKG	Microsoft Developer Studio application extension (similar to a DLL file)
PKR	PGP Public Keyring
PL	Perl program
PLG	File format used by REND386/AVRIL
PLI	Oracle 7 data description
PLM	DisorderTracker2 module
PLS	DisorderTracker2 sample; MPEG PLayList file (used by WinAmp)
PLT	HPGL Plotter drawing; AutoCAD plot drawing; Gerber sign-making software
PM5	Pagemaker 5.0 file
PM6	Pagemaker 6.0 file
PNG	Portable Network Graphics bitmap; Paint Shop Pro browser catalog
PNT, PNTG	MacPaint graphic file
POG	Descent2 PIG file extension
POL	Windows NT policy file
POP	Visual dBASE pop-up file
POT	Microsoft PowerPoint template
POV	Persistence of Vision ray-tracer
PP4	Picture Publisher 4 bitmap
PPA	Microsoft PowerPoint add-in
PPF	Turtle Beach's Pinnacle program file
PPM	Portable Pixelmap bitmap

Extension	Description
PPP	Parson Power Publisher; Serif PagePlus desktop publishing default output
PPS	Microsoft PowerPoint slide show
PPT	Microsoft PowerPoint presentation
PQI	PowerQuest Drive Image file
PRC	3Com PalmPilot resource (text or program) file
PRE	Lotus Freelance presentation
PRF	Windows system file; Macromedia Director settings file
PRG	dBASE, Clipper, and FoxPro program source files; WAVmaker program
PRJ	3D Studio (DOS) project file
PRN	Print table (space-delimited text); DataCAD Windows printer file
PRP	Oberon's Prospero data conversion product saved project file
PRS	Harvard Graphics for Windows presentation
PRT	Print-formatted file; Pro/ENGINEER part file
PRV	PsiMail Internet provider template file
PRZ	Lotus Freelance Graphics 97 file
PS	PostScript-formatted file (a PostScript printer-ready file)
PSB	Pinnacle Sound Bank
PSD	Adobe Photoshop bitmap
PSI	PSION a-law audio
PSM	Protracker Studio Module format; sound data for Epic's games
PSP	Paint Shop Pro image file
PST	Microsoft Outlook Personal Folder file
PTD	Pro/ENGINEER table file
PTM	Polytracker music module (MOD) file
PUB	Ventura Publisher publication; Microsoft Publisher document
PWD	Microsoft Pocket Word document
PWL	Windows 95 password list file
PWP	Photoworks image file (a roll of files that can be viewed using Photoworks)
PWZ	Microsoft PowerPoint Wizard
PXL	Microsoft Pocket Excel spreadsheet
PY	Saved e-messages from Yahoo; Python script file
PYC	Python script file
QAD	PF QuickArt Document
QBW	QuickBooks for Windows file
QDT	QuickBooks data file from the Quicken UK Accountancy/Tax/Invoice program
QD3D	Apple's QuickDraw 3D Metafile format

continues

Extension	Description
QFL	FAMILY LAWYER document
QIC	Microsoft Backup file
QIF	QuickTime-related image (MIME); Quicken Import File
QLB	Quick Library
QM	Quality Motion file
QRY	Microsoft Query
QST	Quake Spy Tab file
QT, QTM	QuickTime Movie
QTI, QTIF	QuickTime-related image
QTP	QuickTime preferences file
QTS	Mac PICT image file; QuickTime-related image
QTX	QuickTime-related image
QW	Symantec Q&A Write program file
QXD	Quark XPress file
R	Pegasus Mail resource file
RA	RealAudio sound
RAM	RealAudio metafile
RAR	RAR compressed archive (Eugene Roshall's format)
RAS	Sun raster images bitmap
RAW	Raw File Format (bitmap); Raw signed PCM data; Raw signed PCM data
RBH	Maintained by RoboHELP, the RBH file adds to the information contained in the Help project file
RDF	Resource Description Framework file (related to XML and metadata)
RDL	Descent Registered Level
REC	Recorder macro; RapidComm voice file
REG	Registration file
REP	Visual dBASE report file
RES	Microsoft Visual C++ resource
RFT	Revisable Form Text (part of IBM's DCA or Document Content Architecture)
RGB, SGI	Silicon Graphics RGB files
RLE	Run-Length Encoded bitmap
RL2	Descent2 Registered Level
RM	RealAudio video file
RMD	Microsoft RegMaid document
RMF	Rich Map Format (used by 3D game editors to store a map)
RMI	MIDI music
ROM	Cartridge-based home video game emulator file (exact copy of ROM contents in cartridges from Atari 2600, Colecovision, Sega, Nintendo, etc.; not interchangeable between emulators)

Extension	Description
ROV	Rescue Rover data file
RPM	RedHat Package Manager package (for Linux)
RPT	Microsoft Visual Basic Crystal Reports file
RRS	Save file for the Ace game Road Rash
RSL	Borland's Paradox 7 reports
RSM	WinWay Resume Writer résumé file
RTF	Rich Text Format document
RTK	Used by RoboHELP to simulate the search feature of Windows Help
RTM	Real Tracker music module (MOD) file
RTS	RealAudio's RTSL document; RoboHELP to speed complex operations
RUL	Extension used in InstallShield
RVP	Microsoft Scan Configuration file (MIME)
R*xx*	RAR compressed files from a multi-volume archive (*xx* = a number from 01 to 99)
S	Assembler source code
S3I	Scream Tracker v3 instrument
S3M	Sound module file for Scream Tracker v3
SAM	Ami Professional document; signed 8-bit sample data
SAV	Saved game file
SB	Raw Signed Byte (8-bit) data
SBK	Creative Labs' Soundfont 1.0 Bank file (Soundblaster)/EMU SoundFont v1.x Bank files
SBL	Shockwave Flash object
SC2	Microsoft Schedule+ 7 file format; SAS catalog (Windows 95/NT, OS/2, Mac)
SC3	SimCity 3000 saved game file
SCC	Microsoft Source Safe file
SCD	Matrix/Imapro SCODL slide image; Microsoft Schedule+ 7
SCF	Windows Explorer command file
SCH	Microsoft Schedule+ 1
SCI	ScanVec Inspire native file format
SCN	TrueSpace2 scene
SCP	Dial-up networking script
SCR	Windows screen saver; fax image; script file
SCT	SAS catalog (DOS); Scitex CT bitmap; Microsoft FoxPro forms
SCT01	SAS catalog (UNIX)
SCV	ScanVec CASmate native file format
SCX	Microsoft FoxPro forms
SD	Sound Designer I audio

continues

Extension	Description
SD2	Sound Designer 2 flattened file/data fork; SAS database (Windows 95/NT OS/2, Mac)
SDF	System Data File Format—legacy Unisys (Sperry) format
SDK	Roland S-series floppy disk image
SDL	SmartDraw library
SDR	SmartDraw drawing
SDS	Raw Midi Sample Dump Standard file
SDT	SmartDraw template
SDV	Semicolon-Divided Values file
SDW	Lotus WordPro graphic file; Raw signed DWORD (32-bit) data
SDX	Midi sample dump standard files compacted by SDX
SEA	Self-expanding archive (used by StuffIt for Macintosh files and possibly by others)
SEP	Tagged Image File Format (TIFF) bitmap
SES	Cool Edit Session file (common digital audio editor file)
SF	IRCAM SoundFile format
SF2	Emu SoundFont v2.0 file; Creative Labs' Soundfont 2.0 Bank file (Sound Blaster)
SFD	SoundStage sound file data
SFI	SoundStage sound file info
SFR	Sonic Foundry Sample Resource
SFW	Seattle Film Works (mangled JPEG)
SFX	RAR self-extracting archive
SGML	Standard Generalized Markup Language
SHB	Corel Show presentation; document shortcut file
SHG	Hotspot bitmap
SHP	3D Studio (DOS) shapes file; format used by some programs for 3D modeling of multipart interactive triangle models
SHS	Shell scrap file; reportedly used to send "password stealers"
SHTML	HTML file containing server-side includes (SSI)
SHW	Corel Show presentation
SIG	Signature file
SIT	StuffIt archive of Mac files
SIZ	Oracle 7 configuration
SKA	PGP secret Keyring
SKL	Macromedia Director resource file
SL	PACT's Save Layout extension
SLB	Autodesk Slide Library file format
SLD	Autodesk Slide file format
SLK	Symbolic Link (SYLK) spreadsheet
SM3	DataCAD symbol file

Extension	Description
SMP	Samplevision format; Ad Lib Gold Sample
SND	NeXT sound; Mac Sound Resource; raw unsigned PCM data; AKAI MPC-series sample
SNDR	Sounder sound file
SNDT	Sndtool sound file
SOU	SB Studio II sound
SPD	Speach Data file
SPL	Shockwave Flash Object; DigiTrakker Sample
SPPACK	SPPack sound sample
SPRITE	Acorn's bitmap format
SQC	Structured Query Language (SQR) common code file
SQL	Informix SQL queries; generally used by database products as an extension for SQL queries (scripts, text, or binary)
SQR	Structured Query Language (SQR) program file
SSD01	SAS data sets (UNIX)
SSD	SAS database (DOS)
SSF	Enable spreadsheet file
ST	Atari ST disk image
STL	Stereolithography file
STM	Shorter suffix for .shtml, an HTML file containing a server-side include (SSI); Scream Tracker v2 music module (MOD) file
STR	Screen saver file
STY	Ventura Publisher style sheet
SVX	Amiga 8SVX sound; Interchange file format, 8SVX/16SV
SW	Raw signed Word (16-bit) data
SWA	Shockwave audio file in Macromedia Director (an MP3 file)
SWF	Shockwave Flash object
SWP	DataCAD Swap file
SYS	System file
SYW	Yamaha SY-series wave files
T64	Commodore 64 emulator tape image file
TAB	Guitar Tablature file
TAR	Tape archive
TAZ	UNIX gzip/tape archive
TBK	Asymetrix Toolbook interactive multimedia files
TCL	Script in the TCL/TK language
TDB	Thumbs Plus database
TDDD	File format used by Imagine and Turbo Silver ray-tracers
TEX	Texture file
TGA	Targa bitmap

continues

Extension	Description
TGZ	UNIX gzip/tape archive
THEME	Windows 95 desktop theme
THN	Graphics Workshop for Windows thumbnail
TIF, TIFF	Tagged Image File Format (TIFF) bitmap
TIG	Tiger file, used by the U.S. government to distribute maps
TLB	OLE type library
TLE	Two-Line Element set (NASA)
TMP	Windows temporary file
TOC	Table of contents of Eudora mailboxes
TOL	Kodak photo enhancer
TOS	Operation System for Atari line of 16/32 and 32/32 computers
TPL	CakeWalk Audio template file; DataCAD template file
TPP	Teleport Pro Project
TRK	Kermit script file
TRM	Terminal file
TRN	MKS Source Integrity project usage log
TTF	TrueType font
TTK	Corel Catalyst Translation Tool Kit
TWF	TabWorks file
TWW	Tagwrite template
TX8	MS-DOS text
TXB	Descent/D2 encoded briefing file
TXT	ASCII text-formatted audio data
TXW	Yamaha TX16W wave files
TZ	Old compression format file
T2T	Sonata CAD modeling software file
UB	Raw unsigned byte (8-bit) data
UDF	Windows NT/2000 uniqueness database file
UDW	Raw unsigned double word (32-bit) data
ULAW	U.S. telephony format (CCITT G.711) audio
ULT	UltraTracker music module (MOD) file
UNI	MikMod UniMod formatted file
URL	Internet shortcut file
USE	MKS Source Integrity file
UU, UUE	UU-encoded file
UW	Raw unsigned word (16-bit) data
UWF	UltraTracker Wave file
V8	Covox 8-bit audio file
VAP	Annotated speech
VBA	VBase file

Extension	Description
VBP	Microsoft Visual Basic project
VBW	Microsoft Visual Basic workspace
VBX	Microsoft Visual Basic custom control
VCE	Natural MicroSystems (NMS) unformatted voice file (used by Cool Edit)
VCF	Virtual card file (Netscape); Vevi configuration file; defines objects for use with Sense8's WorldToolKit
VCT, VCX	Microsoft FoxPro class library
VDA	Targa bitmap
VI	Virtual Instrument file from National Instruments LABView product
VIFF	Khoros Visualisation format
VIR	File identified as a virus-infected file by Norton Anti-Virus and possibly others
VIV	VivoActive Player streaming video file
VIZ	Division's dVS/dVISE file
VLB	Corel Ventura Library
VMF	FaxWorks audio file
VOC	Creative Labs' Sound Blaster audio file
VOX	Dialogic audio file coded using ADPCM; Natural MicroSystems (NMS) formatted voice file; Talking Technology audio file
VP	Ventura Publisher publication
VQE, VQL	Yamaha Sound-VQ Locator file
VQF	Yamaha Sound-VQ file (possible emerging standard)
VRF	Oracle 7 configuration
VRML	Virtual Reality Modeling Language file
VSD	Visio drawing (flow chart or schematic)
VSL	Download list file (GetRight)
VSN	Windows 9x/NT ViruSafe version file, used to keep information about all the files in a directory; when a file is accessed, information is compared with the VSN information to ensure that they match
VSS	Visio stencil file
VST	Targa bitmap
VSW	Visio workspace file
VXD	Microsoft Windows virtual device driver
W3L	W3Launch file
WAB	Microsoft Outlook file
WAD	Large file for DOOM game containing video, player level, and other information
WAL	Quake 2 texture file

continues

Extension	Description
WAV	Windows Waveform sound
WB1, WB2	QuattroPro for Windows spreadsheet
WBK	Microsoft Word backup
WBL	Argo WebLoad II upload file
WBR	Crick Software's WordBar file
WBT	Crick Software's Wordbar template
WCM	WordPerfect macro
WDB	Microsoft Works database
WDG	War FTP remote daemon file
WEB	CorelXARA Web document
WFB	Turtle Beach's WaveFront Bank (Maui/Rio/Monterey)
WFD	Turtle Beach's WaveFront Drum set (Maui/Rio/Monterey)
WFM	Visual dBASE Windows form
WFN	Symbols for use in CorelDRAW
WFP	Turtle Beach's WaveFront Program (Maui/Rio/Monterey)
WGP	Wild Board Games data file
WID	Ventura width table
WIL	WinImage file
WIZ	Microsoft Word wizard
WK1	Lotus 1-2-3 versions 1 and 2 spreadsheet
WK3	Lotus 1-2-3 version 3 spreadsheet
WK4	Lotus 1-2-3 version 4 spreadsheet
WKS	Lotus 1-2-3 spreadsheet; Microsoft Works document
WLD	REND386/AVRIL file
WLF	Argo WebLoad I upload file
WLL	Microsoft Word add-in
WMF	Windows Metafile
WOW	Grave Composer music module (MOD) file
WP	WordPerfect document
WP4	WordPerfect 4 document
WP5	WordPerfect 5 document
WP6	WordPerfect 6 document
WPD	WordPerfect document or demo
WPF	Enable word processing document
WPG	WordPerfect graphic
WPS	Microsoft Works document
WPT	WordPerfect template
WPW	Novell PerfectWorks document
WQ1	Quattro Pro/DOS spreadsheet
WQ2	Quattro Pro/DOS version 5 spreadsheet
WR1	Lotus Symphony
WRG	ReGet document

Extension	Description
WRI	Write document
WRK	Cakewalk music audio project file
WRL	Virtual reality model
WRZ	VRML file object
WS1	WordStar for Windows 1 document
WS2	WordStar for Windows 2 document
WS3	WordStar for Windows 3 document
WS4	WordStar for Windows 4 document
WS5	WordStar for Windows 5 document
WS6	WordStar for Windows 6 document
WS7	WordStar for Windows 7 document
WSD	WordStar 2000 document
WVL	Wavelet compressed bitmap
WWL	Microsoft Word add-in file
X	AVS image format
XAR	CorelXARA drawing
XBM	MIME "xbitmap" image
XI	Instrument sample file for Scream Tracker
XIF	Wang imaging file (comes with Windows 95)
XLA	Microsoft Excel add-in
XLB	Microsoft Excel toolbar
XLC	Microsoft Excel chart
XLD	Microsoft Excel dialog
XLK	Microsoft Excel backup
XLL	Microsoft Excel add-in file
XLM	Microsoft Excel macro
XLS	Microsoft Excel worksheet
XLT	Microsoft Excel template
XLV	Microsoft Excel VBA module
XLW	Microsoft Excel workbook/workspace
XM	FastTracker 2, Digital Tracker music module (MOD) file
XNK	Microsoft Exchange shortcut file
XPM	X bitmap format
XR1	Epic MegaGames Xargon data file
XTP	XTree data file
XWD	X Window dump format
XWF	Yamaha XG Works file (MIDI sequencing)
XY3	XYWrite III document
XY4	XYWrite IV document
XYP	XYWrite III Plus document
XYW	XYWrite for Windows 4.0 document
X16	Macromedia Extra (program extension), 16-bit

continues

Extension	Description
X32	Macromedia Extra (program extension), 32-bit
YAL	Arts & Letters clip art library
YBK	Microsoft Encarta Yearbook
Z	UNIX gzip
ZAP	Windows software installation settings file
ZIP	Zip file
ZOO	Early compressed file format
000-999	Used to number old (backup) versions of files (for example, CONFIG.SYS when changed by an installation program); also used to number related data files for multiple users of a small-scale PC application
12M	Lotus 1-2-3 97 SmartMaster file
123	Lotus 1-2-3 97 file
2D	VersaCAD two-dimensional drawing file
2GR, 3GR	VGA Graphics driver/configuration files under Windows
3D	VersaCAD three-dimensional drawing file
3DM	3D NURBS modeler, Rhino
3DS	File in 3D Studio (for DOS) format
386	File for use in an 80386 or higher microprocessor
4GE	Informix 4GL compiled code
4GL	Informix 4GL source code
669	Composer 669; UNIX Composer music mod file; 669 tracker module
#01 and higher	Method of numbering picture files for a roll of film that has been scanned for computer presentation
$$$	Used by OS/2 to keep track of archived files
@@@	Screen files used in the installation and instruction on use of such applications as Microsoft Codeview for C

B

Complete Answer File Syntax

IN THIS APPENDIX, SECTION HEADINGS CONTAINED within brackets ([ ]) are section headers for the answer file. The subsections within each section list the key names; values within those subsections are possible selections for the specified key.

For example, to assign the `Yes` value to the `AutoLogon` key, the entry should say `AutoLogon=Yes`. Spaces before and after the equal sign (=) are ignored.

> **Microsoft Windows 2000 Guide to Unattended Setup**
> For the most recent information, extract the UNATTEND.DOC file from the \SUPPORT\TOOLS\DEPLOY.CAB file on the Windows 2000 retail CDs.

[Unattended]

This section header is required when creating an unattended install file. If this header isn't present, the answer file won't be processed.

ComputerType

There is no need to specify this key unless you'll be installing a custom, vendor-supplied Hardware Abstraction Layer (HAL).

Key values:

`<HAL>, Retail`	Install the default HAL from the Windows 2000 CD.
`<HAL>, OEM`	Load the OEM-specific HAL. The driver name must be listed subsequently in the `[OEMBootFiles]` section.

DriverSigningPolicy

This key determines how the unattended install process will handle unsigned drivers. Drivers included on the Windows 2000 CD are signed; third-party drivers may or may not be signed. If you select `Ignore`, the system will still warn the user when attempting to install a newer, unsigned version of a driver included on the Windows 2000 CD.

Key values:

`Ignore`	Install unsigned drivers.
`Warn`	Pause installation and prompt the user for action when encountering unsigned drivers. This is the default setting if the key isn't specified.
`Block`	Don't install unsigned drivers.

ExtendOemPartition

For NTFS partitions, the system partition will be expanded into any unused, nonpartitioned disk space. Doesn't work with non–NTFS partitions. If specifying this value in a SYSPREP.INF file, the destination computer's hard drive must have the same capacity as or greater capacity than the master computer.

Key values:

`0`	Don't extend the system partition. This is the default setting if the key isn't specified.
`1`	Extend the system partition.
`<number>`	Increase the system partition size by `<number>` megabytes.

FileSystem

Specifies whether Setup should convert the system partition to NTFS.

Key values:

`ConvertNTFS`	Convert the system partition to NTFS.
`LeaveAlone`	Don't convert the system partition; leave it as is. This is the default setting if the key isn't specified.

InstallFilesPath

This key is valid when used with a SYSPREP.INF answer file. The specified value points to the path of additional files needed during setup, such as language files and files to support Uniprocessor mode when imaging a multiprocessor system.

Key value:

`<path>`	Path string to the support files. This may contain system variables. For example, within the SYSPREP folder, additional support files may be stored in the i386 folder. The path would then be `"%systemdrive%\sysprep\i386"`.

KeepPageFile

This key is valid only for SYSPREP-based installations. This controls whether SYSPREP should regenerate the page file on the first boot of an imaged system. To ensure proper page file regeneration, never specify this key if installing an image on systems with varying RAM sizes.

This key doesn't work quite like other keys. If this key is present at all—regardless of the value—the page file won't be regenerated.

KeyboardLayout

Selects the keyboard layout to install during text-mode setup. This key may be removed in a future release.

Key value:

`<layout description>`	Keyboard layout to use, enclosed in quotes. Must match one of the description strings in the `KeyboardLayout` section of the TXTSETUP.SIF file.

NtUpgrade

If this key is set to `Yes` and setup is started with WINNT32.EXE from Windows NT 3.51, Windows NT 4.0, or Windows 2000, Setup will perform an upgrade rather than a clean install. All user settings will be taken from the current operating system configuration. This setting has no function if you're running WINNT.EXE, installing from the boot disks, installing from the bootable CD-ROM, using SYSPREP, upgrading or installing from Windows 95 or 98, or using Remote Installation Services.

Key values:

`Yes`	Perform an upgrade from a previous installation of Windows NT or Windows 2000.
`No`	Perform a clean install.

OemFilesPath

Points Setup to the location of the \OEM folder, which can contain OEM files and folders not included with the base Windows 2000 code. If the folder exists under the i386 folder of the installation media or distribution share point, you don't need to specify this value.

Key value:

`<path>`	Location of the \OEM folder. Can be a local path or a UNC name.

OemPnPDriversPath

Contains the location of the folders that contain plug and play drivers not included on the Windows 2000 CD. The folders can't contain self-extracting executables, and can't be setup programs.

Key value:

`<folder 1>;<folder 2>`	The value is a list of folders, delimited with semicolons (;), relative to %systemdrive%.

OemPreinstall

Specifies whether to perform an installation from distribution folders or from default media.

Key values:

`Yes`	Any existing subfolders are copied (for example, OEM).
`No`	A standard unattended install is performed.

OemSkipEula

Automatically accepts the End User License Agreement (EULA). End users are required to see and accept this screen. OEMs are not allowed to use this key to bypass the EULA.

Key values:

`Yes`	The person performing the installation and the end user for which Windows is being installed have both read and accepted the terms of the EULA.
`No`	The installer or end user hasn't read the EULA; Setup will pause for the user to read and accept the EULA. This is the default setting if the key isn't specified.

OverwriteOemFilesOnUpgrade

If OEM files have the same name as Windows 2000 system files, they'll be overwritten during an upgrade. This key is present for backward compatibility. If there are unsigned driver files and your `DriverSigningPolicy` key is set to `Block`, OEM files will be overwritten regardless of the value of this key.

Key values:

`Yes`	Overwrite the files. This is the default setting if the key isn't specified.
`No`	Keep the OEM files if conflicts are discovered.

Repartition

Determines whether Setup should delete all partitions on the first drive to create a single partition. This key is valid only when performing an installation by booting from the Windows 2000 CD.

Key values:

`Yes`	Delete other partitions on the first disk.
`No`	Keep existing partitions.

TargetPath

Specifies the installation folder for Windows 2000.

Key values:

`*`	Folder name will be WINNT, unless that folder already exists. If so, Setup will generate a new folder name for the installation named WINNT.*x*, where *x* is the first unused numeric value from 0 to 999.
`<path>`	Specific path into which Windows 2000 should be installed. The drive letter shouldn't be specified; it can be specified using the installation switch `/t` (for WINNT.EXE) or `/tempdrive` (for WINNT32.EXE).

UnattendMode

Specifies the unattended setup mode to use during setup. Any value for this key will run text-mode setup fully automated. Values are listed from least automated to most automated.

Key values:

`GuiAttended`	User must answer all questions presented in GUI-mode setup.

`ProvideDefaults`	User sees all questions presented in GUI-mode setup, but any answers specified in the answer file are provided as defaults. The user can change the default values.
`DefaultHide`	Any tabs for which all answers are supplied through the answer file are not displayed to the end user. Thus, the user can't change specified options. If no questions on a page are answered, the user must complete the answers. If some—but not all—questions on a page are answered, Setup will display the setup screen with defaults filled in for answered questions. In this case, the user must answer any unanswered questions, and can't change the default values for questions on the same page, even if those questions were completed by the answer file.
`ReadOnly`	Similar to `DefaultHide`, except in the case where some—but not all—answers on a page are specified. With `ReadOnly`, the user can't change any default values that have been provided by the answer file.
`FullUnattended`	GUI-mode setup requires no intervention. All answers must be provided by the answer file. If an answer isn't in the answer file, an error message is generated. No user input is allowed when using this setting.

UpdateHAL

This key is valid only when performing a SYSPREP-based installation. This key should be specified only when installing an image created from a uniprocessor master system to a multiprocessor target system. This key notifies Setup to use the Multiprocessor (MP) HAL rather than the Uniprocessor (UP) HAL present when the system was imaged.

Key value:

```
"<hwid>,%windir%\inf\hal.inf"
```

<hwid> specifies `MPS_MP` for an MPS-based multiprocessor HAL or `ACPIAPIC_MP` for the Advanced Configuration and Power Interface (ACPI) Asynchronous Processor Interrupt Controller (APIC) HAL.

UpdateUPHAL

This key is valid only when performing a SYSPREP-based installation. This key should be specified only when installing an image created from a multiprocessor master system using the ACPI APIC HAL to an APIC-compatible uniprocessor or multiprocessor target system. This key notifies Setup to redetect the proper kernel based on the number of processors.

Key value:

`"<hwid>,%systemdrive%\sysprep\i386\Uniproc\Mp2up.inf"`

<hwid> specifies either `MPS_UP` for an MPS-based uniprocessor HAL or `ACPIAPIC_UP` for the Advanced Configuration and Power Interface (ACPI) Asynchronous Processor Interrupt Controller (APIC) HAL. The system will detect whether to use one of these HALs or to use the existing multiprocessor HAL built into the image. If the machine needs the uniprocessor kernel, it will be installed from the %systemdrive%\sysprep\i386\Uniproc folder. You should copy the Uniproc folder from the Windows 2000 source media i386 directory to the i386 directory under the SYSPREP folder of your master machine to prepare your system for imaging before running SYSPREP.

Win9xUpgrade

If this key is set to `Yes` and Setup is started with WINNT32.EXE from Windows 95 or Windows 98, Setup will perform an upgrade rather than a clean install. All user settings will be taken from the current operating system configuration. This setting has no function if you're running WINNT.EXE, installing from boot disks, installing from the bootable CD-ROM, using SYSPREP, upgrading or installing from Windows NT, or using Remote Installation Services.

Key values:

`Yes`	Perform an upgrade from a previous installation of Windows 95 or Windows 98.
`No`	Perform a clean install.

[MassStorageDrivers]

This section lists SCSI drivers that will be loaded and installed during text-mode setup. If this section isn't specified, Setup will attempt to detect the correct SCSI devices on the system and install the retail drivers, if available.

<driver description>

<driver description> must match one of the strings from the right-hand side of the `[SCSI]` section of the TXTSETUP.SIF (from the i386 directory of the Windows 2000 install media) or TXTSETUP.OEM file (possibly included with hardware from an OEM). Multiple instances of the same driver can be specified.

Key values:

`Retail`	Driver was included with the retail Windows 2000 CD (found in the TXTSETUP.SIF file).

`OEM`	Driver wasn't included with the retail Windows 2000 CD, but was supplied by the OEM (found in the TXTSETUP.OEM file). OEM drivers must also be listed in the `[OEMBootFiles]` section (see the following description).

[OEMBootFiles]

Lists boot files supplied by OEMs. Must specify `OemPreinstall = Yes` in the `[Unattended]` section. Files listed under this section must be located in the \OEM\Textmode folder of the distribution media or distribution share point. You don't need this section if you're not specifying values for `ComputerType` or `[MassStorageDrivers]`.

Keys within this section have no values. This section should just list filenames. For example:

```
[OEMBootFiles]
oemscsi.sys
oemscsi.dll
txtsetup.oem
```

<HAL filename>

This should be the same as any HAL specified by the `ComputerType` key in the `[Unattended]` section.

<SCSI driver filename>

This should be the same as any mass-storage device driver description from the `[MassStorageDrivers]` section. If you specified multiple instances of the same description in the `[MassStorageDrivers]` section, you should have the same number of instances for this key.

Txtsetup.oem

This should be a text file containing the descriptions for any OEM-supplied drivers. This file must exist if this section is listed.

[OEM_Ads]

This section allows the administrator to modify the default background bitmap, logo, and background text displayed during the setup process.

Background

Specifies a new background bitmap to display while running Setup. This bitmap will only display at 640 × 480 with 16 colors.

Key value:

`<filename>, <resource ID>`	`<filename>` is the only required field, pointing to a bitmap (*.bmp) located in the OEM folder. If a resource ID is specified, it's a base-10 number representing the resource ID of the bitmap in a DLL file specified by `<filename>`.

Logo

Specifies a small bitmap to display in the upper-right corner of the screen during setup.

Key value:

`<filename>, <resource ID>`	`<filename>` is the only required field, pointing to a bitmap (*.bmp) located in the OEM folder. If a resource ID is specified, it's a base-10 number representing the resource ID of the bitmap in a DLL file specified by `<filename>`.

[GuiUnattended]

This section contains keys used in the automation of the GUI portion of Windows 2000 Setup.

AdminPassword

Sets the password for the local Administrator account. When used in a SYSPREP.INF file for a SYSPREP image, the password on the existing Administrator account must be blank to be changed. If the local Administrator account had a password when the master image was made, all machines set up from the master will have the same password, regardless of the value specified by this key.

Key values:

`<password>`	The password to use for the local administrator account.
`*`	Set a blank password. You can also specify double quotes, as in `AdminPassword = ""`.

AdvServerType

This key is only valid when upgrading Windows 2000 Server, Advanced Server, and Datacenter Server. It has no effect on Windows 2000 Professional.

Key value:

`ServerNT`	This is the only valid value for this key.

Arguments

Use this key if you need to pass arguments to a custom program running with the Windows 2000 setup. See `DetachedProgram` for more information.

Key value:

`<argument>`	`<argument>` is any valid string to pass to the custom program.

AutoLogon

After GUI-mode setup is complete on a new installation of Windows 2000, the computer will automatically log on with the Administrator account. This key has no function for upgrades. If used on a system with a blank administrator password, the system will log on only once. If used on a system with a password specified, the computer will log on repeatedly until the Administrator password has been changed, the `AutoLogon` key has been removed from the registry, or the count specified by `AutoLogonCount` has been reached. The username and password will be stored in the registry in clear text, under this hive:

```
HKLM\SOFTWARE\Microsoft\Windows NT\CurrentVersion\Winlogon
```

The username will be under the `DefaultUserName` registry key, and the password will be under the `DefaultPassword` registry key.

Key values:

`Yes`	Automatically log on as the administrator. If there's a password on the Administrator account, it must be specified in the `AdminPassword` key.
`No`	This is the default setting if the key isn't specified. The system won't attempt to log on automatically.

AutoLogonAccountCreation

This key instructs the setup process to create a local user account automatically for the user specified in the `FullName` key. If an account is generated, it will automatically log onto Windows 2000 at the first boot. This is not controlled by the `AutoLogon` or `AutoLogonCount` key; those options apply only to the Administrator account. This key is not valid for computers joined to a domain—only for those joined to workgroups.

Key values:

`Yes`	Automatically create the local user account. This is the default setting if the key isn't specified.
`No`	Don't create the local user account.

AutoLogonCount

When setting `AutoLogon = Yes` and configuring an Administrator password for the `AdminPassword` key, this key specifies the number of automatic logons using the Administrator account. This number will only decrement with a reboot; simply logging out of the Administrator account won't decrease the count—plus, you'll be logged back on immediately. Using this value with a blank Administrator password will only auto-logon once, regardless of the specified value.

Key value:

<number>	Positive whole number describing the number of times to automatically log on using the local Administrator account.

DetachedProgram

Allows a custom program to run concurrently with the Windows 2000 setup program. Parameters can be passed to the program using the `Arguments` key.

Key value:

<program path>	Specifies the path—including the name of the executable—to run concurrent with the Windows 2000 setup program.

OEMDuplicatorString

This key is only valid when performing a SYSPREP-based installation. The value of this key will be written to the registry under the following hive: `HKLM\System\Setup\OemDuplicatorString`. This allows an administrator to easily identify a machine created from a SYSPREP image.

Key value:

<string>	String to add to the registry. Must be less than 255 characters.

OEMSkipRegional

This key specifies whether to display the Regional Settings page of the GUI-mode setup. You can also use this key in a SYSPREP.INF file to prevent the mini-setup wizard from displaying the Regional Settings page. If you provide values in the `[RegionalSettings]` section, you should set this value to `1`, or Setup will still prompt the user for regional settings.

Key values:

`0`	Display the Regional Settings page. This is the default setting if the key isn't specified.
`1`	Skip the Regional Settings page.

OEMSkipWelcome

Set this key to make Setup skip the GUI-mode Welcome page.

Key values:

`0`	Display the Welcome page. This is the default setting if the key isn't specified.
`1`	Skip the Welcome page.

ProfilesDir

For a new installation of Windows 2000, this key changes the default location for user profiles. The value can contain an environment variable. This key isn't valid for upgrades.

Key value:

`<profile path>`	Complete path to use as the root for user profiles. The default is `"%systemdrive%\Documents and Settings"`. If you want Windows 2000 to use the same profile path as Windows NT 4.0, use `"%systemroot%\Profiles"`.

TimeZone

Specifies the time zone used on the computer.

Key values:

`000`	International Dateline
`001`	Samoa
`002`	Hawaii
`003`	Alaskan
`004`	Pacific
`010`	Mountain (U.S. and Canada)
`015`	U.S. Mountain: Arizona
`020`	Central (U.S. and Canada)
`025`	Canada Central
`030`	Mexico
`033`	Central America
`035`	Eastern (U.S. and Canada)
`040`	U.S. Eastern: Indiana (East)
`045`	S.A. Pacific
`050`	Atlantic (Canada)
`055`	S.A. Western
`056`	Pacific S.A.
`060`	Newfoundland
`065`	E. South America
`070`	S.A. Eastern

073	Greenland
075	Mid-Atlantic
080	Azores
083	Cape Verde Islands
085	GMT (Greenwich Mean Time)
090	GMT Greenwich
095	Central Europe
100	Central European
105	Romance
110	W. Europe
113	W. Central Africa
115	E. Europe
120	Egypt
125	EET (Helsinki, Riga, Tallinn)
130	EET (Athens, Istanbul, Minsk)
140	S. Africa: Harare, Pretoria
145	Russian
150	Arab
155	E. Africa
160	Iran
165	Arabian
170	Caucasus Pacific (U.S. and Canada)
175	Afghanistan
180	Russia Yekaterinburg
185	W. Asia
190	India
193	Nepal
195	Central Asia
200	Sri Lanka
201	N. Central Asia
203	Myanmar: Rangoon
205	S.E. Asia
207	N. Asia
210	China
215	Singapore
220	Taipei
225	W. Australia
227	N. Asia East
230	Korea: Seoul
235	Tokyo
240	Sakha Yakutsk
245	A.U.S. Central: Darwin

`250`	Central Australia
`255`	A.U.S. Eastern
`260`	E. Australia
`265`	Tasmania
`270`	Vladivostok
`275`	W. Pacific
`280`	Central Pacific
`285`	Fiji
`290`	New Zealand
`300`	Tonga

Note: TimeZone indices are as listed in *Microsoft Windows 2000 Guide to Unattended Setup*, distributed with the Windows 2000 retail CD, in the \Support\Deploy.cab UNATTEND.DOC file.

[UserData]

This section contains user- or machine-specific identification information.

ComputerName

Name to use for the computer name. The computer name can't be numeric only; this could cause problems with TCP/IP name resolution, so Setup won't allow numeric-only computer names.

Key values:

`<string>`	Computer name, up to 63 letters and/or numbers.
`*`	Setup will generate a random computer name based on the specified organization name.

FullName

The user's full name, to which Windows 2000 will be registered.

Key value:

`<string>`	Enter the user's name. This parameter must be specified if you want to make setup completely unattended.

OrgName

The organization's full name, to which Windows 2000 will be registered.

Key value:

`<string>`	Enter an organization name. This parameter must be specified if you want to make setup completely unattended.

ProductID

The Microsoft product identification (PID) number, sometimes referred to as a *CD Key*, is usually found attached to the Certificate of Authenticity or on the back of the CD case. Building it into the answer file will assign the same PID to all computers; keep your original licenses and associated PIDs handy, or you may have difficulty getting support from Microsoft. This parameter isn't required if installing Windows 2000 from Microsoft Select CDs.

Key value:

`<string>`	25-character unique (PID) number. This parameter must be specified if you want to make setup completely unattended.

[Proxy]

This section contains proxy settings to use for Internet Explorer, which is included with Windows 2000. This isn't a required section; you could also configure these options through group policy objects.

FTP_Proxy_Server

Sets the Internet Protocol (IP) address or URL for the FTP proxy server on your network.

Key value:

`<address>`	`<address>` can be a URL (`http://proxy:80`) or an IP address (`192.168.0.1:80`).

Gopher_Proxy_Server

Sets the IP address or URL for your Gopher proxy server.

Key value:

`<address>`	`<address>` can be a URL or an IP address.

HTTP_Proxy_Server

Sets the IP address or URL for your HTTP (Web) proxy server. This parameter specifies the value used for all proxy settings when specifying the `Use_Same_Proxy` key.

Key value:

`<address>`	`<address>` can be a URL or an IP address.

Proxy_Enable

Configures Internet Explorer to use a proxy server to connect to the Internet.

Key values:

`0`	Don't use a proxy server.
`1`	Use a proxy server.

Proxy_Override

Defines a list of IP addresses, delimited with semicolons (;), for which to bypass the proxy server.

Key value:

`<list>`	*`<list>`* is a string of IP addresses separated by semicolons and enclosed in quotes. Specify `<local>` (including the angle brackets) to override local addresses. For example: `Proxy_Override = "10.1.1.1; 192.168.0.0; <local>"`

Secure_Proxy_Server

Sets the IP address or URL for your secure (HTTPS) proxy server.

Key value:

`<address>`	*`<address>`* can be a URL or an IP address.

Socks_Proxy_Server

Sets the IP address or URL for your Socks proxy server.

Key value:

`<address>`	*`<address>`* can be a URL or an IP address.

Use_Same_Proxy

Configures Internet Explorer to use the same proxy server for all protocols (FTP, Gopher, HTTP, HTTPS, Socks). If enabled, the value specified in the `HTTP_Proxy_Server` key is used for all protocols.

Key values:

`0`	Configure separate proxy server addresses for each service.
`1`	Use the same proxy server for all services.

[URL]

Configuring options within this section requires including the `[Branding]` section with the `BrandIEUsingUnattended = Yes` option, or the settings will have no effect.

AutoConfig

Configures Internet Explorer to enable browser auto-configuration. If enabled, an auto-config URL must be defined in one of the next two keys (`AutoConfigJSURL` or `AutoConfigURL`).

Key values:

`0`	Don't use automatic browser configuration.
`1`	Use automatic browser configuration.

AutoConfigJSURL

This key points to a JavaScript file to use to auto-configure browser proxy settings.

Key value:

<URL>	Fully qualified URL of an auto-config JavaScript file.

AutoConfigURL

This key points to an automatic configuration *.INS file to use to auto-configure browser proxy settings.

Key value:

<URL>	Fully qualified URL of an auto-config *.INS file.

Help_Page

Takes the user to the defined Web page when he or she selects Online Support from the Help menu of Internet Explorer.

Key value:

<URL>	Complete URL for the user support site.

Home_Page

Sets Internet Explorer's default home page.

Key value:

<URL>	Complete URL for the default IE home page.

Quick_Link

Set default names and targets for the Internet Explorer Quick Links, which are found on the Links toolbar of Internet Explorer. This actually requires a two-part key for each Quick Link entry, with this format:

```
Quick_Link_#_Name = "<link name>"
Quick_Link_# = "<link URL>"
```

For example, to create two Quick Links, one for Microsoft and one for the Ferris Technology Networks, the keys and values would look like this:

```
Quick_Link_1_Name = "Microsoft"
Quick_Link_1 = "http://www.microsoft.com"
Quick_Link_2_Name = "Ferris Technology Networks"
Quick_Link_2 = "http://www.ferristech.net"
```

[FavoritesEx]

This section lets you create default Favorites entries under the Internet Explorer Favorites. Configuring options within this section requires including the `[Branding]` section with the `BrandIEUsingUnattended = Yes` option, or the settings will have no effect.

Keys under the `[FavoritesEx]` section are paired, similar to the `Quicklink` keys under the `[URL]` section. The format is as follows:

```
Title# = "<Link Name>.url"
URL# = "<URL>"
```

For example, to create four entries under Favorites, one for Microsoft, one for Dell Computer Corporation, one for whatis.com, and one for Ask Jeeves, this section would look like the following:

```
[FavoritesEx]
Title1 = "Microsoft.url"
URL1 = "http://www.microsoft.com"
Title2 = "Dell Computer Corporation.url"
URL2 = "http://www.dell.com"
Title3 = "whatis.com.url"
URL3 = "http://www.whatis.com"
Title4 = "Ask Jeeves.url"
URL4 = "http://www.ask.com"
```

[Branding]

This section is required if setting Internet Explorer customizations through the unattended setup process. This section must exist to implement configuration options from the `[URL]` or the `[FavoritesEx]` section.

BrandIEUsingUnattended

Specifies whether to apply Internet Explorer customizations present in the answer file.

Key values:

`Yes`	Customize IE using settings from the `[URL]` and `[FavoritesEx]` sections of the answer file.
`No`	Don't use the answer file for IE customizations. IE will be configured with settings specified in the configuration file from the `IEBrandingFile` key.

IEBrandingFile

This key points to the filename of an Internet Explorer Administration Kit (IEAK) configuration file (*.INS) to use for branding and configuring Internet Explorer. This file must be located at the root of the \OEM folder on the Windows 2000 distribution share point.

Key value:

<filename>	Filename for an *.INS file located at the root of the \OEM folder.

[LicenseFilePrintData]

This section only applies to the Windows 2000 Server family of products. It's not valid for Windows 2000 Professional.

AutoMode

Select the licensing mode in which to install Windows 2000 Server, Advanced Server, or Datacenter Server.

Key values:

`PerSeat`	A separate client access license (CAL) has been purchased for each machine that accesses the server.
`PerServer`	CALs have been purchased for the server to allow up to a specific number of concurrent connections. The `AutoUsers` key must be specified in conjunction with this key.

AutoUsers

This value reflects the number of CALs that were purchased for the server being installed. This key is valid only when the `AutoMode` key is set to `PerServer`.

Key value:

<number>	The number value for this key must be a whole number greater than 5, or unattended setup will fail.

[GuiRunOnce]

Key values listed under this section are formatted as commands. These commands will be copied to the `GuiRunOnce` registry key and executed during the first logon to Windows 2000. These commands will be run under the context of the first user to initiate local logon; as a result, any local user registry settings affect only the initial user account that logs on, rather than all users for the machine. If a command must update registry settings for all users, the command should be executed through the CMDLINES.TXT file, which runs commands and installs applications in the context of a system service.

Entries under this section are in this format:

```
Command# = "<command syntax>"
```

The `#` in `Command#` is an integer, starting with `0` and incremented by one for each additional command line. For example, suppose you want to run two commands during the first user logon for a workstation—one to import settings from a registry file and one to run a batch file. The section would appear as follows:

```
[GuiRunOnce]
Command0 = "reg import BrowserSettings.reg"
Command1 = "cmd /c Cleanup.bat"
```

To ensure automatically running these commands under the local Administrator account, you may want to use this section in conjunction with the `AutoLogon` option (which must be enabled).

[Display]

Configuration options specified under this section must be applicable for the display card installed on target machines. If the options specify invalid values for a target device, Setup will select the closest available option.

BitsPerPel

This key specifies the number of colors used by the display adapter as a value of bits per pixel.

Key value:

<bits>	The number of bits per pixel. Common values are `8` for 256 colors (2^8=256), `15` for High Color with 32,000 colors (2^{15}=32,768), `16` for High Color with 65,000 colors, (2^{16}=65,536), and `24` for True Color (2^{24}=16.7 million).

Vrefresh

Configures a refresh rate for the graphics device. Valid values for your particular configuration can be found on the Monitor tab of the Advanced Display Properties dialog box.

Key value:

`<rate>`	Rate must be a valid refresh frequency, such as `72` for 72 Hertz.

Xresolution

This is the X-axis resolution value. Resolution is usually stated as X-axis by Y-axis, as in 640 × 480 or 800 × 600. In these examples, `Xresolution` is 640 and 800, respectively. The value of this key should be the complementary value to the `Yresolution` setting.

Key value:

`<res>`	Valid resolution setting for the X-axis. Common selections include **`640`**, **`800`**, and `1024`. The valid settings can be different for different graphics adapters.

Yresolution

This is the Y-axis resolution value. Resolution is usually stated as X-axis by Y-axis, as in 640 × 480 or 800 × 600. In these examples, `Yresolution` is 480 and 600, respectively. The value of this key should be the complementary value to the `Xresolution` setting, such as 640 × 480, 800 × 600, 1024 × 768, or another valid resolution pairing for your graphics adapter.

Key value:

`<res>`	Valid resolution setting for the Y-axis. Common selections include **`480`**, **`600`**, and `768`. The valid settings can be different for different graphics adapters.

[RegionalSettings]

This section, which configures regional options such as language and keyboard layout, is optional. To use this section, you must run either WINNT32 with the `/copsource:lang` switch, or WINNT with the `/rx:lang` switch.

InputLocale

This section configures the input locale and keyboard layout combination to be installed with Windows 2000. The combination of *`<locale>`* and *`<layout>`* in this key setting must be supported by language groups defined by the `LanguageGroup` key, or by the default language version of the Windows 2000 installation media you're using. This key won't work if the `Language` key is used. See Microsoft's Web page at this address for current information regarding valid configuration combinations for this key:

`http://www.microsoft.com/globaldev/win2k/setup/default.asp`

Key value:

<locale>:<layout>	*<locale>* is the locale ID, *<layout>* is the keyboard layout ID. Multiple combinations can be entered by separating the entries with commas (,).

Language

This setting should be the language ID of the language or locale of the system on which you're installing Windows 2000. If this key is used, the `InputLocale`, `SystemLocale`, and `UserLocale` keys won't be used. Microsoft recommends using the `Language` key rather than the other three keys to prevent accidentally specifying an invalid combination.

Key value:

<locale>	Locale ID (LCID), as specified at this address: `http://www.microsoft.com/globaldev/win2k/setup/lcid.asp`. Must be supported by language groups defined in the `LanguageGroup` key, or the default language version of the Windows 2000 installation media you're using will be installed.

LanguageGroup

Optional language packages for language groups specified in this key will be installed on the Windows 2000 machine. Multiple values can be specified in a comma-delimited list.

Key values:

1	Western Europe and United States
2	Central Europe
3	Baltic
4	Greek
5	Cyrillic
6	Turkic
7	Japanese
8	Korean
9	Traditional Chinese
10	Simplified Chinese
11	Thai

12	Hebrew
13	Arabic
14	Vietnamese
15	Indic
16	Georgian
17	Armenian

SystemLocale

Specifies the language to use for the display of applications, menus, and dialog boxes. The locale must be supported by one of the language groups from the `LanguageGroup` key. This setting is ignored if the `Language` key is defined.

Key value:

<locale>	A valid locale ID (LCID), as specified at `http://www.microsoft.com/globaldev/win2k/setup/lcid.asp`.

UserLocale

Specifies the format to use for the display of currency, numbers, time, and dates. The locale must be supported by one of the language groups from the `LanguageGroup` key. This setting is ignored if the `Language` key is defined.

Key value:

<locale>	A valid locale ID (LCID), as specified at `http://www.microsoft.com/globaldev/win2k/setup/lcid.asp`.

[TapiLocation]

This section defines TAPI default settings.

AreaCode

This is the telephone area code for phone lines from which the system will be calling.

Key value:

<AreaCode>	Standard telephone area code for your area.

CountryCode

Country code to use with TAPI settings for the country from which the system will be calling.

Key value:

<CountryCode>	Standard telephone country code for your country. The United States is `1`, and you can find other country codes at one of these addresses:
	`http://www.the-acr.com/codes/cntrycd.htm`
	`http://csg.sprint.com/international/int_codes.html`

Dialing

The type of dialing usable on the system's phone lines.

Key values:

`Tone`	Use standard touch-tone dialing using DTMF (Dual Tone Multi Frequency) tones.
`Pulse`	Use older rotary phone dialing.

LongDistanceAccess

Any number or numbers needed to access an outside line.

Key value:

<number>	Enter the number dialed for an outside line. In hotels, this is often `8,` or `9,`; some businesses may require dialing a multiple-digit long distance code to access an outside line. Appending commas after the number creates a two-second pause (per comma) between dialing the access number and dialing the phone number.

[Fax]

This section is optional. You can use this section to enter configuration information for the Windows 2000 Fax Service.

ArchiveFolderName

Folder location for storing outbound faxes. You must set the `ArchiveOutgoing` option to True if you want to use this setting.

Key value:

<path>	Enter the full path to the folder where Windows should save copies of outbound faxes. You can use environment variables, such as `%systemdrive%`.

ArchiveOutgoing

Enable or disable archiving of outbound faxes.

Key values:

`True`	Archive outbound faxes to the folder specified by `ArchiveFolderName`.
`False`	Don't archive a copy of outbound faxes.

Csid

The called subscriber ID (CSID) is sent to the originating fax machine when a receiving fax machine answers a call. This string should be the name of the business or the phone number of the fax machine.

Key value:

<CSID string>	Any string value can be specified here, although it's recommended to use the same value for the transmitter subscriber ID (TSID). The default value of the CSID is `"Fax"`.

FaxNumber

Phone number of your fax line.

Key value:

<Fax Number>	Standard phone number string. The default is `"Fax"`.

FaxPrinterName

Fax printer name. This can't be the same name as the `RoutePrinterName`.

Key value:

<string>	Any desired name for the fax printer. The default is `"Fax"`.

Rings

Sets the number of times the phone will ring before being answered by the Fax Service.

Key value:

<#>	Any valid number of rings. The default is `2`.

RouteFolderName

Folder location for storing incoming faxes. You must set the `RouteToFolder` option to `True` if you want to use this setting.

Key value:

`<path>`	Enter the full path to the folder where Windows should save copies of incoming faxes. You can use environment variables, such as `%systemdrive%`.

RoutePrinterName

Printer name for automatically printing incoming faxes. This value must not be the same as the `FaxPrinterName` setting. You must set the `RouteToPrinter` option to `True` if you want to use this setting.

Key value:

`<printer>`	Either a local printer name or a UNC name for a remote printer.

RouteToFolder

Enables or disables automatic save-to-file for incoming faxes.

Key values:

`True`	Incoming faxes are saved to the folder specified by `ArchiveFolderName`. This is the default setting.
`False`	Incoming faxes are not saved.

RouteToPrinter

Enables or disables automatic printing of incoming faxes.

Key values:

`True`	Incoming faxes are automatically printed to the printer specified by the `RoutePrinterName` key.
`False`	Incoming faxes are not printed. This is the default setting.

TSID

The transmitter subscriber ID (TSID) is sent to the receiving fax machine any time a fax is sent. This string should be the name of the business or the phone number of the fax machine.

Key value:

`<TSID string>`	Any string value may be specified here, although it's recommended to use the same value used for the CSID. The default value of the TSID is `"Fax"`.

[Win9xUpg]

Options specified under this section are used only when upgrading from Windows 95 or Windows 98 to Windows 2000. These settings are invalid when performing a clean install or upgrading from a prior version of Windows NT.

Boot16

Enable MS-DOS boot option on the Windows 2000 Boot Loader menu (boot.ini file). If you convert the drive to NTFS, you won't be able to boot to MS-DOS.

Key values:

`Yes`	Enable boot to MS-DOS mode.
`No`	Don't enable boot to MS-DOS mode. This is the default.

DefaultPassword

Specify a default password for any local accounts created during the upgrade. If this value isn't specified, Setup will prompt for passwords for all local user accounts after the first reboot.

Key value:

<string>	Any valid Windows 2000 non-blank password.

DomainJoinText

Adds the key value to the Domain Join page of the Setup Wizard.

Key value:

<"HTML">	HTML text, enclosed in quotes. The only supported HTML tags are `<A></A>` (URL anchor) and `<B></B>` (bold).

ForcePasswordChange

Forces a password change the first time each local user logs onto the target machine.

Key values:

`Yes`	Require a password change at logon. This is the default.
`No`	Don't require a password change at logon.

ForceWorkgroup

Windows 2000 will run in the Workgroup security mode after the upgrade.

Key values:

`Yes`	Force the system to run in Workgroup mode.
`No`	Don't force Workgroup mode. This is the default.

IgnoreNetworkErrors

If enabled, Setup won't retry a domain connection that fails.

Key values:

`Yes`	If setup attempts to connect to a domain and fails, the system will skip joining the domain and switch to Workgroup mode.
`No`	Setup will retry connecting to the domain. The user will be prompted if this option is set to `No` and the initial connection to the domain fails. This is the default.

KeepBadLinks

If enabled, Setup will keep all shortcuts (*.lnk files).

Key values:

`Yes`	Keep all shortcuts. This is the default.
`No`	Don't keep shortcuts that are incompatible with Windows 2000.

MigrateDefaultUser

Default user settings for Windows 9x will be migrated to the default user settings for Windows 2000 user accounts.

Key values:

`Yes`	Settings will be migrated. This is the default.
`No`	Settings will not be migrated. Standard Windows 2000 defaults will be used. This may cause some applications to fail, if the application relies on settings from the default user account.

MigrateUsersAsAdmin

All accounts created during migration from Windows 9x to Windows 2000 will be added to the local Administrators group.

Key values:

`Yes`	Add all migrated local user accounts to the Administrators group. This is the default.
`No`	Don't add local user accounts to the Administrators group.

MigrateUsersAsPowerUser

All accounts created during migration from Windows 9x to Windows 2000 will be added to the local Power Users group.

Key values:

`Yes`	Add all migrated local user accounts to the Power Users group. This is the default.
`No`	Don't add local user accounts to the Power Users group.

MigrationDlls

Applications that are being migrated from Windows 95 or Windows 98 may include upgrade packs to assist Windows 2000 in the translation of files and configuration information from Windows 9x to Windows 2000. Each upgrade pack includes a unique MIGRATE.DLL file.

Key value:

`<path>`	Path to upgrade packs. Multiple upgrade packs can be added to multiple directories, and the paths specified in a comma-delimited list. Windows 2000 will automatically search subfolders of *`<path>`*. You can add multiple subfolders under a single path, each with a single upgrade pack, but you can't place multiple upgrade packs in a single path or subfolder.

ReportOnly

Setup runs the initial portion of the Setup Wizard, but it only generates an upgrade report containing a list of hardware and software incompatibilities or issues—it doesn't continue with the installation of Windows 2000. This report is saved to the root of the system drive unless an alternate path is provided in the `SaveReportTo` key.

Key values:

`Yes`	Generate an upgrade report only. Don't upgrade the operating system.
`No`	Perform a normal upgrade installation of Windows 2000. This is the default.

SafeMode

With Safe mode, Setup maintains a list of settings when performing an upgrade, and skips any setting that causes problems with the Windows 9x boot process.

Key values:

`Yes`	Run with Safe mode. Setup will need to be run twice.
`No`	Don't run with Safe mode. Setup will need to be run three times. This is the default.

SaveReportTo

Optional path to which an upgrade report should be saved. A report is generated any time Setup is run. Setup will produce only a report if the `ReportOnly` key is enabled.

Key value:

<path>	Path at which to save the upgrade report. This can be a UNC name, and the path can include environment variables (such as `%computername%`).

ScanDrives

Scans drives that would normally be skipped—such as network drives—for software when generating an upgrade report. This option should be used with the `ReportOnly` option.

Key value:

<drive>	*<drive>* is a single drive letter or comma-delimited list of drives to be scanned during setup.

UseLocalAccountOnError

When Windows 2000 attempts to upgrade a Windows 9x machine, it looks at the value of the last valid user who logged onto the machine, and searches for an exact username match in all trusted domains. If successful, Setup uses the domain account for logon. The process will error out if a matching account appears in multiple trusted domains, if the computer account cannot be created in the computer domain, or if a network error occurs. Depending on the value of the key, Setup will behave differently for these error situations.

Key values:

`Yes`	Automatically create a local user account if a conflict or problem occurs determining a domain username.
`No`	Prompt the user for action if an error occurs. This is the default behavior.

UserDomain

If the `UserDomain` key is defined, Setup will search only specified domains for matching user accounts. If an error occurs, Setup acts according to the value set in the `UseLocalAccountOnError` key. Multiple instances of this key can be specified to search multiple domains.

Key value:

<domain>,<username>	*<domain>* is the domain name to search for usernames specified after the comma. Additional usernames can be added to the list and separated by commas (*<domain>,<username>,<username2>*)

UserPassword

Specific passwords can be created for specified local user accounts using this key.

Key value:

`<user>,<password>`	Multiple usernames and passwords can be associated to this key by separating the entries with a comma (,).

[SystemFileProtection]

Windows File Protection, originally called System File Checker (SFC), prevents the deletion or replacement of protected system files. This section is optional.

SFCDllCacheDir

Changes the location of the Windows File Protection cache folder. This folder can't be a UNC; it must be a local path, and environment variables are allowed.

Key value:

`<"path">`	Location for the Windows File Protection file cache, enclosed in quotes. The default location is `%systemroot%\System32\dllcache`.

SFCQuota

Maximum directory size allowed for the Windows File Protection cache files.

Key values:

`<hex>`	The size of the cache files in megabytes, expressed in hexadecimal. For example, `0x64h` is 100MB.
`0x32h`	The default size for Windows 2000 Professional, 50MB.
`FFFFFFFF`	The default size for Windows 2000 Server products. 4,294,967,295MB; all system files will be cached.

> **Converting a Numeric Value to Hexadecimal (Hex)**
>
> The easiest way to convert a numeric value to hex is to use the Windows Calculator. Start Calculator (Start, Run, and type **calc** in the Run box). Select View, Scientific. Make sure the Dec format is selected, and enter a numeric value into the calculator. Now, select the Hex format. The resulting display is the hex value; format it as `0x<value>h` for proper hex notation.

SFCShowProgress

Controls whether Windows File Protection displays a progress meter during file system scans.

Key values:

`0`	Don't show a progress meter. This is the default.
`1`	Show a progress meter during file system scans.

[Components]

This section contains a series of keys used for installing Windows 2000 components. All available components have the same format, `<key> = <value>`, where `<key>` is the component name and `<value>` is one of the following:

`On`	The component will be installed.
`Off`	The component will not be installed.

Rather than restate the key values for each component, the following sections simply define each component's name and default value.

accessopt

Component: Accessibility Wizard.
Default value: `On`

calc

Component: Calculator.
Default value: `On`

cdplayer

Component: CD Player.
Default value: `On`
Note: If Windows 2000 detects a DVD-ROM device during hardware detection, the DVD player is installed separately from the CD player.

certsrv

Component: Certificate Services.
Default value: `Off`

certsrv_client

Component: Certificate Services Web client component.
Default value: `Off`
Options for this component can be specified in the `[Certsrv_Client]` section.

certsrv_server

Component: Certificate Services server component only.
Default value: `Off`
Options for this component can be specified in the `[Certsrv_Server]` section. These components are needed to create a Certification Authority on the server for issuing digital certificates.

charmap

Component: Character Map.
Default value: `On`

chat

Component: Chat.
Default value: `Off`

cluster

This section is valid only when installing Windows 2000 Advanced Server or Datacenter Server.
Component: Cluster service Node and Administration components.
Default value: `On`
Options for this component can be specified in the `[Cluster]` section. This component requires `iis_common`.

deskpaper

Component: Desktop Wallpaper.
Default value: `On`

dialer

Component: Phone Dialer.
Default value: `On`

fp

Component: FrontPage Server Extensions.
Default value: `On` for Windows 2000 Server family; `Off` for Windows 2000 Professional.

freecell

Component: Freecell game.
Default value: `On`

hypertrm

Component: HyperTerminal.
Default value: `On`

iis_common

Component: Common set of Internet Information Server (IIS) files.
Default value: `On` for Windows 2000 Server family; `Off` for Windows 2000 Professional.

iisdbg

Component: Microsoft Script Debugger.
Default value: `On` for Windows 2000 Server family; `Off` for Windows 2000 Professional.

iis_doc

Component: Internet Information Server documentation
Default value: `On` for Windows 2000 Server family; `Off` for Windows 2000 Professional

iis_ftp

Component: IIS FTP server.
Default value: `On` for Windows 2000 Server family; `Off` for Windows 2000 Professional.
Installing `iis_ftp` automatically installs `iis_common` and `iis_inetmgr`.

iis_htmla

Component: IIS HTML-based administration tools.
Default value: `On` for Windows 2000 Server family; `Off` for Windows 2000 Professional.
Installing `iis_htmla` automatically installs `iis_common`, `iis_inetmgr`, and `iis_www`.

iis_inetmgr

Component: IIS Microsoft Management Console-based administration tools.
Default value: `On` for Windows 2000 Server family; `Off` for Windows 2000 Professional.
Installing `iis_inetmgr` automatically installs `iis_common`.

iis_nntp

Component: IIS Network News Transfer Protocol (NNTP) Service.
Default value: `On` for Windows 2000 Server family; `Off` for Windows 2000 Professional.
Installing `iis_nntp` automatically installs `iis_common`, `iis_www`, and `iis_inetmgr`.

iis_nntp_docs

Component: IIS NNTP Service documentation.
Default value: `On` for Windows 2000 Server family; `Off` for Windows 2000 Professional.
Installing `iis_nntp_docs` automatically installs `iis_common`, `iis_www`, and `iis_inetmgr`.

iis_pwmgr

This key is valid only on Windows 2000 Professional.
Component: Personal Web Manager.
Default value: `Off`

iis_smtp

Component: IIS Simple Mail Transfer Protocol (SMTP) Service.
Default value: `On` for Windows 2000 Server family; `Off` for Windows 2000 Professional.
Installing `iis_smtp` automatically installs `iis_common`, `iis_www`, and `iis_inetmgr`.

iis_smtp_docs

Component: IIS SMTP Service documentation.
Default value: `On` for Windows 2000 Server family; `Off` for Windows 2000 Professional.
Installing `iis_smtp_docs` automatically installs `iis_common`, `iis_www`, and `iis_inetmgr`.

iis_www

Component: IIS World Wide Web service.
Default value: `On` for Windows 2000 Server family; `Off` for Windows 2000 Professional.
Installing `iis_www` automatically installs `iis_common` and `iis_inetmgr`.

indexsrv_system

Component: Indexing Service.
Default value: `On` for Windows 2000 Server family; `Off` for Windows 2000 Professional.
Installing `indexsrv_system` automatically installs `iis_common`, `iis_www`, and `iis_inemgr`.
This component provides indexing and searching features for IIS.

LicenseServer

Component: Terminal Services licensing.
Default value: `Off`
This component can only be installed on domain controllers or on a server in a workgroup.

media_clips

Component: Sample sound clips.
Default value: `On`

media_utopia

Component: Utopia sound scheme.
Default value: `On`

minesweeper

Component: Minesweeper game.
Default value: `On`

mousepoint

Component: All available mouse pointers.
Default value: `On`

mplay

Component: Media Player.
Default value: `On`

msmq

Component: Microsoft Message Queuing (MSMQ).
Default value: `Off`

mswordpad

Component: WordPad.
Default value: `On`

netcis

Component: Microsoft COM Internet Services (MS CIS).
Default value: `On` for Windows 2000 Server family; `Off` for Windows 2000 Professional.
Installing `netcis` automatically installs `iis_common`, `iis_www`, and `iis_inetmgr`. MS CIS provides Distributed Component Object Model (DCOM) communication over HTTP for IIS.

netoc

Component: Optional networking components.
Default value: `On`
Additional configuration of optional networking components is handled by the `[NetOptionalComponents]` section.

objectpkg

Component: Object Packager.
Default value: `Off`

paint

Component: Paint.
Default value: `On`

pinball

Component: Pinball game.
Default value: `On`

rec

Component: Sound Recorder.
Default value: `On`

reminst

This component is only valid for the Windows 2000 Server family.
Component: Remote Installation Services.
Default value: `Off`

rstorage

This component is only valid for the Windows 2000 Server family.
Component: Remote Storage Services.
Default value: `Off`

solitaire

Component: Solitaire game.
Default value: `On`

templates

Component: Document Templates.
Default value: `On`

TSClients

Component: Terminal Services client installation disk creator files (10MB).
Default value: `Off`

TSEnable

This component is only valid for the Windows 2000 Server family.
Component: Terminal Services.
Default value: `Off`
Additional configuration of Terminal Services can be performed under the `[TerminalServices]` section.

vol

Component: Volume Control.
Default value: `On`

[Networking]

This section header is necessary to enable unattended installation of network components. It has no specific keys, but the section header still has to be there or network components aren't installed.

[Identification]

This section contains various network identification keys. If this section doesn't exist, the computer will be added to the default WORKGROUP workgroup.

DomainAdmin

This key must specify a valid domain administrator account if the `JoinDomain` key is specified. This value is required even if the computer account has already been created in the domain.

Key value:

<account>	Valid domain administrator account on the specified domain.

DomainAdminPassword

This key must specify the correct password for the Domain Administrator account specified in the `DomainAdmin` key. This value is stored in the answer file as clear text.

Key value:

<password>	Password associated with the account specified in the `DomainAdmin` key.

JoinDomain

This key specifies the name of the domain the computer should join. Don't specify a `JoinWorkgroup` key if you enter a value for this key.

Key value:

<domain>	Valid domain for the computer to join. You must specify a domain administrator account and password in the `DomainAdmin` and `DomainAdminPassword` keys, respectively.

JoinWorkgroup

This key specifies the name of the workgroup the computer should join. Don't specify a `JoinDomain` key if you enter a value for this key.

Key value:

<workgroup>	A workgroup name for the computer to participate in.

MachineObjectOU

If the computer participates in a domain, you can specify the organizational unit (OU) to which the computer belongs.

Key value:

<"*LDAP path*">	Full LDAP path for the OU to which the computer belongs, enclosed in quotes. For example, if your computer participates in the MyCompany.com domain under the Workstations OU, which is under a parent OU named Silicon, the LDAP path would be as follows: `"OU = Workstations,OU = Silicon,DC = MyCompany, DC = com"`

[NetAdapters]

This section is used to specify network adapters to be configured during setup. For each adapter, you must define separate keys and values.

<adapter instance>

The *<adapter instance>* key is a user-selected name for an adapter for which you want to define configuration parameters. The value of this key is the section name for the user-defined section containing parameters for this adapter. For example, if you chose to name the *<adapter instance>* key `PrimaryAdapter` for the first adapter and

`SecondaryAdapter` for the second adapter, the parameters for the adapters will be `params.PrimaryAdapter` and `params.SecondaryAdapter`, respectively. This section will appear as follows:

```
[NetAdapters]
PrimaryAdapter = params.PrimaryAdapter
SecondaryAdapter = params.SecondaryAdapter

[params.PrimaryAdapter]

[params.SecondaryAdapter]
```

[<params.adapter instance>]

An example of this section is displayed in the previous *<adapter instance>* section. Keys under this value are specific to the adapter instance.

ConnectionName

Optional key to provide a friendly name for the network connection specified by `<params.adapter instance>`. For example, `ConnectionName = "LAN"` would change the network adapter name to `LAN`.

Key value:

<"connection name">	Name string, enclosed in quotes.

DMA

Optional key specifying the Direct Memory Access (DMA) channel setting for the adapter. For example, `DMA = 1`.

Key value:

<dma>	DMA channel setting for the network adapter.

DoNotDetectLegacyCards

Legacy cards contained by this optional key will be ignored by Setup. The cards won't be detected, and the drivers won't be installed. Plug and play cards will still be detected, however. For example, `DoNotDetectLegacyCards = *pnp828A` would ignore the Intel 82595-based Ethernet adapter.

Key value:

<ID>	The identifier of the card as specified by the content of the installation *.INF file. Use a comma-delimited list to specify multiple IDs.

InfID

This is the plug and play identifier of a network adapter card that you explicitly want to configure.

Key values:

<PnP ID>	Plug and play (PnP) ID for a specific adapter.
*	Use `InfID = *` in systems with a single network adapter. The first detected network adapter will receive the settings in this section, without requiring advanced knowledge of the types of network cards installed in the system.

IOAddr

Input/output (IO) address, in hexadecimal notation, for a network adapter.

Key value:

<IO address>	This address is specified in hex. For example: `IOAddr = 330`

IRQ

Interrupt number for the network adapter.

Key value:

<IRQ>	This setting should be the IRQ of the network adapter, such as `IRQ = 5`.

MEM

Memory range for the network adapter.

Key value:

<range>	This setting should contain the base memory address setting for the network adapter, such as `MEM = 0xC3fffff`.

NetCardAddress

MAC address for a network adapter. This key is only needed when configuring multiple network cards of the same type on a single box. Each network adapter has a unique MAC address; therefore, this setting, if specified, would need to be changed for each machine or it wouldn't be valid. This parameter is not needed for PCI adapters when the PCI bus number is specified.

Key value:

<MAC address>	Standard network interface card (NIC) MAC address, such as `NetCardAddress = 0x00105A934085`.

PCIBusNumber

Specifies the PCI bus location of the network interface card. If you use this parameter, `PCIFunctionNumber` and `PCIDeviceNumber` are required. If `NetCardAddress` is specified, this key is ignored.

Key value:

<PCI bus number>	PCI bus number in which the adapter is installed.

PCIDeviceNumber

Specifies the PCI device number of the network interface card. If you use this parameter, `PCIBusNumber` and `PCIFunctionNumber` are required. If `NetCardAddress` is specified, this key is ignored.

Key value:

<PCI device number>	PCI device number of the network interface card.

PCIFunctionNumber

Specifies which PCI function number of the PCI card provides network interface card functions. This parameter is `0` on single-function cards, but could be different for multiple-function cards. If you use this parameter, `PCIBusNumber` and `PCIDeviceNumber` are required. If `NetCardAddress` is specified, this key is ignored.

Key value:

<PCI function number>	PCI function number for the function on the card providing network connectivity.

[NetProtocols]

This section contains network protocols to be installed through the unattended setup process. In each of the following keys, you need to replace the italicized key name in angle brackets (*<key name>*) with a valid protocol name. Each of these key names must then be matched by a corresponding parameters section that references the key name. For example, the template for this section looks something like this:

```
[NetProtocols]
<protocol name> = <protocol parameters section>
<protocol 2 name> = <protocol 2 parameters section>

[<protocol parameters section>]
<key> = <value>

[<protocol 2 parameters section>]
<key> = <value>
```

The actual section in the answer file could look something like this:

```
[NetProtocols]
MS_TCPIP = params.MSTCPIP
MS_PPTP = params.MSPPTP

[params.MSTCPIP]
DNSDomain = "MyDomain.com"

[params.MSPPTP]
NumberLineDevices = 15
```

In the following sections, any value that appears in italics and angle brackets (*<value>*) must be replaced with a protocol name, section name, or parameter section fitting the description of the italicized text.

<protocol name>

Various protocols can be listed under this section as keys, with the value pointing to the section where protocol parameters will be defined.

Valid protocol names are as follows:

MS_AppleTalk	AppleTalk protocol.
MS_ATMArps	ATM ARP Server protocol.
MS_ATMLANE	ATM LAN Emulation client.
MS_ATMUni	ATM Call Manager protocol.
MS_DLC	Data Link Control protocol.
MS_L2TP	Layer 2 Tunneling Protocol.
MS_NetBEUI	NetBEUI protocol.
MS_NetMon	Network Monitor agent.
MS_NWIPX	IPX protocol. Installs NWLink IPX/SPX/NetBIOS Compatible Transport Protocol and NWLink NetBIOS Protocol.
MS_PPTP	Point-to-Point Tunneling Protocol.
MS_STREAMS	STREAMS protocol.
MS_TCPIP	TCP/IP protocol. Includes MS_NetBT component.

Key value:

<protocol name> = params.*<protocol name>*

<protocol name> must be one of the protocols listed above. params could be any word of your choosing, but for consistency in the examples, I'd recommend using params.

For example, a key for the TCP/IP protocol would look like this:

```
MS_TCPIP = params.TCPIP
```

[<protocol parameters section>]

This section contains parameters for any protocols specified in the `<protocol name>` sections above.

AdapterSections

Device-specific protocol parameters can be defined through this key.

Key value:

`<section name>`	User-defined adapter-specific section name.

For example, to define adapter-specific TCP/IP settings for the two adapters from the `[NetAdapters]` example and the protocol from the `[NetProtocols]` example, the code would look like this:

```
AdapterSections = params.TCPIP.PrimaryAdapter, params.TCPIP.SecondaryAdapter

[params.TCPIP.PrimaryAdapter]

[params.TCPIP.SecondaryAdapter]
```

[<MS_AppleTalk parameters>]

Keys under this section are used to set configuration options for the AppleTalk protocol on Windows 2000.

DefaultPort

Adapter to which the Services for Macintosh are bound. This key is optional. By default, the default port is the first Ethernet adapter, Token Ring adapter, or LocalTalk adapter—in that order—found on the system.

Key value:

`<adapter>`	A specific adapter name on which the Services for Macintosh should bind.

DefaultZone

Default zone for the network if the adapter is seeding the network. This key is optional.

Key value:

`<zone>`	Text string representing the name of the zone.

DesiredZone

Zone in which the Services for Macintosh are located. This key is optional. If not specified, the default zone will be used.

Key value:

`<zone>`	Text string representing the name of the zone.

EnableRouter

Enables routing for the AppleTalk protocol.

Key values:

`Yes`	Routing is enabled.
`No`	Routing is disabled. This is the default value.

NetworkRangeLowerEnd

Low-value network number of the network range if the network adapter is seeding the network. This is an optional parameter. This parameter is specific to each adapter, and must be used in a section with a `SpecificTo` key.

Key value:

`<value>`	`<value>` is an integer between `1` and `65279`.

NetworkRangeUpperEnd

High value network number of the network range if the network adapter is seeding the network. This is an optional parameter. This parameter is specific to each adapter, and must be used in a section with a `SpecificTo` key.

Key value:

`<value>`	`<value>` is an integer between `1` and `65279`.

SeedingNetwork

Specifies whether the associated network adapter is seeding the network. This is an optional parameter. This parameter is specific to each adapter, and must be used in a section with a `SpecificTo` key.

Key values:

`0`	Don't seed the network. This is the default setting.
`1`	Seed the network.

ZoneList

Specify zone names to use in seeding the network. This is an optional parameter, and should only be specified if `SeedingNetwork = 1`. This parameter is specific to each adapter, and must be used in a section with a `SpecificTo` key.

Key value:

`<zone name list>`	Comma-delimited list of zone names.

[<MS_ATMArps parameters>]

No configuration options are needed for ATM ARP Server. If ATM ARP Server is installed, this section should be added with no keys or values.

[<MS_ATMLANE parameters>]

No configuration options are needed for ATM LAN Emulation. If ATM LAN Emulation is installed, this section should be added with no keys or values.

[<MS_ATMUni parameters>]

No configuration options are needed for ATM Call Manager. If ATM Call Manager is installed, this section should be added with no keys or values.

[<MS_DLC parameters>]

No configuration options are needed for Data Link Control (DLC). If DLC is installed, this section should be added with no keys or values.

[<MS_L2TP parameters>]

Keys under this section are used to configure the Layer 2 Tunneling Protocol.

WanEndpoints

Number of simultaneous VPNs supported by Windows 2000 Server products for L2TP connections.

Key value:

`<integer>`	`<integer>` can be any value from **`0`** to **`30000`**. The default is `5`.

[<MS_NetBEUI parameters>]

No configuration options are needed for NetBEUI. If NetBEUI is installed, this section should be added with no keys or values.

[<MS_NetMon parameters>]

No configuration options are needed for Network Monitor. If Network Monitor is installed, this section should be added with no keys or values.

[<MS_NWIPX parameters>]

These global parameters apply to the IPX protocol.

DedicatedRouter

Use this key to specify a computer being installed as a dedicated router with no other network services.

Key values:

`Yes`	Machine is a dedicated router.
`No`	Other services will run on this machine. This is the default.

EnableWANRouter

This option can be used to enable or disable the RIP router.

Key values:

`Yes`	RIP router is enabled. This is the default.
`No`	RIP router is disabled.

NetworkNumber

Adapter-specific IPX network number. This setting must be specified in a section containing a `SpecificTo` key.

Key value:

`<hexadecimal network number>`	Network number, in hex. The default is `0`.

PktType

Adapter-specific packet type. This setting must be specified in a section containing a `SpecificTo` key.

Key values:

`0`	Ethernet II, applies only to Ethernet adapters.
`1`	Ethernet 802.3, also called IEEE 802.3, applies only to Ethernet adapters.
`2`	802.2, applies to Ethernet, Token Ring, or FDDI adapters.
`3`	SNAP, applies to Ethernet, Token Ring, or FDDI adapters.
`FF`	Autodetect. This is the default.

VirtualNetworkNumber

This key specifies the IPX internal network number, in hexadecimal.

Key value:

`<hex number>`	The default is `0`.

[<MS_PPTP parameters>]

Keys under this section apply to the Microsoft Point-to-Point Tunneling Protocol.

NumberLineDevices

Number of simultaneous virtual private networks (VPNs) supported by Windows 2000 Server products for PPTP connections.

Key value:

`<integer>`	`<integer>` can be any value from `0` to `16384`. The default is `5`.

[<MS_STREAMS parameters>]

No configuration options are needed for STREAMS. If STREAMS is installed, this section should be added with no keys or values.

[<MS_TCPIP parameters>]

In the example given in the `[NetProtocols]` section, this section header would be `[params.TCPIP]`. Information contained in this section globally configures TCP/IP protocol configuration options.

DeadGWDetectDefault

Set this option to `No` if the computer will be used for Routing and Remote Access Services (RRAS). Otherwise, it should not be specified.

Key values:

`Yes`	If Windows 2000 is not used for RRAS, this feature will be enabled by default. When Dead Gateway Detect (DGD) is enabled, the Dial On Demand (DOD) dial-up networking connection will be initialized when TCP/IP routing fails.
`No`	This is the default setting for systems used for RRAS. Specifying `No` prevents DGD from attempting to use a DOD Internet connection when TCP/IP routing fails. RRAS enables DOD through a different mechanism based on least-cost routing metrics.

DNSDomain

Primary Domain Name System (DNS) suffix for the computer, such as MYDOMAIN.COM.

Key value:

`<DNS domain name>`	DNS name to use as the DNS suffix.

DNSSuffixSearchOrder

DNS names to append when resolving machine names without fully qualified domain names (FQDN).

Key value:

`<suffix>`	List of suffixes, in the order they are to be searched, separated by commas.

DontAddDefaultGatewayDefault

This optional key should only be specified for computers that will be used for Routing and Remote Access Services.

Key values:

`Yes`	Use this value if the computer will be used for Routing and Remote Access Services to prevent RRAS from adding a default gateway to the routing table. This is the default.
`No`	You should never specify `No` for this value.

EnableICMPRedirect

This option should only be specified for computers that will be used for Routing and Remote Access Services (RRAS).

Key values:

`Yes`	Enable Internet Control Message Protocol (ICMP) redirection. This should not be used on a server used for RRAS.
`No`	Use this value if the computer will be used for RRAS. This is the default.

EnableLMHosts

Determines whether or not to use an LMHOSTS file for name resolution.

Key values:

`Yes`	Use LHMOSTS file for name resolution. This is the default.
`No`	Don't use LHMOSTS file for name resolution.

EnableSecurity

Configures TCP/IP filtering.

Key values:

`Yes`	Enable TCP/IP filtering.
`No`	Don't enable TCP/IP filtering. This is the default setting.

ScopeID

When using NetBIOS over TCP/IP, this option can be used to set the NetBIOS scope identifier. This option should not be used if DNS is enabled for name resolution.

Key value:

`<string>`	Single-word scope ID.

UseDomainNameDevolution

This key specifies whether the DNS cache resolver should use domain name devolution when provided an unqualified query.

Key values:

`Yes`	Devolve domain names.
`No`	Don't devolve domain names.

[<adapter-specific protocol section>]

The adapter-specific protocol sections are defined in the `AdapterSections` key, as in the `AdapterSections` example. Information in the `[<adapter-specific protocol section>]` sections applies only to the adapter for which each key is defined.

SpecificTo

Settings in this section are specific to the named component. Settings within these sections can only apply to a specific adapter; the `SpecificTo` key is used to denote which adapter is being configured.

Key value:

`<component>`	Network adapter instance defined in the `[NetAdapters]` section. In the examples from this text, valid entries would be `SpecificTo = PrimaryAdapter` or `SpecificTo = SecondaryAdapter`.

DefaultGateway

Default gateway to use for a specific adapter.

Key value:

`<TCP/IP address>`	The TCP/IP address of the default gateway. This isn't necessary if you assign the default gateway using DHCP.

DHCP

Determines whether the specific network adapter being configured should use the Dynamic Host Configuration Protocol (DCHP) protocol for TCP/IP information.

Key values:

`Yes`	DHCP will be used to configure TCP/IP.
`No`	You must manually configure the `IPAddress`, `SubnetMask`, and `DefaultGateway` keys.

DHCPClassId

DHCP user class ID to use when requesting configuration information from a compliant DHCP server.

Key value:

`<string>`	The class ID description, as specified on the DHCP server, for the class from which this network adapter should receive configuration information.

DNSDomain

Connection-specific DNS suffix for the given adapter.

Key value:

`<DNS suffix>`	Valid DNS suffix for this connection.

DNSServerSearchOrder

List of DNS servers to use when resolving computer names. This key may not be necessary if you're using DHCP to assign DNS servers.

Key value:

`<IP address>`	Comma-delimited list of DNS server Internet Protocol (IP) addresses.

IPAddress

If IP addresses are assigned manually rather than through DHCP, specify the address or addresses for the network interface card (NIC) here.

Key value:

`<IP address>`	IP address for the NIC. To assign multiple IP addresses to a single card, separate the addresses with commas (,).

NetBIOSOptions

NetBIOS option to use for this network adapter.

Key values:

`0`	Use NetBIOS setting from the DHCP server.
`1`	Enable NetBIOS over TCP/IP.
`2`	Disable NetBIOS over TCP/IP.

SubnetMask

Subnet mask for the network interface card (NIC). This field isn't needed if you're using DHCP to assign the subnet mask.

Key value:

`<subnet mask>`	Valid subnet mask value.

WINS

Determines whether Windows Internet Naming Service (WINS) will be used for name resolution for the network adapter specific to this connection.

Key values:

`Yes`	Enable WINS for name resolution on this adapter.
`No`	Don't use WINS for name resolution on this adapter.

WINSServerList

IP addresses of the WINS servers for this connection to use with name resolution on the network. This setting has no effect if the `WINS` key is not set to `Yes`.

Key value:

`<IP address>`	IP addresses of WINS servers, separated by commas.

[NetClients]

This section defines network clients to be installed during the unattended setup process.

<network client name>

Various clients can be listed under this section as keys, with the value pointing to the section where client parameters will be defined.

Valid client names are as follows:

`MS_MSClient`	Client for Microsoft Network. Installing this client automatically installs support for NetBIOS. NetBIOS options are set using the `NetBIOSOptions` key under the `[<MS TCPIP parameters>]` section.
`MS_NWClient`	Client for NetWare networks.

Key value:

```
<client name> = params.<client name>
```

`<client name>` must be one of the clients listed above. `params` could be any word of your choosing, but for consistency in the examples, I'd recommend using `params`.

For example, a key for the Microsoft Network client would look like this:

```
MS_MSClient = params.MSClient
```

[<MS_MSClient parameters>]

This section contains client parameters for the `MS_MSClient` Microsoft Network client.

BrowseDomains

This key is valid only for Windows 2000 Server products. It specifies the list of domains the computer is allowed to browse.

Key value:

<domain>	Domain name list, separated by commas.

NameServiceNetworkAddress

Network address for the Name Service provider if `NameServiceProtocol` is set to `ncacn_ip_tcp`.

Key value:

<IP address>	Valid TCP/IP address.

NameServiceProtocol

Protocol used by the name service.

Key values:

`ncacn_np`	Use the NCACN_NP protocol.
`ncacn_ip_tcp`	Use the NCACN_IP_TCP protocol.

[<MS_NWClient parameters>]

This section contains client parameters for the `MS_NWClient` NetWare client.

DefaultContext

Default NetWare context name to use for the NetWare client.

Key value:

<context>	Default logon context string.

DefaultTree

Preferred Netware Directory Services tree.

Key value:

<tree>	String representing the name of the preferred tree.

LogonScript

Determines whether the NetWare client should be configured to run a logon script.

Key values:

`Yes`	Run a logon script.
`No`	Don't run a logon script.

PreferredServer

Preferred NetWare server. If you specify this server, the `DefaultTree` and `DefaultContext` keys should not be defined.

Key value:

`<server>`	String value name of the preferred NetWare server.

[NetServices]

This section defines network services to be installed during the unattended setup process.

<network service name>

Various services can be listed under this section as keys, with the value pointing to the section where service parameters are defined.

Valid service names are as follows:

`MS_NwSapAgent`	SAP agent.
`MS_PSched`	Quality of Service (QoS) Packet Scheduler.
`MS_RasSrv`	Dial-Up Server service.
`MS_Server`	Microsoft File and Print Services.
`MS_WLBS`	Windows Load Balancing Service.

Key value:

```
<service name> = params.<service name>
```

`<service name>` must be one of the services listed above. `params` could be any word of your choosing, but for consistency in the examples, I'd recommend using `params`.

For example, a key for the Microsoft File and Print Services would look like this:

```
MS_Server = params.MSServer
```

[<MS_NwSapAgent parameters>]

No configuration options are available for the SAP agent. If this service is installed, this section should be added with no keys or values.

[<MS_PSched parameters>]

No configuration options are available for the Quality of Service (QoS) Packet Scheduler. If this service is installed, this section should be added with no keys or values.

[<MS_RAS parameters>]

This section, which should have the name assigned in the `ParamsSection` key (in this case, `params.MS_RAS`), contains settings for the Routing and Remote Access Services.

AssignSameNetworkNumber

Specifies whether Routing and Remote Access Services should configure all clients with the same network number. This value is optional.

Key values:

`Yes`	Configure all clients on the same network number. This is the default setting.
`No`	Configure separate network numbers for each client.

AutomaticNetworkNumbers

This value is optional. Specifies whether Routing and Remote Access Services should automatically assign network numbers.

Key values:

`Yes`	Automatically assign network numbers. This is the default setting.
`No`	Don't assign network numbers automatically. In this case, you must also specify the `NetworkNumberFrom` key.

ClientCanRequestIPAddress

Determines whether client computers can request a specific IP address. This key is optional.

Key values:

`Yes`	Clients requesting a specific IP address are granted their request.
`No`	Regardless of the client request, the server automatically assigns clients an IP address. This is the default setting.

ClientsCanRequestIpxNodeNumber

Determines whether client computers can request a specific IPX node number. This key is optional.

Key values:

`Yes`	Clients requesting a specific IPX node number are granted their request.
`No`	Regardless of the client request, the server automatically assigns clients an IPX node number. This is the default setting.

DialinProtocols

This key lists the protocols that will be supported by the Dial-Up Server service. To enable a protocol for the Dial-Up Server service, the protocol must be installed on the server.

Key values:

`All`	All protocols installed on the computer will be enabled for dial-up support.
`AppleTalk`	Dial-up clients can use the AppleTalk protocol.
`IPX`	Dial-up clients can use the IPX protocol.
`NetBEUI`	Dial-up clients can use the NetBEUI protocol.
`TCP/IP`	Dial-up clients can use the TCP/IP protocol. This is the default.

Multiple values can be specified by separating protocol entries with commas (,).

IpAddressEnd

When automatically assigning addresses to clients, this key specifies the last IP address of the assignable range. Only one IP address range can be specified through the unattended install process. This value must be specified if `UseDHCP = No`.

Key value:

`<address>`	Valid, standard format numeric IP address.

IpAddressStart

When automatically assigning addresses to clients, this key specifies the first IP address in the assignable range. Only one IP address range can be specified through the unattended install process. This value must be specified if `UseDHCP = No`.

Key value:

`<address>`	Valid, standard format numeric IP address.

IPXClientAccess

This key should only be specified if IPX is an allowed dial-up protocol. It controls the scope of access granted to a dial-up IPX client.

Key values:

`Network`	IPX clients can access any network resources reachable from the server using the IPX protocol. This is the default setting.
`This Computer`	IPX clients can only access network resources available on this machine.

Multilink

This optional setting is only valid when multiple modems are installed and configured for inbound use with Dial-Up Networking.

Key values:

`Yes`	Dial-up clients can connect using Multilink by combining bandwidth from multiple modem connections. This is the default setting.
`No`	Multilink is not permitted.

NetBEUIClientAccess

This key should only be specified if NetBEUI is an allowed dial-up protocol. It controls the scope of access granted to a dial-up NetBEUI client.

Key values:

`Network`	NetBEUI clients can access any network resources reachable from the server using the NetBEUI protocol. This is the default setting.
`This Computer`	NetBEUI clients can only access network resources available on this machine.

NetworkNumberFrom

Start address of allowed IPX network numbers. This key must be specified if `AutomaticNetworkNumbers = No`.

Key value:

`<network number>`	Hex-format IPX network number from `0x00000001` to `0xFFFFFFFE`.

RouterType

This key determines the configuration used for the Routing and Remote Access Services for Windows 2000 Server products. This parameter is required. No other settings in this section will take effect without specifying a value for this key.

Key values:

`1`	Enable remote access only.
`2`	Enable LAN routing only.
`3`	Enable remote access and LAN routing.
`6`	Enable LAN and WAN routing.
`7`	Enable remote access and LAN and WAN routing.

TcpIpClientAccess

This key should only be specified if TCP/IP is an allowed dial-up protocol. It controls the scope of access granted to a dial-up TCP/IP client.

Key values:

`Network`	TCP/IP clients can access any network resources reachable from the server using the TCP/IP protocol. This is the default setting.
`This Computer`	TCP/IP clients can only access network resources available on this machine.

UseDHCP

TCP/IP clients will automatically receive IP addresses and TCP/IP protocol settings if this key is enabled.

Key values:

`Yes`	TCP/IP configuration is automatically sent to the client when the client connects to the server. This is the default value.
`No`	The client receives an IP address within the range defined by the `IpAddressStart` and `IpAddressEnd` keys. Additional TCP/IP configuration information must be manually entered on the client.

[<MS_RasSrv parameters>]

This section holds a single key, with the value pointing to the section where parameters for the Routing and Remote Access Services will be defined.

ParamsSection

The only valid setting for this key is a pointer to the *`<MS_RAS parameters>`* section. The key should appear like this, where `params.MS_RAS` is the user-selected section name that follows:

```
ParamsSection = params.MS_RAS
```

[<MS_Server parameters>]

This section contains service parameters for the Microsoft File and Print Services.

BroadcastsToLanman2Clients

Specifies whether Microsoft File and Print Services should broadcast browser traffic to LAN Manager 2.x clients. This setting is valid only for Windows 2000 Server products.

Key values:

`Yes`	Enable broadcasts to LAN Manager 2.x clients.
`No`	Disable broadcasts. This is the default setting.

Optimization

Specifies the memory optimization model for Windows 2000 Server family. This setting is valid only for Windows 2000 Server products.

Key values:

`Balance`	Balance memory utilization for a system used for both file and print sharing and network application serving.
`MaxThroughputForFileSharing`	Optimize server for file and print sharing. Use this setting on servers used strictly as file and print servers.
`MaxThroughputForNetworkApps`	Optimize server for network applications, such as Exchange or SQL Server.
`MinMemoryUsed`	Minimize the memory used by the server service.

[<MS_WLBS parameters>]

This section contains configuration options for the Windows Load Balancing Service (WLBS). Windows Load Balancing can only be bound to a single network adapter at a time. The binding must be specified in the `[NetBindings]` section, or Setup will bind to a randomly selected adapter. This section is only valid for Windows 2000 Advanced Server or Windows 2000 Datacenter Server.

AliveMsgPeriod

Time, in milliseconds, between WLBS heartbeats.

Key value:

`<integer>`	Value must be an integer between **`100`** and **`10000`**. The default is **`1000`** (one second).

AliveMsgTolerance

Number of lost heartbeats before the WLBS cluster host fails over.

Key value:

`<integer>`	Value must be an integer between `5` and `100`. The default is `5`.

ClusterIPAddress

Primary IP address for the WLBS cluster. The same address must be specified for all hosts in the WLBS cluster. This is a virtual IP address, and should not be assigned as any actual network adapter's IP address.

Key value:

`<address>`	Primary IP address used to address the WLBS cluster. `0.0.0.0` is the default.

ClusterModeOnStart

Specifies whether the system will automatically join the WLBS cluster, or if it must be manually joined to the cluster.

Key values:

`0`	Join automatically at startup.
`1`	Wait to join the cluster until instructed to join. This is the default value.

ClusterName

Friendly, fully qualified domain name (FQDN) of the cluster to which the primary IP address will resolve.

Key value:

`<FQDN>`	FQDN for the WLBS cluster. The default is `cluster.<domain>.com`.

ClusterNetworkMask

Subnet mask for the WLBS cluster virtual IP address configuration.

Key value:

`<subnet mask>`	Valid subnet mask for the cluster IP address. `0.0.0.0` is the default.

DedicatedIPAddress

IP address for this cluster host.

Key value:

<IP address>	Cluster host's IP address. `0.0.0.0` is the default.

DedicatedNetworkMask

IP subnet mask for this cluster host.

Key value:

<IP address>	Cluster host's subnet mask. `0.0.0.0` is the default.

DescriptorsPerAlloc

Number of connection descriptors created per allocation. This key should not be changed from the default of `512` unless instructed by a message in the Event Log.

Key value:

<integer>	Valid entries for this key are integers between `16` and `1024`. The default is `512`.

HostPriority

Host's cluster priority.

Key value:

<integer>	Valid entries for this key are integers between `1` and `32`. The default is `1`.

MaskSourceMAC

Determines whether MAC addresses for hosts should be masked.

Key values:

`0`	MAC masking is disabled.
`1`	MAC masking is enabled. This allows WLBS cluster hosts to connect to different switch ports.

MaxDescriptorAllocs

Maximum connection descriptor allocations. This key should not be changed from the default of `512` unless instructed by a message in the Event Log.

Key value:

<integer>	Valid entries for this key are integers between `1` and `1024`. The default is `512`.

MulticastSupportEnable

Specifies whether WLBS should allow the use of a multicast MAC address.

Key values:

`0`	Cluster will not use a multicast MAC address.
`1`	MAC address used by cluster can be a multicast address.

NetmonAliveMsgs

Configures heartbeat messages such that they can be captured and viewed by Network Monitor.

Key values:

`0`	Heartbeat can't be captured or viewed by Network Monitor. This is the default configuration.
`1`	Heartbeat can be captured by Network Monitor.

NumActions

Number of actions created per allocation. This key should not be changed from the default of `50` unless instructed by a message in the Event Log.

Key value:

`<integer>`	Integer value between `5` and `500`. The default is `50`.

NumAliveMsgs

Number of heartbeat packet buffers created per allocation. This key should not be changed from the default value of `66` unless instructed by a message in the Event Log.

Key values:

`<integer>`	Integer value between `66` and `660`. The default is `66`.

NumPackets

Number of packets created per allocation. This key should not be changed from the default value of `100` unless instructed by a message in the Event Log.

Key value:

`<integer>`	Integer value between `5` and `500`. The default is `100`.

Ports

This key uses IP protocol and destination ports to distribute IP traffic among WLBS cluster hosts.

Key value:

`<integer>,<integer>,<port type>,<port mode>,<mode parameter>`

Multiple sets of key values can be specified by adding a comma and continuing the format of the key value.

<*integer*> is a port value from `1` to `65535`.

<*port type*> can be `TCP`, `UDP`, or `Both`.

<*port mode*> can be `Disabled`, `Single`, or `Multiple`.

<*mode parameter*> depends on the option selected in <*port mode*>:

For `Disabled` port mode, no mode parameters are specified. For `Single` port mode, the value is an integer between `1` and `32`. For `Multiple` port mode, the value is <*1*>,<*mode parameter 2*>, where <*mode parameter 1*> can be `None`, `Single`, or `ClassC`, and <*mode parameter 2*> can be `Equal` or <*integer*>, where <*integer*> is between `1` and `100`.

For example, HTTP:

```
Ports = 80,80,Both,Multiple,None,Equal
```

Or HTTP and HTTPS:

```
Ports = 80,80,Both,Multiple,None,Equal,443,443,Both,Multiple,Single,Equal
```

RemoteControlEnabled

Enables WLBS remote control features.

Key values:

Value	Description
`0`	WLBS remote control is disabled.
`1`	WLBS remote control is enabled.

RemoteControlPassword

Sets a password that must be entered when connecting to the WLBS over remote control.

Key value:

Value	Description
<*password*>	Any valid password. The default is no password.

RemoteControlUDPPort

Specifies the default UDP port to be used for WLBS remote control connections over IP.

Key value:

Value	Description
<*UDP port*>	This should be an integer between `1` and `65535`, the range of valid UDP ports. The default is `2504`. For security reasons, it's a good idea to select a different port (other than 2504), and make sure it's protected behind a firewall.

[NetBindings]

This section configures bindings for network services, protocols, and adapters. Each key under this section can be listed more than once. When specifying a network binding after these keys, the binding path must be formatted as follows, or it will be disregarded:

```
<key> = <service>, <protocol>, <adapter>
```

For example, the following would be a valid key and value under this section:

```
Disable = MS_Server, MS_NWIPX, PrimaryAdapter
```

Disable

Network binding to disable for a specific network binding.

Demote

Network binding to move to the bottom of the binding order.

Enable

Network binding to enable for a specific network binding.

[NetOptionalComponents]

This section contains a series of keys used for installing optional Windows 2000 network components. All available components have the same format:

```
<key> = <value>
```

where `<key>` is the component name and `<value>` is one of the following values:

`0`	The component will not be installed.
`1`	The component will be installed.

Rather than restate the key values for each component, the following key sections simply define each component's name. Since these are optional components, the default for each key is `0`. Unless otherwise specified, the following components are valid only for the Windows 2000 Server family of products.

ACS

Component: Quality of Service (QoS) Admission Control Service.

DHCPServer

Component: Dynamic Host Configuration Protocol (DHCP) server.

DNS

Component: Domain Name System (DNS) server to resolve Internet names to IP addresses.

IAS

Component: Internet Authentication Services (IAS).

ILS

Component: Internet Location Service (ILS).

If enabled, the `iis_common`, `iis_inetmgr`, `iis_www`, and `netcis` components must all be installed.

LPDSVC

Component: Line Print Daemon (LPD), the TCP/IP print service for UNIX. This component can be installed on Windows 2000 Professional or any of the Windows 2000 Server family of products.

MacPrint

Component: Print services for Macintosh.

MacSrv

Component: Services for Macintosh (SFM).

Netcm

Component: Microsoft Connection Manager Administration Kit and Phone Book service.

If enabled, the `iis_common`, `iis_inetmgr`, `iis_ftp`, and `iis_www` components must all be installed.

NETMONTOOLS

Component: Network Monitor tools.

SimpTcp

Component: Simple TCP/IP Services, such as Chargen, Daytime, Discard, Echo, and Quote.

This component can be installed on Windows 2000 Professional or any of the Windows 2000 Server family of products.

SNMP

Component: Simple Network Management Protocol (SNMP).
This component can be installed on Windows 2000 Professional or any of the Windows 2000 Server family of products.

WINS

Component: Windows Internet Naming Service (WINS) for resolving computer names to IP addresses.

[SNMP]

This section is used to configure the Simple Network Management Protocol service, if the optional network component is installed.

Accept_CommunityName

Specifies community names from which the SNMP service will accept traps.

Key value:

`<community name>:<privilege>`	`<community name>` is a string value for a valid SNMP community. Multiple sets of values can be defined as a comma-delimited list. Each community name must be associated with one of the following privileges: `None`, `Notify`, `Read_Only`, `Read_Write`, or `Read_Create`.

Any_Host

Determines whether the SNMP service should accept SNMP packets from any host.

Key values:

`Yes`	Accept SNMP packets from any host.
`No`	Accept SNMP packets only from hosts specified in the `Limit_Host` key.

Community_Name

SNMP community name for the computer.

Key value:

`<string>`	Valid community name string value.

Contact_Name

Contact name and information for this system.

Key value:

`<string>`	Text string specifying contact information.

Limit_Host

When `Any_Host = No`, this key can be used to specify up to three allowed SNMP host names.

Key value:

`<string>`	Up to three allowed SNMP host names, separated by commas.

Location

Physical location of this system.

Key value:

`<host>`	Text string describing the physical system location.

Send_Authentication

Specifies whether to send an SNMP authentication trap when an unauthorized SNMP host requests information.

Key values:

`Yes`	Send authentication trap.
`No`	Don't send authentication trap.

Service

Available SNMP services to install. Multiple services can be specified as a comma-delimited list.

Key values:

`Applications`	Installed by default. SNMP services for monitoring components at the Applications layer of the OSI model (such as Quality of Service monitors).
`Datalink`	SNMP services for monitoring components at the Datalink layer of the OSI model (such as PPP, the Point-to-Point Protocol).
`End-to-End`	Installed by default. SNMP services for monitoring network communication components from the client to the server.
`Internet`	Installed by default. SNMP services used to monitor network components related to Internet services, such as WWW and FTP service information.

`Physical`	SNMP services for monitoring the physical components of the network (such as the network interface card) as defined by the Open Systems Interconnection (OSI) network communications model.

Traps

IP addresses or IPX addresses to which traps should be sent. To use this key, the `Community_Name` parameter must be specified.

Key value:

<address>	Up to three IP or IPX addresses, separated by commas. Don't mix IP and IPX addresses.

[InternetServer]

This section contains configuration information for the Internet Information Server (IIS) services. This section will not be processed if both the `iis_www` and the `iis_ftp` components are disabled in the `[Components]` section.

PathFTPRoot

Changes the default installation folder for the FTP service. Changing the default location is only possible through the use of an answer file.

Key value:

<"*path*">	Path, in quotes, for the FTP service installation folder. You can use environment variables. The default location is `%systemdrive%\Inetpub\Ftproot`.

PathWWWRoot

Changes the default installation folder for the WWW service. Changing the default location is only possible through the use of an answer file.

Key value:

<"*path*">	Path, in quotes, for the WWW service installation folder. You can use environment variables. The default location is `%systemdrive%\Inetpub\Wwwroot`.

[Cluster]

This section is only valid for Windows 2000 Advanced Server and Windows 2000 Datacenter Server. The Cluster service components will be completely installed if the option is enabled under the `[Components]` section. This section won't run until after setup has completed and a user logs onto the system. To process this section, the following code must exist in the answer file:

```
[GuiRunOnce]
Command0 = "%windir%\cluster\cluscfg.exe -UNATTEND"

[Components]
cluster = on
```

Account

If creating a new cluster (the `Action` key is set to `Form`), this key must specify the Windows 2000 account under which the Cluster service should run.

Key value:

<account>	Valid account name under which the Cluster service should run.

Action

Specify whether Cluster service setup should create a new cluster or join an existing cluster.

Key values:

`Form`	Create a new cluster. The `Account` and `Domain` keys must be specified with this option.
`Join`	Join an existing cluster.

Domain

Domain to which a new cluster belongs.

Key value:

<domain>	Valid domain name.

ExcludeDrive

Drives that should be excluded from available quorum devices.

Key value:

<drive letter>	Comma-delimited list of excluded drive letters.

IPAddr

IP address for the cluster.

Key value:

<IP address>	Valid numeric IP address.

LocalQuorum

This key allows a system drive to be used as a quorum device.

Key value:

`Yes`	Use the system drive as the quorum device. A local quorum resource cannot fail over. This makes the cluster ineffective as a fault-tolerant solution. This setting should only be used for testing purposes.
`No`	Don't allow the system drive to be used as a quorum device. This is the default behavior.

Name

Cluster name.

Key value:

`<name>`	Cluster name string of up to 15 characters.

Network

This key specifies the network adapter name and role used for the cluster communication connection.

Key value:

`<connection name>`, *`<role>`*, *`<priority>`*

`<connection name>` is the name of the network adapter to use for cluster communications.

`<role>`, which can be `All`, `Internal`, or `Client`, specifies the role of the named connection. `All` uses the network connection for intra-cluster communication and client connectivity. `Internal` uses the network connection only for intra-cluster communication. `Client` uses the network connection only for client connectivity.

`<connection name>` and *`<role>`* are required values.

`<priority>`, an optional value, is needed only when setting the role to `Internal`. It specifies the order in which multiple network connections are used for internal communications.

For example, to use the connection named Local Area Connection for internal cluster communication and client connectivity to the LAN, you would specify it as follows:

```
Network = "Local Area Connection", All
```

To use the first network card for internal cluster communication and the second for client connectivity, you would specify it this way:

```
Network = "Local Area Connection", Internal, 1
Network = "Local Area Connection 2", Client
```

Password

Password for the Windows 2000 account specified by `Account`.

Key value:

<string>	Valid account password string specifying the password to the `<account>` value of the `Account` key.

Quorum

Drive letter to use as a quorum device.

Key value:

<drive>	Drive letter, followed by a colon, to use as the quorum device.

Subnet

Subnet mask for the cluster.

Key value:

<mask>	Valid numeric IP address of the subnet mask for the IP address specified by the `IPAddr` key.

[TerminalServices]

Use this section to configure options available under the Windows 2000 Terminal Services component. Terminal Services is only available on the Windows 2000 Server family of products. This section will not be processed if unless `TSEnable = On` under the `[Components]` section.

ApplicationServer

Selects the mode in which to install the Terminal Services Server. Terminal Services Server cannot run in Application Server mode if the Cluster service is installed on the same box.

Key values:

`0`	Install Terminal Services Server in Remote Administration mode. This is a useful remote control tool for remote server administration tasks that can't be performed through the MMC.
`1`	Install Terminal Services Server in Application Server mode.

PermissionsSetting

Selects between Windows 2000 user permission level and Terminal Server 4.0 user permission level.

Key values:

`0`	Windows 2000 user permissions.
`1`	Terminal Server 4.0 user permissions, recommended for backward compatibility with Terminal Server 4.0 applications. This is the default setting.

[Certsrv_Client]

Settings in this section are not processed during unattended setup. These options are configured after the first reboot. This section configures the Certificate Services Web client component. To install this component, set `certsrv_client = On` in the `[Components]` section.

CAMachine

This required parameter specifies the DNS name of an operational Certification Authority computer.

Key value:

<ComputerName>	Certification Authority computer's DNS name.

CAName

This required parameter specifies the name of the Certification Authority running on the machine specified in the `CAMachine` key.

Key value:

<CAName>	Certification Authority name.

[Certsrv_Server]

Settings in this section are not processed during unattended setup. These options are configured after the first reboot. This section can be used to configure Certificate Services on the Windows 2000 Server family of products.

CAType

Type of Certification Authority to install. This parameter requires a value.

Key values:

`EnterpriseRoot`	Install Enterprise Root CA.
`EnterpriseSubordinate`	Install Enterprise Subordinate CA.
`StandaloneRoot`	Install Standalone Root CA.
`StandaloneSubordinate`	Install Standalone Subordinate CA.

Country

Country code to use for the CA, as specified by the International Telecommunication Union Survey Web site at `http://www.itu.int/net/cctlds/index.html`.

Key value:

<country code>	Maximum two-character, non-numeric (alpha only) country code value. The default is determined using the `GetLocalInfo` API call.

CSPProvider

Default cryptography service provider.

Key value:

<"CSP">	Valid CSP name, in quotes. This value is case sensitive. The default is `"Microsoft Base Cryptographic Provider v1.0"`.

Description

Description of the CA.

Key value:

<description>	String value description of the CA. Case sensitive, with a maximum string length is 2048 characters.

Email

Email address for the CA.

Key value:

<email>	Valid email address string. Case sensitive, with a maximum string length of 128 characters.

ExistingKey

Tells the CA to use an existing key.

Key value:

<name>	String specifying the name of an existing key.

HashAlgorithm

Certificate signing hash algorithm supported by the CSP specified in the `CSPProvider` key.

Key value:

<string>	*<string>* must be a valid hash algorithm string or algorithm ID supported by the specified CSP. The default is `SHA1`.

KeyLength

Key length to use for the CA. The default key length of the CSP specified in the `CSPProvider` key is used if this key is not specified.

Key value:

`<length>`	Numeric value to use as the key length for the CA.

Locality

Locality of the CA. This value is required.

Key value:

`<string>`	Specifies the locality of the CA being installed. Case sensitive, with a maximum string length of 128 characters.

Name

This required value specifies the name of the CA.

Key value:

`<name>`	Case-sensitive name string, with a maximum length of 64 characters.

Organization

This required value specifies the organization name of the CA being installed.

Key value:

`<organization>`	Case-sensitive text string, with a maximum length of 64 characters.

OrganizationUnit

This required value specifies the organizational unit of the CA being installed. This term is not related to the organizational unit (OU) concept used in reference to Windows 2000 domains.

Key value:

`<ou>`	Case-sensitive text string, with a maximum length of 32 characters.

ParentCAMachine

Computer name for operational parent CA to use when performing a subordinate CA installation. This value will be ignored for root CA installations. If this string is specified, the `ParentCAName` key should also be defined.

Key value:

`<computername>`	Computer name string for related parent CA.

ParentCAName

CA name for operational parent CA to use when performing a subordinate CA installation. This value will be ignored for root CA installations. If this string is specified, the `ParentCAMachine` key must also be defined.

Key value:

`<computername>`	CA name string for related parent CA.

PreserveDB

This key can be used to preserve an existing certificate database. The `ExistingKey` and `UseExistingCert` keys should also be defined.

Key value:

`Yes`	Preserve existing certificate database.
`No`	Create a new certificate database.

RequestFile

File into which certificate requests should be saved by subordinate CA.

Key value:

`<path>`	Full path to file of existing CA request file on a parent CA. This parameter is ignored if `CAType` is `EnterpriseRoot` or `StandaloneRoot`.

SharedFolder

Folder containing configuration information for a CA.

Key value:

`<path>`	Path to CA configuration information. The default is the registered shared folder (usually `%systemdrive%\CAConfig`).

State

State or province for the CA being installed.

Key value:

`<state>`	This string value is case sensitive, with a maximum of 128 characters. The entire state name should be used, rather than an abbreviation.

UseExistingCert

If a Certification Authority certificate is found that matches the value from the `ExistingKey` key, Setup will use the existing certificate for an existing key.

Key values:

`Yes`	Use the existing CA certificate.
`No`	Don't use an existing certificate.

ValidityPeriod

Number of periods for a CA validity period.

Key value:

<number>	Integer from `0` to `1000`. The default is `2`.

ValidityPeriodUnits

Base unit of measurement expressed by `ValidityPeriod` key.

Key values:

`Years`	This is the default value. The number specified by `ValidityPeriod` is the number of years the certificate will be valid.
`Months`	The number specified by `ValidityPeriod` is the number of months the certificate will be valid.
`Weeks`	The number specified by `ValidityPeriod` is the number of weeks the certificate will be valid.
`Days`	The number specified by `ValidityPeriod` is the number of days the certificate will be valid.

[RemoteInstall]

This section will be generated automatically when creating an image for the Remote Installation Services.

Repartition

Determines whether Setup should delete all partitions on the first drive to create a single partition.

Key values:

`Yes`	Delete other partitions on the first drive.
`No`	Keep existing partitions.

[OsChooser]

This section will be generated automatically when creating an image for the Remote Installation Services.

Description

Description of the RIS image that will appear in the Client Installation Wizard.

Key value:

`<string>`	Description string identifying the RIS image associated with the answer file.

Help

Detailed description of the RIS image that will appear in the Help area of the Client Installation Wizard.

Key value:

`<string>`	Detailed description string identifying the RIS image associated with the answer file.

ImageType

Identifies the installation technology used by the image associated with the answer file.

Key values:

`Flat`	CD-based image.
`Sysprep`	RIPREP image.

LaunchFile

Path to execute when an image is selected from the RIS Client Installation Wizard.

Key value:

`<path>`	Complete path, including the filename.

Version

Version of the operating system or tool associated with the image in the RIS Client Installation Wizard.

Key value:

`<string>`	String description of the OS or tool version.

[DCInstall]

This is an optional section that can be used to automate the installation, configuration, or rollback of an Active Directory controller. This section is valid only for the Windows 2000 Server family of products.

AdministratorPassword

Local administrator password to assign to the Administrator account when rolling back from a domain controller to a member server.

Key value:

`<password>`	Any valid password string. The default is blank.

AutoConfigDNS

The DCPROMO process can automatically install and configure DNS for new domains when Dynamic DNS update capability is not available in the existing DNS.

Key values:

`Yes`	Automatically install and configure DDNS if needed.
`No`	Don't configure DDNS.

ChildName

Domain name to use if this will be a DC for a child domain.

Key value:

`<domain>`	Child domain name string value.

CreateOrJoin

Determines whether DCPROMO will create a new forest or create a new domain in an existing forest.

Key values:

`Join`	Create a new domain joined to an existing forest.
`Create`	Create a new forest.

DatabasePath

Local path to the preferred location of a domain database.

Key value:

`<"path">`	Local path enclosed in quotes, which can include environment variables. The default is `"%systemroot%\NTDS"`. Target location must have at least 20MB of free space for a new domain.

DNSOnNetwork

When creating a new forest, this option determines the behavior of the DNS client configuration.

Key values:

`Yes`	DNS client can be configured during setup. Auto-configuration of DNS is optional. This is the default setting.
`No`	Skip DNS client configuration during setup. Auto-configuration of DNS is forced.

DomainNetBiosName

NetBIOS name of the new domain. This is a required value.

Key value:

<name>	Valid NetBIOS name for the new domain. Must be unique on the network.

IsLastDCInDomain

When demoting a domain controller to a member server, this key specifies whether the computer is the last domain controller in a domain.

Key values:

`Yes`	This machine is the last domain controller in its domain.
`No`	Additional domain controllers are present for this domain.

LogPath

Local path to the preferred location of a domain database log files.

Key value:

<"path">	Local path in quotes, which can include environment variables. The default is `"%systemroot%\NTDS"`. Target location must have at least 10MB of free space for a new domain.

NewDomainDNSName

Use this key to specify a new forest or a new tree in an existing forest.

Key value:

<name>	Domain DNS name string value.

ParentDomainDNSName

The DNS name of an existing parent domain is needed when creating a new child domain.

Key value:

`<name>`	Domain DNS name string for the existing parent domain into which this child domain should be installed.

Password

Password for the Windows 2000 user account with permissions to promote this member server to a domain controller. The `UserDomain` and `UserName` strings should be specified as well.

Key value:

`<password>`	Valid password string value.

RebootOnSuccess

Reboots the computer after successfully completing DCPROMO. The directory services won't start until after the machine reboots.

Key values:

`Yes`	Automatically reboot at completion of the DCPROMO wizard.
`No`	Don't reboot without user interaction. This is the default option.

ReplicaDomainDNSName

When creating a new replica domain by upgrading an existing down-level backup domain controller (BDC), this parameter specifies the DNS name of the domain from which you want to replicate.

Key value:

`<DNS name>`	Valid DNS name of a domain from which to replicate.

ReplicaOrMember

When upgrading an existing down-level BDC, this key determines whether the BDC should be converted to a replica DC or demoted to a member server.

Key values:

`Replica`	Upgrade the BDC to a Windows 2000 replica domain controller.

`Member` — Upgrade the BDC to a Windows 2000 member server. This is the default setting.

ReplicaOrNewDomain

When upgrading an existing down-level BDC, this key determines whether the BDC should be converted to a replica DC or installed as the first DC in a new domain.

Key values:

`Replica`	Upgrade the BDC to a Windows 2000 replica domain controller. This is the default setting.
`Domain`	Upgrade the BDC to a Windows 2000 member server. You must use the `TreeOrChild` key if you select this option.

SiteName

When creating a new domain tree in a new forest of domains, this option selects an existing site in which to place the new domain controller.

Key value:

`<site>`	Name of an existing site. The default is `"Default-First-Site"`.

SysVolPath

Local path to the preferred location of a SysVol database log file. The target drive must be formatted with NTFS 5.0.

Key values:

`<path>`	Local path in quotes, can include environment variables. The default is `"%systemroot%\NTDS"`.

TreeOrChild

Specifies whether a new domain is the root of a new tree or a child domain for an existing domain.

Key values:

`Tree`	The domain is the root of a new tree. The `CreateOrJoin` key must be specified if you select this option.
`Child`	The domain is a child domain for an existing domain. This is the default value.

UserDomain

User domain for the Windows 2000 user account with permissions to promote this member server to a domain controller. The `Password` and `UserName` keys should be present as well.

Key value:

`<domain>`	Valid domain string value from which the user account specified in `UserName` originates.

UserName

Username for the Windows 2000 user account with permissions to promote this member server to a domain controller. The `Password` and `UserDomain` keys should be specified as well.

Key value:

`<account>`	Valid user account with proper permissions from the domain specified in the `UserDomain` key.

[Data]

This section is required when performing an unattended install by booting from the Windows 2000 installation CD.

AutoPartition

Windows 2000 setup can automatically select a partition on which to install. This key must be specified as `AutoPartition = "1"` if you want to perform an unattended install by booting from the Windows 2000 installation CD.

Key values:

`"0"`	Setup will pause and allow the user to select the installation partition.
`"1"`	Setup will select a partition automatically.

MsDosInitiated

When installing by booting from the Windows 2000 installation CD, this key must be `MsDosInitiated = "0"` or setup will fail at the beginning of the GUI-mode setup.

Key value:

`"0"`	The value must be `"0"`. You shouldn't set this value to anything else.

UnattendedInstall

When installing by booting from the Windows 2000 installation CD, this key must be `UnattendedInstall = Yes` or setup will perform a normal attended install.

Key value:

`Yes`	The value must be `Yes`. You shouldn't set this value to anything else.

UseBIOSToBoot

Setup will always use int13 BIOS functions to start the computer, even if Setup detects a device that supports a miniport driver.

Key values:

`0`	Setup will determine whether it should use the BIOS or a miniport driver to boot.
`1`	Setup will always use int13 BIOS functions to boot.

C

Sample Answer Files

THE FOLLOWING SECTIONS PROVIDE SOME SAMPLE answer files to use as starting points when developing your own unattended installs. All of these files should be customized for your environment. At the very least, you should update the username, organization name, domain information, default passwords, domain administration account information, and product ID before attempting to use these files. Although not critical to the success of the installation scripts, you should also update the time zone, TAPI settings, screen resolution, language settings, and network configuration to fit your environment.

These answer files are for unattended clean installs. As such, *they will delete everything on your hard drive.* Do not install Windows 2000 using these answer files unless you need no data or settings from the target machine. The answer files provided are as follows:

- Absolute minimum answer file for unattended setup of Windows 2000 Professional
- Automated install by booting from the Windows 2000 Professional CD
- Answer file to install Windows 2000 Server
- My standard SYSPREP answer file for Windows 2000 Professional

Download These Files

All the answer files in this appendix are available for downloading from the book's companion Web site at `http://www.ferristech.net/win2k`.

Pay attention to the internal comments—text preceded by a semicolon (;)—within the answer files. Comments are included to help identify the effects of various keys and to point out areas of the scripts that must be changed to accommodate different environments.

Absolute Minimum Answer File for Unattended Setup of Windows 2000 Professional

The following sample answer file is the absolute minimum required to perform a successful, completely unattended clean install. To run an install using this file, save the file as UNATTEND.TXT. If running the Windows 2000 installation from DOS with the Windows 2000 CD-ROM mounted to drive D: and the UNATTEND.TXT file on drive A:, the command would be as follows:

```
winnt /s:d:\i386 /t:c /u:a:\unattend.txt
```

To install Windows 2000 Professional from within Windows 95, Windows 98, Windows NT 3.51, or Windows NT 4.0, you would run this command:

```
winnt32 /s:d:\i386 /tempdrive:c /unattend:a:\unattend.txt
```

Note that for either of these scenarios, you must pre-partition and format drive C: in a format recognized by the system from which you will initiate the setup. This is the syntax for the bare minimum answer file:

```
;UNATTEND.TXT Answer File for Windows 2000 Professional
;Clean Install, Base Unattended Setup
;Joined to Workgroup
;Created by Jeffrey Ferris
;Ferris Technology Network
;Version 1.0

[Unattended]
UnattendMode = FullUnattended
NoWaitAfterTextMode = 1
NoWaitAfterGUIMode = 1
OemSkipEula = yes

[GuiUnattended]
AdminPassword = *        ;Blank Administrator Password
TimeZone=20              ;US Central Time Zone
OemSkipWelcome = 1       ;Bypass Welcome screen
OemSkipRegional = 1      ;Skip regional options page

[UserData]
FullName="Ferris Technology Network"
OrgName="Ferris Technology Network"
computername="*"    ;Randomly generate computer name based on organization name
Productid = xxxxx-xxxxx-xxxxx-xxxxx-xxxxx  ;Substitute your unique PID here
```

```
[TapiLocation]
Dialing=Tone
AreaCode=512
LongDistanceAccess=9

[Networking]
InstallDefaultComponents = Yes

[Identification]
JoinWorkgroup = Workgroup


;End of File
```

Automated Install by Booting from the Windows 2000 Professional CD

The following sample answer file is a more customized version of a Windows 2000 Professional answer file. This version joins a domain, installs the NetWare client, adds the IPX protocol, sets display defaults, and customizes some of the components installed with Windows 2000. In addition, the inclusion of the `[Data]` section allows this script to be used as an answer file for a Windows 2000 Professional CD boot-based install. Name this file WINNT.SIF and save it to the root directory of a floppy disk. Insert the Windows 2000 Professional CD, configure your machine to boot to CD, and insert the floppy disk as soon as the system starts to boot from the CD.

```
;WINNT.SIF Answer File for Windows 2000 Professional
;Clean Install, Custom Unattended Setup
;Joined to Workgroup
;Created by Jeffrey Ferris
;Ferris Technology Network
;Version 2.0

;The following [Data] section enables the automated install by booting from
;the CD. If you want to convert this file to a standard UNATTEND.TXT file
;rather than the WINNT.SIF file, simply omit the following section.
[Data]
AutoPartition = "1"
MsDosInitiated = "0"
UnattendedInstall = Yes

[Unattended]
UnattendMode = DefaultHide
NoWaitAfterTextMode = 1
NoWaitAfterGUIMode = 1
OemSkipEula = yes
FileSystem = ConvertNTFS
Repartition = Yes      ;only valid on boot CD installs.
```

```
[GuiUnattended]
AdminPassword = *         ;Blank Administrator Password
TimeZone=20               ;US Central Time Zone
OemSkipWelcome = 1        ;Bypass Welcome screen
OemSkipRegional = 1       ;Skip regional options page

[UserData]
FullName="Ferris Technology Network"
OrgName="Ferris Technology Network"
computername="*"    ;Randomly generate computer name based on organization name
Productid = xxxxx-xxxxx-xxxxx-xxxxx-xxxxx  ;Substitute your unique PID here

[Display]
BitsPerPel=16
Xresolution=800
YResolution=600
Vrefresh=72

[TapiLocation]
Dialing=Tone
AreaCode=512
LongDistanceAccess=9

[Components]
;We're disabling everything "fun."
;This section prevents installation of the CD Player, Character Map,
;Desktop Wallpaper, Phone Dialer, Freecell, HyperTerminal, sound schemes,
;Minesweeper, extra mouse pointers, WordPad, Pinball, Sound Recorder, and
;Solitaire.
cdplayer = off
charmap = off
deskpaper = off
dialer = off
freecell = off
hypertrm = off
media_clips = off
media_utopia = off
minesweeper = off
mousepoint = off
mswordpad = off
pinball = off
rec = off
solitaire = off

[Networking]
InstallDefaultComponents = Yes

[Identification]
;The following information should be changed to reflect your domain environment
JoinDomain = FERRISTECH
```

```
;This should be the username and password for an account with permission to
;add a computer account and join it to the domain.
DomainAdmin = install
DomainAdminPassword = AddW0rkst4ti0ns

[NetAdapters]
Adapter01 = params.LANConnection

[params.LANConnection]
INFID = *               ;Only works in systems with a single NIC.
                        ;Otherwise, you must specify the PnP ID here.
ConnectionName = "LAN Connection"

[NetProtocols]
MS_TCPIP = params.TCPIP        ;install TCP/IP protocol
MS_NWIPX = params.IPX          ;install IPX protocol

;The following options should be changed to reflect your DNS environment.
[params.TCPIP]
DNSDomain = ferristech.net
DNSSuffixSearchOrder = ferristech.net, home.ferristech.net, dev.ferristech.net
EnableLMHosts = No

[params.IPX]
EnableWANRouter = No     ;Disable RIP router.

[NetClients]
MS_MSClient = params.MSClient
MS_NWClient = params.NetWareC        ;don't need this if you don't use NetWare

[params.MSClient]

;Leave out the following section if you don't use NetWare.
[params.NetWareC]
PreferredServer = FTNNWS
LogonScript = No

[NetServices]

[NetBindings]

[NetOptionalComponents]
SimpTCP = 1            ;Installs the Simple TCP/IP Services


;End of File
```

Answer File to Install Windows 2000 Server

In general, I recommend unattended installs for Windows 2000 Server as member servers only. If you want to build an unattended install for a Windows 2000 Server as a domain controller, I recommend building an install to configure a member server with everything you need *except* the domain controller configuration information. When the member server installation is complete, manually run DCPROMO to upgrade your system to a domain controller. Nevertheless, I've included the lines needed to automate the installation of a Windows 2000 Server domain controller. This answer file is formatted for use with the Windows 2000 Server bootable CD installation (WINNT.SIF).

The easiest way to use this answer file to create a DC with no user interaction is to configure your BIOS boot order to CDROM, then HDD, then Floppy (or disable floppy boot entirely). Copy the following WINNT.SIF file to the floppy, insert the floppy and the Windows 2000 Server CD-ROM, and boot the system. Press a key when prompted to start the Windows 2000 Setup. Leave the floppy disk in drive A: until after the first reboot after setup has completed.

The `GuiRunOnce` line references the answer file for the unattended mode DCPROMO execution. DCPROMO will not run until the first boot of the system, at which point AutoLogon will automatically log on as the local administrator. DCPROMO will then execute; it must be able to find the WINNT.SIF file in drive A:, or DCPROMO will fail.

Note: Don't forget to manually configure the DHCP and DNS services; the following answer file only installs the services.

```
;WINNT.SIF Answer File for Windows 2000 Server
;Clean Install, Customized Member Server
;Code included to upgrade to Domain Controller
;Created by Jeffrey Ferris
;Ferris Technology Network
;Version 1.0

;The following section enables the automated installation by booting from
;the CD. If you want to convert this file to a standard UNATTEND.TXT file
;rather than the WINNT.SIF file, simply omit the entire [Data] section.
[Data]
AutoPartition = "1"
MsDosInitiated = "0"
UnattendedInstall = Yes

[Unattended]
UnattendMode = FullUnattended
NoWaitAfterTextMode = 1
NoWaitAfterGUIMode = 1
OemSkipEula = yes
FileSystem = ConvertNTFS
Repartition = Yes
```

```
[GuiUnattended]
AdminPassword = *          ;Blank Administrator Password
AutoLogon = Yes            ;Allow system to autologon one time
                           ;to execute GuiRunOnce commands
TimeZone=20                ;US Central Time Zone
OemSkipWelcome = 1         ;Bypass Welcome screen
OemSkipRegional = 1        ;Skip regional options page

[UserData]
FullName = "Ferris Technology Network"
OrgName = "Ferris Technology Network"
Computername = "FTNDC01"       ;Shouldn't use auto name for domain controllers.
Productid = xxxxx-xxxxx-xxxxx-xxxxx-xxxxx  ;Substitute your unique PID here

[Display]
BitsPerPel=16
Xresolution=800
YResolution=600
Vrefresh=72

[TapiLocation]
Dialing=Tone
AreaCode=512    ;Area code for Austin, Texas. Enter your own area code here.
LongDistanceAccess=9     ;Must dial "9" for long distance.

[LicenseFilePrintData]
AutoMode = PerSeat

[GuiRunOnce]
;The following command can be added to GuiRunOnce if you wish
;to script the upgrade of a member server to a domain controller.
;The floppy containing WINNT.SIF must be in the A:\ drive when the
;server boots the first time after completing Setup.
;You can use a different answer file if you wish. Simply copy the
;required [DCInstall] section to the answer file.
Command0 = "dcpromo /answer:a:\winnt.sif"

[Components]
;No need for any of these components on a Windows 2000 Server DC.
;This section prevents installation of the CD Player, Character Map,
;Desktop Wallpaper, Phone Dialer, Freecell, HyperTerminal, sound schemes,
;Minesweeper, extra mouse pointers, WordPad, Pinball, Sound Recorder, and
;Solitaire.
cdplayer = off
charmap = off
deskpaper = off
dialer = off
freecell = off
hypertrm = off
media_clips = off
media_utopia = off
```

```
minesweeper = off
mousepoint = off
mswordpad = off
pinball = off
rec = off
solitaire = off

;These are the Server-specific components.
iis_nntp = off          ;Disable Network News Transfer Protocol
iis_nntp_docs = off     ;Don't install NNTP Documentation
iis_smtp = off          ;Disable Simple Mail Transfer Protocol
iis_smtp_docs = off     ;Don't install SMTP Documentation
indexsrv_system = off   ;Disable IIS Indexing Service
TSClients = on      ;Install files needed to make Terminal Services Client disks
TSEnable = on       ;Install Terminal Services.  We'll use this for remote admin

[Networking]

[NetAdapters]
Adapter01 = params.LANConnection

[params.LANConnection]
INFID = *               ;Only works in systems with a single NIC.
                        ;Otherwise, you must specify the PnP ID here.
ConnectionName = "LAN Connection"

[NetClients]
MS_MSCLIENT = params.MSCLIENT

[params.MSCLIENT]

[NetProtocols]
MS_TCPIP = params.TCPIP

[params.TCPIP]
AdapterSections = params.TCPIP.LANConnection

[params.TCPIP.LANConnection]
;These settings are specific to the first adapter.
DHCP = No                     ;Since this is a server, configure manual IP info.
SpecificTo = Adapter01
IPAddress = 192.168.0.2       ;Set this to the static IP address for the server.
DefaultGateway = 192.168.0.1  ;Set this to the default gateway for your subnet.
SubnetMask = 255.255.255.0    ;Subnet mask for this subnet (if needed).
DNSDomain = ferristech.net    ;This is a global setting.
;The following line should list your DNS servers, separated by commas.
;Since this box is a DNS server, include its IP in the list.
DNSServerSearchOrder = 192.168.0.2, 192.168.0.51
```

```
[NetServices]
MS_Server = params.MSServer

;config MS File and Print Service
[params.MSServer]
Optimization = Balance

[Identification]
;this is overridden when DCPROMO runs
JoinWorkgroup = Workgroup
[NetOptionalComponents]
SimpTCP = 1            ;Installs the Simple TCP/IP Services
DHCPServer = 1         ;Installs DHCP. Configure after first boot.
                       ;Don't forget to authorize DHCP in AD.
DNS = 1                ;Installs DNS. Configure after first boot.


;The following section configures Terminal Services for remote administration.
[TerminalServices]
ApplicationServer = 0  ;Install TS in Remote Administration mode.

;The following section includes parameters needed to upgrade
;the member server to a domain controller after unattended install
;successfully completes.  To install a base member server, remove
;this section.

;This section is used during DCPROMO.
;In this example, the script will create a new forest of domains.
[DCInstall]
;I have found that DCPROMO fails if this section has comments
;on the same lines as keys.  Comments precede applicable keys.

;Create a new forest of domains.
CreateOrJoin = "Create"

;Unique downlevel domain name
DomainNetBiosName = "FerrisTech"

;Full DNS name of new domain.
NewDomainDnsName = "win2000.ferristech.net"
RebootOnSuccess = "Yes"

;This is the first DC in the new domain.
ReplicaOrNewDomain = "Domain"

;New domain is the root of a new Tree.
TreeOrChild = "Tree"

;End of File
```

My Standard SYSPREP Answer File for Windows 2000 Professional

Here's the answer file I'm currently using. Right now, this one is tuned for a SYSPREP image install from a multiprocessor ACPI workstation. For security purposes, I've changed a few values, such as IP addresses, passwords, domains, usernames, and sections that might otherwise expose risks to my client. In addition, I've added comments, preceded by a semicolon (;) for this sample file. Normally, comments should be put on lines by themselves. Since I use the same image for a large number of different hardware platforms, I run SYSPREP using the `-pnp` switch to force full plug and play hardware redetection at the first reboot of an imaged system.

```
;Sysprep to load every mass storage driver that would
;ever possibly be used by FerrisTech.
;(And certainly a few extras)

;SYSPREP.INF for Sysprep 1.1
;Created by Jeffrey Ferris
;Ferris Technology Network
;January 1, 2000
;Version 2.0
;ACPI MP image for Windows 2000, Build 2195

[Unattended]
UnattendMode = FullUnattended
OemPreinstall = Yes
NoWaitAfterTextMode = 1
NoWaitAfterGUIMode = 1
OemSkipEula = yes
InstallFilesPath = "%systemdrive%\sysprep\i386"
OemPnPDriversPath = "\sysprep\drivers"
ExtendOemPartition = 1
UpdateUPHAL = "ACPIAPIC_UP,%systemdrive%\sysprep\i386\uniproc\mp2up.inf"
FileSystem = ConvertNTFS

[OEM_Ads]
Banner = "Ferris Technology Network Windows 2000 Setup"

[GuiUnattended]
AdminPassword = *         ;Set admin password on master image
TimeZone=20               ;US Central Time Zone
OEMDuplicatorString = "FTN Sysprep Image v2.0"
OemSkipWelcome = 1        ;Bypass Welcome screen
OemSkipRegional = 1       ;Skip regional options page

;This key is valid only when performing a SYSPREP-based installation.
;This key should be specified only when installing an image created
;from a uniprocessor master system to a multiprocessor target system.
;This key notifies Setup to use the Multiprocessor (MP) HAL rather than
;the Uniprocessor (UP) HAL present when the system was imaged.
;You should not reapply this image to a Uniprocessor machine,
```

```
;or there will be a noticeable hit to performance
;Enable next line ONLY if building master on UP to apply to MP.
;UpdateHAL=ACPIAPIC_MP,%windir%\inf\hal.inf

;This key is valid only when performing a SYSPREP-based installation.
;This key should be specified only when installing an image created from
;a multiprocessor master system using the ACPI APIC HAL to an APIC-compatible
;uniprocessor or multiprocessor target system. This key notifies Setup to
;redetect the proper kernel based on the number of processors.
;Enable next line if building master image on MP machine to apply the image
;to either MP or UP machines.
;UpdateUPHAL=ACPIAPIC_UP,%systemdrive%\Sysprep\i386\Uniproc\mp2up.inf

[UserData]
FullName="Ferris Technology Network"
OrgName="Ferris Technology Network"
;The next line randomly generates a computer name based on organization name
computername=*Productid = xxxxx-xxxxx-xxxxx-xxxxx-xxxxx
;Substitute your unique PID here

[Display]
;This is the lowest common denominator for display resolution
;True Color, 800x600, 72 Hertz refresh rate
BitsPerPel=16
Xresolution=800
YResolution=600
Vrefresh=72

[TapiLocation]
Dialing=Tone
AreaCode=512
LongDistanceAccess=9

[Networking]
InstallDefaultComponents = Yes


[GuiRunOnce]

;For Sysprep v1.0 (the version included with Windows 2000), you
;will not need the following sections.

;I use [Data] with Sysprep v1.1, because of the UseBiosToBoot key.
;The hard disks on the destination computers must be accessible through
;extended INT13 BIOS functions. The target computers must be able to start
;with a boot.ini that uses the multi() syntax.


[data]
;Force systems supporting extended INT13 BIOS calls to use the multi() syntax
UseBIOSToBoot = 1
UnattendedInstall = Yes
```

```
;The following key is only supported by Sysprep v1.1.
;This section allows a SYSPREP image to install on a machine
;with any of the drive controller types matching the
;plug and play IDs of the lines below.
;
;Format of this section is:
;   <PlugAndPlayID> = <location of supporting *.INF file>
;
;Any lines ending in MSHDC.INF are for IDE drive support.
;Any lines ending in SCSI.INF are for SCSI drive support.

[SysprepMassStorage]
PCMCIA\*PNP0600=%systemroot%\inf\mshdc.inf
*PNP0600=%systemroot%\inf\mshdc.inf
PCMCIA\KME-KXLC005-A99E=%systemroot%\inf\mshdc.inf
PCMCIA\_-NinjaATA—3768=%systemroot%\inf\mshdc.inf
PCMCIA\FUJITSU-IDE-PC_CARD-DDF2=%systemroot%\inf\mshdc.inf
*AZT0502=%systemroot%\inf\mshdc.inf
PCI\CC_0101=%systemroot%\inf\mshdc.inf
PCI\VEN_10B9&DEV_5215=%systemroot%\inf\mshdc.inf
PCI\VEN_10B9&DEV_5219=%systemroot%\inf\mshdc.inf
PCI\VEN_10B9&DEV_5229=%systemroot%\inf\mshdc.inf
PCI\VEN_1097&DEV_0038=%systemroot%\inf\mshdc.inf
PCI\VEN_1095&DEV_0640=%systemroot%\inf\mshdc.inf
PCI\VEN_1095&DEV_0646=%systemroot%\inf\mshdc.inf
PCI\VEN_0E11&DEV_AE33=%systemroot%\inf\mshdc.inf
PCI\VEN_8086&DEV_1222=%systemroot%\inf\mshdc.inf
PCI\VEN_8086&DEV_1230=%systemroot%\inf\mshdc.inf
PCI\VEN_8086&DEV_7010=%systemroot%\inf\mshdc.inf
PCI\VEN_8086&DEV_7111=%systemroot%\inf\mshdc.inf
PCI\VEN_8086&DEV_2411=%systemroot%\inf\mshdc.inf
PCI\VEN_8086&DEV_2421=%systemroot%\inf\mshdc.inf
PCI\VEN_8086&DEV_7199=%systemroot%\inf\mshdc.inf
PCI\VEN_1042&DEV_1000=%systemroot%\inf\mshdc.inf
PCI\VEN_1039&DEV_0601=%systemroot%\inf\mshdc.inf
PCI\VEN_1039&DEV_5513=%systemroot%\inf\mshdc.inf
PCI\VEN_10AD&DEV_0001=%systemroot%\inf\mshdc.inf
PCI\VEN_10AD&DEV_0150=%systemroot%\inf\mshdc.inf
PCI\VEN_105A&DEV_4D33=%systemroot%\inf\mshdc.inf
PCI\VEN_1106&DEV_0571=%systemroot%\inf\mshdc.inf
PCI\VEN_8086&DEV_1960&SUBSYS_11111028=%systemroot%\inf\scsi.inf
PCI\VEN_8086&DEV_1960&SUBSYS_11121111=%systemroot%\inf\scsi.inf
PCI\VEN_8086&DEV_1960&SUBSYS_11111111=%systemroot%\inf\scsi.inf
PCI\VEN_8086&DEV_1960&SUBSYS_04671028=%systemroot%\inf\scsi.inf
*ADP1540=%systemroot%\inf\scsi.inf
*ADP1542=%systemroot%\inf\scsi.inf
*ADP4215=%systemroot%\inf\scsi.inf
DETECTEDIsa\aha154x=%systemroot%\inf\scsi.inf
SPARROW_SCSI=%systemroot%\inf\scsi.inf
DETECTED\sparrow=%systemroot%\inf\scsi.inf
```

```
*ADP1502=%systemroot%\inf\scsi.inf
*ADP1505=%systemroot%\inf\scsi.inf
*ADP1510=%systemroot%\inf\scsi.inf
*ADP1512=%systemroot%\inf\scsi.inf
*ADP1515=%systemroot%\inf\scsi.inf
*ADP1520=%systemroot%\inf\scsi.inf
*ADP1522=%systemroot%\inf\scsi.inf
*ADP3015=%systemroot%\inf\scsi.inf
*ADP3215=%systemroot%\inf\scsi.inf
*ADP6360=%systemroot%\inf\scsi.inf
*ADP6370=%systemroot%\inf\scsi.inf
PCMCIA\Adaptec__Inc.-APA-1460_SCSI_Host_Adapter-BE89=%systemroot%\inf\scsi.inf
PCMCIA\Adaptec__Inc.-APA-1460_SCSI_Host_Adapter-B67E=%systemroot%\inf\scsi.inf
PCMCIA\Adaptec__Inc.-APA-1460_SCSI_Host_Adapter-6F71=%systemroot%\inf\scsi.inf
PCI\VEN_9004&DEV_5075=%systemroot%\inf\scsi.inf
PCI\VEN_9004&DEV_5175=%systemroot%\inf\scsi.inf
PCI\VEN_9004&DEV_5275=%systemroot%\inf\scsi.inf
PCI\VEN_9004&DEV_5375=%systemroot%\inf\scsi.inf
PCI\VEN_9004&DEV_5475=%systemroot%\inf\scsi.inf
PCI\VEN_9004&DEV_5575=%systemroot%\inf\scsi.inf
PCI\VEN_9004&DEV_5675=%systemroot%\inf\scsi.inf
PCI\VEN_9004&DEV_5775=%systemroot%\inf\scsi.inf
PCI\VEN_9004&DEV_5078=%systemroot%\inf\scsi.inf
PCI\VEN_9004&DEV_5178=%systemroot%\inf\scsi.inf
PCI\VEN_9004&DEV_5278=%systemroot%\inf\scsi.inf
PCI\VEN_9004&DEV_5378=%systemroot%\inf\scsi.inf
PCI\VEN_9004&DEV_5478=%systemroot%\inf\scsi.inf
PCI\VEN_9004&DEV_5578=%systemroot%\inf\scsi.inf
PCI\VEN_9004&DEV_5678=%systemroot%\inf\scsi.inf
PCI\VEN_9004&DEV_5778=%systemroot%\inf\scsi.inf
PCI\VEN_9004&DEV_7860=%systemroot%\inf\scsi.inf
PCI\VEN_9004&DEV_6078=%systemroot%\inf\scsi.inf
PCI\VEN_9004&DEV_6178=%systemroot%\inf\scsi.inf
PCI\VEN_9004&DEV_6278=%systemroot%\inf\scsi.inf
PCI\VEN_9004&DEV_6378=%systemroot%\inf\scsi.inf
PCI\VEN_9004&DEV_6478=%systemroot%\inf\scsi.inf
PCI\VEN_9004&DEV_6578=%systemroot%\inf\scsi.inf
PCI\VEN_9004&DEV_6778=%systemroot%\inf\scsi.inf
PCI\VEN_9004&DEV_7078=%systemroot%\inf\scsi.inf
PCI\VEN_9004&DEV_7178=%systemroot%\inf\scsi.inf
PCI\VEN_9004&DEV_7278=%systemroot%\inf\scsi.inf
PCI\VEN_9004&DEV_7478=%systemroot%\inf\scsi.inf
PCI\VEN_9004&DEV_7578=%systemroot%\inf\scsi.inf
PCI\VEN_9004&DEV_7678=%systemroot%\inf\scsi.inf
PCI\VEN_9004&DEV_7778=%systemroot%\inf\scsi.inf
PCI\VEN_9004&DEV_8078=%systemroot%\inf\scsi.inf
PCI\VEN_9004&DEV_8178=%systemroot%\inf\scsi.inf
PCI\VEN_9004&DEV_8278=%systemroot%\inf\scsi.inf
PCI\VEN_9004&DEV_8478=%systemroot%\inf\scsi.inf
PCI\VEN_9004&DEV_8578=%systemroot%\inf\scsi.inf
PCI\VEN_9004&DEV_8678=%systemroot%\inf\scsi.inf
```

```
PCI\VEN_9004&DEV_8778=%systemroot%\inf\scsi.inf
PCI\VEN_9004&DEV_8878=%systemroot%\inf\scsi.inf
PCI\VEN_9004&DEV_7891=%systemroot%\inf\scsi.inf
PCI\VEN_9004&DEV_7892=%systemroot%\inf\scsi.inf
PCI\VEN_9004&DEV_7896=%systemroot%\inf\scsi.inf
PCI\VEN_9004&DEV_7897=%systemroot%\inf\scsi.inf
PCI\VEN_9004&DEV_3B78=%systemroot%\inf\scsi.inf
PCI\VEN_9004&DEV_EC78=%systemroot%\inf\scsi.inf
PCI\VEN_9004&DEV_6075=%systemroot%\inf\scsi.inf
PCI\VEN_9004&DEV_6075&SUBSYS_75609004=%systemroot%\inf\scsi.inf
PCI\VEN_9004&DEV_3860=%systemroot%\inf\scsi.inf
PCI\VEN_9005&DEV_0010=%systemroot%\inf\scsi.inf
PCI\VEN_9005&DEV_0020=%systemroot%\inf\scsi.inf
PCI\VEN_9005&DEV_0030=%systemroot%\inf\scsi.inf
PCI\VEN_9005&DEV_001F=%systemroot%\inf\scsi.inf
PCI\VEN_9005&DEV_002F=%systemroot%\inf\scsi.inf
PCI\VEN_9005&DEV_003F=%systemroot%\inf\scsi.inf
PCI\VEN_9005&DEV_0050=%systemroot%\inf\scsi.inf
PCI\VEN_9005&DEV_0051=%systemroot%\inf\scsi.inf
PCI\VEN_9005&DEV_005F=%systemroot%\inf\scsi.inf
*FDC0000=%systemroot%\inf\scsi.inf
DETECTEDPci\Fd16_700=%systemroot%\inf\scsi.inf
FD16_700_SCSI=%systemroot%\inf\scsi.inf
PCI\VEN_1036&DEV_0000=%systemroot%\inf\scsi.inf
DETECTED\fd16_700=%systemroot%\inf\scsi.inf
GEN_SCSIADAPTER=%systemroot%\inf\scsi.inf
PCI\VEN_1014&DEV_002E=%systemroot%\inf\scsi.inf
PCMCIA\IBM-PCMCIA_Portable_CD-ROM_Drive-84E3=%systemroot%\inf\scsi.inf
PCMCIA\IBM-PCMCIA_CD-ROM_DRIVE_CD-400-5AFA=%systemroot%\inf\scsi.inf
PCMCIA\IBM-PCMCIA_Portable_CD-ROM_Drive-84E2=%systemroot%\inf\scsi.inf
PCI\VEN_1077&DEV_1020=%systemroot%\inf\scsi.inf
PCI\VEN_1077&DEV_2100&SUBSYS_00011077=%systemroot%\inf\scsi.inf
PCI\VEN_1077&DEV_1240=%systemroot%\inf\scsi.inf
PCI\VEN_1077&DEV_1080=%systemroot%\inf\scsi.inf
PCI\VEN_1000&DEV_0001=%systemroot%\inf\scsi.inf
PCI\VEN_1000&DEV_0002=%systemroot%\inf\scsi.inf
PCI\VEN_1000&DEV_0003=%systemroot%\inf\scsi.inf
PCI\VEN_1000&DEV_0004=%systemroot%\inf\scsi.inf
PCI\VEN_1000&DEV_0005=%systemroot%\inf\scsi.inf
PCI\VEN_1000&DEV_0006=%systemroot%\inf\scsi.inf
PCI\VEN_1000&DEV_000B=%systemroot%\inf\scsi.inf
PCI\VEN_1000&DEV_000C=%systemroot%\inf\scsi.inf
PCI\VEN_1000&DEV_000D=%systemroot%\inf\scsi.inf
PCI\VEN_1000&DEV_000F=%systemroot%\inf\scsi.inf
PCI\VEN_105A&DEV_4D38=%systemroot%\inf\scsi.inf

;End of File
```

Glossary

$$Rename.txt Text file needed to convert short filenames into long filenames when performing an unattended install.

OEM folder Folder structure used to include third-party files with a DSP-based or SYSPREP-based Windows 2000 unattended installation.

%systemdrive% Environment variable that translates to the volume letter of the drive on which Windows 2000 was installed. If Windows 2000 is installed to the default location, this environment variable would equate to C:.

%systemroot% Environment variable that translates to the install location of Windows 2000. If Windows 2000 is installed to the default location, this environment variable would equate to C:\WINNT.

%username% Environment variable that translates to the user account name of the associated user. This variable is often entered as a path to the user's profile, used in logon scripts, or referenced in batch files.

%userprofile% Environment variable that translates to the path of the current user's local profile. For example, with the default configuration of a clean install, this variable translates to C:\Documents and Settings\%username%.

ACPI see *Advanced Configuration and Power Interface*

Active Directory (AD) Directory service that is the core of Windows 2000 domain-based networking. AD provides a hierarchical view of the network with a single point of administration for all network objects. The Active

Directory acts as a programmatically accessible information repository for all network objects, including user accounts, computer accounts, network shares, and printers.

AD see *Active Directory*

administrative template File containing policy template definitions for generating policy files or configuring group policy objects through the Administrative Templates hive of the Group Policy Editor. Administrative templates are plain-text files ending with an *.ADM extension.

Advanced Configuration and Power Interface (ACPI) Industry specification for power management and plug and play compatibility. ACPI-enabled systems allow for better power management—including Standby and Hibernate modes—and plug and play device compatibility under Windows 2000.

Advanced Power Management (APM) A legacy power management standard being replaced by ACPI. APM is less robust, less configurable, and less reliable than ACPI.

answer file The text file that facilitates customized or unattended installs of Windows 2000 by providing values for questions asked during the setup process. Examples of answer files include UNATTEND.TXT, WINNT.SIF, SYSPREP.INF, and REMBOOT.SIF.

APM see *Advanced Power Management*

auditing Tracking security events and permission usage by recording selected types of events in the Event Viewer security log.

BINL see *Boot Information Negotiation Layer*

Boot Information Negotiation Layer (BINL) The boot server service used by RIS. Interacts with the AD controller, Domain Name System (DNS), DHCP, and other boot servers to remotely install a client requesting service.

boot partition The volume or partition that contains the Windows 2000 operating system and related support files (for example, the \WINNT directory). The boot partition is sometimes called the *boot volume.*

boot volume see *boot partition*

DC see *domain controller*

DDNS see *Dynamic Domain Name System*

default profile Base local-user profile used as a template in the creation of all user profiles.

Device Manager Provides similar functions in Windows 2000 as in Windows 95 and Windows 98. Device Manager was not included in Windows NT 4.0. With Device Manager, you can view, update, configure, or remove devices and the associated device drivers for both local and remote computers.

DFS see *Distributed File System*

DHCP See *Dynamic Host Configuration Protocol*

Distributed File System Allows you to distribute files across a logically centralized file share. Files from the multiple servers all appear to be located in the same share point.

distribution share point (DSP) Location on a network from which Windows 2000 install files have been copied, enabling network-based automated installation.

domain controller (DC) A Windows 2000 server that hosts an Active Directory database, which stores all information about users, groups, computers, group policy objects, and more in a centralized directory service.

domain Under Windows NT Server environments, a centrally administered group of networked computers and users. On the Internet, domains are the company name portion of a URL, such as FerrisTech in `www.ferristech.net`. Windows 2000 domains can use the same domain name on an internal Windows domain as on the external Internet domain name.

Domain Name System (DNS) A TCP/IP name resolution service that translates fully qualified domain names to IP addresses.

DNS see *Domain Name System*

DSP see *distribution share point*

dual boot A workstation configuration in which multiple operating systems are installed, usually in separate partitions of a single machine. For example, if a machine can boot to either Windows 9x or Windows 2000, the computer is configured to dual boot.

dynamic disk Physical disk that is managed through the Windows 2000 Disk Management MMC. Dynamic disks cannot be accessed through DOS. They cannot contain partitions or logical drives; only dynamic volumes.

Dynamic Domain Name System Similar to DNS, this TCP/IP name resolution service translates fully qualified domain names to IP addresses, and allows clients to dynamically enter and update name translation information in the DNS database.

Dynamic Host Configuration Protocol (DHCP) Protocol to dynamically assign IP addresses and IP configuration information to TCP/IP client machines.

dynamic volume Logical volume created through the Windows 2000 Disk Management MMC. Dynamic volumes can include simple, spanned, striped, mirrored, and RAID5. These volumes can exist only on dynamic disks.

EAP see *Extensible Authentication Protocol*

EFS see *Encrypted File System*

Encrypted File System (EFS) Enhancement to the NTFS file system allowing secure encrypted files and folders viewable only by the owner and the recovery key holder.

Extensible Authentication Protocol (EAP) Extension to PPP (Point-to-Point Protocol) that provides enhanced user authentication for remote-access users, such as tokens, Smart Cards, or biometric devices.

FAT see *File Allocation Table*

FAT32 32-bit version of the File Allocation Table disk format; FAT32 volumes are supported on Windows 95 OSR2, Windows 98, and Windows 2000.

File Allocation Table (FAT) A table associating filenames to the location of each file's clusters on a disk. FAT volumes are supported on many operating systems, including DOS, Windows 3.1, Windows 9x, Windows NT 3.x, Windows NT 4.0, and Windows 2000.

forest Collection of one or more Windows 2000 domains or domain trees with disjointed name space, but which share a common global catalog and schema. If there are multiple domains, they must be linked with two-way transitive trusts.

GC see *global catalog*

ghost image One of the common types of system images used with SYSPREP-based installs. Ghost images are created using the Norton Ghost utility. Often, the filenames end in *.GHO.

global catalog (GC) Active Directory domain controller that contains a partial replica of every domain in the Active Directory forest. The global catalog stores only the fields and values most frequently required in search operations, such as a user's first and last names, as well as the unique identifier attributes required to locate a full replica of the object, such as the user's unique account name. Fields to be included in the GC are customizable.

global group Security group in a Windows 2000 domain that can be granted rights and permissions and that can be added to local groups within the same domain. Global groups can be granted permissions to resources on any member resource within the same domain. A global group cannot contain accounts from outside the local domain.

Global Unique Identifier (GUID) Theoretically unique identification number associated with document types, group policy objects, control registrations, and other items requiring unique identification.

GPC see *group policy container*

GPE see *Group Policy Editor*

GPO see *group policy object*

GPT see *group policy template*

group policy container (GPC) Stores the version number, status, and policy information for each policy by GUID in the Active Directory. The GPC maintains version numbering, status information, and policy information. For policies to apply, the GPC must be in sync with the associated group policy template.

Group Policy Editor (GPE) MMC console accessed through the Group Policy MMC snap-in or through the Group Policy tab of an applicable Active Directory container used for modifying group policy configuration settings.

group policy object (GPO) A collection of group policy settings, assigned a global unique identifier (GUID) and stored in the Active Directory. A GPO can be applied to sites, domains, or organizational units (SDOUs). In addition, there is one local group policy object stored on every computer affecting only settings specific to that local machine.

group policy setting User or computer configurations that are applied to the user's desktop. You change the group policy settings through the Group Policy Editor.

group policy template (GPT) Stores policy information. Can be found on any domain controller under the `\\`*<MACHINE_NAME>*`\SYSVOL\`*<DOMAIN_NAME>*`\Policies` folder. Folders named with GUIDs represent the GPTs; these GUIDs match the GPT to an associated GPC. Under each GPT folder is a GPT.INI file containing a version number. If you define administrative templates (*.ADM files) for a GPO, they will be stored in the GPT folder under an ADM subfolder. Startup and shutdown scripts are stored under the Machine\Scripts subfolder. Logon and logoff scripts are stored under the User\Scripts subfolder.

group policy Group of technologies through which group policy objects, which contain group policy settings, are created, edited, and applied to Windows 2000 users and computers.

GUID see *Global Unique Identifier*

Hardware Compatibility List (HCL) The list maintained by Microsoft of all systems and drivers certified compatible with Microsoft products. You can find the Hardware Compatibility List online at `http://www.microsoft.com/hcl`.

HCL see *Hardware Compatibility List*

Hibernate A power-management mode in which the memory is saved to a special location on the hard disk (%systemdrive%\hiberfil.sys) before system shutdown. System state, including running applications and open documents, is maintained throughout the power cycle. When the system is powered back on, the memory is read from the hibernation file, and the system resumes where it left off.

IntelliMirror A suite of technology functions in Windows 2000 domains that enable policy-based Software Installation and Maintenance, User Data Management, and User Settings Management. IntelliMirror coupled with the Remote Installation Services makes up the Windows 2000 Change and Configuration Management model.

Internet Protocol Security (IPSec) Standard defining a suite of cryptography-based services and security protocols to provide end-to-end security, privacy, and integrity of network communication.

IPSec see *Internet Protocol Security*

Kerberos A standard security protocol developed at the Massachusetts Institute of Technology (MIT) for user and machine authentication. Kerberos is defined in detail by RFC 1510. In the past, Kerberos was commonly used on the Internet and for UNIX-based authentication. Windows 2000 can now authenticate using Kerberos V5. In addition, Windows 2000 can interoperate with UNIX-based Kerberos V5 authentication systems.

L2TP see *Layer 2 Tunneling Protocol*

Layer 2 Tunneling Protocol (L2TP) Packet-oriented Point-to-Point Tunneling Protocol, similar to PPTP but with greater security and flexibility, used in virtual private networking communications.

local group A type of security group used in Windows NT. Windows 2000 Server products, Windows 2000 Professional, and Windows 2000 domains can all have local groups. User accounts, global groups, and universal groups from local or trusted resources can be added to local groups.

logoff script Batch file or executable that runs during the user account logoff process.

logon script Batch file or executable that runs during the user account logon process.

Microsoft Management Console (MMC) The common administrative interface for Windows 2000 GUI-based administrative tools, called *consoles*.

MMC see *Microsoft Management Console*

NT File System (NTFS) File system used by Windows NT and Windows

2000, allowing for account-level security, compression, and addressing of larger disk sizes. Windows 2000's version of NTFS provides encryption via the Encrypted File System.

NTFS see *NT File System*

Point-to-Point Protocol Remote access serial interface connectivity protocol supporting dynamic IP configuration and error detection. PPP is commonly used for dial-up connections to Internet service providers (ISPs).

PolEdit The Windows NT policy editor, used to import *.ADM files to create domain policy files. This type of policy management has been replaced by group policy objects.

policy A specific configuration setting in a group policy object.

PowerQuest Drive Image One of the common types of system images used with SYSPREP-based installs. PowerQuest Drive Images are created using the PowerQuest Drive Image utility. Often the filenames end in *.PQI.

PPP see *Point-to-Point Protocol*

Pre-boot Execution Environment (PXE) Provides a standard mechanism for connecting to the network by booting directly from a PXE ROM on a network interface card (NIC). Windows 2000 provides the option of booting to a PXE ROM emulator from a floppy disk. PXE is required when installing systems using RIS.

profile Collection of user environment settings, including display preferences, desktop arrangement, Start menu programs, and application settings, that the user can change.

PXE see *Pre-boot Execution Environment*

RAID see *Redundant Array of Independent (or Inexpensive) Disks*

RBFG see *Remote Boot Floppy Generator*

Redundant Array of Independent (or Inexpensive) Disks (RAID) Standardized categorization of fault-tolerant disk systems. Windows 2000 provides three levels of software RAID—Level 0 (striping, no fault tolerance), Level 1 (mirroring), and Level 5 (striping with rotating parity). Only RAID 0 is supported on Windows 2000 Professional; the Windows 2000 Server family supports RAID 0, 1, and 5.

RegEdit Registry Editor. Running REGEDIT.EXE opens the Registry Editor utility, through which you can view, change, or export registry settings. RegEdt32, another utility for editing the registry, provides these features as well as the ability to set NTFS security access permissions on individual keys and values.

REMBOOT.SIF Common answer file used to provide configuration options to a RIS-based install of Windows 2000 Professional.

Remote Boot Floppy Generator (RBFG) Utility provided with the Windows 2000 Server RIS service with which a PXE Boot ROM Emulator can be created on a floppy disk. See *Pre-boot Execution Environment* and *Remote Installation Services.*

Remote Installation Services (RIS) Windows 2000 Server service providing network boot (PXE) based installation of Windows 2000 Professional workstations. RIS uses the BINL and TFTP protocols.

Resultant Set of Policies (RSoP) Net result of group policies on a user or computer after applying all group policy objects that pertain to that object.

RIPREP The Remote Installation System Preparation Wizard; the Remote Installation Services implementation of SYSPREP.

RIS see *Remote Installation Services*

RISetup Server-side wizard used to complete the installation of the Remote Installation Services.

RSoP see *Resultant Set of Policies*

schema Similar to a database, the Active Directory schema holds a description of all object classes and attributes stored in the Active Directory.

ScriptIt Utility available from Microsoft to assist with scripted unattended installation of applications. See the following URLs to download the distribution and for sample usage guidelines:

`http://support.microsoft.com/support/kb/articles/Q191/6/05.ASP`

`http://technet.microsoft.com/cdonline/Content/Complete/windows/winnt/Winntas/tools/scriptit.htm`

`http://www.microsoft.com/NTServer/nts/deployment/custguide/scriptit3.asp`

SDOU Stands for *sites, domains, and organizational units*, the basic hierarchy of containers under Active Directory.

security identifier (SID) Theoretically unique identification number associated with Windows 2000 security principals (users, groups, and machines). When building machines using a system image, the SID is regenerated by the SYSPREP utility. Without regenerating the SID, there is a strong potential for security problems.

shutdown script Batch file or executable that runs when a computer shuts down.

SID see *security identifier*

Single Instance Storage (SIS) Windows 2000 service used to reduce disk space requirements on the boot server by removing duplicate files from RIPREP images and replacing them with pointers to files in a common file store. SIS is installed when RIS is configured.

SIS see *Single Instance Storage*

SMS package The basic unit of the Microsoft Systems Management Server (SMS) software distribution. Packages contain source files for the program and configuration files to direct the distribution.

SMS Senders A component of the Microsoft Systems Management Server (SMS) package used to replicate files to specific heterogeneous locations in a network environment.

Standby A power-management mode in which the system remains running, but all processes are suspended and the machine uses the absolute minimum amount of power required to keep information in RAM active. System state, including running applications and open documents, is maintained. The system can be revived quickly from standby mode (resumed), and the system is in the same state as it was before entering standby mode. Standby allows notebook users to save battery life with a near-shutdown mode, while still allowing almost instant reactivation of a suspended system.

startup script Batch file or executable that runs when a computer starts up.

SYSDIFF The System Differential utility, which can be used to take a snapshot of a system before and after modifications, and then compare those snapshots to discern registry and file differences. Those differences are packaged into a Difference Package, which can then be applied to additional machines.

SYSPREP.INF Required name of an answer file that can be used to answer questions posed by the mini-setup wizard that runs after the application of a SYSPREP image to a target machine.

system files The files needed to load, configure, and run Windows 2000.

system partition The volume or partition that contains the hardware-specific boot files needed to boot Windows 2000, such as NTLDR, BOOT.INI, and NTDETECT.COM. The system partition is sometimes called the *system volume.*

system volume see *system partition*

TFTP Trivial File Transfer Protocol. Client/server protocol used by RIS to transfer RIS-based Windows 2000 setup files from the RIS server down to the client machine.

TFTPD Trivial File Transfer Protocol Daemon. Server-side service used to transfer files needed during RIS-based installs to client machines.

tree One or more Windows 2000 domains linked with two-way transitive trusts with a common global catalog and schema. Domains form a hierarchical structure within a tree, creating a contiguous namespace.

UDF see *uniqueness database file*

UNATTEND.TXT Standard filename used for an answer file when performing an install using the WINNT or WINNT32 executables from a distribution share point or CD-based (but not CD-boot) install.

UNC see *Universal Naming Convention*

uniqueness database file (UDF) When performing an unattended install using an answer file, the UDF can provide machine-specific customizations without requiring the regeneration of an entire customized answer file.

universal group A Windows 2000 domain security group. Universal groups are not available in mixed-mode domains; only when the domain has been converted to native mode can you create and utilize universal groups. Universal groups can be used anywhere in a domain tree or forest, and can include other user accounts, global groups, local groups, or universal groups from any domain in the tree or forest. Universal groups can be members of domain local groups and universal groups, but not global groups.

Universal Naming Convention (UNC) Standard method of accessing servers and shares on a network. The format is \\<*servername*>\<*share*>.

Universal Serial Bus (USB) A plug and play interface between a computer and a peripheral hardware device that doesn't require an adapter card and can install without powering down the machine. USB 1.1 supports device connection speeds of up to 12 Mbps with up to 127 simultaneously connected devices.

The devices often obtain power from the USB port to which they are connected, so as not to require additional power supplies for each USB device.

USB see *Universal Serial Bus*

WDM see *Windows Driver Model*

Windows Driver Model (WDM) Provides a common set of I/O services and device drivers based on the class/minidriver structure for both Windows 98 and Windows 2000 operating systems.

WINNT.SIF Required name of an answer file used when performing unattended or scripted installations of Windows 2000 by booting from the CD. WINNT.SIF must be located in the root folder of a floppy disk in the A:\ drive. The file must be present when Windows 2000 starts to boot from the installation CD.

Index

Symbols

A

C

D

E

F

G

H

I

J-K

L

N

O

Q-R

S

T

U

V

W

X-Z

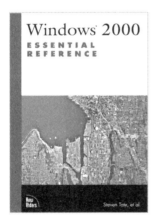

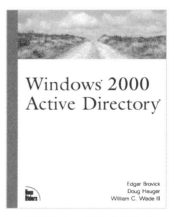

Books for Networking Professionals

Windows NT Titles

Windows NT TCP/IP

By Karanjit S. Siyan, Ph.D.
1st Edition
460 pages, $29.99
ISBN: 1-56205-887-8

If you're still looking for good documentation on Microsoft TCP/IP, look no further—this is your book. *Windows NT TCP/IP* cuts through the complexities to provide the most informative and complete reference on Windows-based TCP/IP. Concepts essential to TCP/IP administration are related to the practical use of Microsoft TCP/IP in a real-world networking environment. The book begins by covering TCP/IP architecture and advanced installation and configuration issues. Then it moves on to routing with TCP/IP, DHCP Management, and WINS/DNS Name Resolution.

Windows NT DNS

By Michael Masterson, Herman Knief, Scott Vinick, and Eric Roul
1st Edition
340 pages, $29.99
ISBN: 1-56205-943-2

Have you ever opened a Windows NT book looking for detailed information about DNS only to discover that it doesn't even begin to scratch the surface? DNS is probably one of the most complicated subjects for NT administrators, and there are few books on the market that address it in detail. This book answers your most complex DNS questions, focusing on the implementation of the Domain Name System within Windows NT. Written from the viewpoints of experienced Windows NT professionals, this book covers the details of how DNS functions within NT and then explores specific interactions with critical network components. Proven procedures to design and set up DNS are demonstrated. You'll also find coverage of related topics, such as maintenance, security, and troubleshooting.

Windows NT Registry: A Settings Reference

By Sandra Osborne
1st Edition
550 pages, $29.99
ISBN: 1-56205-941-6

The NT Registry can be a very powerful tool for those capable of using it wisely. Unfortunately, there is little information regarding the NT Registry due to Microsoft's insistence that their source code be kept secret. This book covers critical issues and settings used for configuring network protocols, including NWLink, PTP, TCP/IP, and DHCP. It discusses the problems related to a particular component and then discusses settings, which are the actual changes necessary for implementing robust solutions.

Windows NT Performance: Monitoring, Benchmarking, and Tuning

By Mark T. Edmead and Paul Hinsberg
1st Edition
288 pages, $29.99
ISBN: 1-56205-942-4

Performance monitoring is a little like preventive medicine for the administrator: No one enjoys a checkup, but it's a good thing to do on a regular basis. This book helps you focus on the critical aspects of improving the performance of your NT system by showing you how to monitor the system, implement benchmarking, and tune your network. The book is organized by resource components, which makes it easy to use as a reference tool.

Windows NT Terminal Server and Citrix MetaFrame

By Ted Harwood
1st Edition
400 pages, $29.99
ISBN: 1-56205-944-0

It's no surprise that most administration headaches revolve around integration with other networks and clients. This book addresses these types of real-world issues on a case-by-case basis, giving tools and advice for solving each problem. The author also offers the real nuts and bolts of thin client administration on multiple systems, covering relevant issues, such as installation, configuration, network connection, management, and application distribution.

Windows NT Power Toolkit

By Stu Sjouwerman and Ed Tittel
1st Edition
800 pages, $49.99
ISBN: 0-7357-0922-X

This book covers the analysis, tuning, optimization, automation, enhancement, maintenance, and troubleshooting of Windows NT Server 4.0 and Windows NT Workstation 4.0. In most cases, the two operating systems overlap completely and are discussed together. Where the two systems diverge, each platform is covered separately. This advanced title comprises a task-oriented treatment of the Windows NT 4 environment. By concentrating on the use of operating system tools and utilities, Resource Kit elements, and selected third-party tuning, analysis, optimization, and productivity tools, this book will show its readers how to carry out everyday and advanced tasks.

Windows NT Network Management: Reducing Total Cost of Ownership

By Anil Desai
1st Edition
450 pages, $34.99
ISBN: 1-56205-946-7

Administering a Windows NT network is kind of like trying to herd cats—an impossible task characterized by constant motion, exhausting labor, and lots of hairballs. Author Anil Desai knows all about it; he's a consulting engineer for Sprint Paranet, which specializes in Windows NT implementation, integration, and management. So, we asked him to put together a concise manual of the best practices—a book of tools and ideas that other administrators can turn to again and again in managing their own NT networks.

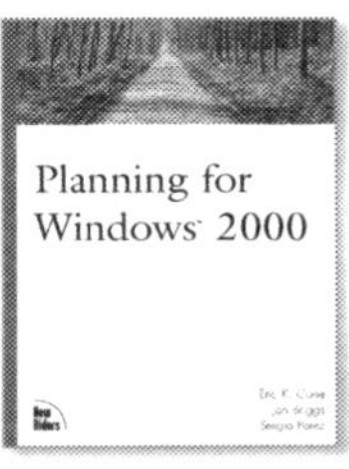

Planning for Windows 2000

By Eric K. Cone, Jon Boggs, and Sergio Perez

1st Edition

400 pages, $29.99

ISBN: 0-7357-0048-6

Windows 2000 is poised to be one of the largest and most important software releases of the next decade, and you are charged with planning, testing, and deploying it in your enterprise. Are you ready? With this book, you will be. *Planning for Windows 2000* lets you know what the upgrade hurdles will be, informs you how to clear them, guides you through effective Active Directory design, and presents you with detailed rollout procedures. Eric K. Cone, Jon Boggs, and Sergio Perez give you the benefit of their extensive experiences as Windows 2000 Rapid Deployment Program members by sharing problems and solutions they've encountered on the job.

Inside Windows 2000 Server

By William Boswell

1st Edition

1533 pages, $49.99

ISBN: 1-56205-929-7

Finally, a totally new edition of New Riders' best-selling *Inside Windows NT Server 4*. Taking the author-driven, no-nonsense approach we pioneered with our *Landmark* books, New Riders proudly offers something unique for Windows 2000 administrators—an interesting, discriminating book on Windows 2000 Server written by someone who can anticipate your situation and give you workarounds that won't leave a system unstable or sluggish.

BackOffice Titles

Implementing Exchange Server

By Doug Hauger, Marywynne Leon, and William C. Wade III

1st Edition

400 pages, $29.99

ISBN: 1-56205-931-9

If you're interested in connectivity and maintenance issues for Exchange Server, this book is for you. Exchange's power lies in its capability to be connected to multiple email subsystems to create a "universal email backbone." It's not unusual to have several different and complex systems all connected via email gateways, including Lotus Notes or cc:Mail, Microsoft Mail, legacy mainframe systems, and Internet mail. This book covers all of the problems and issues associated with getting an integrated system running smoothly, and it addresses troubleshooting and diagnosis of email problems with an eye toward prevention and best practices.

Exchange System Administration

By Janice Rice Howd

1st Edition

300 pages, $34.99

ISBN: 0-7357-0081-8

Okay, you've got your Exchange Server installed and connected; now what? Email administration is one of the most critical networking jobs, and Exchange can be particularly troublesome in large, heterogeneous environments. Janice Howd, a noted consultant and teacher with over a decade of email administration experience, has put together this advanced, concise handbook for daily, periodic, and emergency administration. With in-depth coverage of topics like managing disk resources, replication, and disaster recovery, this is the one reference every Exchange administrator needs.

SQL Server System Administration

By Sean Baird, Chris Miller, et al.
1st Edition
352 pages, $29.99
ISBN: 1-56205-955-6

How often does your SQL Server go down during the day when everyone wants to access the data? Do you spend most of your time being a "report monkey" for your coworkers and bosses? *SQL Server System Administration* helps you keep data consistently available to your users. This book omits introductory information. The authors don't spend time explaining queries and how they work. Instead, they focus on the information you can't get anywhere else, like how to choose the correct replication topology and achieve high availability of information.

Internet Information Services Administration

By Kelli Adam
1st Edition,
200 pages, $29.99
ISBN: 0-7357-0022-2

Are the new Internet technologies in Internet Information Services giving you headaches? Does protecting security on the Web take up all of your time? Then this is the book for you. With hands-on configuration training, advanced study of the new protocols the most recent version of IIS, and detailed instructions on authenticating users with the new Certificate Server and implementing and managing the new e-commerce features, *Internet Information Services Administration* gives you the real-life solutions you need. This definitive resource prepares you for the release of Windows 2000 by giving you detailed advice on working with Microsoft Management Console, which was first used by IIS.

SMS 2 Administration

By Michael Lubanski and Darshan Doshi
1st Edition
350 pages, $39.99
ISBN: 0-7357-0082-6

Microsoft's new version of its Systems Management Server (SMS) is starting to turn heads. Although complex, it allows administrators to lower their total cost of ownership and more efficiently manage clients, applications, and support operations. So if your organization is using or implementing SMS, you'll need some expert advice. Darshan Doshi and Michael Lubanski can help you get the most bang for your buck with insight, expert tips, and real-world examples. Darshan and Michael are consultants specializing in SMS and have worked with Microsoft on one of the most complex SMS rollouts in the world, involving 32 countries, 15 languages, and thousands of clients.

UNIX/Linux Titles

Solaris Essential Reference

By John P. Mulligan
1st Edition,
300 pages, $24.95
ISBN: 0-7357-0023-0

Looking for the fastest, easiest way to find the Solaris command you need? Need a few pointers on shell scripting? How about advanced administration tips and sound, practical expertise on security issues? Are you looking for trustworthy information about available third-party software packages that will enhance your operating system? Author John Mulligan—creator of the popular "Unofficial Guide to The Solaris™ Operating Environment" Web site (`sun.icsnet.com`)—delivers all that and more in one attractive, easy-to-use reference book. With clear and concise instructions on how to perform important administration and management tasks and key information on powerful commands and advanced topics, *Solaris Essential Reference* is the book you need when you know what you want to do and only need to know how.

Linux System Administration

By M Carling, Stephen Degler, and James Dennis
1st Edition
450 pages, $29.99
ISBN: 1-56205-934-3

As an administrator, you probably feel that most of your time and energy is spent in endless firefighting. If your network has become a fragile quilt of temporary patches and work-arounds, this book is for you. Have you had trouble sending or receiving email lately? Are you looking for a way to keep your network running smoothly with enhanced performance? Are your users always hankering for more storage, services, and speed? *Linux System Administration* advises you on the many intricacies of maintaining a secure, stable system. In this definitive work, the authors address all the issues related to system administration, from adding users and managing file permissions, to Internet services and Web hosting, to recovery planning and security. This book fulfills the need for expert advice that will ensure a trouble-free Linux environment.

GTK+/Gnome Application Development

By Havoc Pennington
1st Edition
492 pages, $39.99
ISBN: 0-7357-0078-8

This title is for the reader who is conversant with the C programming language and UNIX/Linux development. It provides detailed and solution-oriented information designed to meet the needs of programmers and application developers using the GTK+/Gnome libraries. Coverage complements existing GTK+/Gnome documentation, going into more depth on pivotal issues, such as uncovering the GTK+ object system, working with the event loop, managing the Gdk substrate, writing custom widgets, and mastering GnomeCanvas.

Developing Linux Applications with GTK+ and GDK

By Eric Harlow
1st Edition
490 pages, $34.99
ISBN: 0-7357-0021-4

We all know that Linux is one of the most powerful and solid operating systems in existence. And as the success of Linux grows, there is an increasing interest in developing applications with graphical user interfaces that take advantage of the power of Linux. In this book, software developer Eric Harlow gives you an indispensable development handbook focusing on the GTK+ toolkit. More than an overview of the elements of application or GUI design, this is a hands-on book that delves deeply into the technology. With in-depth material on the various GUI programming tools and loads of examples, this book's unique focus will give you the information you need to design and launch professional-quality applications.

Linux Essential Reference

By Ed Petron
1st Edition
350 pages, $24.95
ISBN: 0-7357-0852-5

This book is all about getting things done as quickly and efficiently as possible by providing a structured organization for the plethora of available Linux information. We can sum it up in one word—value. This book has it all: concise instructions on how to perform key administration tasks, advanced information on configuration, shell scripting, hardware management, systems management, data tasks, automation, and tons of other useful information. All of this coupled with an unique navigational structure and a great price. This book truly provides groundbreaking information for the growing community of advanced Linux professionals.

Lotus Notes and Domino Titles

Domino System Administration

By Rob Kirkland, CLP, CLI
1st Edition
850 pages, $49.99
ISBN: 1-56205-948-3

Your boss has just announced that you will be upgrading to the newest version of Notes and Domino when it ships. How are you supposed to get this new system installed, configured, and rolled out to all your end users? You understand how Lotus Notes works—you've been administering it for years. What you need is a concise, practical explanation of the new features and how to make some of the advanced stuff work smoothly by someone like you, who has worked with the product for years and understands what you need to know. *Domino System Administration* is the answer—the first book on Domino that attacks the technology at the professional level with practical, hands-on assistance to get Domino running in your organization.

Lotus Notes & Domino Essential Reference

By Tim Bankes, CLP and Dave Hatter, CLP, MCP
1st Edition
650 pages, $45.00
ISBN: 0-7357-0007-9

You're in a bind because you've been asked to design and program a new database in Notes for an important client who will keep track of and itemize a myriad of inventory and shipping data. The client wants a user-friendly interface that won't sacrifice speed or functionality. You are experienced (and could develop this application in your sleep) but feel you need something to facilitate your creative and technical abilities—something to perfect your programming skills. The answer is waiting for you: *Lotus Notes & Domino Essential Reference*. It's compact and simply designed. It's loaded with information. All of the objects, classes, functions, and methods are listed. It shows you the object hierarchy and the relationship between each one. It's perfect for you. Problem solved.

Networking Titles

Cisco Router Configuration & Troubleshooting

By Mark Tripod
1st Edition
300 pages, $34.99
ISBN: 0-7357-0024-9

Want the real story on making your Cisco routers run like a dream? Why not pick up a copy of *Cisco Router Configuration & Troubleshooting* and see what Mark Tripod of Exodus Communications has to say? They're the folks responsible for making some of the largest sites on the Net scream, like Amazon.com, Hotmail, USAToday, Geocities, and Sony. In this book, they provide advanced configuration issues, sprinkled with advice and preferred practices. You won't see a general overview on TCP/IP. This book addresses more meaty issues, like security, monitoring, traffic management, and more. In the troubleshooting section, the author provides a unique methodology and lots of sample problems to illustrate. By providing real-world insight and examples instead of rehashing Cisco's documentation, Mark gives network administrators information they can start using today.

Network Intrusion Detection: An Analyst's Handbook

By Stephen Northcutt
1st Edition
267 pages, $39.99
ISBN: 0-7357-0868-1

Get answers and solutions from someone who has been in the trenches. The author, Stephen Northcutt, original developer of the Shadow intrusion detection system and former Director of the United States Navy's Information System Security Office at the Naval Security Warfare Center, gives his expertise to intrusion detection specialists, security analysts, and consultants responsible for setting up and maintaining an effective defense against network security attacks.

Other Books By New Riders

Windows Technologies

Internet Information Services Administration
0-7357-0022-2
SMS 2 Administration
0-7357-0082-6
Planning for Windows 2000
0-7357-0048-6
Windows NT Network Management: Reducing Total Cost of Ownership
1-56205-946-7
Windows NT DNS
1-56205-943-2
Windows NT Performance Monitoring, Benchmarking, and Tuning
1-56205-942-4
Windows NT Power Toolkit
0-7357-0922-X
Windows NT Registry: A Settings Reference
1-56205-941-6
Windows NT TCP/IP
1-56205-887-8
Windows NT Terminal Server and Citrix MetaFrame
1-56205-944-0
Implementing Exchange Server
1-56205-931-9
Inside Window 2000 Server
1-56205-929-7
Exchange Server Administration
0-7357-0081-8
SQL Server System Administration
1-56205-955-6
Windows 2000 Active Directory
0-7357-0870-3

Networking

Understanding Directory Services
0-7357-0910-6
Understanding the Network
0-7357-0977-7
Domino System Administration
1-56205-948-3
Cisco Router Configuration and Troubleshooting
0-7357-0024-9
Understanding Data Communications, Sixth Edition
0-7357-0036-2
Network Intrusion Detection: An Analyst's Handbook
0-7357-0868-1

Certification

A+ Certification TestPrep
1-56205-892-4
A+ Certification Training Guide, 2E
0-7357-0907-6
A+ Fast Track
0-7357-0028-1
MCSD Fast Track: Visual Basic 6, Exam 70-176
0-7357-0019-2
MCSE Fast Track: Internet Information Server 4
1-56205-936-X
MCSE Fast Track: Networking Essentials
1-56205-939-4
MCSE Fast Track: TCP/IP
1-56205-937-8
MCSD Fast Track: VB 6, Exam 70-175
0-7357-0018-4
MCSE Fast Track: Windows 98
0-7357-0016-8
MCSE Fast Track: Windows NT Server 4
1-56205-935-1
MCSE Fast Track: Windows NT Server 4 Enterprise
1-56205-940-8
MCSE Fast Track: Windows NT Workstation 4
1-56205-938-6
MCSE Simulation Guide: Windows NT Server 4 Enterprise
1-56205-914-9
MCSE Simulation Guide: Windows NT Workstation 4
1-56205-925-4
MCSE TestPrep: Networking Essentials, Second Edition
0-7357-0010-9
MCSE TestPrep: TCP/IP, Second Edition
0-7357-0025-7
MCSE TestPrep: Windows 98
1-56205-922-X
MCSE TestPrep: Windows NT Server 4 Enterprise, Second Edition
0-7357-0009-5
MCSE TestPrep: Windows NT Server 4, Second Edition
0-7357-0012-5
MCSE TestPrep: Windows NT Workstation 4, Second Edition
0-7357-0008-7
MCSD TestPrep: VB 6 Exams
0-7357-0032-X
MCSE Training Guide: Networking Essentials, Second Edition
1-56205-919-X
MCSE Training Guide: TCP/IP, Second Edition
1-56205-920-3
MCSE Training Guide: Windows 98
1-56205-890-8
MCSE Training Guide: Windows NT Server 4, Second Edition
1-56205-916-5
MCSE Training Guide: Windows NT Server Enterprise, Second Edition
1-56205-917-3
MCSE Training Guide: Windows NT Workstation 4, Second Edition
1-56205-918-1
MCSD Training Guide: VB 6 Exams
0-7357-0002-8

Graphics

Inside 3D Studio MAX 2, Volume I
1-56205-857-6
Inside 3D Studio MAX 2, Volume II: Modeling and Materials
1-56205-864-9
Inside 3D Studio MAX 2, Volume III: Animation
1-56205-865-7
Inside 3D Studio MAX 2 Resource Kit
1-56205-953-X
Inside AutoCAD 14, Limited Edition
1-56205-898-3
Inside Softimage 3D
1-56205-885-1
HTML Web Magic, Second Edition
1-56830-475-7
Dynamic HTML Web Magic
1-56830-421-8
Designing Web Graphics.3
1-56205-949-1
Illustrator 8 Magic
1-56205-952-1
Inside trueSpace 4
1-56205-957-2
Inside Adobe Photoshop 5
1-56205-884-3
Inside Adobe Photoshop 5, Limited Edition
1-56205-951-3
Photoshop 5 Artistry
1-56205-895-9
Photoshop 5 Type Magic
1-56830-465-X
Photoshop 5 Web Magic
1-56205-913-0

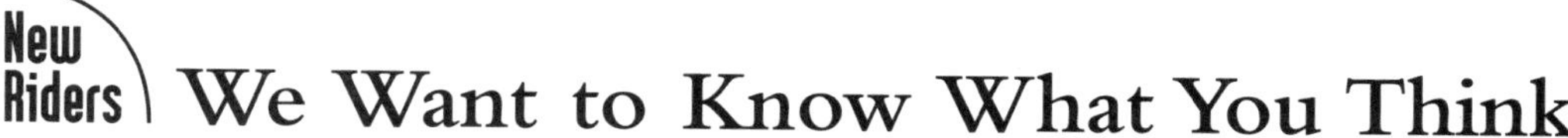

We Want to Know What You Think

To better serve you, we would like your opinion on the content and quality of this book. Please complete this card, and mail it to us or fax it to 317-581-4663.

Name ____________________

Address ____________________

City ________ State ________ Zip ________

Phone ____________________

Email Address ____________________

Occupation ____________________

Operating system(s) that you use ____________________

What influenced your purchase of this book?

- ❑ Recommendation
- ❑ Cover Design
- ❑ Table of Contents
- ❑ Index
- ❑ Magazine Review
- ❑ Advertisement
- ❑ New Riders' Reputation
- ❑ Author Name

How would you rate the contents of this book?

- ❑ Excellent
- ❑ Very Good
- ❑ Good
- ❑ Fair
- ❑ Below Average
- ❑ Poor

How do you plan to use this book?

- ❑ Quick Reference
- ❑ Self-Training
- ❑ Classroom
- ❑ Other

What do you like most about this book? Check all that apply.

- ❑ Content
- ❑ Writing Style
- ❑ Accuracy
- ❑ Examples
- ❑ Listings
- ❑ Design
- ❑ Index
- ❑ Page Count
- ❑ Price
- ❑ Illustrations

What do you like least about this book? Check all that apply.

- ❑ Content
- ❑ Writing Style
- ❑ Accuracy
- ❑ Examples
- ❑ Listings
- ❑ Design
- ❑ Index
- ❑ Page Count
- ❑ Price
- ❑ Illustrations

What would be a useful follow-up book for you? ____________________

Where did you purchase this book? ____________________

Can you name a similar book that you like better than this one, or one that is as good? Why?

____

How many New Riders books do you own? ____________________

What are your favorite computer books? ____________________

What other titles would you like to see us develop? ____________________

Any comments for us? ____________________

Windows 2000 Deployment & Desktop Management:
0-7357-0975-0

www.newriders.com • Fax 317-581-4663

Fold here and tape to mail

Place
Stamp
Here

New Riders Publishing
201 W. 103rd St.
Indianapolis, IN 46290

How to Contact Us

Visit Our Web Site

www.newriders.com

On our Web site you'll find information about our other books, authors, tables of contents, indexes, and book errata.

Email Us

Contact us at this address:

nrfeedback@newriders.com

- If you have comments or questions about this book
- To report errors that you have found in this book
- If you have a book proposal to submit or are interested in writing for New Riders
- If you would like to have an author kit sent to you
- If you are an expert in a computer topic or technology and are interested in being a technical editor who reviews manuscripts for technical accuracy

nrfeedback@newriders.com

- To find a distributor in your area, please contact our international department at this address.

nrmedia@newriders.com

- For instructors from educational institutions who want to preview New Riders books for classroom use. Email should include your name, title, school, department, address, phone number, office days/hours, text in use, and enrollment, along with your request for desk/examination copies and/or additional information.
- For members of the media who are interested in reviewing copies of New Riders books. Send your name, mailing address, and email address, along with the name of the publication or Web site you work for.

Write to Us

New Riders Publishing
201 W. 103rd St.
Indianapolis, IN 46290-1097

Call Us

Toll-free (800) 571-5840 + 9 + 4511
If outside U.S. (317) 581-3500. Ask for New Riders.

Fax Us

(317) 581-4663